WHY PARTIES?

CHICAGO STUDIES IN AMERICAN POLITICS

A series edited by Benjamin I. Page, Susan Herbst,
Lawrence R. Jacobs, and James Druckman

WHY PARTIES?
A Second Look

JOHN H. ALDRICH

THE UNIVERSITY OF CHICAGO PRESS

Chicago and London

JOHN H. ALDRICH is the Pfizer-Pratt University Professor of Political
Science at Duke University. He is the author and coauthor of numerous
books and articles, as well as a Fellow of the American Academy of
Arts and Sciences and recipient of the American Political Science
Association's Samuel J. Eldersveld Career Achievement Award.

The University of Chicago Press, Chicago 60637
The University of Chicago Press, Ltd., London
© 1995, 2011 by The University of Chicago
All rights reserved. Published 2011.
Printed in the United States of America

20 19 18 17 16 15 14 13 12 11   1 2 3 4 5

ISBN-13: 978-0-226-01273-5 (cloth)
ISBN-13: 978-0-226-01274-2 (paper)
ISBN-10: 0-226-01273-5 (cloth)
ISBN-10: 0-226-01274-3 (paper)

Library of Congress Cataloging-in-Publication Data

Aldrich, John Herbert, 1947–
Why parties? : a second look / John H. Aldrich.
p. cm. — (Chicago studies in American politics)
Includes bibliographical references and index.
ISBN-13: 978-0-226-01273-5 (hardcover : alk. paper)
ISBN-10: 0-226-01273-5 (hardcover : alk. paper)
ISBN-13: 978-0-226-01274-2 (pbk. : alk. paper)
ISBN-10: 0-226-01274-3 (pbk. : alk. paper) 1. Political parties—United
States—History. 2. United States—Politics and government. I. Title.
II. Series: Chicago studies in American politics.
JK2261.A458 2011
324.273—dc22
2010042778

♾ This paper meets the requirements of ANSI/NISO Z39.48-1992

In memory of

Herbert and Ruth Aldrich

and Robert and Irene Aldrich

CONTENTS

ACKNOWLEDGMENTS

Research, and the publications it produces, is a collective enterprise. This fact is especially true for this book, which represents the combination, and culmination, of several different projects. Therefore these acknowledgments run long, and I am certain I have forgotten to note the help and advice of several people. To them, please accept my apologies.

A large number of institutions provided substantial assistance. The research reported in this book has no clear starting point, but one strong candidate for beginnings is the research I did with the support of the National Science Foundation (SES-8108548). Both the University of Minnesota and Duke University provided grants and generous leaves, and both added supportive and congenial working environments, as well as the advice and assistance of many of their members and staffs. Many of the data used in this project were made available through the University of Michigan's Inter-university Consortium for Political and Social Research and the National Elections Studies. A great many university departments (mostly, but happily not always, political science departments) suffered through presentations of various parts of this project. Among them are Carnegie Mellon; the University of California (Davis, Los Angeles, and San Diego); California Institute of Technology; the University of Florida; the University of North Carolina, Chapel Hill; Stanford; the University of Rochester; Wisconsin; Yale; and of course Minnesota and Duke. Two institutions deserve special notes of appreciation. The Center for Advanced Study in the Behavioral Sciences (with, in my case, support from NSF, BNS87-00864) provided its usual stimulating intellectual and collegial environment, making for the most enjoyable and rewarding year of my professional life. Phil Converse, Bob Scott, and entire staff, and of course an amazing collection of fellows made it so. The Department of Government at Harvard offered me a rare and special week to discuss this book. Special thanks to Jim Alt and Ken Shepsle for that opportunity and to the Harvard community for helping to make me spend a few more years completing this book, and making the result much better.

I have had the good fortune to learn about politics and political parties from some of the masters of the subject, whether as formal teachers or as colleagues. John Kessel trained me uncommonly well early on, and he has remained a constant source of wisdom and, I am pleased to say, friendship throughout my professional career. Each department where I have worked has provided a major figure on party politics whose influence should be evident throughout this book. My appreciation therefore to Joe Schlesinger and Frank Sorauf. Allan Kornberg not only served that role at Duke but made Duke attractive and welcoming to me and a wonderful place to live and work. Bill Riker's impact is perhaps most evident of all, but even that greatly understates his importance to me, as to so many others.

Many people have offered substantial comments on parts of the work in progress. These include Lance Banning, David Baron, Bob Bates, Ira Berlin, Bill Bianco, David Brady, Dean Burnham, David Canon, Gary Cox, John Ferejohn, Mo Fiorina, Ruth Grant, Gary Jacobson, Cal Jillson, Bill Keech, Morgan Kousser, Keith Krehbiel, Peter Lange, Matt McCubbins, Terry Moe, Mike Munger, Dick Niemi, Sam Popkin, Wendy Rahn, Tom Schwartz, Lloyd Shapley, Theda Skocpol, John Sullivan, Jack Walker (whose untimely passing left too much unsaid), Tom Weko, Rick Wilson—and the list goes on. Michael Gillespie listened to my often breathless meanderings as we ran, as well as in more usual venues, and he always had sound advice and insightful facts and opinions to offer, as well as detailed comments. Barry Weingast is quite remarkable. While he has, of course, a lot to offer, what makes him special is both his ability to see to the heart of the matter quickly, and when he has criticisms, to make them be seen positively rather than as the devastating critiques they could be. Two stand out for their genuine friendship and professionalism. Dave Rohde and Ken Shepsle were not just willing to read and comment as often as asked, they also listened, supported, and discussed for many hours over many years.

Another long list of people provided more direct assistance in this project—rather embarrassing, because some did so as graduate students and are now senior faculty. Mike McGinnis and John Williams fit that bill most directly. Wendy Rahn soon will. Mike Alvarez, Jacquie

Pfeffer, Pat Sellers, and Mat Schousen provided more than "merely" their fine assistance at Duke. A special note of thanks, as well, to Jim Granato, Michael Layton, and Regina Smyth, as well as to students who read drafts of chapters in a course. Ben Page and Charles Stewart read the manuscript with care and strengthened it considerably.

None of these institutions and none of these people, mentioned and unmentioned, have any responsibility for the content of this book. At the University of Chicago Press, John Tryneski, Alice Bennett, and the rest of the staff are, however, responsible. They are responsible for bringing this book to reality, making it as attractive as it is, and making it, clearly, a better book.

My family is the reason I have achieved whatever I have accomplished. Cindy is the love of my life and my best friend. She has made my entire adult life joyful. It is hard to believe that David is about to leave us as an adult, although he is in many ways already mature. My appreciation for the love, caring, and wisdom my parents have always given me grows every year. Mom and Dad, it is my honor and privilege to dedicate this book, with love, to you.

THE NEW EDITION

One of my greatest professional pleasures has been my good fortune to get to work with some wonderful people who are (or were) graduate students. This has always been true, and remains so as I look back over the process leading to this revision. I particularly would like to thank John Griffin, Brad Gomez, and Jeff Grynaviski for work they did on projects that appear in this revised version, but even more for their own work that has helped shape my thinking over the past fifteen years. Vicky DeFrancesco Soto, Jill Rickershouser Carvalho, Monique Lyle, and Jennifer Merolla not only began as students and became friends, but they also pushed my thinking in a number of very helpful ways. Then there are the comparativists: Alberto Dias, Renan Levine, Beatriz Magaloni, Tom Scotto, Laura Stephenson, and Liz Zechmeister. To them, and to Paul Abramson, Andre Blais, Abraham Diskin, and Indridi Indridason, I propose that the next version will show more full integration into comparative themes. Recent and current graduate students who have done work more particularly for this book—even while starting to turn my thinking much as did John, Brad, and Jeff—include Michael Brady, Brad Bishop, Chris DeSante, Rebecca Hatch, Dan Lee, Ian McDonald, Jacob Montgomery, Brendan Nyhan, Brittany Perry, David Sparks, and Michael Tofias. Special thanks go to David Brady for, among other things, making it possible for me to spend time at the

Hoover Institution, Stanford University, an unparalleled place to think and write, and to Norm Schofield for working at such a spectacular level on many of the same problems that interest me. Gary Cox, Mo Fiorina, Mat McCubbins, Ken Shepsle, and Barry Weingast have both pushed and pulled me along, perhaps without their noticing. But of all of these, Dave Rohde has been friend and colleague in virtually every aspect of the revisions of this book, far beyond what anyone could ever ask, including reading the revisions and improving them. John Tryneski remains both a fine editor and friend, but I was especially pleased to get to know Kailee Kremer and have her improve the manuscript so much.

Much has happened in the fifteen years since *Why Parties?* was first published. David has not only matured to be a remarkable young (or not so very young) adult, but he has added Whitney to our family. Cindy simply remains the center and greatest joy and love of my life. Sadly, my mother and father, to whom the first edition was dedicated, have both passed on, as have all of their generation in my family, and all but one in Cindy's. Thus, I dedicate this book to the memory of all of them but in particular to the memory of Cindy's and my parents.

PART ONE

POLITICAL PARTIES AND DEMOCRACY

1 POLITICS AND PARTIES IN AMERICA

Political parties lie at the heart of American politics.[1] E. E. Schattschneider (1942, 1) claimed that "political parties created democracy, and . . . democracy is unthinkable save in terms of parties." A fair, if minimal, paraphrase would be to say that democracy is *unworkable* save in terms of parties. All democracies that are Madisonian, extended republics, which is to say all democratic nations, have political parties. To be truly democratic it is necessary for any nation's leadership to be harnessed to public desires and aspirations, at least in some very general sense. The elected leaders, being granted political power by the public, must ultimately be held accountable to that public. It may be that each official can be held accountable for his or her own personal actions by the constituency that elects and reelects that official. But government policy is determined by the collective actions of many individual officeholders. No one person either can or should be held accountable for actions taken by the House, Senate, and president together. The political party as a collective enterprise, organizing competition for the full range of offices, provides the only means for holding elected officials responsible for what they do collectively. Morris P. Fiorina has written (1980, 26) that "the only way collective responsibility has ever existed, and can exist, given our institutions, is through the agency of the political party; in American politics, responsibility requires cohesive parties."

But perhaps there is more. The scholars mentioned above used the plural, "parties." It may be, as V. O. Key Jr. argued (1949), that at least two parties are necessary, that it is the plural parties that lie at the heart of, that make workable, and that provide responsibility for democracy.

Indeed, we might have to go even further. It may not be the mere presence of two parties at any one time that matters, for sometimes and in some places parties arise and then disappear from electoral competitiveness rapidly, as the American Independent Party and the Reform Party did in the United States in the 1960s and 1990s, respectively. What matters is the sustained competition that comes from the interaction between or among durable parties, such that it is the fact that any winning party must seriously consider the prospect of losing an election before democracy becomes tenable. A necessary condition for effective democracy, in this view, is that there must be a *party system*, an ongoing set of parties in sustained competition for access to power.

Of course, to think about a system of parties requires understanding the basis of individual political parties. Most of this book examines why the political party exists. It is important to know what the answer to this question is, because it is then a much shorter step than before toward understanding why a party system exists, and hence why some democracies are tenable and potentially durable. In this chapter, we begin by examining the political party and the elements that go into a theory of the political party, from which we can then consider what a party system might be.

THE POLITICAL PARTY

With the ability to shape competition for elected office comes responsibility. Many people, whether academics, commentators, politicians, or members of the public, place the political ills of the contemporary scene—a government seemingly unable to solve critical problems and a public distrustful of, apathetic toward, or alienated from politics—on the failures of the two great American parties. Members of Congress are too concerned with their own reelection, in this view, to be able or willing to think of the public good. The president worries about his personal popularity, spends too little time leading the nation, and when he does turn to Congress, finds it impossible to forge majorities—primarily partisan majorities—to pass his own initiatives or to form workable compromises with Congress. Elections are candidate centered, turning on personality, image, and the latest, cleverest ad. Party platforms are little more than the first order of business at national conventions, only to be passed quickly and, party leaders hope, without controversy or media attention, so that the convention can turn to more important business. Ultimate blame for each of these rests, from this perspective, on the major American party.

With few, if important, exceptions, in the 1970s and 1980s the scholarly study of American parties turned from foundational theory to an examination of what appeared to be the central set of issues of the day concerning political parties: party decline, decay, and decomposition.[2] Since then, parties have revitalized. But now there are new ills—extremely polarized "red and blue" politics, bitter public debates that are essentially demagoguery, intractability, and failure to find compromise regardless of the consequences for the public. Where is the bipartisanship of that era of decline, decay, and decomposition? Parties are, in this view, the problem, whether they are too weak or too strong. And yet, whether stronger or weaker, they are there, and thoughtful observers see them as essential.

To address these two questions—how do we understand and evaluate political parties, and how do we understand their role in democracy—I return to consider the foundations of the major American political party and the two-party system (or, more generally, the multiparty system). My basic argument is that the major political party is the creature of the politicians, the partisan activist, and the ambitious office seeker and officeholder. They have created and maintained, used or abused, reformed or ignored the political party when doing so has furthered their goals and ambitions. The political party is thus an "endogenous" institution—an institution shaped by these political actors. Whatever its strength or weakness, whatever its form and role, it is the ambitious politicians' creation.

These politicians, we must understand from the outset, do not have partisan goals per se. Rather, they have more personal and fundamental goals, and the party is only the instrument for achieving them. Their goals are several and come in various combinations. Following Richard Fenno (1973), they include most basically the desire to have a long and successful career in political office, but they also encompass the desire to achieve policy ends and to attain power and prestige within the government. These goals are to be sought in government, not in parties, but they are goals that at times have best been realized *through* the parties. The parties are, as we will see, shaped by these goals in their various combinations, and particularly in the problems politicians most typically encounter when seeking to achieve their goals. Thus, there are three goals, three problems, and three reasons why politicians often turn to the organized party in search for a sustainable way to solve these problems and thus be more likely to achieve these goals.

Ambitious politicians turn to the political party to achieve such goals only when parties are useful vehicles for solving problems that cannot be solved as effectively, if at all, through other means. Thus I believe that the political party must be understood not only in relation to the goals of the actors most consequential for parties, but also in relation to the electoral, legislative, and executive institutions of the government. Fiorina was correct: only given our institutions can we understand political parties.

The third major force shaping the political party is the historical setting. Technological changes, for instance, have made campaigning for office today vastly different than it was only a few decades ago, let alone in the nineteenth century. Such changes have had great consequences for political parties. In the nineteenth century, political parties were the only feasible means for organizing mass elections. Today's technologies allow an individual member of Congress to create a personal, continuing campaign organization, something that was simply unimaginable a century ago. But there is, of course, more to the historical context than technology.

Normative understandings have changed greatly. Even Ronald Reagan, who claimed that "government is not the solution to our problems, government *is* the problem," also held to the value of a "social safety net" provided by the government that is far larger than even the most progressive politician of the nineteenth century could have imagined. Ideas, in short, matter a great deal. Founders had to overcome antipathy verging on disgust over the very idea of political parties in order to create them in the first place, and Martin Van Buren's ideas about the nature and value of the "modern mass party" greatly shaped the nature of Jacksonian Democracy and political parties generally for more than a century. Neither Van Buren nor anyone else set out to create a system of competing mass parties (although he and others of that era recognized the importance of sustained partisan competition, they merely—but always—wanted to win that competiton). But the creation of the modern mass party led quickly to the creation of the first modern mass two-party system.

History matters in yet another way, beyond the ideas, values, and technological possibilities available at any given historical moment. The path of development matters as well. Once a set of institutional arrangements is in place, the set of equilibrium possibilities is greatly reduced, and change from the existing equilibrium path to a new and possibly superior one may be difficult or impossible. In other words, once there are two major parties, their presence induces incentives for ambitious politicians to affiliate with one party or the other, and some of these incentives emerge only because of the prior existence of these two parties.

The combination of these three forces means that the fundamental syllogism for the theory of political parties to be offered here is just what Rohde and Shepsle (1978) originally offered as the basis for the rational-choice-based new institutionalism: political outcomes—here political parties—result from actors' seeking to realize their goals, choosing within and possibly shaping a given set of institutional arrangements, and so choosing within a given historical context.

Before outlining this theory I provide a brief overview of the three major approaches that have long dominated the study of political parties. These prepare the way for understanding the theory of the political party, as each focuses attention on a different aspect and often on a different goal of politicians and their motivation to create or maintain a political party. I then turn to the question asked primarily in this chapter, briefly in chapter 2, and then more fully again in chapter 9 about the necessity of a system of political parties for an effective, functioning democracy. These preliminaries will provide a better sense of just what is at stake in the attempt to make sense of the major American party. Chapter 2 asks the most fundamental theoretical question: why are there parties? This discussion introduces three major theoretical problems that I believe have guided ambitious politicians as they have created, reformed, used, or ignored political parties. Part 2 puts the three major theoretical claims to test. Chapter 3 examines the origins of the first two political parties in the 1790s, emerging out of the legislative arena, attempting to solve a fundamental problem of social choice, and "completing ratification" by deciding just how strong and active the new national government was to be. Chapter 4 looks at the formation of the modern mass political party by focusing on its hallmark, the mobilization of the electorate—perhaps the most evident example of collective action and its inherent problems. Chapter 5 examines the other side of the Democratic and Whig parties of this period, the complex institutional arrangements these two parties helped shape that effectively kept the slavery issue off the agenda, making the union viable into the 1850s. That chapter then turns to the breakup of that party system and the rise of the Republican Party, looking especially at the interplay between the career goals of ambitious politicians and the slavery issue that culminated in the Civil War. The three chapters in part 2 conveniently illustrate the three theoretical problems that parties have been employed to attack (when it has been in the interests of politicians to use the parties), cover the formative period of political parties ending with the establishment of competition between Democrats and Republicans, and establish the form of parties and the basic nature of the historical path that survived, albeit with many important changes, through the post–World War II era.

Part 3 turns to the modern era. In this section I analyze the contemporary scene generally but look especially at the changes wrought in elections, governance, and hence parties in the 1960s. It was this set of changes that set in motion the empirical patterns that some saw as the decline (dealignment, decay, even decomposition) of parties but culminated in the rise of polarized parties. Chapter 6 examines the "party-in-elections." Chapter 7 develops the theory of the party-in-government, in light of the electoral forces. Chapter 8 looks at the oft-ignored party-as-organization and the new form of party I argue emerged in response to the politics of the 1960s and 1970s. The lacuna that many noted as the decline of parties was not, by this account, so much simply decline as the change from what I call the "party in control" of its ambitious office seekers and holders to the "party in service" to them. Chapter 9 concludes by reexamining the historical dynamics of the post–World War II era and considers the role of a party system in American democracy.

PREVIOUS APPROACHES TO THE STUDY OF AMERICAN POLITICAL PARTIES

Parties as Diverse Coalitions, Aggregating and Articulating the Interest in and of the Public

There are three basic views or understandings of major political parties in America.[3] The first is most often associated with V. O. Key Jr. (e.g., 1964), Frank Sorauf (1964; now Hershey 2009), Samuel Eldersveld (1964, 1982), and others. The major American party, to them, is a broad and encompassing organization, a coalition of many and diverse partners, that is commonly called umbrella-like. In seeking to appeal to a majority of the public, the two parties are based on similar values, roughly defining the "American creed." McClosky (1969) said of political (which is to say partisan) elites, "The evidence suggests that it is the [political elites] rather than the public who serve as the major repositories of the public conscience and as the carriers of the Creed. Responsibility for keeping the system going, hence, falls most heavily upon them" (286). His basic finding was that such elites share most elements of this "creed."

On many policy issues, however, there are clear and sometimes sharply drawn lines between the two parties. What Benjamin I. Page (1978) referred to as "partisan cleavages" are possible, even likely. On civil rights, as on many other issues, the Democratic Party has been more liberal than the Republican Party for decades, and on New Deal economic issues even a generation longer. In chapter 6 we will see a great deal of evidence that Democratic officeholders and activists are, in fact, more liberal than comparable Republicans on many issues and that the public perceives those differences (see table 6.1). The line of cleavage now is especially sharp, but it has been clearly discernible for a long time, even when parties were at their most diverse.

On other issues the line is less sharp and at times all but invisible. Even in this era of resurgent polarization between the two parties, many (and often most) roll call votes are not partisan. Survey researchers rarely choose to ask about issues that do not divide parties, but table 6.1 illustrates several policies on which the two parties are less clearly distinguished. Although both parties value democratic principles, the free market, equal opportunity, and the like, and though both adhere to the principles of a strong economy, peace maintained by a defense adequate for that purpose, and so on, they differ in the relative emphasis they place on such values, and they differ even more in the means or policies they consider appropriate for achieving those ends. Thus the Democrats are more likely to favor the active intervention of the government, especially the national government, on economic and social welfare issues, whereas the Republicans are much less so inclined. Democrats have long appealed to the poor, the working class, and Franklin Roosevelt's "common man." Republicans have sought support from the middle class and up, suburbanites, and the burgeoning Sun Belt.

With few exceptions these distinctions between the two major parties are tendencies, not certainties, and differing values are typically matters of emphasis rather than fundamental disagreements. As a consequence, with the exception of race, socioeconomic groups divide their votes broadly between the candidates of both parties. As Abramson, Aldrich, and Rohde report (2010, 128–29, table 5-2), excepting only race, the proportions of major socioeconomic groups voting for one presidential nominee compared with the other rarely reached or exceeded a difference of twenty percentage points from 1952 through 2008. Thus, in a close election, a group that split its vote by as much as, say, 60–40 would be understood as giving a very large vote for one party, but the disadvantaged party nonetheless would be supported by a substantial minority of that group.[4]

Each party is a coalition of many and diverse groups. This is most evident in the New Deal coalition Roosevelt forged in creating a working Democratic majority in the 1930s. It consisted of the then-solid South, cities, immigrants, blacks, ethnic and religious groups of many types, the working class and unions, and so on. Over half a century later this "coalition of minorities" has frayed considerably; some parts of it have exited from the coalition entirely, and the remnants are no longer capable of reaching majority size in presidential elections. Although some elements have left entirely or their loyalties have weakened, they have been replaced by others. For example, the Democratic coalition may no longer be home to as much of the South or as many blue-collar voters, but teachers' unions, women's groups, and organizations representing blacks, Hispanics, gays, environmentalists, and many others have been added since the 1960s to the panoply of voices seeking to be heard at their national convention. The Republican Party may once have been defined more easily by what wasn't included in the New Deal coalition, but it too has attracted a range of groups and interests. At Republican conventions one can find both Wall Street and Main Street fiscal conservatives, and westerners who seek to remove government interference in their lives (and lands), but also southerners who are social conservatives, the latter including pro-life groups, fundamentalist Christians, and so on, who seek active government intervention in behalf of their central concerns.

Although there are good reasons why these groups are allied with their particular parties, there is still great diversity within each party. There are even apparent contradictions latent—and at critical moments active—within each party. Blacks and white southerners may have found alliance comfortable when both were so deeply affected by the Great Depression, but when civil rights made it onto the national agenda in the 1950s and 1960s, the latent tensions in their respective views become active and divisive. Recent Republican conventions may have been noncontroversial, but fundamentalists and Wall Street business leaders, or other pairings, may well find that latent disagreements will become just as divisive when circumstances and the political agenda change. As of this writing, "tea party" and other conservative activists are engaging the Republican "regulars" on many such fronts.

In this view James Madison was correct. There is no small set of fixed interests; there are, rather, many and diverse interests in this extended Republic. He argued that a fundamental advantage of the new Constitution in creating a stronger federation was that the most evident and serious concern about majority rule—that a cohesive majority could tyrannize any minority—would be alleviated because there could be no cohesive majority in an extended republic. So too could no political party, no matter how large, rule tyrannically, because it must also be too diverse.

In a truly diverse republic, the problem is the opposite of majority tyranny. The problem is how to form *any* majority capable of taking action to solve pressing problems. A major political party aggregates these many and varied interests sufficiently to appeal to enough voters to form a majority in elections and to forge partisan-based, majority coalitions in government. In this view, parties are intermediaries that connect the public and the government. Parties also aggregate these diverse interests into a relatively cohesive, if typically compromise, platform,[5] and they articulate these varied interests by representing them in government. The result, in this view, is that parties parlay those compromise positions into policy outcomes, and so they—a ruling, if nonhomogeneous and shifting, government majority—can be held accountable to the public in subsequent elections.

The diversity of interests a party must seek to aggregate and the diversity of actors in the party lead to an equally diverse set of party arrangements. Key's (1964) and Sorauf's (1964; Hershey 2009) long influential texts, for example, have presented the political party as divided into three parts: the party-in-the-electorate, the party-in-government, and the party-as-organization, meant to provide some coherence for understanding the wide variety of activities parties must engage in. These diverse structures make possible the key concepts of the party in this view: interest articulation and aggregation and electoral accountability (see Eldersveld 1964).

The Responsible Party Thesis

If the first view of interest aggregation and articulation was primarily empirical but with normative overtones (if parties are a major way by which the public interacts with and shapes its government, then that must be a good thing, right?), the second view, that of responsible parties, is primarily normative and aspirational, with critique of the empirics of party politics thrown in. This thesis is most directly associated with E. E. Schattschneider (1942) and the Committee for a More Responsible Two-Party System, sponsored by the American Political Science Association, that he chaired (1950). But this view has deeper historical roots. Woodrow Wilson's *Congressional Government* (1881), for example, included a plea for parties more in the responsible party mold, and as Ranney (1975) and Epstein (1986) report, prominent political scientists at the beginning of the twentieth century were much enamored of this doctrine.

Ranney (1975, 43) lists four criteria that define responsible parties. Such parties (1) make policy commitments to the electorate, (2) are willing and able to carry them out when in office, (3) develop alternatives to government policies when out of office, and (4) differ sufficiently between themselves to "provide the electorate with a proper range of choice between alternative actions."[6] This doctrine derives from an idealized (and more closely realized) form of the British system, what Lijphart (1984, 1999) calls the "Westminster model." As a normative standard, it has several obvious defects. For example, it reduces choices for the public to exactly two. If the United States is a diverse and extended Madisonian republic, it is not obvious that the public would find its views adequately articulated by exactly two options, no matter how clear and distinct. A mélange of compromise proposals may be more suitable. Alternation of parties in office may also make policy trajectories shift dramatically back and forth. And if one party does capture a longtime working majority, majority tyranny could follow. This is a normative standard that thus places great weight on the accountability of elected officials, through their party's control of office, and less weight on interest articulation. In more practical terms, it is an idealization that fits more readily with a unified, essentially unicameral assembly that combines the legislative and executive branches and that is elected all at once. It fits more poorly with a government designed around the principles of separated but intermingled powers, with officials elected at different times from differently defined constituencies for the Madisonian purpose of making ambition check ambition.

Notwithstanding these problems, the responsible party thesis retains its attractiveness to many. In the 1970s, when parties seemed in more serious decline than usual, electoral accountability was seen as not just weakened but virtually nonexistent (e.g., Fiorina 1980). Such pressing problems as the budget deficit could not be solved because of too-weak and nonresponsible parties—as contrasted to today, where budget deficits are seen as insoluble because of too-strong and nonresponsible parties. Campaigns seemed to turn on the trivial, the personal, and the irrelevant, leaving debate—let alone action—on significant problems off the agenda. Finally, the public perceived the government as increasingly ineffective and incompetent. Cynicism was up, trust and confidence in the government were down. Alienation increasesd, participation decreased (see Abramson 1983; Lipset and Schneider 1987). And the public came to see the political parties as increasingly irrelevant to elections and to governance (see Wattenberg 1990; this volume, chap. 6). When the parties' candidates did address issues, it is often felt, they were too similar. Conservative Republicans in the 1940s and 1950s complained that the dominant, moderate wing of their party engaged in "me-too-ism"; whatever Democrats said, the moderate Republicans responded "me too!" Or as George Wallace, the once and future Democrat, claimed in his third-party presidential campaign in 1968, "there ain't a dime's worth of difference" between the two parties. It was not always so, responsible party advocates claimed. In other eras parties were stronger, and they were stronger in the sense of responsible parties. At the very least they were sufficiently united in office to "be willing and able to carry out" whatever policy commitments the majority party chose. They may not have been then, and today may not truly be, responsible parties, consistent with that doctrine, but they once were stronger, more effective, and more easily held accountable. Perhaps they could become so again.

The advocates had a point. In much of our partisan history, American parties were stronger than when Schattschneider, Ranney, et al., were writing. The Republicans and Democrats have competed nationwide since the end of Reconstruction. Beginning in the late 1930s, these two parties began parallel declines, at least by some measures such as the level of party voting in Congress (see chap. 7), bottoming out in the early 1970s. Both then started to climb back toward what now appear to be the historically more common levels of partisan "polarization." It so happens, by this account, that the 1950s and 1960s were the historical anomaly, and part of the anomalous and unique nature of this period was that it was far from fulfilling Ranney's four conditions.

And, from a normative perspective, if my claim is correct that a party system is necessary for effective democracy, the major but partial defect in our democratic system was coming home to roost. That defect was the systematic violation of the principles of democratic competition in the South. This had long been a problem, of course, but the elevation of concerns about those systematically excluded by presumptively unconstitutional law and by force was moving up onto the national agenda. As a result, the weakness of one-third of the nation's failure to be democratic was being revealed, in large part, through its party system.

The previous paragraphs illustrated a number of the concerns raised by the decline of parties thesis, and that thesis often has some version of responsible parties as the standard for measuring the extent of the claimed decline. Not all agreed that the parties had declined—at least as much as, or in the same sense as, was held by the major adherents of decline. One characteristic of the older, stronger party periods was that large regions of the country were dominated by a single party. The South was solidly Democratic for a century, machines ruled in many cities and in some rural areas, and in such areas of one-party dominance there was for long periods effectively no competition for office by the opposing party. Thus articulation, aggregation, and accountability were all lost. Today both parties can seriously imagine competing effectively—and possibly winning—in every region of the nation.[7] And genuine competition for elective office has long been claimed as one of the most important virtues of political parties. As Hofstadter argued (1969), the legitimation of opposition made possible the success of the young Republic, solving perhaps the greatest internal threat to any nation by making possible the peaceful, legitimate transfer of power. The emergence of the Federalist and Jeffersonian Republican Parties made legitimation of opposition possible and effected such a transfer in 1800 (see chap. 3). The absence of regular—and that means partisan—competition for elective office, moreover, risks tyranny or corruption (that is the simplest statement of Key's argument [1949], which I expand upon below and in chap. 9).

Parties and Electoral Competition

The third view of parties focuses on the importance of this competition for office. Of course both earlier views also saw electoral competition as a central characteristic of partisan politics. But this third view sees competition for office as the singular, defining characteristic of the major American political party. The most rigorous advocates of this position are Anthony Downs (1957) and Joseph A. Schlesinger (1991; see also Demsetz 1990). Both are rational choice theorists, positing that actors are goal seekers and that their actions, and eventually the institutional arrangements they help shape, are the product of their attempts to realize their goals. At the center of their theory are the partisan elites: the aspiring office seekers and the successful officeholders. Their theories rest, moreover, on a simple assumption about the goal of each such partisan elite, office seeking and holding per se. That is, party leaders are motivated to win elections. As a result a party is, in the words of Downs (1957, 25), "a team seeking to control the governing apparatus by gaining office in a duly constituted election." The political party therefore is the organization that team uses to realize its goals. Electoral victory is paramount; other motives are at most secondary. Most important, as Downs puts it, parties formulate policies to win elections rather than winning elections to promulgate policies. In a two-party system, the "health" of the system is measured by how competitive the two parties are for a wide range of elective offices over a long period. In Schlesinger's view (1991), the hallmark of a party is its ability to channel the competing career ambitions of its potential and actual officeholders, forming them into an effective electoral machine. More accurately, he argued that each office and its partisan seeker serves as one "nucleus" of a party, and a strong party is one that has many strong nuclei connected to each other for the purpose of supporting its ambitious partisan office seekers.

The genius of democracy, in this view, is rather like the genius Adam Smith found in the free market. In Smith's case individuals acting in their own self-interest turn out to be guided, as if by some unseen hand, to act in the economic interests of the collective. In Schlesinger's case ambitious politicians, seeking to have a long and successful career, are all led by the necessity of winning broad support in the face of stiff competition to reflect the desires of those citizens who support them. Without competition for office—without at least minimally strong political parties—career ambition is not necessarily harnessed to reflect the desires of the public. In elections, political parties serve the Madisonian principle of having ambition clash with, and thereby check, ambition. Seeking popular support in the face of competition yields officeholders who find it in their self-interest to respond to the wishes of the public so that that public will continually reelect them, thereby satisfying their career ambition. All else about parties flows from this Schumpeterian view. Office seekers will try to create a strong electoral machine for mobilizing the electorate, but only if competition forces them to do so. Thus will the party-as-organization flow from competition for office. So too will the party-in-government flow naturally from electoral competition—but only so long as it is in the long-term career interests of office seekers and holders to do so. Only so long, that is, as there is a shared, collective interest in working together in office, and doing so to remain in office.[8] And that collective interest must come from a common electoral fate.

These, then, are the three major views or understandings of political parties. I will offer a fourth. Like those of Downs and Schlesinger, it will be a rational choice theory, and it will be one that takes career ambitions of elective office seekers and holders as one of its central building blocks. It will differ, however, in seeing office seeking as only one of several goals held by those with political ambitions. To be sure, winning elections is an intermediary end on its way to achieving power and policy in addition to being an end in itself. Motivations for policy ends and for power and prestige in office, that is, require electoral victory. But for many, winning office per se is not the end of politics but the beginning. As we will see, this leads naturally and inevitably to drawing from the other views of parties, and it will be necessary to trace the historical, "equilibrium" path of development. My aim is also to develop a theoretical account of parties that can help us make sense of the widest possible array of empirical findings relevant to party politics. Understanding the nature of the political party, however, takes us only part of the way to understanding the party's role in democracy. For parties are engendered by but also reflect back on democratic politics. But it is not any one party alone that can achieve that reflection. Indeed, democracy fails when there is but one party. Instead it is necessary to have a party system, an ongoing competition between two or more durable parties.

A THEORY OF POLITICAL PARTIES

These and other astute observers might come to very different conclusions, but they all agree that the political party is—or should be—central to the American political system. Parties are—or should be—integral parts of all political life, from structuring the reasoning and choice of the electorate, through all facets of campaigns and seemingly all facets of the government, to the very possibility of effective governance in a democracy.

How is it, then, that such astute observers of American politics and parties, writing at virtually the same time in the 1970s and 1980s and looking at much the same evidence, come to such diametrically opposed conclusions about the strength of parties? Eldersveld provided an obvious answer. He wrote that "political parties are complex institutions and processes, and as such they are difficult to understand and evaluate" (1982, 407). As proof, he went on to consider the decline of parties thesis. At one point he wrote, "The decline in our parties, therefore, is difficult to demonstrate, empirically or in terms of historical perspective" (417). And yet he then turned to signs of party decline and concluded his book with this statement: "Despite their defects they continue today to be the major instruments for democratic government in this nation. With necessary reforms we can make them even more central to the governmental process and to the lives of American citizens. Eighty years ago, Lord James Bryce, after studying our party system, said, 'In America the great moving forces are the parties. The government counts for less than in Europe, the parties count for more. . . .' If our citizens and their leaders wish it, American parties will still be the 'great moving forces' of our system" (1982, 432–33).

The "Fundamental Equation" of the New Institutionalism Applied to Parties

That parties are complex does not mean they are incomprehensible. Indeed complexity is, if not an intentional outcome, at least an anticipated result of those who shape the political parties. Moreover, they are so deeply woven into the fabric of American politics that they cannot be understood apart from either their own historical context and dynamics or those of the political system as a whole. Parties, that is, can be understood only in relation to the polity, to the government and its institutions, and to the historical context of the times.

The study of political parties is also necessarily a study of a major pair of political *institutions*. Indeed, the institutions that define the political party are unique, and as it happens they are unique in ways that make an institutional account especially useful. Their establishment and nature are fundamentally extralegal; they are nongovernmental political institutions. Instead of statute, their basis lies in the actions of ambitious politicians who created them and who maintain them. They are, in the parlance of the new institutionalism, *endogenous institutions*—in fact, the most highly endogenous political institutions of any substantial and sustained importance.

By endogenous I mean it was the actions of political actors that created political parties in the first place, and it is the actions of political actors that shape and alter them over time. And political actors have chosen to alter their parties dramatically at several times in our history, reformed them often, and tinkered with them constantly. Of all major political bodies in the United States, the political party is the most variable in its rules, regulations, and procedures—that is to say, in its formal organization—and in its informal methods and traditions. It is often the same actors who write the party's rules who then choose the party's outcomes, sometimes at nearly the same time and by the same method. Thus, for example, on one night, national party conventions debate, consider any proposed amendments, and then adopt their rules by a majority vote of credentialed delegates. The next night these same delegates debate, consider any proposed amendments, and then adopt their platform by majority vote, and they choose their presidential nominee by majority vote the following night.

Who, then, are these critical political actors? Many see the party-in-the-electorate as comprising major actors. To be sure, mobilizing the electorate to capture office is a central task of the political party. But America is a republican democracy. All power flows directly or indirectly from the great body of the people, to paraphrase Madison's definition. The public elects its political leaders, but it is that leadership that legislates, executes, and adjudicates policy. The parties are defined in relation to this republican democracy. Thus it is political leaders, those Schlesinger (1975) has called "office-seekers"—*those who seek and those who hold elective office*—who are the central actors in the party.[9]

Ambitious office seekers and holders are thus the first and most important actors in the political party. A second set of important figures in party politics comprises those who hold, or have access to, critical resources that office seekers need to realize their ambitions. It is expensive to build and maintain the party and campaign organizations necessary to compete effectively in the electoral arena. Thomas Ferguson, for example, has made an extended argument for the "primary and constitutive role large investors play in American politics" (1983, 3; see also Ferguson 1986, 1989, 1991). Much of his research emphasizes this primary and constitutive role in party politics in particular, such as in partisan realignments. The study of the role of money in congressional elections has also focused in part on concentrations of such sources of funding, such as from political action committees (e.g., Sorauf 1988), which political parties have come to take advantage of (for early accounts see Hernnson 1988; Kayden and Mayhe 1985). Elections are also fought over the flow of information to the public. The electoral arm of political parties in the eighteenth century was made up of "committees of correspondence," which were primarily lines of communication among political elites and between them and potential voters, and one of the first signs of organizing of the Jeffersonian Republican Party was the hiring of a newspaper editor (see chap. 3). The press was first a partisan press, and editors and publishers from Thomas Ritchie (see chap. 4) to Horace Greeley long were critical players in party politics. Today those with specialized knowledge relevant to communication, such as pollsters, media and advertising experts, and computerized fund-raising specialists, enjoy influence in party, campaign, and even government councils that greatly exceeds their mere technical expertise (see Aldrich 1992).

In more theoretical terms, this second set of party actors include those Schlesinger (1975) has called "benefit seekers," those for whom realization of their goals depends on the party's success in capturing office. Party activists shade from those powerful figures with concentrations of, or access to, large amounts of money and information, as described above, to the legions of volunteer campaign activists who ring doorbells and stuff envelopes and are, individually and collectively, critical to the first level of the party—its office seekers. All are critical because they command the resources, whether money, expertise, and information, or merely time and labor, that office seekers need to realize their ambitions. As a result, activists' motivations shape and constrain the behavior of office seekers, as their own roles are, in turn, shaped and constrained by the office seekers. In chapter 6 I argue that the changed incentives of party activists have played a significant role in the fundamentally altered nature of the contemporary party, but the impact of benefit seekers will be seen scattered throughout this account.

Voters, however, are neither office seekers nor benefit seekers and thus are not a part of the political party at all, even if they identify strongly with a party and consistently support its candidates.[10] Voters are indeed critical, but they are critical as the targets of party activities. Parties "produce" candidates, platforms, and policies. Voters "consume" by exchanging their votes for the party's product (see Popkin et al. 1976). Some voters, of course, become partisan benefit-seekers by becoming activists, whether as occasional volunteers, as sustained contributors, or even as candidates. But until they do so, they may be faithful consumers, "brand name" loyalists as it were, but they are still only the targets of partisans' efforts to sell their wares in the political marketplace.

Why, then, do politicians create and recreate the party, exploit its features, or ignore its dictates? The simple answer is that it has been in their interests to do so. That is, this is a *rational choice* account of the party, an account that presumes that rational, elective office seekers and holders use the party to achieve their ends.

I do not assume that politicians are invariably self-interested in a narrow sense. This is not a theory in which elective office seekers simply maximize their chances of election or reelection, at least not for its own sake. They may well have fundamental values and principles, and they may have preferences over policies as means to those ends. They also care about office, both for its own sake and for the opportunities to achieve other ends that election and reelection make possible. In chapters 3–5, I recount several historical cases in some detail. None of these make sense under the assumption of a single-minded office-seeking goal. All are understandable as the rational actions of goal-seeking politicians using the political party to help achieve their ends. Their ends are simply more numerous, interesting, and political than mere careerism. Just as winning elections is a means to other ends for politicians (whether career or policy ends), so too is the political party a means to these other ends.[11]

Why, then, do politicians turn to create or reform, to use or abuse, partisan institutions? The answer is that parties are designed as attempts to solve problems that current institutional arrangements do not solve and that politicians have come to believe they cannot solve. These problems fall into three general and recurring categories.[12]

The Problem of Ambition and Elective Office Seeking

Elective office seekers, as that label says, want to win election to office. Parties regulate access to those offices. If elective office is indeed valuable, there will be more aspirants than offices, and the political party and the two-party system are means of regulating that competition and channeling those ambitions. Major party nomination is all but a necessary condition for election in America, and partisan institutions have been developed—and have been reformed and re-reformed—for regulating competition. Intrainstitutional leadership positions are also highly valued and therefore potentially competitive. There is, for example, a fairly well-institutionalized path to the office of Speaker of the House trod by Speakers from Sam Rayburn to Nancy Pelosi. It is, however, a Democratic Party institution. Elective politicians, of course, ordinarily desire election more than once. They are typically careerists who want a long and productive career in politics. Schlesinger's ambition theory (1966), developed and extended by others (see especially Rohde 1979), is precisely about this general problem. Underlying this theory, though typically not fully developed, is a problem. The problem is that if office is desirable, there will be more aspirants than there are offices to go around. When stated in rigorous form, it can be proved that in fact there is no permanent solution to this problem.[13] And it is a problem that can adversely affect the fortunes of a party. In 1912 the Republican vote was split between William Howard Taft and Theodore Roosevelt. This split enabled Woodrow Wilson to win with 42 percent of the popular vote. Not only was Wilson the only break in Republican hegemony of the White House in this period, but in that year Democrats increased their House majority by sixty-five additional seats and captured majority control of the Senate. Thus failure to regulate intraparty competition cost Republicans dearly.

For elective office seekers, regulating conflict over who holds those offices is clearly of major concern. It is ever present. And it is not just a problem of access to government offices but is also a problem internal to each party as soon as the party becomes an important gateway to office.

The Problem of Making Decisions for the Party and for the Polity

Once in office, partisans determine outcomes for the polity. They propose alternatives, shape the agenda, pass or reject legislation, determine how to implement what they enact, and oversee that implementation. The policy formation and execution process, that is, is highly partisan. The parties-in-government are more than mere coalitions of like-minded individuals, however; they are enduring institutions. Very few incumbents change their partisan affiliations. Most retain their partisanship throughout their careers, even though they often disagree (i.e., are not uniformly like-minded) with some of their partisan peers. When the rare incumbent does change parties, it is invariably to join the party more consonant with that switcher's policy interests. This implies that there are differences between the two parties at some fundamental and enduring level on policy positions, values, and beliefs. When incumbents do change parties, they almost invariably lament (often correctly) that they did not change their ideas or beliefs, but it was their party that changed and thus moved away from them. They were surprised by these important but occasional changes, reflecting the prevailing belief of partisan stability.

Thus, parties are institutions designed to promote the achievement of collective choices—choices on which the parties differ and choices reached by majority rule. As with access to office and ambition theory, there is a well-developed theory for this problem: social choice theory. Underlying this theory is the well-known problem that no method of choice can solve the elective officeholders' problem of combining the interests, concerns, or values of a polity that remains faithful to democratic values, as shown by the consequences flowing from Arrow's theorem (Arrow 1951). Thus, in a republican democracy politicians may turn to partisan institutions to solve the problem of collective choice. In the language of politics, parties may help achieve the goal of attaining policy majorities in the first place, as well as the often more difficult goal of maintaining such majorities. To the extent that this problem tends to reside most often in policy choices, it tends to be the problem that is confronted most often by legislative parties, although it certainly applies to electoral and organizational aspects of the parties, as well.

The Problem of Collective Action

The third problem is the most pervasive and thus the furthest-ranging in substantive content. The clearest example, however, is also the most important. To win office, candidates need more than a party's nomination. Election requires not only persuading members of the public to support that candidacy but also mobilizing as many of those supporters as possible. Mobilizing is perhaps the quintessential problem of collective action. How do candidates get supporters to vote for them—at least in greater numbers than vote for the opposition—as well as get them to provide the cadre of workers and contribute the resources needed to win elections? The political party has long been the solution.

As important as wooing and mobilizing supporters are, collective action problems arise in a wide range of circumstances facing elective office seekers. Party action invariably requires the concerted action of many partisans to achieve collectively desirable outcomes. Jimmy Carter was the only president in the 1970s and 1980s to enjoy unified party control of government. Democrats in Congress, it might well be argued, shared an interest in achieving policy outcomes. And yet Carter was all too often unable to get them to act in their shared collective interests. In 1980 not only he but the Democratic congressional parties paid a heavy price for failed cooperation. The theory here, of course, is the theory of public goods (Samuelson 1954) and its consequence, the theory of collective action (Olson 1965).

The Elective Office Seekers' and Holders' Interests Are to Win

Why should this crucial set of actors, the elective office seekers and officeholders, care about these three classes of problems? The short answer is that these concerns become practical problems to politicians when they adversely affect their chances of winning. Put differently, politicians turn to their political party—that is, use its powers, re- sources, and institutional forms—when they believe doing so increases their prospects for winning desired outcomes, and they turn from it if it does not.[14]

Ambition theory is about winning per se. The breakdown of orderly access to office risks unfettered and unregulated competition. The in- ability of a party to develop effective means of nomination and sup- port for election therefore directly influences the chances of victory for the candidates and thus for their parties. The standard example of the problem of social choice theory, the "paradox of voting," is paradoxi- cal precisely because all are voting to win desired outcomes, and yet there is no majority-preferred outcome. Even if there happens to be a majority-preferred policy, the conditions under which it is truly a stable equilibrium are extremely fragile and thus all too amenable to defeat. In other words, majorities in Congress are hard to attain and at least as hard to maintain. And the only reason to employ scarce campaign resources to mobilize supporters is that such mobilization increases the odds of victory. Its opposite, the failure to act when there are broadly shared interests—the problem of collective action—reduces the pros- pects of victory, whether at the ballot box or in government. Scholars may recognize these as manifestations of theoretical problems and call them "paradoxes," or "impossibility results," to emphasize their generic importance. Politicians recognize the consequences of these impos- sibility results by their adverse effects on their chances of winning—of securing what it is in their interests to secure.

So why have politicians so often turned to political parties for solu- tions to these problems? Their existence creates incentives for their use. It is, for example, incredibly difficult to win election to major office without the backing of a major party. It is only a little less certain that legislators who seek to lead a policy proposal through the congressional labyrinth will first turn to their party for assistance. But such incentives tell us only that an ongoing political institution is used when it is useful. Why form political parties in the first place? The answer is what part 1 of this book is about, and the theory will be developed in the next chapter and tested in the following three. A brief statement of three points will give a first look at the argument.

First, parties are institutions. This means, among other things, that they have some durability. They may be endogenous institutions, yet party reforms are meant not as short-term fixes but as alterations to last for years, even decades. Thus, for example, legislators might create a party rather than a temporary majority coalition to increase their chances of winning not just today but tomorrow and into the future. Similarly, a long and successful political career means winning office today, but it also requires winning elections throughout that career. A standing, enduring organization makes that goal more likely.

Second, American democracy chooses by plurality or majority rule. Election to office therefore requires broad-based support wherever and from whomever it can be found. So strong are the resulting incentives for a two-party system to emerge that the effect is called Duverger's Law (Duverger 1954). It is in part the need to win vast and diverse support that has led politicians to create political parties.

Third, parties may help officeholders win more, and more often, than alternatives. Consider the usual stylized model of pork barrel politics. All winners get a piece of the pork for their districts. All funded projects are paid for by tax revenues, so each district pays an equal share of the costs of each project adopted, whether or not that district receives a project. Several writers have argued that this kind of legislation leads to "universalism," that is, adoption of a "norm" that every such bill yields a project to every district and thus passes with a "universal" or unanimous coalition. Thus everyone "wins." Weingast proved the basic theorem (1979). His theorem yields the choice of the rule of universalism over the formation of a simple majority coalition, because in advance each legislator calculates the chances of any simple majority coalition's forming as equal to that of any other. As a result, expecting to win only a bit more than half the time and lose the rest of the time, all legislators prefer consistent use of the norm of universalism.[15] But consider an alternative. Suppose some majority agree to form a more permanent coalition, to control outcomes now and into the future, and develop institutional means to encourage fealty to this agreement. If they successfully accomplish this, they will win regularly. Members of this institutionalized coalition would prefer it to universalism, since they always win a project in either case, but they get their projects at lower cost under the institutionalized majority coalition, which passes fewer projects.[16] Thus, even in this case with no shared substantive interests at all, there are nonetheless incentives to form an enduring voting coalition—to form a political party. And those in the excluded minority have incentives to counterorganize. United, they may be more able to woo defectors to their side. If not, they can campaign to throw those rascals in the majority party out of office.

In sum, these theoretical problems affect elective office seekers and officeholders by reducing their chances of winning. Politicians therefore may turn to political parties as institutions designed to ameliorate them. In solving these theoretical problems, however, from the politicians' perspective parties are affecting who wins and loses and what is won or lost. And it is to parties that politicians often turn, because of their durability as institutionalized solutions, because of the need to orchestrate large and diverse groups of people to form winning majorities, and because often more can be won through parties. Note that this argument rests on the implicit assumption that winning and losing hang in the balance. Politicians may be expected to give up some of their personal autonomy only when they face an imminent threat of defeat without doing so or only when doing so can block opponents' ability to build the strength necessary to win.

This is, of course, the positive case for parties, for it specifies conditions under which politicians find them useful. Not all problems are best solved, perhaps even solved at all, by political parties. Other arrangements, perhaps interest groups, issue networks, or personal electoral coalitions, may be superior at different times and under different conditions (see Hansen 1991, for example). The party may even be part of the problem. In such cases politicians turn elsewhere to seek the means to win.[17] Thus this theory is at base a theory of ambitious politicians seeking to achieve their goals. Often they have done so through the agency of the party, but sometimes, this theory implies, they will seek to realize their goals in other ways.

The political party has regularly proved useful. The permanence of parties suggests that the appropriate question is not "When parties?" but "How much parties and how much other means?" That parties are endogenous implies that there is no single, consistent account of the political party—nor should we expect one. Instead, parties are but a (major) part of the institutional context in which current historical conditions—the problems—are set, and solutions are sought with permanence only by changing that web of institutional arrangements. Of these the political party is by design the most malleable, and thus it is intended to change in important ways and with relatively great frequency. But it changes in ways that have, for most of American history, retained major political parties and, indeed, retained two major parties.

PARTY COMPETITION AND DEMOCRACY

And it is here, at this point, that the question of a party system arises. John Griffin and I (2010) recently published the account I paraphrase in this section. We argued that not only is a party system in equilibrium but also that, in two-party systems such as in the United States, each of the two major parties forms its own organizational complex, and that complex is also in equilibrium. Hence, there is a three-part equilibrium, with each party organization being in equilibrium in and of itself, and with the two parties forming a party system that is also in equilibrium. Further, we argued that an individual party is in equilibrium when its label conveys meaning to voters (i.e., the party stands for something), and it is sufficiently attractive to enough voters so as, in turn, to attract ambitious politicians to affiliate with it and its label. Given the goals of an ambitious politician in a two-party system, the individual party is in equilibrium when it can offer its candidates an even chance of election. In a two-party system, then, each of the parties is in equilibrium when elections are competitive. The important point is that each and every incumbent fears losing the next election, and indeed they should because the opposition has a credible chance of winning. What the equilibrium of the two-party system looks like will be considered in the next chapter.

Some have contended that in the absence of a competitive party system, intraparty competition among party factions might play the same role as parties in tying government policies to citizens' interests. For instance, Benedict (1985, 386) assessed mid-nineteenth-century factionalism and concluded that "factional competition provided another opportunity for the public, and especially active partisans, to influence policy." But this was just what Key (1949, see especially 302–6) strongly objected to as being almost exactly the opposite of a political party, at least in the early to mid-twentieth-century South. Factions, he claimed, were "ill-designed to meet the necessities of self-government" (1949, 310–11), lacking continuity in name, in leadership, and in the political candidates they presented to the public. As a result of factions' lack of continuity, the electorate necessarily becomes confused by the absence of a clear set of options, sustained over time. Parties and parties alone, he believed, are able to be held responsible and therefore forced to exercise at least a modicum of responsibility. Factions cannot be held responsible, he argued. This he demonstrated convincingly by examining one southern one-party state after another. Therefore, his argument continued, no elected official or his party will exercise responsibility, and he also demonstrated that southern Democrats did not, in fact, do so. With factions, there is not a loyal opposition that will search for issues to bring up in an attempt to oust the governing party. Factions lack "collective spirit," a sense of duty and obligation, and any sense of "joint responsibility" between governor and legislature as well. In sum, factional politics undermines each part of Key's party triad (i.e., the party in the electorate, in government, and as an organization), both in the short term and, more worrisomely, in the long term.

It might seem that the voter in a one-party (which was, to Key, a "no party") system could still be a "rational God of vengeance or reward," in the sense of retrospective voting that Key developed (1966). Not so, he argued. Retrospective voting needs a competitive alternative. At the same time, he extended his argument about how the lack of organized parties undermines the development of responsible leadership and affects the choices of those ambitiously seeking to enter politics.

The problem Key identified with factional politics was that it does not stand for any of three things that we might believe partisan contests for control of electoral offices to be about. Factions do not stand for ideas or policies that would help the voter distinguish one from another in the voting booth. Neither do they stand unified with ambitious politicians in seeking joint control of a large swath of offices, who therefore could be seen as bound together across the legislature, the executive branch, and in other offices chosen directly by election, or chosen indirectly by political appointment by elected officials. Third, factions do not typically, in Key's account, stand for control of the same office over time, making the transition from one occupant of that office to the next unconnected with what had transpired in that office, and thus denying the voter the ability to hold the party and its ambitious politicians accountable for conduct while in office.

Griffin and I thus contended that a competitive party system is a necessary ingredient of democratic politics. Meaningful party labels allow voters to play a substantial role in selecting the direction of policy and holding politicians accountable. Ambitious politicians affiliate with parties that create those meaningful (and, if they are good enough, popular) labels. A party will be competitive when its label attracts a sufficient number of voters and ambitious candidates, and a pair of competitive parties consists of two such parties, each of which is in such an individual equilibrium. They form a two-party system when each party acts and reacts to the actions of the other, thus integrating their choices into a system of strategic interaction. And it is at that point, and only at that point, of existence of a party system that democracy can be effective, at least in an extended republic.

2 WHY PARTIES FORM

Ratification of the Constitution launched America's "great experiment," testing the viability of democracy. This experiment began before national political parties were invented. The founders held deep sentiments against parties, yet many of them were instrumental in creating parties, justifying them as temporary necessities to make the great experiment succeed, as we will see in chapter 3. In the 1820s what effectively had become a one-party system led to a revival of concerns that the viability of the republic was threatened (see chap. 4). Martin Van Buren and others sought to revive the old party principles of Jefferson and Madison through a new form that historians have come to call the "modern mass party," and with formation of the Whigs this led to the first full flowering of a two-party system. Even with collapse of the Whigs, incentives for political parties were sufficiently strong that politicians turned almost immediately to the formation of the Republican and American ("Know Nothing") Parties. With the ascendance of the Republicans over the Americans, a two-party system was maintained (see chap. 5).

In these crucial moments, ambitious politicians sought durable solutions to what they perceived as critical problems. New partisan institutions were their chosen means. In each case not only were these problems seen as threatening the Union, but it was the politicians' seeking to achieve their goals—seeking to win—that led them to create parties.

In this chapter I will develop a theoretical account of the origins of political parties by demonstrating that there exists a set of incentives for ambitious politicians to "turn to parties." In particular, a series of problems that necessarily arise in elections and in governance make it possible for politicians to win more of what they seek to win, more often, and over a longer period by creating political parties. The historical context determines when, and in what form, these theoretical possibilities actually arise. This theoretical inquiry produces "possibility" results that imply political parties may be a solution. It is not necessary or inevitable that politicians will turn to parties. These theoretical circumstances are, however, regular and recurring rather than rare and occasional, so the possibility that politicians will seek to achieve their goals through political parties will also recur.

The situations that give rise to incentives for turning to parties are problems endemic to republican government.[1] That is, each of the three problems is deeply interwoven into the choices a society might make and thus into our theoretical understanding of social decision-making. All are so significant that there are theories about each: the theory of public goods and collective action, the theory of social choice and voting, and the theory of political ambition. A second purpose of this chapter is to develop the technical tools, language, and logics that their theoretical study has produced. These tools and logics need to be understood on their own terms if we are to comprehend the role of each in the theory of political parties. I have simplified presentation as much as possible, and I hope to provide readers unfamiliar with the technical literature enough of the insights and results already achieved to make them useful for understanding.[2]

I also hope to show that each is indeed relevant to the question of why ambitious politicians might choose to create and use political parties. Of course politicians confront such circumstances not as theoretical insights, but as practical, substantive problems affecting their ability to achieve their goals. The task therefore is to demonstrate that they perceive political parties as a possible institutional means to solve the particular (theoretical) problem that has arisen.

COLLECTIVE ACTION PROBLEMS WITHIN THE GOVERNMENT

The Problem of Collective Policymaking

Parties-in-government consist of officeholders who have preferences. It could be that parties are no more than a convenient coalition of those who share preferences most closely: shared preferences are important bases of political parties. Parties-in-government are also institutions with rules and procedures for selecting leaders, providing them with powers and resources, and structuring Congress and government more

Table 2.1 A Collective Action Problem and Incentives for Party Formation

	Bill		
Legislator	X	Y	Z
A	4[a]	3	−9
B	3	−9	4
C	−9	4	3

Independent voting Outcome: All bills pass. Payoff (−2, −2, −2)[b]
Pareto optimal result Defeat all bills. Payoff (0, 0, 0)
Party of A and B Outcome: Pass only X. Payoff (4, 3, −9)

[a]Denotes payoff to legislator if bill is passed.
[b]Denotes typical payoffs to legislators A, B, and C, respectively.

generally. The goal here is to see what the incentives are for creating or affiliating with institutional parties in addition to any sharing of preferences. Let us begin with a simple "government," in which whatever a unicameral legislature passes becomes law, but let us also assume as great a divergence in preferences as we can. That is, are there incentives for partisan activity even when preferences are not closely shared?

Consider distributive or "pork barrel" legislation—legislation that concentrates benefits in one or only a few districts but distributes costs broadly, perhaps equally, across all districts. One such example is shown in table 2.1, adapted from Schwartz (1989), whose account this section relies on.

In table 2.1 there are three legislators, A, B, and C, and three bills, X, Y, and Z. The entry is the value to the legislator (or the district represented) if the bill passes. Thus the 4 in row A, column X indicates that A receives a payoff of 4 if X passes. The three bills are symmetric, each legislator (or district) winning 4 with one bill, 3 with another, and −9 with the third. Any bill that fails gives each a payoff of 0.

Suppose these legislators act independently and arrive at their choices by looking only at the value to them of the bill currently under consideration. If so, all three bills pass by a 2–1 vote, and all three legislators receive a total payoff of −2. This is worse for all three of them than defeating all bills, yielding each 0. Defeating all bills is said to be "Pareto superior" to passing all three.

Even knowing this result, legislators cannot ensure the Pareto superior outcome when acting independently. Suppose the bills are taken up in alphabetical order. No matter what happens with bills X and Y, by the time Z is taken up B and C have a clear incentive to vote for passage, as they gain 4 and 3, respectively, no matter whether X and Y have won or lost. So too A and C would rationally choose to vote for Y, whenever it would come up for a vote. In similar fashion, A and B independently conclude that they should vote for X. The equilibrium in behavior for independent legislators, therefore, is to pass each bill, even though all three might know full well that doing so makes them worse off.

This is the problem of collective action, and it arises when rational behavior, in equilibrium, leads to results that are Pareto inferior to at least one other possible outcome. A, B, and C are led by their individual, rational decisions to a behavioral equilibrium that passes all three bills. They unanimously prefer defeat of all bills to their adoption, however, and yet that Pareto superior outcome cannot be attained by rational, independent action.

The Nature of the Collective Action Problem

Collective action arises in a large variety of political contexts, owing to the nature of the goods governments deal with. These are "public goods" rather than the "private goods" of economic theory. Pure public goods exhibit "jointness of supply," meaning that one person's use or consumption of the good does not reduce the amount available for others, and "nonexcludability," meaning that it is very difficult to keep those many from consuming the good (see, for example, Barry and Hardin 1982). Indeed it is often impossible to avoid consuming a public good provided by the government even for those who do not want it. A lighthouse illustrates jointness of supply, since one ship's use of the light does not affect others' ability to see and use that light. National defense is nonexcludable, since if it protects one family, it is effectively impossible to keep from protecting their neighbors as well. And the president is everyone's president, so citizens cannot avoid "consuming" this public good whether they like it or not.

Collective action is needed to secure nearly all public goods, and this is especially true in democracies, where governments all but invariably act collectively, such as in voting to select representatives or to pass legislation. Political parties, moreover, are collections of individuals, so that virtually everything they do involves collective action, and they provide public goods for their members, since much of what they do affects many, if not all, partisans. To be sure real, rather than theoretically pure, public goods typically have private goods dimensions—some firm receives the contract to build a bridge or jet fighter—and this private dimension is often critical in producing public goods. Additionally, the "public" that benefits from the public good may not include all citizens: for example, agricultural subsidies are a public good available primarily to farmers. Nonetheless, effectively everything governments and thus political parties produce constitutes goods that are primarily public, and collective action is required to secure them.

The problem of collective action—the potential that individually rational decisions lead to Pareto inferior outcomes—is ever present in the provision of public goods. This problem can be studied in two forms. One is game theoretic, typified by the "prisoners' dilemma game" (see Luce and Raiffa 1957). The other is based on the theory of individual decision making, typified by the expected utility model of turnout called the "calculus of voting." The expected utility form will be taken up later in this chapter. The game theoretic form is examined here.

Table 2.2 provides a standard illustration of a two-player prisoners' dilemma, similar to but simpler than that in table 2.1. Here player 1 chooses the upper or lower row while player 2 chooses the left or right column. The entry lists the payoffs to the two players for the particular combination of choices, with player 1's payoff first and player 2's second. Note that no matter what player 2 chooses, player 1 is always better off by picking the bottom row. Similarly, player 2 always receives a better payoff for choosing the right over the left column, no matter what player 1 chooses. The result therefore is a behavioral equilibrium of choosing bottom and right, respectively. The bottom right outcome, however, yields both players less than in the upper left cell, and thus the dilemma is that the equilibrium in behavior is Pareto inferior. The choices in table 2.2 are labeled to reflect the usual interpretation of choosing to "cooperate" with the other player or choosing to "defect" from cooperation. If both cooperate, they receive the Pareto superior outcome. Acting independently, they are rationally led to defect and, in equilibrium, fail to realize their potential joint gains.

There are two ways to achieve cooperation. One way is to agree to cooperate during play. For example, legislators interact repeatedly over a relatively long period. Axelrod (1984), Hardin (1982), and Taylor (1976) studied repeated play, and they show roughly that as long as interaction is ongoing and as long as the players place enough value on payoffs in the future, it can be individually rational to cooperate. A very closely related idea is that politicians might find it valuable to develop a reputation for being cooperative; if they do, they can achieve

Table 2.2 The Two-Person Prisoners' Dilemma Game

Player 1's choice	Player 2's choice	
	Cooperation	Defection
Cooperation	(3, 3)	(1, 4)
Defection	(4, 1)	(2, 2)

more by obtaining cooperative outcomes in the face of incentives to defect. This is one interpretation of Sam Rayburn's famous dictum that representatives can "get along by going along."

The problem with these ideas is a result known as the "folk theorem" (so called because the originator is unknown; see Bianco and Bates 1990; Fudenberg and Maskin 1986). The folk theorem says, in effect, that though the cooperative outcome is a behavioral equilibrium to the repeated prisoners' dilemma game, so too is *every* set of outcomes that yields the players at least what they get from defecting. Instead of the defection outcome being the single behavioral equilibrium, as in the single play game, the folk theorem concludes that essentially everything is a possible equilibrium in the repeated version of this game. The Axelrod-Hardin-Taylor results are thus only one set out of the many possible equilibriums, just as always defecting is also an equilibrium outcome, and many others are in equilibrium as well. In this case, actors may choose to create institutions, because institutional arrangements can help specify which of the equilibrium outcomes is actually chosen.

The second way to achieve the cooperative outcome is to agree in advance to do so. Saying so is insufficient, however, for both players have every reason to defect from that agreement, and even if they intend to honor it, they would recognize that the other player might take advantage of the situation and defect, making them the "sucker."[3] To be effective any a priori agreement requires a binding commitment. One possibility is some form of institutional arrangement that provides a basis for commitment.[4] In either single or repeated play, then, institutions can be important in resolving collective action problems.

Incentives for Party Formation

With legislators acting independently, each bill in table 2.1 passed with a minimal winning coalition. One alternative to acting independently is to form what Schwartz calls a "broad" coalition, one larger than required for minimal winning. To do so the legislators would have to have some means of binding each other ex ante, but suppose they can solve this problem. One agreement they could reach would be to agree to vote for a bill only if it made each one of them better off (or no one worse off). In the example in table 2.1, "broad" means "unanimous," and this rule would lead to them defeating each bill. This would solve the collective action problem, for only Pareto superior bills could pass under unanimity. Of course, as the filibuster politics in the Senate reminds us, supermajority rules can easily lead to no bill being passed at all.

Another alternative is to form what Schwartz calls a "long" but narrow coalition. Two legislators could agree to form an enduring coalition to pass any bill that made both of them better off and to defeat all others. Schwartz, indeed, defines a political party as a long coalition. As in the first case, there would have to be some means of ensuring commitment, one primary purpose of institutionalizing the party. Suppose A and B enter into a long coalition. They would agree to pass bill X and defeat bills Y and Z. Each would get positive payoffs, 4 and 3 respectively (and C would lose −9). Society would not be better off, but both members of the majority coalition are better off than by acting independently or in a unanimous coalition.[5] To be sure, A prefers the A-B coalition, B prefers the B-C coalition, and C prefers A-C. The central point, however, is that members win more in this "party" than in the unanimous coalition or by acting independently. It is not necessarily the case that a party will form, but it is possible, and it is possible because partisans win more in a party than by other arrangements.

Table 2.3 provides a second example. Here, with independent voting, all bills fail, and each legislator nets 0. It is Pareto superior for each bill to pass, yielding each legislator 1. Thus a broad coalition will pass all three. A two-person party will yield each of its members 2 and the excluded member −2. This particular case illustrates the conditions of Weingast's universalism theorem (1979); "universalism" means passing substantive legislation unanimously, or nearly so, within this pork barrel setting. The basic idea is that in a universal coalition, each legislator gets a "pet project" to take back to the district.

Central to his theorem is his assumption that, a priori, each member expects a minimal winning coalition to form but no member has any idea which one, so that (Weingast assumes) every minimal winning

Table 2.3 A Second Collective Action Problem with Incentives for Party Formation and for a Norm of Universalism via Weingast's Theorem

Legislator	Bill		
	X	Y	Z
A	3	−1	−1
B	−1	3	−1
C	−1	−1	3

Independent voting   Outcome: All bills fail.   Payoff (0, 0, 0)
Pareto optimal result   Pass all bills.   Payoff (1, 1, 1)
Universalism norm   Outcome: Pass all bills.   Payoff (1, 1, 1)
Party of A and B   Outcome: Pass bills X and Y.   Payoff (2, 2, −2)
Universalism theorem (Weingast, 1979)
Outcome: Pass all bills. Ex ante payoff   (2/3, 2/3, 2/3)

coalition is equally likely. In this case there is a two-thirds chance of each legislator being in a minimal wining coalition, with an ex ante expected payoff of 2/3.[6] This expected payoff is, indeed, less than the payoff of universalism, in which all bills pass and each receives a payoff of 1. Again, some form of a priori commitment is necessary, and universalism theorems show that it is possible, but not necessary, for a "norm" of universalism to develop.

As we saw above, forming a (minimal winning) party yielded the winners a payoff of 2 each. This is not a counterexample to Weingast's theorem, because the formation of a party means there is ex ante certainty about which coalition will form, not the equal probability of his theorem. That, of course, is the point. The reason to enter a party is to win more, and here that means reducing uncertainty over future outcomes. The majority party can pass any bill, so it can yield each more than acting independently, more than forming majority coalitions piecemeal, and more than under a universalism norm. It is thus possible that rational legislators would choose to form a party, because they would win more than otherwise.

We have seen that pork barrel legislation gives an incentive for a political party to form. That incentive exists whether or not there is a collective action problem. Consider table 2.3 again, but suppose that the winner receives 2. This is not a collective action problem, for each receives the same payoff if all bills pass or if none do, but there is still an incentive for a long, narrow coalition. The two, say A and B, would agree to pass the two bills that give each one a payoff of 2, and each would receive a payoff of 1, better than they could get playing individually or in a universal coalition.

Is this set of examples at all general? Schwartz proves that as long as the bills are distributive policies, there will be incentives for a majority to form a minimal winning party. Suppose there are n legislators, and m denotes (minimal) majority size. Passing any bill yields benefits to a winner of, say, b. If costs, c, are divided equally, each pays a cost of c/n. Each legislator, if choosing independently, will vote for any bill for which $b - c > 0$. If a simple majority forms, they will pass pork barrel legislation such that $b - mc > 0$ for all members of the coalition. The rest lose an amount of $-mc$. What Schwartz shows is that it is better for winners to be in a permanent coalition a priori, that is, in the majority party. Whatever the situation, each member can calculate that there is an a priori probability, p, of being in the winning coalition. If only minimal winning coalitions will form, each expects to receive an amount equal to $pb - mc$. Weingast's theorem assumes that p is based on every minimal winning coalition's being equally likely and thus assumes its lowest value. The larger p is, the higher each winner's payoff. When p equals 1, each of the m winners expects to receive a full b – mc. Thus members of the majority each prefer to know with certainty that they are the winning coalition. These m individuals will be worse off with *any* degree of uncertainty. That is the incentive for forming a binding coalition—for forming a political party.

One might argue that there are transactions costs that must be paid for forming and maintaining a party coalition. Although this is true, there are also transactions costs for forming each winning coalition. No one knows how large either set of costs is, but it is likely that transactions costs for parties are far less, at least over the long haul, than those for forming new majorities for each piece of legislation. Thus an additional incentive for intralegislative party formation is to reduce costs of legislative coalition formation over the long haul.

We can also exploit the structure of bicameralism to extend Schwartz's argument. Suppose there are two chambers and the two have to agree for a bill to become law. An example similar to the United States House and Senate is displayed in table 2.4. Here, the seven-member House faces proposals like those in table 2.3. The Senate comprises three members whose states are composed of House districts. Thus, Q's state consists of the House districts, A, B, and C, and so on. Senators' payoffs are assumed to be the sum of those in the component House district. Here, if a party of D, E, F, and G forms in the House, it will pass bills W, X, Y, and Z, with each partisan receiving +4 and the rest receiving –4. R and S have an incentive to join the House's majority party, since they would like to pass the same bills and reject the rest. R and S would then receive +8, while Q receives a payoff of –12. With geographic definitions of districts and of the distribution of legislative benefits, we would expect parties to form along regional lines, and bicameralism would accentuate the value of partisan regional bases.[7]

SOCIAL CHOICE PROBLEMS WITHIN THE GOVERNMENT

The Social Choice Problem in Policymaking

Social choice theory in political science concerns Arrow's general possibility theorem and its implications for the theory of majority voting (1951; see also Riker 1982a). Its typical example, the "paradox of voting," is illustrated in table 2.5. Here there are three alternatives— say, a bill, an amendment, and the status quo (or reversion outcome). The three legislators have preferences over these outcomes. Suppose

Table 2.4 An Example of Bicameralism with Districts Defined
Geographically and with Incentives for Regional Party Bases

	Bill						
	T	U	V	W	X	Y	Z
House							
A	7	−1	−1	−1	−1	−1	−1
B	−1	7	−1	−1	−1	−1	−1
C	−1	−1	7	−1	−1	−1	−1
D	−1	−1	−1	7	−1	−1	−1
E	−1	−1	−1	−1	7	−1	−1
F	−1	−1	−1	−1	−1	7	−1
G	−1	−1	−1	−1	−1	−1	7
Senate[a]							
Q (= A + B + C)	5	5	5	−3	−3	−3	−3
R (= D + E)	−2	−2	−2	6	6	−2	−2
S (= F + G)	−2	−2	−2	−2	−2	6	6

Independent Voting   Outcome: All bills fail with a payoff of 0 to all.
Pareto optimal result   All bills pass with a payoff of 1 to all.
"Natural" geographic basis for parties   Suppose D-E-F-G and R-S formed a party,
passing (W, X, Y, Z). Then:
A, B, and C receive −4; D, E, F, and G receive +4 each
Q receives −12;   R and S receive +8 each
This is the highest these parties could have obtained, and it is higher than either inde-
pendent voting or the Pareto optimal (universalism) outcome.
Other parties are possible, but only those with a geographic basis are of much value.
For example, suppose the House majority party was A-B-D-F. By passing (T, U, W,
Y), each of them would receive +4, while the others in the House would receive −4.
Q would be a winner in the Senate (+4), while R and S would receive 0. Alternatively,
the majority A-B-C-D could form a party and pass (T, U, V, W) in the House. Q
would win 12, R would receive 0, and S would get −8. Thus the nongeographic coali-
tion in the House could succeed there but would get support in the Senate only from
Q. The last, which is also a geographic coalition, shows that not all are advantaged.
Rather, the small state coalition in the House is, when interchamber majorities are
necessary. Although both of these examples *could* yield interchamber parties, only the
first is truly advantageous for all members.

[a]Senate payoffs are the sum of the payoffs to that state's House districts.

that voting is by round-robin majority rule and that each legislator votes
for the preferred alternative at each vote. Then X beats Y by a 2–1 vote,
and Y defeats Z 2–1. We might expect transitivity to hold, so that if X
beats Y and Y beats Z, then X should defeat Z. In fact, Z defeats X 2–1.
This is called a majority "cycle," since voting can cycle the social choice
from Z to Y to X and back to Z.

Payoff values are assigned to the alternatives in table 2.5, with 4 for
the most preferred alternative, 3 for the second most preferred, and
−9 for the least liked alternative. Note that these reproduce the payoffs from table 2.1, except over competing versions of the same bill

rather than three different bills. Thus, at least in this case, the same preferences that led to a collective action problem also lead to a social choice problem. Table 2.5 does not look like pork barrel preferences, and indeed it has many interpretations in addition to preferences for pork. In other words, preferences that could lead to a collective action problem need not be of distributive policies, so that the previous section is actually more general than it appears.

The Nature of the Social Choice Problem

Arrow's general possibility theorem is essentially that cycles are always possible—not that they *must* exist, but that they can never be ruled out. His theorem is about preferences. All legislators have noncyclical preferences. Is there a sense in which we could say that this three-person society also has noncyclical preferences? Is there a socially preferred outcome? Round-robin majority voting (or the method of majority voting generally; see Sen 1970; Riker 1982a), if it is used to define "social

Table 2.5 A Social Choice Problem and Incentives for Party Formation

	Preference ranking		
	1st	2nd	3rd
Legislator			
A	X	Y	Z
B	Z	X	Y
C	Y	Z	X
Utility value	4	3	−9

Round-robin tournament, voting independently and sincerely
X beats Y (A, B)   Y beats Z (A, C)   Z beats X (B, C):   **Outcome: ?**
Sequential agenda: sincere voting

1st vote	Final vote outcome	Payoff to (A, B, C)
a. $(X,Y) = X^a$	$(X, Z) = Z$	(−9, 4, 3)
b. $(X, Z) = Z$	$(Z, Y) = Y$	(3, −9, 4)
c. $(Y, Z) = Y$	$(Y, X) = X$	(4, 3, −9)

Sequential agenda: sophisticated voting

a. $(X,Y) = Y$	$(Y, Z) = Y$	(3, −9, 4)
b. $(X, Z) = X$	$(X, Y) = X$	(4, 3, −9)
c. $(Y, Z) = Z$	$(Z, X) = Z$	(−9, 4, 3)

Equiprobable order of voting   Expected outcome: (2/3, 2/3, 2/3)
Temporary coalitions A and B coalesce, yielding X;
       C offers to coalesce with B, yielding Z;
       A offers to coalesce with C, yielding Y;
       B offers to coalesce with A again.
       Thus, there is a cycle in coalitions.
Party of A and B   Outcome: Pass X.   Payoff (4, 3, −9)

a(X,Y) = X, for example, denotes that alternative X is voted against Y with X winning. Boldface denotes the final, winning outcome.

preference," says no. Arrow's theorem says no method of choosing can guarantee that noncyclical social "preferences" can be obtained from noncyclical individual preferences.[8]

Voting theory is about how preferences lead to choices, that is, about behavior, as well as about the normative questions Arrow considered. In the example, legislators always choose to vote for the preferred alternative in any pair, illustrating how Arrow's theorem can be translated into a form for studying behavior. This has been done mostly in terms of majority voting procedures, either in large electorates or in "committees," that is, smaller bodies such as legislatures. The central problem in this literature is a search for equilibriums in behavior, and the literature divides into two streams of research.

One stream consists of what may be referred to as the "positive" results. It seeks conditions that yield a behavioral equilibrium, which would tell us what society would choose. The most famous result is Duncan Black's "median voter" theorem (1958). This theorem says that if it is possible to arrange alternatives so that every voter's preferences are "single peaked" in one dimension, then there is a behavioral equilibrium.[9] Calling each voter's most preferred alternative an "ideal point," the result is that the ideal point of the median voter is the equilibrium. Black proved this result for the case of committees, and Anthony Downs (1957) provided the comparable result for large electorates. Two candidates competing along a single dimension (e.g., a left/right ideological dimension) and seeking only to win the election would be led to "converge" to the ideal point of the median voter (see chap. 6 for further development). Some generalization is possible, but these results are marginal emendations of Black's theorem (see Sen 1970). Black's theorem has been employed in a variety of forms. For example, Shepsle (1979) used the median voter theorem as his institutional model of a legislature with a committee system, and there are a number of other results that involve voting on one dimension at a time or that in some other way constrain multidimensional choice settings to single dimensions. In general, however, the median voter result is extraordinarily fragile, itself, as deviation from exact unidimensionality utterly destroys equilibrium (Kramer 1973).

Black also searched for equilibrium in multidimensional spaces.[10] Stated more generally by Plott (1967), this attempt to generalize the median voter theorem effectively requires the existence of a multivariate median.[11] A multivariate median, however, exists only in symmetric distributions (e.g., of ideal points). Davis and Hinich (e.g., 1966; see also Davis, Hinich, and Ordeshook 1970) extended the Downsian spatial model to multiple dimensions, and they also needed symmetry conditions to yield a behavioral equilibrium.[12]

This apparent necessity for symmetry underlies the second, "negative," stream of research. Unidimensionality cannot be assumed; it is empirically rare if not nonexistent. Most certainly, symmetry of preferences can be dismissed as wildly implausible. Thus the failure to find a multidimensional generalization of Black's theorem in anything like a useful set of conditions means that cycling in social choices holds almost invariably. One must begin with the premise that there is no behavioral equilibrium. Thus Plott's basic argument was that disequilibrium was ordinarily the case, and the two-candidate spatial model also foundered on such impossibility results.

More "impossibility" results followed. It was shown, for example, that Arrow's theorem was coincident with the nonexistence of the game theoretic solution concept of the core, thus providing a formal tie between Arrow's preference cycling and behavior.[13] Kramer (1973) then showed that the median voter result was just as rare and fragile, as noted above. The ultimate in negative results are the series of "chaos" theorems (e.g., McKelvey 1976; Schofield 1978; McKelvey and Schofield 1986). These showed that if there was no behavioral equilibrium, majority voting could lead from any one outcome to any other, no matter how far apart, even to alternatives that were unanimously disfavored. Pairwise majority voting, they showed, *could* result in "anything happening."[14] In fact, even in his initial paper, McKelvey (1976) argued that this result did not lead to "chaos" but instead provided the opportunity for institutional effects, illustrating his claim by use of agenda setting. This stream of research was effectively summarized by Riker's calling politics "truly the dismal science" (1980).[15]

Give the implausibility of a single dimension of choice and of multidimensional symmetry, the presumed pervasiveness of disequilibrium has led to two newer directions in research. One is the new institutionalism, such as the work of Shepsle and Weingast. This is in part the search for equilibriums due to the combination of preferences and institutional arrangements (called "structure-induced equilibriums" or SIEs), with the knowledge that equilibriums under majority rule based on preferences alone ("preference-induced equilibriums," or PIEs) are virtually nonexistent. This will be explored in the party setting in chapter 7. The second has examined choice without imposing (much in the way of) institutional arrangements. The search, instead, is for alternative solution concepts. Most notable here are such concepts as the "uncovered set" (e.g., McKelvey 1986) or the "minmax set" (e.g., Kramer 1977). The general thrust of this literature is that though there may be no equilibrium akin to Black's median voter theorem, all of these concepts tend to lead to voting outcomes near the center. Perhaps, then, there may be some weaker form of generalization of the median voter revealing a tendency toward choice at, or convergence to, the policy center.

Incentives for Party Formation in the Presence of a Social Choice Problem

Table 2.5 was used to illustrate the paradox of voting with round-robin voting. Legislatures, of course, adopt rules for determining the agenda, such as that the first vote is on the amendment, equivalent to voting for the unamended versus the amended bill. The winner then faces the status quo, which determines the final outcome.

Cyclical preferences would not be revealed with such an agenda, since not all pairs are matched. This does not mean the paradoxical arrangement of preferences is inconsequential. To examine this, we need a behavioral rule to guide us in understanding how rational legislators would choose. There are two commonly used choice rules, called "sincere" and "sophisticated" voting. Voting is sincere if legislators always vote for whichever alternative they prefer. Voting is sophisticated if legislators look ahead to see the consequences of their current votes for later choices. One might vote against a preferred alternative early on to avoid ending up with an even worse outcome at the end of the process (see Clinton and Meirowitz 2004 for application). Obviously sophisticated voting requires, in addition to anything else, information about the preferences of the other votes. Thus sincere voting is plausible when legislators or voters know little about each other, whereas sophisticated voting is more likely when legislators or voters know each other well.[16]

Under sincere voting as shown in table 2.5, the status quo always wins. For example, if X is an amended form of bill Y, X wins in the first vote but loses to the status quo (Z) in the second vote. Any of these three alternatives can win, depending only on the order in which they are voted on, with the winner being the last one to enter voting. Under sophisticated voting, any of the three alternatives can win, although in this case the status quo (that is, the last alternative to enter voting) always loses. Thus, with the same preferences, the outcome depends on the order of voting, sometimes called "path dependence" because the outcome depends on the "path" or agenda followed. The outcome also depends on whether voters are sincere or sophisticated and thus presumably on the availability and costs of information, among other things.

In table 2.6 there is a behavioral equilibrium in preferences. In this case X defeats Y and Y defeats Z, as before, but X also defeats Z. That is, X defeats both alternatives in pairwise voting and is called a "Condorcet winner." X is also the median voter result, with A the median voter. X is chosen under any of the three methods of voting: the round-robin

Table 2.6 The Absence of a Social Choice Problem and the Absence of Incentives for Party Formation

	Preference ranking		
	1st	2nd	3rd
Legislator			
A	X	Y	Z
B	Z	X	Y
C	Y	X	Z
Utility value	4	3	−9

Round-robin tournament, voting independently and sincerely
X beats Y (A, B)   Y beats Z (A, C)   X beats Z (A, C):   **Outcome: X**
Sequential agenda: sincere voting

1st vote	Final vote outcome	Payoff to (A, B, C)
a. (X, Y) = X[a]	(X, Z) = **X**	(4, 3, 3)
b. (X, Z) = X	(X, Y) = **X**	(4, 3, 3)
c. (Y, Z) = Y	(Y, X) = **X**	(4, 3, 3)

Seqential agenda: sophisticated voting

a. (X, Y) = X	(X, Z) = **X**	(4, 3, 3)
b. (X, Z) = X	(X, Y) = **X**	(4, 3, 3)
c. (Y, Z) = Y	(Y, X) = **X**	(4, 3, 3)

Random, equiprobable, ordering of voting   All pass X Payoff (4, 3, 3)
Temporary coalitions (A, B), (B, C), (A, C) pass X   Payoff (4, 3, 3)
Party of A and B   Outcome: X   Payoff (4, 3, 3)
This is true for any party of two. Thus, there is no incentive for a party (or for a universalism norm, etc.) with a voting equilibrium.

[a](X, Y) = X, for example, denotes that alternative X is voted against Y with X winning. Boldface denotes the final, winning outcome.

tournament, the sequential agenda with sincere voting, or the agenda with sophisticated voting. The choice no longer depends on the path or on the decision rules followed by the actors.

What, then, of parties? Here "length" is not meaningful, since these are three alternatives under simultaneous consideration. Think first of a party as a coalition, say of A and B. In the situation depicted in table 2.5, A and B could agree to support X over the other two bills, and as a majority they could ensure that X passes, yielding payoffs to A of 4, B of 3, and C of −9. If this were a mere coalition, however, it would be vulnerable: C could offer to join with B, agreeing on passage of Z. This would make them both better off, giving B 4 and C 3. Now A could offer to join with C, making both better off, giving C the 4 payoff and A the 3. But then B could reoffer the A-B coalition. In short, if a party were a mere coalition formed around a single issue, there would be a cycle among coalitions, mirroring the cycle in preferences. To be a party, then, must mean more than being a temporary coalition of immediate interests. It could be a long coalition, in which A and B would agree to commit to a coalition over a series of bills, and anytime such a case of cycling arose, they would determine a joint course of action. In this particular case B could do better, but by entering the A-B party, B could ensure never being in C's circumstance of being the worst off. Again, the value of the party would be to institutionalize for the long haul (and over issues) and reduce uncertainty, ensuring each member some benefits for being in this party, such as here in avoiding the worst outcome.

In table 2.6, *any* two-legislator coalition will agree on X. That is, there is nothing to be gained by coalition, and thus by forming a political party. The virtue of an equilibrium due to preferences alone is that the PIE will be chosen under a wide array of institutional rules added to majority rule. When there is a well-defined sense of what the majority prefers, the majority will work its will.[17]

Is this at all general? Consider the five-person legislature in figure 2.1, where with single-peaked preferences, C is the median voter. As long as C's most preferred option is proposed at all, it will be chosen under majority rule.

We can divide all winning coalitions into two classes, those that include C and those that do not. C has no incentive to form such a coalition, since his or her ideal policy will be chosen without doing so. Coalescing with, say, A and B might lead that majority to agree on C's ideal point, but it might also choose some other option. It might, for example, agree to choose B's ideal point, since that is the median position in the coalition, thereby making C worse off. Even if the median, or C's ideal point, wins in coalition, forming a coalition would involve paying needless transactions costs, and it might be that the median would not win, thus making C worse off.

Consider, then, coalitions that exclude C. Any majority coalition that excludes C has to include legislators on both "sides" of C. Suppose A, B, and D form a coalition. Anything that A and B find more attractive than C's ideal point, D likes less, and vice versa. As Axelrod

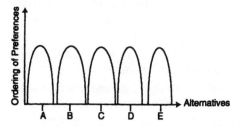

Figure 2.1. An example of single-peaked preferences.
Source: Compiled by author.

pointed out (1970), the coalition that has the least internal conflict of interest (or in other words has the most in common) is "connected," having adjacent ideal point locations. Any such connected coalition must therefore include C. Skipping over C, such as forming A-B-D, involves greater conflict of interest than, say, forming A-B-C or B-C-D, and A-B-D may be able to agree to no more than selecting C's ideal point, which they could get without coalescing.[18]

Thus there is no incentive to form a coalition when there is an equilibrium. From a social choice theory perspective, the existence of incentives to form a political party is found in the absence of an equilibrium (whereas, for the collective action problem, incentives came in trying to upset an inferior equilibrium). Social choice theory, however, tells us that most of the time we should expect there to be no voting equilibrium, which means, then, that there generally are incentives to form a long coalition, that is, a party. One might argue that if a coalition such as A-B-D has formed for other reasons, it might face the possibility of figure 2.1 sometime in the future. Even so, the coalition of A-B-D can always agree on C's ideal point—or equivalently, agree not to act in coalition on this policy—and the members will receive no worse than they would have without forming (or employing) the party. They will have won at least as much as they would have without the party, and in the presumably common cases where there is a paradoxical arrangement of preferences, they can win more.

If the lesson of voting theory in committee settings is that PIEs are rare, then there are always incentives to form a party. Riker's dismal conclusion turns out to provide a strong case for the formation of political parties.

The new institutionalism (e.g., Shepsle 1979) emerged in response to the ordinary absence of (pure) voting equilibriums. Two points discussed below and in later chapters are also relevant here. First, many different institutional arrangements can be sufficient to yield (structure-induced) equilibriums, such as committee systems, agenda designs, and separated powers. None of these are necessary—like parties, all yield possibility results. Second, partisan institutions are virtually always one of those institutions.

COLLECTIVE ACTION AND ELECTORAL MOBILIZATION

The Problem of Collective Action in Elections

The Federalist and Jeffersonian Republican Parties began with the government as a means of solving a social choice problem (see chap. 3).

Such parties-in-government may also become electoral parties. The most obvious motivation lies with the minority. The examples above demonstrated incentives for some majority to form a party. If this happens, some or all of those excluded might form a party in reaction, seeking to become the legislative majority. Failing to reach majority size, the minority would naturally turn to the public, seeking to elect more of its members. That is essentially what the Jeffersonians did when facing a Hamiltonian majority. Later parties, notably the Jacksonian Democratic party, formed more directly for electoral purposes (see chap. 4). The question for this section and the next, then, is what set of incentives candidates for elective office might have that would lead them to form or join a political party. In this section we examine incentives that arise from attempting to mobilize the electorate. Mobilizing the electorate by definition is getting the public to turn out to vote for, or otherwise support, a candidate. Examining the logic of voting among citizens introduces the second form in which problems of collective action are studied, and in this case turnout is the quintessential example.

The Nature of the Problem of Collective Action and Mobilization

Turnout is ordinarily seen as a problem in individual decision making, unlike the prisoners' dilemma. Both can be put in game theoretic terms, but in the latter case, the strategic interaction between the players is central. Both players have an immediate and direct impact on the outcome, and each player would be wise to at least consider the strategic possibilities of the other player. In large electorates the outcome depends on the actions taken by all, but strategic interaction is so remote that it can be effectively ignored: how one citizen decides to act has very little effect on the decisions of any others. Sheer size all but eliminates strategic interaction, reducing the problem to one of individual decision making.

The standard theory, called the "calculus of voting," employs expected utility maximization (see Downs 1957; Riker and Ordeshook 1968, 1973). If there are two candidates, the calculus, like all rational choice models, predicts voting for the more preferred one. The question is whether to vote at all. The calculus for choosing whether one votes or abstains is

(2.1) $$R = PB + D - C.$$

R denotes the reward (expected utility) for casting a vote, and one votes if R is positive and abstains if not. P represents the probability that the vote will affect the outcome, roughly the probability of casting the vote that makes or breaks a tie.[19] B represents the differential benefit the citizen receives from the election of the more preferred candidate. The D term, for duty, measures any positive rewards received from the act of voting itself, which may include the satisfaction of having done one's duty as a citizen, the value of expressing support for the preferred candidate or party, and so on. Finally, C stands for the costs of voting, including the time and effort needed to register and go to the polls and the costs of decision making.[20] C and D, therefore, come with the act of voting itself and do not depend on the outcome. Only B depends on the outcome, and it is discounted by the impact of P, the effect this one vote would have on determining that outcome.

This calculus is a typical example of expected utility maximizing. It thus serves as a template for a large number of other expected utility maximization problems. One example is the "calculus of candidacy" that will be examined in the next section. It also serves as a calculus for political participation more generally. Olson (1965) analyzed the problem of collective action for participating in interest groups, for example, and his logic is effectively equivalent to this calculus.

The calculus is a model of individual decision making, but the outcome sought is a public good. The winning candidate is "jointly supplied," no one can be excluded from "consuming" the good, and indeed no one can avoid consuming it, no matter whether they voted for or against the winner or did not vote at all. The question, then, is under what conditions it is rational for the individual to contribute to (or "cooperate in") the provision of this public good.

The collective action problem follows immediately from the calculus and the observation that, in any large group, the P term is almost invariably very small. A near-zero P makes the PB term tiny unless B is immense. Thus all those who share an interest in seeing a candidate elected nonetheless are motivated to act primarily on the D and C terms, that is, the intrinsic costs and benefits to voting, and very little in terms of their collectively shared interest in the candidate. If we set aside the D term for the moment (as Barry [1970] and others argue should be done), then one votes if PB > C. If P is effectively zero, then no one should vote. As in the prisoners' dilemma, the rational citizen should "defect" by abstaining.[21]

The calculus of voting includes a second, prior "collective action" problem: becoming informed. A citizen concerned about the electoral outcome needs to determine what outcome is desired. Which candidate, in other words, does the citizen want to see elected, and how important is the outcome—that is, how large is the B term?

The citizen must expend decision-making costs to gather and process information to determine this, but if a vote has a negligible impact on the outcome, why should anyone pay these costs? Downs (1957) explained why it is rational for citizens to be ill informed except as they "accidentally" acquire information or obtain it for other reasons.

Incentives for Candidates in Electoral Mobilization

Candidates want to win elections. To do so, they need to convince more citizens to prefer them than prefer their opponent(s), and they need to convince these supporters to vote in greater numbers than their opposition. Citizens may not have incentives to turn out or even to ascertain their preferences over candidates. Candidates, however, *do* have strong personal incentives to solve these collective action problems for citizens, if only for their supporters. Campaigns therefore can be understood as attempts to create supporters and get them to turn out in the face of these two collective action problems.

There are a number of ways candidates can generate supporters and get them to vote, and these can be seen as attempts to manipulate terms in the calculus of voting. Most important are the common efforts to lower the costs of voting, such as exhortations to register and vote and formally organized mobilization drives. Candidates also can lower decision-making costs for voters by providing as much information as possible in a readily available form, seeking to "instruct" voters that the candidate values what they do, thus also seeking to generate a favorable B term as well as lowering C. At the same time, "allocating emphasis," to use Page's term (1976), or even outright exaggeration, may make the B differential appear large.

Exhortations that all citizens should do their duty by voting seek to increase the intrinsic rewards of voting, while claims that "everyone's vote counts" seek to make the P term seem high. These claims strike everyone, however, opponents and supporters alike, so candidates typically leave them to editorial writers and the League of Women Voters. But candidates do manipulate the P, B, C, and D terms more selectively. Thus candidates and parties focus their campaign appeals and mobilization drives on those they believe already are, or are most likely to become, their supporters.

Although candidates employ many particular tactics to make it seem in their supporters' personal interests to turn out and vote, the general points are that candidates have private incentives to seek to overcome these collective action problems, and that these tactics, to be successful, must be chosen in light of the collective action problems facing the electorate. Implementing these tactics takes resources. It is probably not very expensive to generate the largely private benefits sufficient for overcoming the free riding incentives an individual citizen faces, but these small per capita costs become substantial in a large electorate. Yet as a great deal of empirical work has demonstrated (e.g., Patterson and Caldeira 1983; Rosenstone and Hansen 1993), wise expenditures of resources pays off in increased turnout.

Incentives for Party Affiliation for Candidates

That candidates have private incentives to reduce collective action problems among their supporters does not necessarily mean they have incentives to form a party. Today's elections are typically described as "candidate centered," and a large part of that claim is that it has become feasible for individual candidates to raise and expend resources on their own (see chap. 6 and 8). So part of the answer must be historically contingent, but part must continue to apply, since candidates with any serious hopes are almost invariably partisan.

Affiliation with a party provides a candidate with, among other things, a "brand name." In advertising, successful brand names convey a great deal of information cheaply: they cue an established reputation (see Downs 1957). Travelers, for example, know little about a local hamburger stand but know that McDonald's provides a certain type of product with standards for cleanliness, service, and so on. A party label can convey a great deal of information as well. *The American Voter* popularized the view that political parties provide cues and partisan images (Campbell et al. 1960). Key (1966) referred to party identification as a "standing decision": partisans vote for their preferred party's candidates until and unless given good reasons not to.

In the last few years, several important game theoretic models of party reputation have advanced the technical understanding of the value of a reputation to a party's candidates (see, for example, Snyder and Ting 2002; Grynaviski 2010). They have also examined some of the conditions under which they are useful to such candidates, particularly so for less well-known and experienced candidates, who can use the party's reputation to establish a basis of choice among their constituents. Of course, if the reputation is a negative for the candidate (the party is liberal, while the constituents are not, and so on), then the reputation is harmful. And, if they were to successfully develop a different reputation, doing so weakens the value of the party label for all others, as it signifies less certainly what the party stands for. Some therefore have argued that there are really two possibilities. One possibility is that (nearly) every candidate and officeholder hews closely to the party reputational positions in their own personal campaigns, thereby maintaining a high value to the reputation (clarity of party positioning) for everyone. The other is that defections from that position by well-known figures weaken the reputation for everyone else, leading to further defections, such that the value of the party position as a reputation is low for all (see, for example, Castanheira and Crutzen, 2009). The conditions under which politicians choose a strong reputation for the party (that is, adopt something very close to the party platform as their own) is when there is relatively high agreement on that platform a priori. A divided party would choose to let the party stand for little, with every partisan running on their own best choice of platform for winning office. This is very similar to the argument about "conditional party government" that will be discussed in later chapters.

The candidate's party affiliation therefore provides a very inexpensive way to infer a great deal: assumptions about what a typical Democrat or Republican is like. To be sure, other sources of reputation could serve much the same as party affiliation. A reputation as a liberal or conservative, for example, is a similar cost-saving device for voters. The empirical dominance of party cues (and their not coincidental relation to what is popularly understood by "liberal" and "conservative") in the public suggests, of course, that the affiliation of a candidate with a party has proved useful. Thus the collective action problem for voters of becoming sufficiently informed to make a (possibly preliminary) determination of whom they favor is greatly attenuated, given party affiliation and perhaps other reputational cues. This effect is exaggerated to the extent that voters' choices are correlated among candidates of the same party. The correlation is, of course, partially endogenous to the actions and the stances of a party's candidates (as well as to institutional features such as ballot forms that ease or hinder split-ticket voting). Even today, however, many vote straight tickets, or close to it, and as Cox and McCubbins (1993) have shown, there is a substantial impact of party identification on even the highly candidate-centered (especially incumbent-centered) voting for Congress.

Affiliation with a party not only brings the candidate a "natural" reputation, it also provides economies of scale. This is especially important for turnout. Campaigns may reduce free riding incentives in the public, but they are costly for the candidates. The campaign budget imposes real constraints, especially at lower levels of office and for nonincumbents. A turnout drive by the party's presidential nominee reduces or eliminates the costs of getting partisans to the polls for other candidates of that party, for example. Once the voter is there, the additional costs of voting for remaining offices are very small, especially if party-line votes are possible. Thus the tide of partisans turning out to vote for president lifts the boats for all of the rest of that party's nominees.

The combination of office-seeking ambition and the very nature of electoral institutions generates incentives for candidates to solve the two collective action problems affecting voters: becoming informed and turning out to vote. Candidates have two kinds of incentives to affiliate with a political party, ameliorating both of the public's collective action problems. Party affiliation provides an initial reputation that reduces decision-making costs and provides a core of likely supporters. Long-term incumbents may develop their own personal reputations in addition to partisan reputations, and this fact has been of great empirical significance for understanding the U.S. House in particular (see Jacobson 2008). Many offices have shorter tenures, with ambitious politicians therefore seeking to climb higher up the list of offices. Each time they strike out into a new electorate, party reputations become more valuable again.

Party campaign efforts, whether conducted by the party organization itself or by its various candidates, provide economies of scale for all of the party's candidates as they seek to reduce the costs and increase the benefits for supporters to come to the polls. As before, these incentives create the possibility that candidates might want to affiliate with a party. There are other means of reaching the same ends. Moreover, affiliation is not costless. The reputational effects of being a Democrat or Republican need not be entirely positive and at times can be quite negative. Until recently being a Republican in the South provided a reputation, but one that made winning all but impossible. Any partisan image undoubtedly mixes positives and negatives for any candidate. Yet the ambitious politician seeking a long and successful career almost invariably affiliates with one or the other major party, in part owing to reputational effects and economies of scale.

One of the tensions facing partisan candidates is the need to solve another collective action problem, that of generating the many activists needed to secure the labor and financial (and other) resources needed to achieve mobilization. This may yield tension, because the best appeal to activists may differ from what would best mobilize voters. Indeed, these (commonly) opposing forces of appealing to the base versus appealing to the independent or unaffiliated voter yield some of the highest levels of tension, requiring a careful balancing of centripetal and centrifugal forces in the contemporary era. Resolution of such competing pressures depends in part on the activists' incentives. For example, political machines generated selective incentives for securing activists' support that were largely independent of policy appeals to the public. The reduction of such private incentives is a substantial part of the forces that reduced or eliminated partisan machines. In place of the private benefit seekers of the machine era are today's more policy-motivated activists. The consequences of such activists for inducing more divergence between candidates of opposing parties is developed and tested in chapter 6.

AMBITION AND INCENTIVES FOR PARTY AFFILIATION

The Problem of Ambition Theory

Joseph A. Schlesinger began his theory of political ambition by asserting, "Ambition lies at the heart of politics. Politics thrive on the hope of preferment and the drive for office" (1966, 1). Schlesinger's ambition is the ordinary drive for a long and successful career, in this case a career in elective office. This ambition constrains office seekers and holders to promise what the public wants and to deliver what the public finds at least minimally satisfactory. It also provides incentives for ambitious politicians to affiliate with a major party.

Black (1972) and Rohde (1979) modified ambition theory, casting it in expected utility maximizing form, the "calculus of candidacy." It can be illustrated using Rohde's example of an incumbent member of the House considering whether to run for reelection, run for the Senate, or retire.[22] There are three outcomes, $\{O_n, O_h, O_s\}$, denoting holding no office, keeping the current House seat, and gaining a Senate seat. Ambition theory assumes that all prefer holding a higher office to a lower office and prefer that to holding no office, or $U(O_s) > U(O_h) > U(O_n)$.[23] It will be convenient to set $U(O_n) = 0$. The candidate chooses an action, $\{a_n, a_h, a_s\}$, to run for no office, run for reelection, or run for the Senate. It is very costly to run for office, and presumably more so for the Senate than the House, so costs may be written $C_s > C_h > C_n = 0$. Expected utility maximization requires calculating the probability of each possible outcome, given each possible action. Many are zero, of course. The two critical probabilities are P_s and P_h, the probability of election to the Senate (or House) if the candidate runs for that office, with $(1 - P_s)$ and $(1 - P_h)$, the respective probabilities of defeat, being the remaining nonzero probabilities. The P, B, and C terms discussed so far mirror those in the calculus of voting. The voting calculus also includes a D term. Here, though there may be intrinsic benefits for running for office, they are likely to be so small for ambitious politicians that they can be ignored.

The calculus can be simplified to:

(2.2a) $EU(a_n) = 0$

(2.2b) $EU(a_h) = P_h U(O_h) - (1 - P_h)U(O_n) - C_h$

(2.2c) $EU(a_s) = P_s U(O_s) - (1 - P_s)U(O_n) - C_s$

or, with $U(O_n) = 0$, to:

(2.2a) $= 0$

(2.2b) $= P_h U(O_h) - C_h$

(2.2c) $= P_s U(O_s) - C_s.$

The expected utility maximizing candidate chooses whichever yields the highest expected return. Thus the candidate retires if the costs of running for each office exceed its expected benefits. If not, the candidate runs for whichever office yields the larger expected net benefits. For incumbent members of the House, the probability of reelection (barring indictment) is so high that $EU(a_h)$ is almost always positive, so premature retirement is rare. The probability of winning a Senate race is usually much lower than for the House, and the costs of running are much higher. Candidates therefore must either have very strong ambition or pick the timing of a Senate race very carefully, looking for circumstances that make P_s unusually high. Of course all terms, P, B, and C, may vary across contests, for example, in large compared with small states. Finally, although there are strong parallels to the form of the calculus of voting, there is no collective action problem, since the outcome of holding office is a private good for the candidate, even though it may be a public good for fellow partisans in office, among activists, and in the electorate.

Incentives for Party Affiliation among Ambitious Politicians

In most applications, as above, the question is which office a candidate seeks. Party affiliation is taken for granted and not even considered a matter of choice. Although recognizing their importance, Schlesinger deferred consideration of parties until the end of his study, because ambition and its theoretical consequences are features of the actors and government, independent of party. This point reflects, of course, my claim that parties are the consequences of the actions of political elites in a republican democracy. It is also true that in ordinary circumstances very few political careerists change their party affiliation.

Yet as Schlesinger recognized, affiliation with a major party is close to a necessary condition for access to elective office, and even closer to a necessary condition for a long, successful career in politics. At base, party affiliation is a choice made by ambitious politicians, even if often made before entering politics. At critical times, such as during major upheavals (e.g., in the 1850s; see chap. 5) or with the rise of the Republicans to competitive status in the South, significant numbers do change their party affiliation, and more consider doing so. Moreover, Schlesinger noted the irony that in the age of party decline and candidate-centered elections in which he wrote, politicians' affiliation with a major party had increased (to over 99 percent since World War II; see Schlesinger 1984). Why then are politicians affiliating with major parties more today, if they need them less? It seems quite evident that the conditional is wrong—ambitious politicians do *not* need parties less; they need them, if anything, even more. Party affiliation therefore should be derived from the theory rather than be assumed by the theory a priori. In the terms used in this chapter, the question is, what incentives are there for political careerists to form ties with a major political party?

To begin to analyze the incentives that may have produced these results, consider what the calculus of candidacy looks like when party affiliation, rather than level of office, is the variable of choice. In chapter 5 we will examine the demise of the Whigs and the rise of the Republican Party, so I will use that notation for illustration, although the form is general (for formal development, see Aldrich and Bianco 1992). Consider a candidate deciding whether to run for office as a Whig or a Republican and therefore facing three outcomes, $\{O_W, O_R, O_n\}$, where O_W denotes serving as a Whig, O_R serving as a Republican, and O_n not serving at all. Let $U(O_j)$ denote the utility for outcome j. There are three actions, $\{a_w, a_r, a_n\}$, and each has a cost, $\{C_w, C_r, C_n\}$. Finally, there will be a set of probabilities, P_{jk}, denoting the probability of outcome j given that action k has been taken. This is generally written

$$(2.3) \qquad EU(a_j) = \Sigma P_{jk} U(O_k) - C_k,$$

and expected utility maximizing candidates choose action j, such that

$$(2.4) \qquad \text{Max } EU(a_j).$$

This calculus can be simplified by three assumptions (see Aldrich and Bianco 1992 for details). First, pure office-seeking ambition implies in its strongest and simplest form that no politicians care which party they join based on policy concerns. Second, we can easily assume that the candidate will not win election as a W(R) if he or she runs as an R(W). Finally, we can also assume that net costs of running are positive and (less obviously) constant across parties. Differing costs across parties are likely to be negatively correlated with probabilities of success (that is, extra effort will make up for lower probabilities), so that variable costs are likely to accentuate any findings reached. Aldrich and Bianco show that the full expression of this model (1992, 105), combined with the simplifications above, leads to (106):

(2.5a) $EU(a_n) = 0;$
(2.5b) $EU(a_w) = P_{WW}U(O) - C;$
(2.5c) $EU(a_R) = P_{RR}U(O) - C.$

Rational (pure) office seekers will run if at least one party offers a positive expected return, and they will then choose to run in whichever party offers the higher (highest) probability of victory. Note that, with simplifying assumptions, the calculus of candidacy and the calculus of party choice are identical in form. In either case it is the consequence of ambition that the candidate desires as great a certainty of holding office as possible and acts so as to minimize the risk of defeat.

What about running as a candidate independent of any party? For a single election to a single office for one who cares only about holding office and not at all about using it, the calculus could be written as $EU(a_I) = P_IU(O) - C_I$, where I denotes independence. In this case it is thus an empirical question whether P_I is less than P_{WW} or P_{RR}, or if C_I is less than C, or both. The empirical answer is almost certainly yes in both cases, probably decisively so. Still, it is an empirical question. The value of independence compared with party affiliation will, however, be quite different if the candidate values the potential for repeated election to office, or the use of office, or both.

Ambition is for a career. To that end, victory in the immediate election is crucial, for any defeat greatly reduces the prospects for a long career. So too, however, are the prospects for continued election critical. This is true for the selection of what office to seek, but the advantages of incumbency mean that victory in the current election will yield (for most offices, at least) a relatively high probability of reelection later. Choice of party, however, depends even more on future as well as current prospects. Thus, for example, Whigs in the 1850s differed in their assessments of the future. Some apparently believed it was more likely that the Republican Party would join the Democrats as the two major parties than that the Whigs would remain a major party. Senator William Seward (NY), even though antislavery himself, believed the prospects of the Whig party were better and remained a Whig longer than others for that reason.

Consider, then, calculations over a career. Even maintaining the pure office-seeking model, future party switching opens up a huge array of possible strategies. The two most important to consider are choosing to affiliate with one party or the other and expecting to continue that affiliation for the foreseeable future. Aldrich and Bianco (1992) demonstrate that future choices of this simple sort do not change the fundamentals: the ambitious candidate affiliates with the party that offers the higher probability of a continuing career.

This narrowly career-oriented form of ambition has been developed on the grounds that if we can find incentives for affiliating with a party with this self-interested motivation, explaining why ambitious politicians who also have policy goals affiliate with a party will be even easier. The model so far, however, explains which party ambitious politicians join, but it does not explain why they join any party, or why they might have formed a party in the first place.

The answer to these more fundamental questions focuses on the same central variable, the probability of election. The argument proceeds in three steps. The first is to assume—and to justify the assumption—that the probability of election for any candidate is higher with a party than without. The second step is to show that the probability is higher by affiliating with a major party than with a minor party. The final step is to show that there will be two such major parties—Duverger's Law.

The probability of election is a summary measure of expected choices of the electorate. As I argued earlier, the electorate faces two collective action problems, and candidates who affiliate with a party receive (at least potentially) two resources for ameliorating those problems. They receive, that is, an initial reputation (and hence a bloc of potential supporters) and a set of resources for identifying and helping to bring out those supporters. The purely ambitious candidate is assumed to place no particular value on the reputation itself, although candidates with policy motivations might be attracted to (or repelled by) one or another party by its reputation. The advantage of assuming a reputation by affiliating with a party is efficiency in attracting support. Economies of scale simply make it more attractive to participate in a political party than to go it alone. This of course was especially consequential in earlier periods, when political parties were the nearly exclusive source of the funding and labor needed to compete effectively, reinforced when voting was not secret and was cast by party-strip ballots. Even without such an effective monopoly, however, it follows that it is possible that there are incentives for affiliating with a political party. Indeed, Aldrich and Bianco (1992) provide a simple, game theoretic model that combines choice of party with the Black-Rohde model of office seeking from which they derive such incentives.

Combined with the electoral credibility that comes with having achieved a party's nomination for office, reputation and resources more easily explain why candidates affiliate with existing parties than why they form them in the first place. In particular, the formation of a party, even if the potential advantages are fully appreciated, raises a collective action problem of its own. Chapters 4 and 5 will provide detailed accounts of the ways the (Jacksonian) Democratic and Republican Parties were able to surmount these collective action problems and form in the first place. In the latter chapter I will use the calculus of party affiliation, but we will also see that it needs to be understood as a problem in strategic interaction, requiring a game theoretic explanation, rather than as a problem in individual decision making. We will also see not only that it took ambitious politicians to create the two American mass political parties, but that it also took a conjunction of particular conditions to make collective action possible.

What was especially important in the Jacksonian case was that office seekers were also benefit seekers—seeking, that is, the benefits that come from other partisans' holding office. In this case it was to be through a new party, forged primarily by incumbent representatives and senators (along with other high-level benefit seekers) seeking, with the aid of the popular presidential candidacy of Jackson, the dual benefits of spurred mobilization for all Democrats and an incumbency that could provide selective benefits for these Jacksonian Democratic congressmen. Thus the spoils of office, whether in controlling jobs or in distributing the benefits of legislation, could become a full spoils *system* only by means of an organized party controlling a majority in Congress and, above all, capturing the presidency. Even if Jacksonian Democrats were merely ambitious office seekers, control over the spoils of victory would make holding office more valuable and more certain over the long term. This combination of access to the spoils of office and the consequent development of a party reputation shows with empirical content and specificity why affiliation tends to be with a major rather than minor party and, even more importantly, illustrates Schwartz's insight into the value of a long coalition.

The remaining problem, then, is to explain why there are, have been, and are likely to be exactly two major parties in America. This problem is one of the central problems in the study of political parties in a comparative context. While this book is primarily about American political parties, this comparative question is sufficiently important (and sheds sufficient light on American parties) as to justify separate consideration.

Party Systems

To this point, we have looked at political parties as individual entities. A major defining characteristic of American democracy, as with all other democracies of which I am aware, is not that there are a number of discrete parties, or that there is a Democratic and a Republican Party, but that there there are two (or more) durable parties that define a system. We call ours a "two-party system," and Hofstadter titled his book *The Idea of a Party System* (1969). We ask three questions in this section (following the presentation in Aldrich 2007). What is a party system, why does America have a two-party system, and given that it does, with what effects?

If one were to take the literature at face value, there are two unrelated definitions of "party system." In comparative politics, a party system is defined in comparison across nations, typically by the number of political parties, or at least the number of major or durable political parties. Thus, Anglo-American democracies are generally two-party systems, and European parliamentary democracies, which use some form of proportional voting, are typically multiparty systems. This view directs attention to two other considerations.

One is the nature (and sometimes origin) of social cleavages. Are they many, deep, crosscutting, reinforcing? Attention often turns to electoral rules (winner-take-all or proportional) or other forms of democratic institutions thought relevant to the number of parties, such as centralized powers versus decentralized or federal governments, unicameral or bicameral legislatures, presidential or parliamentary systems, and so on (Lijphart 1999).

The second is apparently unique to the literature about American political parties, where "party system" means the long-term structure of the parties' electoral coalitions (perhaps akin to the electoral version of Schwartz's long coalitions). Thus, while the Democratic and Republican Parties have been the two major parties since 1860, their coalitional compositions have changed dramatically over that century and a half. Sometimes, there is a rapid and dramatic change in coalitions, such as at the creation of the New Deal—such changes are referred to as "party realignments" (e.g., Sundquist 1983). Sometimes they are less comprehensive; an example is the move for the Democrats to become the party in favor of civil rights in the 1960s, which some refer to as an "issue evolution" (Carmines and Stimson 1989). In either case (or other forms), the major characteristic is the over-time durability of the electoral coalition, and thus the novel event is its change.

In fact, of course, it would make sense to have a definition of a party system that encompassed both perspectives. It makes sense to say that the Dutch multiparty system is indeed considerably different from the British "two-plus" party system. And it makes sense to explicate durable patterns, especially of political characteristics such as the social composition or policy views of parties' electoral support, and thus to have a historical dimension.

Rational choice theory again provides a useful way to think about these questions, and its (rather limited) range of applications helps us understand why the United States has a two-party system. What might a party system be? Politics in general and just about everything of interest about political parties in particular is about strategy. The key to understanding how strategic action differs from its nonstrategic equivalent is that the outcome depends upon the choices of all the actors in the system. If someone can "rationally" determine what to do with reference only to their own preferences and without regard to what others think or do, and in turn, their actions have no effect on the choices of others, that person is not a part of the strategic system. What outcome occurs in the above examples, such as the prisoners' dilemma, depends not just on what the row chooser did but also on what the column chooser did.

Thus, we can define a party system by its strategic interaction. The system of political parties consists of all and only those parties whose actions help determine the outcome, and whose actions are contingent upon the (anticipated) actions of all other parties, and vice versa. (There is one addition to this definition, as discussed below.) In 2008, John McCain and Barack Obama were locked in a two-candidate election. Their actions were based in part on what they expected their opponent to do, and vice versa, and the outcome depended not just on what Obama did but also on what McCain did. There were eleven other presidential candidates on at least some ballots in 2008, but their actions did not shape McCain's or Obama's choices, nor did they affect the outcome. It was a pure two-person contest. This reflects a two-party system, in that exactly the same was true for the Democratic and Republican Parties in 2008. The two parties form a system because these two parties are durable in strategic interaction and are expected to be so into the future. While a third party or candidate occasionally is a strategic actor in presidential politics (Ralph Nader in 2000 but not in 2008, for instance), no third party or candidate is so over time. Thus, we have a two-party system.

A system of parties is thus defined as those parties engaged in strategic interaction from election to election, competing for popular support. Notice that the public is, in the aggregate, a strategic actor as well. That is, each member of the public conditions his or her choices on the strategies of the parties (who do they nominate, what do they propose to do if elected, and so on), and parties condition their choices not only on what they expect the other party in the system to do but also with respect to their anticipated response from the public. Thus parties, candidates, and voters are engaged in strategic interaction. But it is precisely this strategic interaction among voters and parties (that is, their candidates and officeholders) that defines what we mean by democratic governance, as well. A party system, that is, is embedded in and is a necessary ingredient of an effective democracy.

Duverger's Law, that elections decided by plurality or majority rule yield a two-party system, is an empirical observation.[24] As Riker pointed out (1982b), it becomes a scientific law only when given theoretical underpinnings. He pointed to two possible sources of a rational basis for the law. One resides in the electorate and is manifested in the "wasted vote" logic, that is, the decisions of voters to choose between only the two leading candidates or parties. Palfrey (1989) and Feddersen (1992) provide formal demonstrations of this account. Abramson et al. (1992) provide evidence that voters avoided "wasting" votes on other than the two major contenders in presidential primaries, and Black (1978) and Cain (1978) provide comparable evidence for the "wasted vote" logic in Canada and in Britain. Still, the formal demonstration rests on the problematic assumption that voters base their decisions on the probability of making or breaking ties (but see Aldrich 1993b). Nonetheless, even a weak tendency of voters to act in this "sophisticated" fashion will encourage two-partyism.

The stronger force, Riker believed, lies with the political elites. Certainly it is in the party's interests—in the collective interests of its key members—to be one of the two major parties. Thus any party will seek to recruit, train, and support the strongest candidates it can. Just as surely, it is in the interests of the two strongest candidates to ensure, as far as possible, that the choice reduces to just those two.[25] The advantage for the possible or actual candidates lies, however, not (or not only) in the advantages major party affiliation affords them for the immediate election. The advantage lies in the long-term career prospects of relatively high likelihood of continued access to office over the course of a political career and of the heightened ability to use that office for whatever goals are desired. It is the reduction of uncertainty in repeated electoral contests, just as in repeated policymaking contests, that yields the great advantage of affiliation with, and even the creation of, a major party.

Cox (1997), among others, demonstrated that rational voters could indeed yield a two-party system. His general and elegant result is that voters' choices in a district that selects, say, M winners will, if they choose rationally, support M+1 candidates. This result means that in single-member district systems such as (most of) the United States, rational voters will act so as to lead to two candidates being the appropriate number. Sometimes in the United States and often in other nations (particularly interesting is Japan), voters in one district select more than one candidate for office, and in those districts "Duvergerian" results lead to more (precisely to M+1) candidates or parties able to sustain candidacies.

This result, however, is about voting and choices at the district level. There is no reason in this logic to lead to each district having the same two parties. Indeed, as Chhibber and Kollman show (2004), India is best described as a system with single-member districts but a multiparty system. However, they also show that in most districts there is a two-party system. The Congress Party is one of the two major parties in most districts, but the other major party differs from place to place.

In Japan, the Liberal Democratic Party (LDP), until only recently the long-dominant party, had to solve the problem of how to ensure that they put forth just the right number of candidates to compete effectively in multimember districts. Too few, and they would not win all of the seats they could. Too many, and they would divide votes among too many candidates, diluting their strength and risking losing seats they could have won. In discussing how the LDP addressed this problem, Reed (2009) contrasts explanations that focus on the party as an actor with his own explanation that it was the choices of individual candidates that eventually solved the M+1 rule problem for the LDP. In his account it was, therefore, the decentralized actions of individual, rational candidates that eventually converged on the appropriate decisions.

The study of a party system, therefore, needs to include examination of not only the incentives toward a two-party or multiparty system, but also the manner in which major parties create national organizations across districts, or how and why they fail to do so. Here, the incentives to have a strong party reputation and the incentives to create a single, national party, uniting potentially disparate organizations (not unlike Van Buren did in 1828–36 as we will see in chap. 4), come together.

While Duverger's Law is discussed as deducing that plurality elections yield two-party systems, the results actually are about a system with three parties. In particular, the two parties choose locations based not only on what their opponent does (in light of anticipated electoral choices), but also in reaction to the threat of possible entry of some (unknown, unspecified) third party. Thus, as in Palfrey's original one-dimensional model (1989), the two parties do not converge to the median, as they do in the median voter theorem (Black 1978) or its electoral competition version (Downs 1957). Instead they (symmetrically) diverge in equilibrium just enough so that both still continue to expect to tie each other, but so that there is also no policy position for a new, third party to adopt that allows them to enter and win the election. This sort of result, then, provides an explanation for why two parties are different from each other—they are positioning themselves to maintain their duopoly status, making both better off, while also competing against the other duopoly-party.

Dan Lee and I (Aldrich and Lee, forthcoming) show that if there are multiple policy dimensions, there are two-party results (with the two parties positioning themselves to foil the ability of any third party to compete, as in Palfrey), but there are also combinations in which there can be three and even four parties in equilibrium in a plurality system. This result, then, pushes the question back to that asked in light of Cox's work (1997). The two-party result does not only answer Cox's question concerning organizing across districts to transform the local incentives toward two parties into a national two-party system, but also shows the importance of coordination between the two parties to block entry of third or even fourth parties when there is more than one issue dimension. That is, the two major parties in a two-party system also have incentives to try to reduce the policy space to be approximately one dimensional, so they can maintain their duopoly, or at least to make one dimension the primary dimension of party competition, so that any other dimension is insufficiently salient to the public to make entry of new parties viable. In chapter 5, we will see how the Democrats and Whigs acted in a fashion that seems quite consistent with this account, maintaining the line of party cleavage on economic development and not allowing the issue of slavery to become very consequential in electoral politics.

POLITICAL PARTIES AND THE NEW INSTITUTIONALISM

The last few sections have demonstrated that the nature of forming electoral and legislative majorities in a republican democracy induces incentives for the possible formation of political parties. The nature of these incentives invariably entails that politicians stand to win more—achieve more of their goals or be more likely to achieve their goals—through a party than otherwise. Rational choice theory since Riker's classic argument (1962) has moved away from this emphasis on winning per se to become more concerned with the problems of social choice and collective action—that is, to search for conditions that generate equilibrium outcomes or that yield equilibrium outcomes with desirable properties, especially Pareto optimality. I have argued in this chapter that winning—that is, achieving one's goals—and establishing (desirable) equilibriums are closely related in republican democracies. To achieve an equilibrium at all or to attain a desirable outcome is often precisely the same thing as winning, whether that means securing office, using office for other purposes, or both.

Saying that politicians might find it in their interests to create or to use a political party is not the same thing as saying they will choose to do so. A political party is a collective enterprise, subject to significant collective action problems in forming and maintaining it. Moreover, there may be other means of achieving the politicians' goals, and parties may not always be a means to desirable outcomes. In chapter 8 I will argue that contemporary, candidate-centered elections have become more desirable to ambitious candidates than the traditional "party-centered" elections. Since forming or even affiliating with a political party is a voluntary choice of a politician, it is critical to examine the particular setting to see if (1) there is an incentive for politicians to turn to parties, (2) it is feasible (not, for example, a potential solution that founders on a collective action problem), and (3) there are no superior solutions—or at minimum that politicians actually did act on the incentives by creating or employing the agency of a party.

Political parties are "solutions" of a particular kind. They must be institutions that are enduring, or at least that politicians expect to endure, if they are to be successful in achieving their goals. Although long a part of the rational choice tradition, the "new institutionalism" became a self-consciously identified entity only with publication of Shepsle's famous paper (1979).[26] Shepsle's work examined one of the two great problems that structure the analysis of how institutions affect outcomes by developing his notion of structure-induced equilibrium, or SIEs. The problem is to investigate the equilibrium in outcomes, given the preferences of the actors and the institutional rules. There are two major streams to the study of SIEs.

The first, illustrated by Shepsle, is motivated by Arrow's theorem and searches for the existence of equilibrium, virtually any equilibrium, when it is generally expected that there would be none. The second stream of research concerns public goods and collective action. Thus, for example, Olson (1965) not only developed the problem of collective action but also considered institutional solutions to that problem.

The goal here is not to find just any equilibrium, but to develop means to achieve a desirable equilibrium when an undesirable one (notably a Pareto inferior one) would otherwise be expected. Although differing in these ways, these two streams investigate the combination of actors' goals and institutional arrangements in achieving political outcomes. This problem may be referred to as investigation of institutional equilibrium.

The second great problem Shepsle (1986) called that of equilibrium institutions. Instead of asking what equilibrium it is that institutional arrangements and preferences produce, the question is what institutional arrangements are chosen in the first place. This is the question that motivated this chapter: why or under what conditions would rational actors choose to turn to parties? What was shown here was that, if rational politicians did turn to parties, those parties might have beneficial effects—that is, they might help politicians achieve their goals. The equilibrium institutions question, then, is whether rational politicians would indeed choose that institutional arrangement. It rests, of course, on the presumption that politicians can choose such institutional arrangements (i.e., they are endogenous institutions). Parties meet this criterion, perhaps more commonly than most institutions studied. Thus politicians *can* choose to create or modify partisan institutions, and this chapter has demonstrated that they might *want* to create or modify them. The problem of equilibrium institutions, then, asks whether politicians *do* so choose, given that they can and might want to.

As with institutional equilibrium, there are two streams to the equilibrium institutions literature, one concerning social choice problems and the other addressing public goods and collective action problems. Analysis of equilibrium institutions proceeds by assuming that at least one important reason actors may choose an equilibrium institution is its desirable consequences, for example, in solving social choice or collective action problems. It may well be that adopting any new or altered rules will have unanticipated consequences and that their institutional equilibrium consequences may be only one of many reasons that rules were adopted or changed. Still, the presumption is that their anticipated equilibrium consequences are important motivations for adoption.

The first stream, social choice, faces the "inheritability problem" (first posed by Riker, 1980). If it is true that rules are adopted to yield SIEs, because there is no equilibrium in preferences alone, then the choice of rules may be affected by, or inherit, the disequilibrium of choices over outcomes. We saw in the paradox of voting example above that forming temporary coalitions was unsatisfactory precisely because those temporary coalitions cycled themselves. There is as yet no general answer to this problem. It may be that Arrow's theorem extends back, so that the "answer" to the inheritability problem is another impossibility result. Just as Arrow's theorem can be proved using an infinite regress approach (see MacKay 1980), so may the choice of rules yield an infinite regress. There may be ways around this problem. For example, the Constitution may end the infinite regress. Legislation is enacted by simple majorities, whereas the Constitution may be changed only by extraordinary majorities—and by extraordinary majorities fashioned in states as well as the nation. Therefore disequilibrium over legislation would not be expected to reflect back into disequilibrium over constitutional amendments, owing to the differing rules of selection and the larger set of actors involved in amending (see Aldrich 1993a).

Party rules, however, are often changed by the same procedures and the same actors that determine outcomes. A simple majority of national convention delegates is needed to nominate candidates, but the same people use the same procedure at virtually the same time to choose the party's rules.[27] So too does a party's congressional caucus decide on rules governing itself and on policy outcomes it seeks.

Constitutional rules and party rules share another characteristic: they define institutions. The idea of institutionalizing something is to give its rules and procedures some permanence. If disequilibrium were a problem in choosing some political outcome, it does not follow immediately, if at all, that the choice of rules to specify how this *and other outcomes* are to be chosen would also cycle. Different decision criteria are involved: choice of the specific outcome at hand, and choice of rules to affect choices of outcomes over some time horizon. That does not mean there will be equilibrium in the choice of rules where there is none in the choice of particular outcomes. It does mean that the choice of rules will not, in general, inherit the disequilibrium associated with the choice of these particular outcomes. Moreover, the argument made here is not that actors turned to parties for the mere purpose of resolving cyclicality. Rather, it is that the actors had the purpose of winning, and that happens to include buttressing their side from the threat of losing owing to manipulation of cycling by opponents. They seek not just to end the threat of cycling, but to yield particular resolutions that further their particular goals. The choice of rules, whether constitutional or partisan, is typically justified on ethical or moral grounds, in addition to any practical considerations. Whether or not advocates believe in those normative arguments, their regularity suggests that advocates consider them useful in convincing others. To that extent, normative grounds invoke alternative goals and values, also breaking the immediate inheritability of outcome cycling.

The problems posed by public goods and collective action provide the second stream of research into equilibrium institutions. Here the vast literature that Axelrod's (1984) and Taylor's (1976) research has spawned often deals with institutional or normative arrangements that promote more optimal outcomes than would be expected in their absence. This literature faces the problem of the folk theorem, in which differing institutional arrangements are capable of supporting virtually any set of outcomes in equilibrium. In general, however, the problem is how to sustain any outcome superior to what would happen "naturally," in the absence of institutional arrangements. Thus the problem is that there are shared preferences that go unrealized, and the equilibrium institutions problem is to aid the realization of unanimously desired outcomes that are not otherwise sustainable.

The next three chapters are empirical examinations of times in which politicians did turn to parties. Their first purpose is to show that the theoretical possibilities developed in this chapter appeared to hold in the particular historical contexts studied. Their second purpose is to demonstrate that the relevant political actors realized the theoretical problems in the form generally realized by politicians, the opportunity to win or lose on important issues.[28] The purpose of these chapters, in other words, is to put the possibility claims made in this chapter to the test. Parties were chosen institutions, these chapters argue, in the spirit of equilibrium institutions. These parties were chosen because of their consequences for winning, thereby creating institutional equilibriums.

PART TWO

PARTY FORMATION IN AMERICA,
1790–1860

PROLOGUE

In part 2, I analyze three historical instances when politicians faced the theoretical concerns examined in part 1, albeit facing them as practical political problems. The case studies demonstrate that, when confronting these theoretical possibility results (or incentives), political elites did in fact turn to the political party as a solution. The three cases are also instances when the party solution worked, which need not always be true. And conveniently, the three cases illustrate incentives drawn from, in the sequence of the chapters to follow, social choice, collective action, and ambition theoretic incentives.

In chapter 3 I show that the Federalist and Republican Parties can be understood in large part as institutional solutions that emerged from the actions of Hamilton, Jefferson, Madison, and others who were facing a social choice problem. The practical manifestation of that problem was addressing what I call the "great principle"—how large and active the new central government would be, and in their competing views *must* be—to make the great experiment in republican democracy viable. I add a coda to this analysis of parties and the "great principle." The presidential election of 1800 was one of the most interesting, complex, and important in American history. The one strand I pull out of the complexity of 1800 demonstrates that, by the end of the century, the newly created political parties had become the site of terrific competition and strategy as each party sought (often successfully) to revise more to its favor state laws governing the election of presidential electors.

In chapter 4 I show that Martin Van Buren explicitly planned, and that he and others implemented, the creation of the Jacksonian Democratic Party to solve, in part, a series of collective action problems. Their practical problem was to gather the resources sufficient to mobilize an increasingly far-flung electorate, so that Democrats could capture and use office for partisan purposes over a series of elections. To do so they invented the modern mass political party and, along with the Whigs, created what was unequivocally the first two-party system. These parties and the system they formed not only sought solutions to these practical forms of collective action problems but, I show in the first part of chapter 5, were also complex institutions designed to maintain national unity by avoiding division among regions, especially over slavery. The demise of the Whig party broke that apparent two-party equilibrium. Van Buren had warned years earlier that with the loss of the intersectional party distinctions realized in the Democratic and Whig parties, "geographic divisions founded on local interests, or what is worse prejudices between free and slave holding states will inevitably take their place." Prejudices between free and slaveholding states did in fact take their place. The result was that a new major party arose, and with it the third party system. It was, I show in the rest of chapter 5, the combination of policy concerns over the slavery issue and the actions of ambitious politicians seeking political careers that generated the new Republican Party and the new partisan alignment.

This, then, adds up to the "positive" case for political parties, in the sense that solving the problems of the time led these politicians, positively, toward the creation of political party institutions. There is nothing in the theory that says politicians will always find it in their interests to create or maintain partisan institutions. Such arrangements could be part of the problem, as, in the 1850s, antislavery advocates found that the Whig party and the second party system were part of the problem in seeking a solution to the slavery issue—at least on terms congenial to antislavery advocates. Or parties could simply become less useful, ineffective, or in the extreme, irrelevant. As a result, politicians might find it useful to let the old partisan arrangements atrophy. It is a bit too simple, but not too far off the mark, to say that the decline and eventual demise of the Federalist Party in national politics was due to its ineffectiveness, if not irrelevance.

Although the primary purpose of the case studies is to articulate and exemplify the theoretical account, they serve further purposes as well. First, the case studies, though not complete explanations of the politics of any of the periods, nonetheless provide insight into the origins of all major parties in American history. Second, they detail the development of the first form of parties and then the creation of the "modern mass party," the second form of American political party that would serve this republic until about 1960. Third, the case studies provide an account of the development of the American two-party system, particularly major aspects of the first three party systems and the critical eras demarcating each.

The cases make one further point. These were rational political actors struggling to achieve their political goals. But in none of the three cases could the goals be understood as the narrow self-interest of ambitious politicians. To be sure, there were narrow political aims involved. Hamilton desired to see his plan enacted. Van Buren wanted to win elections. Republicans wanted to win office. Institutional solutions were used in these cases and were not just short term. Actors in the first party system wanted, among other things, to establish a lengthy series of precedent-setting outcomes. Democrats and Whigs, just like Republicans, wanted to win election repeatedly and to make politics a genuine career opportunity. But there was more in the creation of partisan institutional arrangements than seeking long-term rather than short-term victories. The aims of the actors were not merely to win elections and control offices; their goals invariably included achieving policy objectives, indeed, seeking to win on struggles over principles. The first party system can be understood only as based in part on seeking to ensure that the actors' beliefs about the appropriate size and power of the new federal government would be realized. The Jacksonian Democratic Party can be understood only as an attempt to enact the "party principle." And the second party system can be understood only as its creators' seeking in part to avoid the slavery issue and the threat it posed to the Union. The third party system, and especially the actions of those who would become Republicans, can be understood only as in part the attempt to move in an increasingly antislavery direction. To be sure, winning in the narrow sense and winning in the short term were constantly involved, but so too were winning in the longer term and winning on the principles or policies involved. These rational political actors were self-interested in the narrow sense, but not merely that. They were also actors with broader and richer goals, and their actions could be understood only by the interplay of these two sorts of motivations.

3

FOUNDING THE FIRST PARTIES
Institutions and Social Choice

Thomas Jefferson, then secretary of state, hosted Treasury Secretary Alexander Hamilton and Representative James Madison for dinner on or about June 20, 1790. The second of three sessions of the First Congress was nearing its end. Amid continuing and frequently acrimonious debate, two matters, location of the capital and disposition of Hamilton's fiscal plan, had reached an impasse that the dinner was intended to resolve. These three agreed on a plan to trade votes in Congress, and by August 12, 1790, the issues were decided on terms close to those forged that night.

There is no denying that these issues were crucial affairs, that the impasse on each was of long standing, or that firm decisions were needed. The symbolic importance of the capital for any new nation is evident, and the economic and political benefits to the chosen location, whether in the North or the South, would be substantial. Its location had been disputed for a decade, and it accounted for over one-third of all roll call votes cast in the House in its first session under the new constitution.[1] In September the House had reached an agreement to locate the capital in Pennsylvania and moved on to other matters. The Senate could not agree, however, and the House and Senate had to reopen debate. This time the House stalled action. On June 10 its members defeated a measure to consider the location question in committee of the whole, effectively postponing further congressional action until later in the summer.

The second great dispute concerned Hamilton's plan for the nation's economy, at this time focusing on whether the national government should assume the debts states had incurred in and after the Revolution.[2] Opposition was led in the House by Madison himself. Hamilton's supporters initially defeated a series of amendments that Madison and his allies introduced to weaken or eliminate assumption, but slowly Madison's proposals gathered strength. On June 2, shortly after three new representatives from North Carolina were seated, Hamilton's opponents called the question on assumption and defeated it 31–29. The plan was sent to the Senate with assumption stricken. Like the capital location, division on the assumption question was broadly North against South; but the voting groups, and their underlying motivations, were far more complicated than that.

Economic difficulties that led to the plan had long been important. They were, for example, an important impetus to the call for a convention to amend the Articles of Confederation. Should the new government fail to solve the very issues that had undermined the old order, the new order would likely fail. Hamilton believed that quick, decisive action by the national government was needed. Substantively, his plan would affect some differently than others, and congressional disagreement in part reflected these local interests. Some also believed it was inappropriate for the federal government to take such far-reaching actions and assume what they believed to be the prerogatives of individual states.

Thus by June 1790 even the most optimistic of the framers could no longer hope that the new constitutional design would generate unity over America's "great experiment" of democracy in an extended republic. Establishing sufficient unity to solve these most difficult problems was the motivation for the dinner of June 20. And this unusual step appeared to work.

In fact, of course, the trade that night did not end disagreement between Hamilton, John Adams, and others on the one hand, and Jefferson, Madison, and their supporters on the other. Continuing disagreement took a turn that in time would culminate in the creation of a new form of organization that would forever alter democracy as these founders saw it. Instead of solving problems by vote trades among opposing leaders or by other forms of piecemeal, issue-by-issue compromise, these leaders—first Hamilton, then Jefferson and Madison—turned to organizing their supporters. In time these organizations would strengthen and would widen their scope with respect to both members and issues, to become the first political parties of modern democratic form in this or any nation. In 1790 none of the principals either foresaw the invention of parties or had any master partisan design in mind, but the path they set out on culminated in modern political parties.

I argue that these efforts were driven by the consequences of majority instability, that is, by the social choice problem. In one sense the instability of temporary majority coalitions revealed itself in the difficulties encountered in resolving these and other pressing problems facing the new nation. The fundamental problem, however, was to establish in practice just how strong and active the new federal government was to be. Basic differences on this, which I call the "great principle," rested on differing views of how to make the new republic most likely to succeed. Failure to establish a clear basis of precedent would leave this great principle unresolved and risk revealing the unworkability of an extended republic. These failures over immediate policy concerns and over establishing the long-run viability of the federal government were due, I argue, to the instability of majority rule as demonstrated by Arrow's theorem and its extension to voting theory (see chap. 2).

UNSTABLE MAJORITIES IN THE FIRST CONGRESS

The two problems of location of the capital and of fiscal policy were not new to the First Congress (see Aldrich, Jillson, and Wilson 2002; Jillson and Wilson 1994). They had been repeatedly considered throughout the 1780s in the Continental Congresses. The location of the capital had been debated and left unresolved in several of the Continental Congresses, with numerous locations proposed, just as in the First Congress. Funding had, of course, been a considerable concern throughout the Revolution and the 1780s. In 1781 Robert Morris, superintendent of finance, had proposed a "Report on the Public Credit" that was very similar to Hamilton's plan, including calls for assumption of state debt, measures to alleviate the national debt, and formation of a national bank. Delegate Hamilton had been one of Morris's strongest supporters in the Congress, albeit in a losing effort. Jillson and Wilson (1994) demonstrate that the structure of the confederal government required near unanimity among the state delegations to adopt any motion—an effective unanimity that was impossible to achieve. Thus the events that led to the proposed vote trade in the First Congress essentially replayed events that had helped lead to the call for revision of the Articles.

These events displayed another way in which policy and procedural disputes were intertwined. Up to this point, in the new as in the confederal Congress, policies were first raised and discussed in Committee of the Whole (involving few rules and a nearly "pure" democracy). In this relaxed setting, concerns were raised, a committee was designated for formulating an actual proposal, if there was sufficient interest expressed, and the ad hoc committee's bill was then discussed again in Committee of the Whole, often with amendments and final passage effectively agreed to.

As Bill Granstaff puts it (pers. comm.), the Congress (usually in Committee of the Whole) agreed there was a "cause" for considering legislation and then chose the "effect" (the bill). In September of 1789, however, the Congress deviated from this process over the question of the location of the capital. Meeting separately from the Congress itself ("out of doors"), supporters of what would become Hamilton's coalition met and crafted an effect (that is, a bill) before the Congress had agreed on the cause. This deviation in process as well as disagreement over the resulting bill led Madison to conclude that "all was lost in the House." A major step toward the formation of both parties was thus taken.

Historians dispute the terms of the vote trade agreement discussed above. In some accounts (e.g., Bowling 1971), Jefferson and Madison agreed to prevail upon Daniel Carroll and George Gale of Maryland and perhaps Richard Bland Lee and Alexander White of Virginia to pass assumption in the House.[3] Switching four votes would be more than sufficient to reverse the 31–29 vote of June 2. Hamilton agreed, in this account, to prevail on the Senate for approval of Philadelphia as a temporary capital, with permanent location on the banks of the Potomac; to modify requirements for reporting state debt; and to make various other changes to his plan so that more of the southern states' debt would quality for assumption. If Hamilton did try to change any votes, they most likely would have been those of Tristram Dalton and Caleb Strong of Massachusetts. If so, he was unsuccessful. Bowling (1971) argued that it was more likely that Hamilton's role on the capital question was to ensure that the Massachusetts delegation, while continuing to vote against the agreed-upon plan, would not repeat its efforts to upset the supporting coalition in the Senate.

Jacob Cooke (1970, 1971) argued that the trade agreement was primarily (perhaps exclusively) about assumption.[4] He further argued that the trade was not consummated. Hamilton, he presumed, did not try to change any votes and, had he tried, would have failed for lack of influence. Finally, Cooke believed, the trade was not needed anyway, since agreements and changes struck elsewhere determined the outcome. He did not dispute that a trade was agreed to, or that votes did change so that the outcomes sought at the dinner became law. In between, though, he argued, a complicated set of maneuvers and compacts among small numbers of individuals led to a great many shifts in votes on these two concerns, with just enough changes to pass the capital and assumption bills.

Whether the vote trade was effective or the questions were resolved through many shifts and bargains is immaterial for the argument pre-

sented here. It is sufficient that the leaders of the two principal groupings in government—and perhaps many others as well—believed such
unusual steps were needed. Either version, I argue, is just what one
would expect to happen in a government without stability-enhancing
institutions, facing problems that many or all care deeply about and
foundering on the absence of equilibrium. It was because of such events
as those described so far that leaders not only sought means to circum-
vent the effects the social choice problem was having on these and other
issues, but also sought to solve them so that they could win a more
lasting set of outcomes.

The costs owing to instability and associated uncertainty about winning were even greater than the costs that would have been exacted for
failure to resolve these particular issues. These costs included uncertainty in the nation about the effectiveness and even the feasibility of
the new constitutional order and, more directly, resolution of remaining
ambiguity over the Constitution itself. The question, the "great principle," was exactly how powerful and positive the new federal government was to be or, even more deeply, what sort of nation America was
to be. It was on this great principle, I argue, that Jefferson and Madison
divided from Hamilton and Adams. On this great principle, compromise, such as vote trades, was at best a short-term palliative that could
not be sustained. And it was on this great principle that these leaders
gradually moved toward the formation of the first political parties.

The argument, then, is that what eventually became political parties in the modern sense were the solutions to one of the remaining
great constitutional questions. Resolution of this great principle could
be achieved only by the realization of policy outcomes. How strong,
effective, and positive the federal government was to be would be demonstrated only by what the new government actually did. On this principle, every political elite may be assumed to have had preferences. If
preferences guided action, then it would be reasonable to expect that
actual outcomes revealed which position—a stronger or a more limited
national government—had greater support, with the outcome being the
equilibrium of the median voter theorem. Votes in Congress did not
occur on the great principle alone, however. Rather, each substantive
action had its own values, consequences, and interests. As a result, pure
majority rule did not just reflect sentiment on the great principle, but
disclosed preferences over the great principle and preferences over the
substance of the particular outcomes.

In such a setting, we know there should be no equilibrium of preferences alone. In fact there was no equilibrium, and vote trades, politicking, and the like revealed and reflected the instability of simple majority

rule. The problem then was how to ensure not just passage of individual bills but achievement of the entire stream of policy—to win on the great principle. Parties, therefore, eventually formed as institutional solutions to the instability of majority rule so that policies chosen or denied would reflect, in the main, just how strong and active the new national government was to be.

By 1790, with passage of the Bill of Rights, the remaining and most pressing unsettled issue about the new order was the great principle. It was unsettled by ratification because even an amended Constitution was necessarily (and likely purposefully) ambiguous over the power to be wielded at the national level. As Anti-Federalist Luther Martin put it during ratification, the new Constitution might be "just so much federal in appearance" as to deceive the unwary but "so predominantly national as to put it in the powers of its movers, whenever the machine shall be set agoing, to strike out every appearance of being federal, and to render it wholly and entirely a national government" (in Storing 1981, 12).

What position the Constitution implied on the great principle dimension was inherently ambiguous, as Martin foresaw, because it depended not just on the written document but on how the new government would in fact be used, and that further depended in large part on the preferences of its new representatives. A national government filled with Anti-Federalists would use the apparatus of government to do less than would one filled with nationalists. The first few Congresses would be critical, for actions taken—or refrained from—in its earliest years would set the clearest precedents for just what power resided in and would be acted upon by the new national government.

The great principle can be thought of as a dimension beginning at one end with the arrangements under the Articles of Confederation. Virtually all agreed that the Continental Congress possessed too little power. Many believed that relatively small adjustments to strengthen national power would be sufficient. Delegates to the Constitutional Convention, however, generally agreed that a whole new structure of government was necessary but disagreed over the power it should exercise, with Hamilton at the extreme, desiring great strengthening. Thus preferences defined positions along a dimension that ranged from the Articles at one end to a powerful, unified national government at the other.[5]

If preferences were arrayed along a single dimension, and if the issue was purely what position on that dimension should be chosen, there would be a well-defined social choice, an equilibrium based on Black's median voter theorem.[6] But the Constitution did not, perhaps could not, precisely define the powers the new government might employ. The ambiguity remaining in the Constitution meant that resolution of the great principle must await actions taken in the first few Congresses.

The members elected or appointed to the First Congress were a diverse lot. Although those like Patrick Henry, whose ideal was closest to the Articles, disproportionately chose to remain outside the new government, some opposed to ratification were participants: fourteen of the sixty-five members elected to the first House were Anti-Federalists (those who had opposed ratification), and two were selected to the Senate (see Aldrich and Grant 1993). Their goal on the great principle was to seek outcomes that rendered the new government as limited as possible.

Largely owing to such Anti-Federalists, a great many proposals were debated on just these grounds. As Aldrich and Grant put it (1993, 310), "Even seemingly noncontroversial proposals were greeted by antifederalist objections or treated as constitutional questions, perhaps as a result of excessive fear that dangerous precedents would be established." Examples included the power of the president to declare a day of thanksgiving at the close of the first session, the authority of Congress to require state officers to swear allegiance to the Constitution, the ability of the House to grant the president the authority to deal with Indians, and the propriety of providing the president with furniture and china. Every proposal, that is, had the potential of raising the great principle, and many, even innocuous ones, were considered on those grounds. As these were often "housekeeping" proposals that arose in establishing the government at all, and as these had scant policy content, it may well be that differences in voting on them were almost exclusively due to differences over the great principle, unlike the mixture of principle and policy that came later, when more substantively weighty policies were under consideration.

With the new machine in motion, every action, whether successful or defeated, defined a specific instance of just what powers the government held and would use. Where ardent Anti-Federalists might see power lurking behind the decision to buy George Washington a desk, both Jeffersonians and Hamiltonians might not. But when it came to Hamilton's ambitious fiscal policy, Jeffersonians might well disagree.

But proposals were not simply precedents revealing the scope and power of the government. They were also substantive legislative proposals in their own right, with their own intrinsic merits and demerits, differentially affecting the values and the interests of the members and those they represented. Representatives and senators, therefore, necessarily judged such proposals in part on their own merits and in light of their own values and interests. The more consequential the matter, the more it needed to be judged on its own grounds rather than purely and simply on its implications for the great principle.

Proposals were therefore multidimensional. Indeed, because they were seen to have implications for the great principle and to set precedents on it, proposals were *necessarily* multidimensional. Perhaps, indeed, controversies concerning a day of thanksgiving or furniture for the president could be decided on great-principle grounds alone, precisely because of their low intrinsic content. But the location of the capital, disposition of Hamilton's plan, and other weighty issues could not be decided solely on those grounds.[7]

These issues were decided by majority voting in the House and Senate. If important issues are necessarily multidimensional, then the voting equilibrium due to unidimensionality disappears, and impossibility results, agenda control, coalitional manipulation, and "chaos" theorems become relevant.

One way to see this instability is to consider the findings of scholars who have analyzed roll call votes in the first Congresses. Any review reveals a very muddled literature, especially with respect to the first two Congresses. Grant (1977), reviewing work through the mid-1970s, found two major classes of interpretations.[8] Some discovered voting blocs. Ryan (1971), for example, saw two blocs based on sectionalism, and Bowling (1968) also found two, but these appeared to him to be pro- and antiadministration. Henderson (1974), conversely, discovered three sectional blocs: northern, southern, and middle states. Others such as Libby (1912) and Bell (1973) could observe only "different factional groupings formed around each issue" (Grant 1977, 37). Bell, for example, found clear factions on the votes concerning the Bill of Rights and the removal power issue but found no structure at all on votes for the capital. He uncovered four blocs on funding and assumption votes, with nearly every state delegation being divided on these issues regardless of state interests. Hoadley (1980, 1986) found that the first two Congresses were highly factionalized, and his graphs indeed illustrate widely dispersed scatters (see, for example, 1986, figs. 19, 20, and 26 for the first two Congresses). By the Third Congress, factionalism gave way to increasing polarization and to party politics. The dispersed scatter of congressmen and senators of the first two Congresses becomes, in the Third Congress, a much tighter clustering into two clear and quite separate blocs (see especially fig. 27, the House; and fig. 28, the Senate), and those two blocs are not just polarized but also very strongly related to partisan affiliations.

Illustrative, finally, is the fate of particular pieces of legislation. Consider, for example, the House votes on assumption. Assumption failed in the House on April 12, 1790, by an unrecorded vote of 29–31, and it passed on July 26 by a (recorded) vote of 34–28, although the critical vote was an unrecorded one in Committee of the Whole on July 24 by a 32–29 tally. Bowling's reconstruction of these votes (1971) showed that only four states (Massachusetts and Connecticut in the affirmative and Maryland and Georgia in the negative) voted as unified delegations on April 12. All others (except, of course, Delaware with its one representative) were divided on this particular vote. He then recorded fourteen changes in the vote count, including at least nine congressmen who actually changed sides on the issue by July 24, and two more changes, one of them a vote switch, by July 26. He recorded this set of changes in his defense of the simpler vote trade by Hamilton, Jefferson, and Madison. It was Cooke (1970) who, in rebutting Bowling's claims, saw the politicking, maneuvering, and changing as even more complicated.

Thus majority voting was highly unstable, shifting, and chaotic— just what would be expected in multidimensional choices that lack preference-based equilibrium. This was especially so in the voting on the major issues of the First Congress: location of the capital and Hamilton's plan.

Although both issues were successfully resolved by the end of the second session of the First Congress (August 12, 1790), their resolutions were achieved only through compromise, if not actual vote trades. Any compromise or trade means that each side paid some price, because neither got its most preferred outcome. Transaction costs in salvaging half loaves case by case are high. Moreover, political maneuvering was at best a necessary but unpalatable means, and especially at that time such politicking was generally understood to be inimical to social and political consensus. The very notion of politicking and stratagem (which founders disparaged as "cabal and intrigue") risked—and in fact engendered—outrage on the floor of Congress and in the nation.

Great costs were also exacted on the great principle. The most important and contentious issues were being resolved by provisional, issue-specific compromises. Such resolutions left uncertainty about what would happen in the future, and policy was evolving with no guarantee of long-term consistency or clarity of principle. The results were the absence of a clear signal to the nation about how strong and active the new government was and would be, and their precedent-setting value was necessarily undercut. Although decision by stratagem was costly on principle and inherently unpalatable to all, the costs likely were highest to Hamilton. He could count a majority in both chambers who supported his plan and, presumably, his vision of the proper role of the national government, but Madison's strategizing had divided his majority and nearly cost his plan assumption.[9] Indeed, Madison's temporary success in blocking assumption was accomplished by creating a coalition of minorities, just as Downs (1957) described, and doing so required both multidimensional choices and lack of a voting (or preference-induced) equilibrium. All, therefore, saw the need for a new basis for structuring decision making in the government, and Hamilton, whose goals were closest to realization and therefore most at risk, had the most to gain by taking new initiatives.

ORGANIZING TO INDUCE STABILITY

By the Second Congress (1791–93), most officeholders could be identified as Federalists or (Jeffersonian) Republicans (see Martis 1989).[10] By the Third Congress, voting patterns can be identified as polarized, broadly along party lines (as in Hoadley 1980, 1986). The presidential elections of 1796, following the announcement of Washington's retirement, were organized by the two parties, and by 1800 elections were publicly and undeniably partisan, as will be discussed below. Although no precise date can be given for the formation of these gradually strengthening political parties, they clearly emerged early in the new order, impelled by the attempts of Hamiltonians and Jeffersonians to win a consistent pattern of victories on policy—in reaction to the instability apparent in the First Congress—and to establish undeniable precedents on the great principle. These efforts are consistent with one solution to this problem of disequilibrium, examined in chapter 2, by establishing institutional constraints or incentives for themselves so that they would more often find it in their interest to vote according to the great principle rather than on other grounds. That is, institutional arrangements could induce equilibrium where preferences alone would not. These arrangements were designed to create a "long" coalition, as Schwartz (1989) defined a party, and they were needed, in the face of disequilibrium, because there was stiff competition seriously affecting the chances of the Hamiltonian majority-in-preference to win.

The presence of incentives does not by itself guarantee that the incentives will be acted on. Those who desire to organize majorities necessarily face a collective action problem. Hamiltonians might have known they shared interests collectively. They may have understood that, as a majority, they stood to benefit the most from organizing, and they surely recognized that they had the most to lose by failing to organize. Madison's minority had exploited the instability of preference-based majorities to wrest victory temporarily from them on debt assumption. Such knowledge does not guarantee that they had incentives, individually, to expend the time, effort, and resources needed to translate that collective interest into an organization.[11] Frohlich and Oppenheimer (1970) proposed that a political entrepreneur might be willing to exert the effort to create and maintain an organization in exchange for the leadership values he would accrue. According to Alvarez (1989), Hamilton was that figure. Chambers (1963) writes of Hamilton:

> Throughout the long shaping of the Federalist formulation, Hamilton played a curious though commanded role. In effect, he had initiated the whole effort with his vision and advocacy, and throughout its early years he stood forth as the party's unquestioned spokesman and leader. . . . His proposals, as he saw them, were to point the new nation in the "right" direction, place its new government on firm foundations, mobilize support for his management in that government, and thwart such political foes as might appear.

On September 1, 1789, Congress resolved that the secretary of the treasury should prepare a plan on the public debt, which Hamilton submitted in January 1790. Thus, at least in part, leadership was thrust on him, but it also provided him with a key resource. He could, and aggressively did, seize the initiative to define the agenda, enabling him "to frame the policy responses to the economic crises" (Alvarez 1989, 27). Second, whereas formal caucusing risked revelation of "cabal and intrigue," informal caucusing was common from the outset. Hoadley (1986, 53) points to caucuses in this period as showing "the need for the party to provide a degree of coordination in its legislative strategy." Although not yet constituting a party, they at least partially achieved coordination of strategy. In the House, for example, Fisher Ames and Theodore Sedgwick of Massachusetts and Jonathan Trumbull of Connecticut served as Hamilton's lieutenants on the chamber floor, exercising some control over what proposals were made and how they were voted on by coordinating Hamilton's supporters in the House. Hamilton, though strengthened by his office and his influence with the president, was prohibited from the chamber floor, but he sat in the gallery throughout the debate over his plan, often conferring with his supporters. In short, the first signs of a party-in-government appeared as early as the First Congress.

The effects of this tentative organizing became clearer in the third session, after the vote trade agreement. Hamilton was instructed by Congress to prepare a second report for the third session of the First Congress. He used the opportunity to propose a system of taxation, a mint, and a national bank in December 1790 and January 1791. The proposed mint passed easily. A solid southern bloc led opposition to the plan for taxation, pushing to keep taxes as low as possible. Madison, however, supported this part of Hamilton's plan, and it passed (albeit in the Second, not First, Congress) with only slight modifications.

The bank bill raised more substantial opposition in the Senate and later, when opponents' numbers proved too small there (it was passed largely unchanged in late January 1791), in the House. House members objected to locating the main branch in Philadelphia, the temporary capital. Southerners, who all along had feared acquiescing even to temporary location of the capital in the North, saw locating the central bank there as a threat to building a permanent capital on the Potomac. There was also substantial opposition "to the general principle of Congress creating a separate institution" (Alvarez 1989, 23). Madison led this opposition, arguing that Congress lacked the power to charter a corporation, even though this has been seen by some as contradicting the implied powers clause of the Constitution Madison himself defended in *Federalist* 44. As before, Ames and Sedgwick defended Hamilton's plan against Madisonians. The bank bill passed 30–20, reflecting the Hamiltonians' majority-in-preference in the House and their ability to hold their supporters in line, with all but one nay coming from southern representatives.

Washington was concerned that Madison's questioning of the constitutionality of the bank required legal rather than merely political defense. Attorney General Edmund Randolph (Virginia), joined by Jefferson, agreed with Madison's analysis. Hamilton wrote the opposing brief, arguing (as he had in *Federalist* 23) that if the end was constitutional, if the measure was relevant to that end, and if the proposed means were not directly prohibited by the Constitution, then the means were constitutional. Washington was persuaded by Hamilton's brief (which may be seen as a paraphrase of Madison's arguments in *Federalist* 44) and signed the measure into law. It thus appears that, over the course of the first two Congresses, Hamilton was a sufficiently active entrepreneur to shape his majorities-in-preference into actual voting majorities and, by this time, to have established an emerging pattern of victories on substance and therefore on the great principle. This rudimentary organization had become something closer to a party-in-the-government.

At the end of the Second Congress, therefore, "Madison and Jefferson decided they must organize an opposition" (Fribourg 1872, 76). Jeffersonians had, like Hamiltonians, sought to coordinate their legislative plans, control the agenda, and seek votes and victories on the floor.[12] Hamilton and his closest allies simply held more votes.

Madison and Jefferson had lost in Congress. They had won permanent victory only on the capital and temporary victory on assumption.

Hamilton's plan eventually was carried, however, with only a few weakening amendments. By this time, that is, a clearer pattern of precedents were being set, and Jeffersonians realized that strategizing to upset majority coalitions in Congress was too frail a reed to support their central hopes of a more limited government than Hamiltonians desired and could, with effort, achieve. Although a disorganized majority could be split and thereby defeated, a more organized majority could be divided less often. There is an alternative in a republic, however, and that is to seek to capture a majority in Congress by popular election.

Fribourg, at least, actually saw a formal plan for creating an opposition political party (1872, 76). She argued that Jefferson and Madison intended to "blend" landed gentry from the South with dissatisfied groups in the large northern cities into a "new force." To do this, Jefferson secured a part-time job in the government for Madison's college friend Philip Freneau. This kept at hand the editor of the *National Gazette*, which served as the Republicans' first and most important partisan newspaper. Before the Third Congress, Madison and Jefferson vacationed in New York, where they allegedly met with Aaron Burr and George Clinton, who opposed Hamilton. It is disputed whether these Virginians and New Yorkers forged their intersectional alliance there, but it was done in time for elections to the Third Congress. Hofstadter (1969) observes that "committees of correspondence" first appeared in that election. Such committees were the closest thing to electoral organizations of that era, and they were disproportionately Republican.[13] Jeffersonians' efforts led to their winning a majority of House seats in the Third Congress (57–48) but not dominating the Senate and resulted in the more fully polarized parties of the Third Congress.

By about the Third or Fourth Congress, then, political parties had come into existence. Shifting factions became settled. Hamiltonians had established a clear pattern of victories on the floor on the most important matters. These victories, moreover, were clearly more in the direction of the Hamiltonians' preferences than the earlier compromises the full chamber yielded. Jefferson and Madison reached out beyond their section and beyond their closest set of acquaintances. They had a plan for an intersectional alliance, and they united the two largest states. They had a partisan press and rudimentary campaign organizations. Opposition to Hamiltonians spread in numbers, and gradually new issues were also included.

Foreign policy questions began to separate Jeffersonians from Hamiltonians, especially over whether the United States should be more closely allied with Britain or France. Some mark the true emergence of a partisan spirit with these concerns, especially the Jay Treaty (1795) and later the XYZ Affair and the Alien and Sedition Acts (1798). In the Third Congress, the House used its role as the body most closely tied to the public to express public displeasure with the Jay Treaty that had been passed in secret in the Senate, and to attempt to halt its implementation. In this Third Congress, the House also voted on actions to be taken against British seizure of merchant ships and over payment of debt to France.

The connection between the great principle and foreign affairs is not as immediately obvious, since no one disagreed that these were national affairs, appropriately acted on by the central government in general and by the president and Senate in particular.[14] That it directly raised the principle at all was more symbolic, with Federalists preferring to align with the British government and act in the Senate and executive branch (which they held), whereas Republicans preferred to align with France (and act in the House, where they were strongest and actually held a majority in this Third Congress). It is, in fact, more a measure of the growing importance of partisan spirit and organization that all consequential matters were becoming polarized around the emerging political parties.

Organizing continued for some time, and there is dispute about just when these efforts were sufficient to call them political parties. The important point is that—even if tentatively—by the Third Congress officeholders were divided into two recognizable, broad, intersectional alliances, and the range of partisan interests extended to virtually all consequential matters under consideration. Basic electoral institutions and partisan presses appeared. The totality of these partisan organizations was sufficient to create the incentives to keep partisans voting more or less directly along party lines. By the time Hamiltonians could be called Federalists and Jeffersonians could be called Republicans, both had achieved enough organization to coordinate presidential elections, extend their concern over issues, and capture the affiliation of essentially all national politicians on one side or the other and the affiliations of many outside the national government. In short, many of the elements we identify with political parties today had appeared, if tenuously, by the Third Congress.

SOME SYSTEMATIC TESTS OF THE EMERGENCE OF POLITICAL PARTIES

In this section, I compare roll call voting in the House on selected key issues.[15] The basic hypothesis is that votes on key issues important in the development of the first parties should be different in the largely preparty First Congress than in even the Third Congress, after the out-lines of the two parties had emerged. In that sense this is a conservative test, because the parties, though visible in the Third Congress, became much more visible soon thereafter. Thus, if there are differences be-tween these two Congresses consistent with the theory, they should be expected to be even stronger if the First Congress is compared with later ones.

Data

Systematic data about this period are limited. Recorded roll call votes are, of course, available.[16] Assignment of partisan affiliation continues to be a contended issue today, even for members elected well into the nineteenth century, let alone in the preparty period when they, of course, did not even have parties to affiliate with. Fortunately, Martis (1989) has recently reexamined the various measures of partisanship compiled over the years and produced the best measure of affiliation available. "Partisan affiliation" in the First Congress is conventionally referred to as "pro- and antiadministration," that is, supporters and opponents of Washington's administration (and thus of Hamilton). I will refer to them by their later names of Federalist and (Jeffersonian) Republican Parties, respectively.

The final data necessary to conduct this analysis concern the prefer-ences of members on the great principle and on other matters. Prob-lematic even in the contemporary era (see Jackson and Kingdon 1992, for example), estimates of preferences are even more so in the early Congresses, and there are precious few data for indirect evidence. I have therefore chosen to use estimates from a procedure developed by Poole and Rosentahl (1985; Poole 1988). Their procedure estimates the ideal point locations of members on underlying dimensions, based on the totality of their actual roll call votes recorded. I am especially grateful to Keith Poole for conducting this analysis and providing esti-mates for three dimensions of preferences for each Congress. Estimated dimensions are not interpreted, and a part of this exercise will be to demonstrate that their first dimension (which, analogous to principal components analysis, is the dimension that emerges as the strongest single dimension structuring the voting patterns) is, or can be inferred as, the great principle dimension. Since their estimates are based on the full set of recorded votes cast, the standard problem of using votes to infer preferences to, in turn, relate to votes is minimized by analyz-ing the relation of preferences to a single vote at a time and to a small set of votes overall. Their procedure is derived from a theory of choice that assumes that preferences are single peaked over the dimensions recovered (here, three) and thus matches the theory to be tested. These are, of course, revealed preferences, so that the inferred preferences include any impact parties may have had in constraining or otherwise affecting their choice. In that sense the statistical analysis of any added impact of party is even more conservative.

The purpose of the exercise is to see what role the great principle, other bases of preferences (whether countervailing values, particular interests, or whatever), and party organizing may have had in shaping outcomes. If there were parties in any sense in the First Congress, they would have concerned actions taken on Hamilton's plan. Ten votes on this plan were recorded and were sufficiently divided to analyze. The two concerns of Hamilton's plan and of foreign affairs were analyzed in the Third Congress, covering all five recorded, divided votes on foreign policy and the five recorded, divided votes most directly addressing remaining issues about the plan. These twenty votes are detailed in the appendix to this chapter.

There are, of course, missing data owing to abstentions on individual votes, and some representatives missed so many roll calls (especially in the First Congress) that they could not be included in the Poole-Rosenthal estimation procedure. Of 65 members in the First Congress, only 36 can be analyzed: 24 "Federalists," 6 "Republicans," and 6 Anti-Federalists.[17] Of 105 members in the Third Congress, 66 can be included: 34 Republicans and 32 Federalists.[18]

Hypotheses

More specific hypotheses include the following, most of which are obviously implied. First, preferences in either Congress will be related to roll call choices. Second, in both Congresses preferences will be multidimensional, thus raising the possibility of disequilibrium. Third, the most important dimension will be best understood as the great principle dimension, while other dimensions of preference capture other bases of choice.

Fourth, party affiliation should be closely related to the great principle dimension in both Congresses. It was, I argue, on preferences concerning the great principle that the Federalist and Jeffersonian Republican Parties formed and voting polarized in the Third Congress. By the Third Congress, only the great principle dimension should be related to partisan affiliation, if that was the basis of formation, and if this formation was consequential.

Fifth, party voting should have increased substantially between the First and Third Congresses. Although there might be "party" votes in the First Congress, such votes would be the "incidental" consequence of a majority of those who supported Federalist principles "happening" to vote, by virtue of their balancing of several preferences, in opposition to how a majority of those with Republican sympathies would by weighing their preferences, "happen" to vote.[19] If by the Third Congress increasingly organized parties induced incentives for their members to weigh their great principle preferences more heavily than other preferences, then individual party votes and aggregate party voting should become more commonplace. Indeed, it should become increasingly difficult to disentangle party affiliation from beliefs about the great principle, even though other dimensions of preferences should remain consequential to choosers.

Analysis

The Poole-Rosenthal data provided estimated ideal point positions on three dimensions, and of these the first appears to be the great principle dimension. Such a conclusion can be based only on inference, of course, and I will so argue owing to the pattern of findings obtained. A first indication is that, for members serving in at least two of these three Congresses, correlations (Pearson's r) between ideal point positions in pairs of Congresses are high in absolute terms and high in comparison with correlations of ideal point positions on the other two dimensions. The correlations for this dimension are .89 (First and Second Congresses), .61 (First and Third), and .57 (Second and Third). Comparable correlations for the second dimension are .20, .34, and .46, and for the third are .56, .16, and .28.

If this is the great principle dimension and if it served as the basis for party development, then it should be related to party affiliation. This can be seen in two complementary ways. Mean ideal point positions for party members on each of the three dimensions in each of the three Congresses are reported in table 3.1. In each case it is the first or great principle dimension that most consistently, clearly, and significantly differentiates Federalists from Republicans.[20] A second and related way to examine this question is to estimate the relation between preferences on dimensions and (Federalist or Republican) party affiliation. Dichotomous probit estimates yielded a statistically significant coefficient for the great principle dimension (-0.381, -0.933, and -1.333 for the First through Third Congresses, respectively).[21] The effect of this dimension on partisan affiliation increases substantially with each Congress. In comparable estimations using all three dimensions of preferences, the first dimension coefficient is large and is the only significant estimate in the Second and Third Congresses, but it is not significant in the First.[22] It thus appears that the first dimension was clearly related to partisan

Table 3.1 Mean Ideal Point Positions on Dimensions in the United States House, by Party Affiliation, First through Third Congresses

	Dimension					
	1 (GP)[a]		2		3	
	Mean	(s.d.)	Mean	(s.d.)	Mean	(s.d.)
First Congress						
Republican	0.544	(0.565)	0.294	(0.363)	0.757	(1.10)
Federalist	−0.383	(1.03)	1.039	(1.35)	−0.181	(0.838)
Total[b]	−0.157	(1.08)	0.518	(1.47)	−0.083	(0.950)
Second Congress						
Republican	0.486	(0.648)	0.374	(1.08)	−0.183	(0.845)
Federalist	−0.665	(1.05)	0.552	(0.614)	−0.383	(0.855)
Total	−0.372	(1.23)	0.488	(0.807)	−0.311	(0.859)
Third Congress						
Republican	0.733	(0.977)	0.157	(0.814)	−0.194	(0.729)
Federalist	−1.039	(0.885)	0.713	(0.828)	−0.232	(0.722)
Total	−0.256	(1.53)	0.427	(0.861)	−0.212	(0.720)

[a]Great principle.
[b]Includes Anti-Federalists in totals only.

affiliation in each of the three Congresses. It became increasingly clarified, however, as the most, and perhaps only, important basis of partisanship in the Second and especially the Third Congress. In sum, the first, or great principle, dimension is relatively stable over time, it alone is associated with party affiliation in the latter two Congresses, and it is so in the First Congress as well, if less strongly and uniquely.

The fundamental assumption of the "new institutionalism" is that political outcomes depend on the goals and thus the preferences of the actors involved and on the institutional setting in which such choices are made. Here this means that roll call votes of members of the First and Third Congresses depended on their preferences, as summarized by their ideal positions on the three dimensions, and they depended on the emergence of a new institutional arrangement in the Third Congress—the rudimentary political parties—that was absent in the First. Moreover, if the first is the great principle dimension, it should consistently have been a very important determinant of choice on key votes, such as the twenty analyzed here. But if parties arose in reaction to disequilibrium, other dimensions of preferences should have been consequential, at least from time to time, sufficiently so that choice was based on multidimensional preferences. In the First Congress, party should be largely irrelevant, since there was no genuine organization. Great principle and other preferences alone should be relevant. By the Third Congress, both party and great principle preferences should be relevant and be pulling in essentially the same direction, while other dimensions should be relevant at least from time to time, else there would be no need for party organizations, at least on these particular votes. The principles above concern individual choices. We would further expect these efforts to accumulate, so that party votes would be relatively common in the Third Congress, more so than in the First.

Using one standard definition of a "party vote," in which a majority of one party opposes a majority of the other, these expected patterns are indeed found. In the First Congress, two of the ten votes were party votes by this standard, and on one of them a bare majority of "Federalists" opposed a bare majority of "Republicans." Eight of the ten key votes were party votes in the Third Congress. Opposing partisan majorities were large on all five foreign affairs votes. The strength of the party vote increased over time on the five fiscal policy issues. Federalists were consistently united on all of these. Republicans were deeply divided on the first such vote, and a narrow majority voted with the Federalists. The second vote was more consensual, with substantial majorities in both parties voting together. The final three were party votes. On the first two, however, Republicans were still clearly divided. The final vote saw a substantial majority of Republicans opposing a massive majority of Federalists. Overall a 20 percent rate of party voting on key issues is low even by American standards, whereas 80 percent is unusually high. Although not providing a census of all votes, the evidence nonetheless clearly implies that parties were not voting coalitions in the First Congress but had emerged as central coalitional features in the Third Congress.

This net accounting is if anything illustrated even more dramatically at the individual level. Probit estimates indicate the effect of party (Federalist or Republican) on the roll call vote. In the First Congress, party was not significantly related to the vote in *any* of the ten cases (with an average t-statistic of 0.41). Party was significantly related to the vote in *all* ten cases in the Third Congress (with an average t-statistic of 4.26). Clearly, at the individual as at the aggregate level, the impact of party was much stronger in the Third Congress than in the First Congress.

Vote choice, of course, is assumed to be based on preferences, in addition to any incentives induced by the rise of at least partially organized parties. Three kinds of probit analyses investigate this fundamental basis of choice. First, estimates using just the first, great principle, dimension provide an initial assessment of its relation to choice. Second, the three preference dimensions were included to provide a fuller examination of the effect of preferences on choice and to judge the impact of the first dimension relative to and controlling for other dimensions of preference. Finally, the effects of party affiliation and preferences together were estimated, testing the full specification expected to hold in the Third Congress.

The first, or great principle, dimension should be related to choice on virtually all key votes in both Congresses. In the First Congress, it was significantly related in eight of ten cases in bivariate probit estimations. In one case, ideal point location on that dimension perfectly predicted roll call votes.[23] In the Third Congress, ideal preference on this dimension is significantly related to choice in all ten cases. Knowledge of a member's stance on the great principle, that is, provides significant information about his choice on eighteen of twenty key votes in these two Congresses.

The more fully specified model estimates, based on all three dimensions of preference, are reported in tables 3.2 and 3.3. Besides the one vote in the First Congress already excluded owing to perfect predictability on the great principle dimension alone, a second vote in that Congress cannot be estimated owing to perfect predictability in the three-dimensional model. This leaves eighteen votes that I can analyze in detail. The other two votes are excluded, of course, because of their perfect relationship to preferences.

The first question concerns the effect of the great principle. That dimension's coefficient estimate is statistically significant in fifteen of the remaining eighteen votes: its coefficient is significantly or perfectly related to roll call choices on seven of the ten votes in the First Congress and is nearly so (very close to significant at the more generous .10 level) on an eighth. Preferences on this dimension were significantly related to choice on all ten votes in the Third Congress. It also appears that this dimension exerts a larger and more consistent effect in the Third Congress than in the First, which is consistent with the argument that preferences on this principle were important but more heavily traded off against other concerns in the First Congress, lacking additional incentives from parties.

The question turns, therefore, to whether other concerns did matter. If only one dimension "mattered"—if the several dimensions reduced to one effective dimension—then there would regularly be an equilibrium based on preferences, requiring no partisan or other institutional devices. An appropriate and stringent test of this hypothesis is to ask whether adding the other two dimensions of preference to the probit estimates based on the first dimension alone yields a statistically significant improvement.[24] There are nine testable cases in the First Congress. One went from less than perfectly to perfectly predictable

Table 3.2 Probit Estimates of Effect of Three Dimensions of Preferences on Roll Call Votes, First Congress

| Roll call vote number | Constant | (s.e.) | Dimensions, MLE | | | | | | (χ^2_4) $-2 \times$ LLR | Percentage correctly predicted | N |
			First	(s.e.)	Second	(s.e.)	Third	(s.e.)			
HO 12004	-1.499	(0.703)	-2.749	(1.264)[c]	-0.242	(0.187)	0.468	(0.586)	26.82[c]	86.7	30
HO 12009	0.378	(0.250)	-0.381	(0.228)[b]	-0.345	(0.178)[c]	0.209	(0.258)	6.92 (n.s.)	67.6	34
HO 12040	0.941	(0.294)	0.173	(0.251)	0.042	(0.192)	0.229	(0.301)	13.70	80.6	31
HO 12042			[Perfect fit with first dimension only]						—	(100)	36
HO 12045	25.525	(50.919)	34.643	(69.175)	-2.447	(5.557)	16.055	(32.319)	43.78	94.4	36[a]
HO 12046	0.369	(0.289)	1.054	(0.323)[d]	0.0996	(0.158)	0.337	(0.290)	18.58	83.3	36
HO 13006			[Perfect fit with all three dimensions]						—	(100)	34
HO 13007	-0.105	(0.246)	0.688	(0.243)[d]	-0.147	(0.180)	0.296	(0.279)	14.00	83.3	36
HO 13008	-0.970	(0.366)	-0.913	(0.370)[d]	0.268	(0.201)	-0.635	(0.357)[c]	18.84	75.8	32
HO 13009	-0.333	(0.280)	0.459	(0.257)[c]	-0.642	(0.335)[c]	0.045	(0.297)	18.08	81.8	33

Note: Critical value for χ^2_4, .01 level, is 13.28. MLE stands for maximum likelihood estimate.

[a]One case short of perfect fit, thus large parameter estimates and standard errors.

[b]Significant at .10, one-tailed.

[c]Significant at .05, one-tailed.

[d]Significant at .01 or better, one-tailed.

[e]Perfect if Anti-Federalists excluded.

Table 3.3 Probit Estimates of Effect of Three Dimensions of Preferences on Roll Call Votes, Third Congress

Roll call vote number	Constant (s.e.)	Dimensions, MLE						(χ^2_4) $-2 \times$ LLR	Percentage correctly predicted	N
		First	(s.e.)	Second	(s.e.)	Third	(s.e.)			
Fiscal policy										
HO 31011	-1.300 (0.324)	1.110	(0.280)[d]	0.726	(0.246)[d]	-0.964	(0.389)[d]	44.28	84.1	63
HO 31029	1.610 (0.383)	-0.949	(0.229)[d]	-1.622	(0.414)[d]	1.163	(0.399)[d]	48.14	85.0	60
HO 31031	-2.306 (0.657)	2.211	(0.620)[d]	1.735	(0.528)[d]	-1.939	(0.584)[d]	59.02	94.7	57
HO 31033	3.836 (1.755)	-5.792	(2.763)[c]	-4.881	(2.479)[c]	3.289	(1.461)[c]	66.46	94.8	58[a]
HO 32012	-1.185 (0.836)	4.956	(2.370)[c]	1.918	(1.518)	0.162	(0.500)	69.90	94.8	58[a]
Foreign policy										
HO 31012	0.370 (0.305)	1.971	(0.460)[d]	-0.525	(0.390)[b]	0.246	(0.434)	64.32	93.8	64
HO 31013	0.565 (0.288)	1.737	(0.379)[d]	-0.405	(0.332)	0.218	(0.401)	60.20	90.8	65
HO 31014	1.267 (0.379)	0.956	(0.210)[d]	-1.458	(0.439)[d]	0.833	(0.478)[c]	49.52	90.2	61
HO 31040	-1.247 (0.421)	1.445	(0.464)[d]	0.312	(0.450)	0.635	(0.585)	35.72	84.8	46
HO 31046 (France)	7.719 (4.227)	6.392	(3.375)[c]	-2.767	(1.529)[c]	-0.664	(0.893)	63.32	94.3	53[a]

Note: Critical value for χ^2_4, .01 level, is 13.28. MLE stands for maximum likelihood estimate.
[a]Close to perfect prediction, thus yielding large parameter estimates and standard errors.
[b]Significant at .10, one-tailed.
[c]Significant at .05, one-tailed.
[d]Significant at .01 or better, one-tailed.

with the addition of the other two dimensions. Although not formally testable, it obviously supports the hypothesis. Two other votes led to rejection of the null at the .05 level and another at the .10 level, and still another was very close to that level. On at least half of the votes in the First Congress, that is, the hypothesis of multidimensional rather than single-dimensional preferences is supported. In the Third Congress the null hypothesis is rejected on all five fiscal policy votes and on two of five foreign policy votes—on seven of ten votes overall. In sum, choice was multidimensional on a clear majority of the votes. Thus, even if some key votes were essentially unidimensional, this could not be guaranteed in advance. Politicians had to prepare to face all the time, and apparently did face most of the time, choices based on multiple dimensions of preferences. Thus there generally was no equilibrium due to preferences alone.

The final question was whether preferences and structure together were related to choice. The hypothesis for the First Congress is that parties were not organized, so adding partisan identification (not yet known by the member himself) to preferences would add little to the explanation. The hypothesis is indeed supported. The party affiliation coefficient estimates were always very small and statistically insignificant.[25] The Third Congress results were different, as expected. These are reported in table 3.4. Party was not a significant addition to the preference equation estimates (table 3.3), and its coefficients are not statistically significant on the five votes on foreign affairs. That variable is, however, a significant addition at the .05 level on two fiscal policy votes, and it is so at the .10 level on a third. In these cases the party coefficient estimate is relatively large, while the great principle dimension estimate is relatively small. This pattern is consistent with the argument. Parties were created to help constrain voting to be based more heavily on the great principle, in large measure by relating all other issues to the partisan great-principle dimension. Sometimes, the estimates imply, that effect was so strong that party affiliation alone provides sufficient information to predict vote choices from the (collinear) complex of party and great principle. At other times it is primarily that dimension alone, but in all cases it is some combination of that pair that matters—and matters strongly.

No part of this analysis of House members' preferences, partisanship, and choices provides definitive proof of the argument. Yet there is strong support for each hypothesis. The result is a pattern of evidence that is sufficiently clear to lend support to the argument about the preferences and behavior of House members. This implies, that is, that the emergence of partisan organizations helped induce their members to adhere more closely to the great principle and to weigh

Table 3.4 Probit Estimates of Effect of Three Dimensions of Preferences and Party Affiliation on Roll Call Votes, Third Congress

Roll call vote number	Constant	(s.e.)	Dimensions, MLE[a]						Party	(s.e.)	$-2 \times$ LLR (χ_5^2)	Percentage correctly predicted	N
			First	(s.e.)	Second	(s.e.)	Third	(s.e.)					
Fiscal policy													
HO 31011	-1.012	(0.388)	0.883	(0.337)[d]	0.838	(0.270)[d]	-0.913	(0.391)[d]	-0.918	(0.667)[b]	46.34	82.5	63
HO 31029	0.760	(0.535)	-0.049	(0.435)	-4.219	(1.861)[c]	3.519	(1.634)[c]	6.175	(2.808)[c]	63.56	88.3	60
HO 31031	-2.116	(0.791)	2.152	(0.823)[d]	2.080	(0.735)[d]	-2.169	(0.703)[d]	-1.575	(1.107)[b]	61.78	96.5	57
HO 31033	5.139	(2.728)	-8.727	(4.896)[c]	-7.699	(3.959)[c]	5.331	(3.072)[c]	3.676	(2.382)[b]	72.40	96.6	58
HO 32012	-1.219	(0.883)	4.994	(2.355)[c]	1.875	(1.679)	0.182	(0.509)	0.146	(1.609)	69.90	94.8	58
Foreign policy													
HO 31012	-0.123	(0.515)	2.834	(0.964)[d]	-0.846	(0.508)[b]	0.419	(0.498)	1.444	(1.270)[b]	65.94	95.3	64
HO 31013	0.473	(0.443)	1.871	(0.610)[d]	-0.452	(0.371)	0.229	(0.407)	0.256	(0.897)	60.30	90.8	65
HO 31014	1.736	(0.528)	0.605	(0.310)[c]	-1.173	(0.481)[d]	0.631	(0.492)	-1.164	(0.788)[b]	51.72	90.2	61
HO 31040	-1.349	(0.552)	1.553	(0.594)[d]	0.271	(0.466)	0.681	(0.604)	0.279	(0.939)	35.82	84.8	46
HO 31046 (France)	3.687	(18.624)	6.399	(3.382)[c]	-2.771	(1.533)[c]	-0.674	(0.896)	4.033	(19.177)	63.32	94.3	53

Note: Critical value for χ_5^2, .01 level, is 15.09.
[a]MLE stands for maximum likelihood estimate.
[b]Significant at .10, one-tailed.
[c]Significant at .05, one-tailed.
[d]Significant at .01, one-tailed.

other dimensions less substantially in deciding how to vote on major issues of the day. Combined with a comparable pattern of evidence in the actions taken by party leaders—by Hamilton, Jefferson, and Madison in particular—it is reasonable to conclude that parties arose out of the step-by-step strengthening of factions into political parties as a means of avoiding the consequences of voting disequilibrium and, in particular, setting a clear pattern of precedents on the revealed power and energy of the new national government. That is, parties emerged out of disequilibrium to resolve ambiguity inherent in the new constitutional order and to win on the great principle.

PARTY AND DESIGN IN THE PRESIDENTIAL ELECTION OF 1800

The two parties might have organized over the great principle. That does not, however, mean that their actions were principled as each sought to defeat its opponent on that principle. By 1800, each party was orchestrating its actions throughout the nation as it sought to change state laws wherever possible to make conditions most favorable for its winning the presidential vote in the Electoral College.

The enormous respect and affection for George Washington rendered the first two presidential elections uninteresting and uninformative about the true nature of political disagreement in the land. It was only after his decision to retire after his second term that the question arose of how the curious design of the Electoral College would actually work in practice. In 1796, as we saw above, the two parties were emerging, and each did coordinate its supporters around presidential and vice-presidential standard bearers. Thus, even in its first true test, the original plan of the selection of well-informed and wise Electors from the great body of the people to refine public sentiment into a sound choice for president was undermined. Electors were, instead, to support their party's choice, no matter what their personal views or those of their constituents might be. And Electors indeed proved faithful to their party. In turn, those voters who did have a say over who would be Electors sensibly enough tended to support those Electors who would faithfully back their party's predetermined choices for highest office.

While Electors backed their party's presidential choice in 1796, the same was not true for the party's selection for vice president. Indeed, the Federalists' failure to hold fast to both of their party's choices led to the vote total for Thomas Pinckney (SC) to fall behind that of Jefferson, and in turn led to the split result of a Federalist winning the presidency and a Republican winning the vice presidency (and, in total, thirteen people receiving at least one electoral vote each). While that might have meant election of the most distinguished pair in history, neither party nor either individual was at all pleased by the pairing over the next four years.

By 1800, the parties appear to have resolved this issue, because all Electors supported both candidates of their preferred party, except one Federalist from Rhode Island who supported John Jay over Charles Cotesworth Pinckney (SC), the presumed "running mate" of Adams. The failure of even one Jeffersonian to vote for someone other than Aaron Burr meant that Jefferson and Burr tied in the Electoral College vote (at 73 votes apiece, with Adams receiving 65). As a result the Electoral vote was indeterminate, and the top two candidates, the two Jeffersonians, were submitted to the U.S. House for selection. The result was yet another major, exciting chapter on this election. (For more on the 1800 election, see Ferling 2004; Larson 2007; Weisberger 2000.)

By the end of the century, then, the two parties had emerged even more firmly. Leaders of both parties knew that they were locked in a close battle for the presidency. Both had strong candidates (Adams and Jefferson), so each could make a strong case for support, making it likely that they would realize that potential for a close contest. And close it was. The 1800 contest is a very strong contender, in addition, for being the nastiest and most bitter campaign in American history. Both parties saw reason, therefore, to organize carefully, well in advance.

Of the many interesting stories about 1800, I choose but one of them here to illustrate a point: By 1800, there were two parties politicking in a fashion easily understood in today's partisan era (see Aldrich 2007 for details). There was much at stake in addition to winning. The great principle reached something of a zenith in this election, as both sides claimed that the election of the other would doom this great experiment in republican democracy. Federalists, Jeffersonians argued, would push too far toward a British-style central government, while Jeffersonians, Federalists claimed, risked leading the United States down the French path of empowering the mob and leading to tyranny. The former were decried as monarchists, the latter as Jacobins.

The Electoral College presented both parties with a unique opportunity to shape electoral outcomes. The Constitution left selection of Electors up to the states. States could choose Electors in the state legislature, giving the public no direct say in either the Electors or, more realistically, the party's choice for president, knowing that Electors would likely be faithful to their party's choice. Even if the state decided to have Electors chosen by public vote, the legislature would choose how this election would be decided. The first of the two choices for voting was a statewide plurality system. This is a winner-take-all election. That is, whoever got the most votes in the state won election, and if, as was increasingly true, each party had, in effect, a slate of Electoral candidates, whichever party got more votes in the state would win every contest for Elector. It is the system used by all but two states today. The alternative was the system currently used by Maine and Nebraska, in which constituents in each congressional district would elect one Elector, while the statewide plurality winner would get two additional Electoral seats. The key difference is that the district-level selection plan was much more likely to result in a state choosing at least some Electors from each party. None but the smallest states were so dominated by one party that, at least in a close election such as 1800, it would be very likely that one party would sweep all seats.

Each party would thus prefer the district-level allocation in those states in which it was likely to come in second place. Conversely, if it were the more popular party, it would prefer winner-take-all. Even better for a party that held unified control over the state government was to select Electors in the legislature, where they were already assured a majority and could be confident of holding every Electoral vote. There was always at least a small risk of defeat in public voting in a close contest.

And so, both parties had means, motive, and opportunity to revise laws to help their chances, or, at least, they did in some states. Every state offered the means to revise its rules for choosing Electors, because that required simply passing a law through the legislature by simple majority vote. Some states, of course, had no motive for change, because the current law (the one used in the 1796 election) was already favorable. Parties in some states did not have the opportunity, because they did not hold control over the state legislature and could not pass a new law rigging the system favorably. But some did have all three.

Five of the sixteen states changed their laws that either removed power from the public's hands or concentrated it, by changing from the district to winner-take-all procedure. In each of four states (Georgia, Massachusetts, New Hampshire, and Virginia), one party held unified control. Virginia changed from district to winner-take-all; the other three changed from popular vote to legislative selection. All of these were cases of the larger party taking advantage of its status to enhance its electoral vote total.

In New York, Republicans proposed moving from winner-take-all to the district plan, but this was defeated by the majority Federalists. The Federalists then lost their majority to the Republicans in July, with the result that Federalists' use of their majority position led to their seeing all of the state's electoral votes being cast for Jefferson and Burr. They quite probably would have won enough Electoral votes via the district plan in New York that they had just defeated to have changed the national outcome and reelected Adams. There was split control in Pennsylvania, and the two chambers deadlocked. In time a compromise was reached in that state that did not reflect the will of the public or the size of the majority, but the simple fact of divided control.

As Noble Cunningham notes, political elites were well aware of where the presidential votes were coming from, as he quotes Thomas Boylston Adams writing to his brother John Quincy (who was in Berlin at the time), "It is perfectly well understood that the tiral [sic] of strength between the two Candidates for the chief magistracy of the Union is to be seen, not in the choice of electors by the people, but in the complexion and character of the individual legislatures" (1971, 105).

The net effect of these changes on the outcome is hard to calculate. But my reconstruction (Aldrich 1997) suggests that each of the changes in the state laws changed the distribution of votes cast from the state. Centralizing power worked, giving the majority party more votes than it would have had otherwise. The two parties were in such close balance, however, that the net estimate is that these changes exactly canceled each other out. At least, the changes were sufficiently balanced that they were highly unlikely to have been able to make a difference, electing Adams instead of Jefferson.

CONCLUSION

A common way to introduce studies of the origins of the Federalist and Republican Parties is to present their emergence as a puzzle. Why did they emerge so rapidly when many individuals, including their founders, publicly claimed to despise the very idea of political parties? Madison had warned of the dangers of party and faction in *Federalist* 10. Jefferson wrote in 1789 that "such addiction [to a political party] is the last degradation of a free and moral agent. If I could not go to heaven but with a party, I would not go there at all." Franklin warned of "the infinite mutual abuse of parties, tearing to pieces the best of characters," and Washington spoke, even as they were emerging, of the "baneful effects of the Spirit of Party" in his Farewell Address. As Hofstadter put it, "But here we are brought face to face with the primary paradox of this inquiry: Jefferson, the . . . co-founder of the first modern popular party, had no use for political parties . . . the creators of the first American party system on both sides, Federalists and Republicans, were men who looked on parties as sores on the body politic" (1969, 2).

Proposed resolutions of this paradox are of three types—roughly "principle," "interest," and "institutional" explanations (see Aldrich and Grant 1993). The explanation offered here unites all three: the great principle, combined with sectional and related interests, yielded disequilibrium, and an institutional form was required to reduce its baneful effects and provide at least a first approximation to solving the great principle. All three parts, that is, are necessary to the explanation I offer, and none of the three, taken alone, provides a sufficient resolution of this paradox.

Principle is necessary, and the great principle, I argue, was the dominant, general one involved. As Grant puts it (1977, 2), "Once the conflict is identified as a contest between enduring principles, one need seek no further for an explanation of the rapid rise of party activity." This may explain party activity, for surely some great principle is needed to explain why Jefferson would not only eschew heaven but actively conspire in creating that device that would send him to the devil. It does not explain why someone with such a keen appreciation of the importance of institutional structure as Madison would risk institutionalizing that evil. Indeed, if it is "only" principle at stake, identification of who is on which side—that is, forming informal coalitions—would be sufficient, because there would be a purely preference-induced equilibrium due to Black's median voter theorem. It was only because there was more at stake that principle did not transform itself directly into vote choice.

Interests, therefore, are necessary to explain why principle was not the exclusive basis of action. One does not need the extreme interpretation of Beard (1941), since the more temperate account of, say, Binkley (1962) is sufficient to show that there were sectional and other interests at stake on many issues. Since interests, whether sectional or class or other, were likely to endure, institutionalizing them into partisan organizations is not difficult to imagine. If it were only interests at stake, it is harder to explain why the founders would invent and maintain what they themselves believed to be evil, to be "sores on the body politic." Even more important, if parties formed solely to promote interests, it is very hard indeed to explain why Federalists simply acceded (albeit not altogether happily) to their minority status in the early years of the nineteenth century. Why institutionalize one's interests and then give up institutional efforts, if interests do not fade?

The usual institutionalist's account (e.g., Hofstadter 1969) resolves the paradox by pointing out that these political parties were very different forms from the parties or factions that Madison sought to avoid. Factions were traditional, interest-based, personalized cliques not unlike today's "special interest" groups, and the only recent experience of a national party when Madison wrote was a traitorous organization revolting against the sovereign. The newly invented political party was, in the institutionalists's accounts, a rationalized, legal entity, one that evolved consistently with the rationalized, legal form of government just created, a form that formally located sovereignty in its people. These accounts, then, view the Federalist and Republican Parties as first forms of the modern mass democratic party, much as we know it today.

The problem such accounts face, however, is that these first parties fell far short of the true modern political party. Most prominently, these national parties were not much in the way of electoral parties (although more local and state factions and parties were) seeking to mobilize the public, provide voice for the new democracy, and aggregate the public's interests. To be sure, committees of correspondence and partisan presses did provide means of campaigning, and Fourth of July festivities became partisan celebrations in this early period. But a commitment to fully democratic politics, tying the party to the people, was weaker in this era than it would be in the Jacksonian era or in the "full flowering" of competition between two mass-based democratic parties at the height of the Democratic-Whig period, such as with the 1840 "Log Cabin and Hard Cider" campaign (see chap. 4). Thus institutionalists debate whether these two "really" were political parties. They were not fully so; such parties did not emerge until later, when Martin Van Buren and others invented this new form. Although the Federalists and Jeffersonian Republicans were political parties, they were primarily "parties-in-government" and primarily organizations of political elites. They functioned not to reflect the new democracy but to resolve policies to yield a clear pattern of support for the governing partisan's position on the great principle, a majority-in-preference threatened by the disequilibrium induced by choice based on both principle and interests. Especially as electoral parties, these became more focused on the strength of personalities than on the "party principle" Van Buren and others sought to control. They sought to control personalized electoral politics in part because the system risked tyranny. The "real" political parties these institutionalists look for did emerge in the Jacksonian era. This new form of party was consciously designed, and its invention was intended to solve a different theoretical problem—that of collective action. They were created to mobilize the electorate, in particular, so that elections in this Jacksonian era of an increasingly diverse democratic nation could be won more often.

Appendix: House Votes from First and Third Congresses Analyzed

Number	Date	Ayes/Nays	Description
First Congress			
HO 12004	4/15/90	33/23	To form committee of the whole to hear first report on public credit from Hamilton
HO 12009	5/26/90	31/25	To amend HR 63 (re United States debt) to issue certificates for bills of credit issued by Congress
HO 12039	7/19/90	40/15	To pass bill on public debt, to provide for payment of debts of United States
HO 12042	7/24/90	29/32	To oppose Senate amendment to debt bill, which would provide for assumption of state debt
HO 12045	7/26/90	34/28	To agree to amended Senate amendment to debt bill
HO 12046	7/29/90	33/27	To adhere to amendment to debt bill for interest on assumed state debt, effective in seven years
HO 13006	2/1/91	23/34	To recommit with instructions an act of Senate to incorporate subscribers to the Bank of the United States
HO 13007	2/3/91	21/38	To recommit bank bill with certain instructions
HO 13008	2/8/91	38/20	To order previous question on passage of bank bill
HO 13009	2/8/91	39/20	To pass bank bill
Third Congress			
Fiscal policy			
HO 31011	4/8/94	39/56	To appoint committee to report on practicality of obtaining statement on settlement of accounts of states with the general government
HO 31029	5/14/94	52/37	To put main question on engrossment of third reading of HR 39
HO 31031	5/14/94	33/53	To postpone third reading of HR 39
HO 31033	5/16/94	52/33	To pass HR 39
HO 32012	2/21/95	39/49	To amend HR 110 (a bill to provide support of public credit and redemption of public debt) to reduce or eliminate role of commissions in debt redemption
Foreign policy			
HO 31012	4/15/94	53/44	To put main question on passage of resolution to prohibit all commercial intercourse between citizens of United States and subjects of Great Britain
HO 31013	4/18/94	57/42	To consider report of Committee of the Whole on resolution concerning Great Britain

Appendix: *continued*

Number	Date	Ayes/Nays	Description
HO 31014	4/21/94	58/38	To pass resolution concerning Great Britain
HO 31040	5/23/94	24/46	To pass resolution to suspend all commerce with British West Indies until Great Britain assumed intention to compensate United States citizens for injuries caused by its warships and privateers
HO 31046	5/31/94	55/23	To pass HR 57, providing payment of money due to French republic

4

JACKSONIAN DEMOCRACY
The Mass Party and Collective Action

Andrew Jackson stood for president for the second time in 1828. Four years earlier he had faced John Quincy Adams, Henry Clay, and William Crawford. This time, now-incumbent Adams was his sole major opponent. "Old Hickory" drew support from a variety of sources, some positively supporting him, others turning to him primarily out of opposition to the incumbent. Martin Van Buren, recently reselected to the Senate from New York, not only switched his own support and that of his state political organization, the Albany Regency, from Adams to Jackson, but also brought into being a new force in national politics. Largely through his efforts, the Democratic Party, the first national, mass-based party in history, was invented. To be sure, Jacksonian Democracy was still only in the process of organizing in 1828 and a far cry from the party it would become even four years later. But the birth of party politics in a form recognizable even today can fairly be dated to 1828.

In many ways this mass-based party can be seen as an extension of prior party practices, and Van Buren himself referred to it as a revival of the old party principles of Jefferson and Madison. The extension was so substantial, however, and the institutionalization eventually so massive, that it was a difference in degree that amounted to a difference in kind. The earlier parties, as we saw in the previous chapter, had been primarily parties-in-government, formulated over differences between their leaders in the new national government. Electoral politics in the first parties, while assuming many of the same forms to come later, simply paled in comparison with the electoral organization of Jacksonian Democracy. The new mass party penetrated deeply into states, localities, and in many ways into the very fabric of the ordinary life of voters. Rather than relating primarily to the "natural aristocracy" and the national government they led, the new parties were rooted in the masses, seeking to win their support, mobilize it on election day, and obtain control over the spoils of office such victories could bring the party.

From a theoretical perspective, electoral mobilization is seen by many as the quintessential example of the problem of collective action. The Democratic, the Whig, and eventually the Republican Parties were in important ways institutions designed to solve this collective action problem. This chapter will focus on this aspect of the new parties. Since the Democratic Party was the first such enterprise, and for nearly a decade the only significant such national organization, their efforts will be analyzed carefully and provide the test case of parties as solutions to collective action problems. Although turnout is regarded as the quintessential collective action problem, I argue that mobilization was neither the first nor the most difficult such problem the Democrats had to solve—that problem was the formulation of the Democratic Party as an organization. With solution of this prior problem, using that organization to increase mobilization was relatively straightforward— and highly successful.

FROM FEDERALIST AND REPUBLICAN TO DEMOCRATIC AND WHIG PARTIES

The election of 1800 brought the Jeffersonian Republicans to national power. The members of the "Virginia Dynasty"—Thomas Jefferson, James Madison, and James Monroe—were elected president for two successive terms each. The Federalists' opposition waned to the point that by 1820 they failed even to propose an opponent to Monroe.[1] Similarly, Jeffersonian Republicans won control of the House and Senate in 1800, never to lose those majorities to Federalists. The Federalists did continue to contest, holding 26 seats in the House and 4 in the Senate as late as the Eighteenth Congress (1823–25), but those numbers paled in comparison with the 187 House and 44 Senate seats the Jeffersonians held. The Federalists had effectively ended as a national party, in part by being on the wrong side of the "War Hawk" election leading to the War of 1812. With senators selected by state governments, their small Senate delegations imply that they also lost much ground in the states in the first two decades of the nineteenth century.

Monroe considered filling the lacuna in competitive, partisan elections by transforming the Jeffersonians into the National Republicans, a party of national unity. The "Era of Good Feelings" was also called that of "no party politics," although it was actually a period of one-party politics. Whatever its title, it ended quickly when an economic downturn eliminated good feelings. With no clear successor to the last of the Virginia Dynasty in 1824, so also was the one-party politics Monroe's plan saw as necessary to maintain national unity. With disunity instead, a small portion of the Republican congressional caucus nominated William Crawford (GA), secretary of the treasury, for president. State legislatures nominated Adams, Jackson, and Clay, while John C. Calhoun declined the honor. The most important remaining institution of the old form of parties, the congressional caucus, was derided as "King Caucus," an elite oligarchy arbitrarily and capriciously wielding its powers. This last vestige of the old form of national parties ended in 1824 in the face of the weak showing of its nominee.

Jackson won a popular vote plurality (41 percent) in 1824 but failed to attain an electoral vote majority. Amid charges of a "corrupt bargain," the House elected Adams president after Clay threw his support to Adams and before Adams selected Clay as his secretary of state, the then-conventional stepping-stone to the presidency. Thus motivated, anti-Adams forces won a majority in the 1826 congressional elections. In 1828 state legislatures again nominated slates, Adams and Clay on one side and Jackson and Calhoun (Adams's vice president) on the other.

In December 1827 Van Buren came over to Jackson and began his efforts to revitalize the old party principles in a new form to mobilize elite support and resources for Jackson. Those resources were then used to create a new electoral organization for mobilizing the electorate to win the presidency for Jackson and the spoils of office for those who supported him.

Van Buren's efforts and the resulting Democratic Party worked. In 1824, under 30 percent of those eligible voted for president. In 1828, turnout for president increased to over 50 percent of the eligible electorate, and that came with only one mass party taking the field and with less than a year to begin the complex process of creating a new party form. Two mass parties would be largely in place by 1840, and in that year turnout increased to over 78 percent of the eligible electorate.

The new party that made possible this "mighty democratic uprising," as Schlesinger called it (1947, 36), differed from the old. Unlike its predecessors, the Democratic Party was carefully planned. More important, it was not the instrument of the natural aristocracy but brought to power a new breed of middle-class (some would say uncouth) and, all agreed, personally ambitious men. Instead of serving the natural aristocracy, Van Buren's party was intended to be—and in important ways proved to be—more important than the men in it, including Jackson and Van Buren. Many would say, with some justice, that the new party could not serve anyone's principles, natural aristocrat or otherwise, for it *had* no principles—other than winning elections (but see below and chap. 5). Finally, and most important here, it was not just a new form of party; it was a mass party. This modern form centered on winning elections with a view that control of a majority in the public brought control of office, and with that, control of policy and the spoils of office. It was, at base, hugely successful in solving the central problem the mass party was designed to solve—mobilization of the electorate.

COLLECTIVE ACTION, ELECTORAL MOBILIZATION, AND PARTY ORGANIZATION

The problem of collective action, as described in chapter 2, arises in its most apparent form when there are shared interests—ends that all value within some collectivity—but when it is not in people's individual interests to contribute to those ends. In the language of the theory, this is a Pareto inferior behavioral equilibrium, and the problem of collective action is how to make it behaviorally consistent to act to achieve Pareto superior outcomes. Since elections are means of choosing among alternative public goods—the president is everyone's president whether they voted for or against the winner or did not vote at all—voting is often considered the archetypal example of the collective action problem.

The calculus of voting illustrates this problem clearly (see Downs 1957; Riker and Ordeshook 1968, 1973; Aldrich 1993b). Note that the choice between candidates in a two-candidate contest is straightforward: vote for the more preferred candidate, because voting for the less-preferred candidate never helps and sometimes hurts in achieving one's goals. The question, then, is whether one votes at all. The turnout equation derived from the calculus of voting provides the answer:

$$(4.1) \qquad R = PB + D - C$$

R denotes the reward from voting, and one rationally chooses to vote when $R > 0$, abstaining otherwise. P represents the probability that the vote cast is efficacious. If the only thing that matters is who wins the election, then P represents the probability that a vote will make or break a tie. B stands for the differential benefits of voting—how much one candidate is preferred to the other. D designates the intrinsic value, if any, that comes with voting, regardless of outcome (where it stands for citizen duty, possibly the most important such intrinsic value). Finally, the costs of voting, C, are subtracted, because the costs of deciding what to do and casting the ballot must be paid no matter who wins the election. Note the similarity of this model to those discussed in chapter 2.

This equation is typical of expected utility-maximizing models of rational choice.[2] What makes it different from the theory of individual decision making, however, is that the outcome of the election is determined by collective action. That the collectivity, the mass electorate, is especially large leads many to conclude that the P term must be very, very small no matter what the decision maker chooses. If P is effectively zero, then so too must PB be essentially zero unless B is immense. As a result, even relatively low costs of voting (net of any D value) will make R negative for many, leading them to abstain. They fail to contribute their vote to the collective outcome; instead they take a "free ride" on the actions of others.

As a general framework, the calculus of voting captures many of the features found in contemporary campaigns and elections. Consider the costs of voting. If PB is typically small, then C looms relatively large in the equation. Political parties have long relied on cost-reduction techniques as the centerpieces of their turnout drives. Providing transportation to the polls, supplying information on when and where to register and vote, giving information and sample ballots suggesting how to vote, and the like are all tried-and-true techniques. Costs of voting in early nineteenth-century America, as in the twentieth century, were not overwhelming for many. To be sure, distance to the polls, transportation costs, and even the lack of free time to devote to voting were greater obstacles then than now for many. Lower literacy rates made becoming informed more difficult. Still, the costs were not very high for a great proportion of the electorate, and party organizations could offset enough of them to help make participation worthwhile. Perhaps most important were speechmaking, rallies, bonfires, and the like that provided information about the election, the contenders, and the stakes involved, lowering decision costs.[3]

These very same techniques were also designed to generate enthusiasm for the contest, the party, and its candidates, thereby giving them a second and likely even more important dimension affecting the D term. Political campaigns became an important form of entertainment, generating interest and enthusiasm that spilled over into participation. Jacksonian Democrats employed many of these techniques as early as 1828 (raising hickory poles to honor and advertise Old Hickory). They were used extensively on both sides in the "Log Cabin and Hard Cider" campaign of 1840. In terms of the calculus of voting, Fiorina (1976) has argued that an important intrinsic value to voting is affirming support for the voter's favored party or candidate, whether in victory or defeat. His suggestion is to add the extent to which a voter prefers one candidate over the other to the D term, the intrinsic benefits that come from casting the vote per se. Although not theoretically different from the original calculus, it is substantively important, leading to the modified equation:[4]

(4.2) $R = PB + B + D - C.$

The interpretation is that a voter might want to stand up and be counted as a Jackson man in 1828, especially plausible in an age without the secret ballot. This addition clearly reduces the problem of mobilization, because turnout is now based in part on the relative valuation of candidates undiscounted by a (likely small) P value, and the campaign hoopla of the age can easily be seen as an attempt to highlight the social, political, and personal value of being known to be on the right side.

Overblown campaign rhetoric accentuates, if it does not outright exaggerate, the importance of the stakes, and negative campaigning portrays the choice as truth, justice, and virtue versus lies, corruption, and scandal. Both of these, of course, are attempts to convince the public that the difference between the contenders, the B term, is vast. Campaign rhetoric was particularly virulent in the United States in the early nineteenth century, and the 1828 campaign was among the most negative of all. John Quincy Adams, Democrats claimed, gambled in the White House at public expense, and it was even alleged that he procured for the czar of Russia. Jackson, in turn, was declared a murderer who had married a bigamist.[5]

With neither costs nor (expected) benefits especially high, turnout is actually atypical of many collective action problems, where the problem is severe when potential collective gains are very large but so are individual costs. Substantively, this relatively low cost-benefit calculation for many typical voters is precisely what makes campaign effort worthwhile. Investments of even small resources per capita by parties can be consequential in turning out supporters.

The party's problem is that relatively small per-capita costs add up to substantial sums needed to mobilize large electorates. In this sense the collective action problem of creating and sustaining a campaign organization is a more typical example of the theory of collective action, one with large costs and large potential benefits. The problem is further complicated in that the campaign organization does not want to increase turnout in general. The goal is to mobilize the party's supporters to win elections. Expending scarce resources in an area of opposition strength is obviously unwise, but so too is mobilizing the party's own supporters where they are not needed. A strategic party should allocate resources where its efforts could make the difference between winning and losing. It is therefore better to invest in a contest expected to be close than in one where the party is confident of either victory or defeat.

This "strategic parties hypothesis," that party resources should follow cost-benefit principles, provides a solution to a paradoxical set of empirical findings in the contemporary literature. Those who analyze the turnout decisions of individuals often find that P term measures, such as individuals' perceptions of how close the election will be, are only weakly related to turnout or not related at all (see Ferejohn and Fiorina 1974, 1975; Aldrich 1976, 1993b). Conversely, those who study aggregate rates of participation (e.g., among states, districts, or localities) find a very strong relation between the closeness of the election and the level of turnout (see Barzel and Silberberg 1973; Silberman and Durden 1975; Cox and Munger 1989). Although these paradoxical findings may be traced to several factors, one important explanation is the strategic parties hypothesis. Individuals may assess PB to be very nearly zero and therefore choose primarily on the basis of the C, D, and B terms in equation 4.2.[6] But partisan groups and other campaign organizations invest their resources wisely and thus deploy them in contests likely to be close. Relatively high effort expended in close contests has its intended effect of stimulating turnout by increasing the intrinsic values of voting, that is, by increasing perceived benefits or sense of duty or by reducing the costs of voting. Thus a greater proportion of individuals turn out in these close contests than in one-sided ones, because their actual costs and intrinsic benefits of voting have been affected by strategic parties' heavy investment in resources in the close races regardless of individuals' valuation of the PB term.[7]

In the ordinary case, both parties recognize which elections are expected to be close and which one-sided. Both invest more heavily in the close contests. Strategic parties may therefore be caught in a prisoners' dilemma. If neither mobilizes, the election will be close and not very costly, whereas if both invest, the mobilization will be balanced between the two parties, keeping the outcome close but costly. Neither can risk not investing in close contests, however, because if only the opposition did so, the increased turnout for that party could turn the vote in its favor. With resources used to stimulate turnout on both sides, the election that was thought to be close remains so, but it is a tight race with higher turnout. It therefore follows that we should see parties investing heavily in elections expected to be competitive, and we should observe high rates of participation in those races, whether or not voters turn out just because of that closeness.[8]

In 1828 and 1832, only the Democratic Party was organizing extensively to mobilize the electorate. To be sure, local supporters of Adams and Clay undoubtedly attempted to counter Democrats' efforts, but in these years Democrats more or less chose where the mobilizing efforts were to be made. Even by 1836 the Whig party was just beginning to organize and remained considerably behind in its development. It was not until 1840 that both parties had come close to being fully organized national, mass-based parties. As a result, we can investigate the efforts of strategic parties in these years of asymmetric party development in ways unavailable in the more fully developed two-party system that followed.

This, then, provides a theoretical account of how political parties could solve their major collective action problem, mobilization of the electorate. We should expect that turnout would be higher in those states in which the Democratic party was organized, in which the differential benefits of the election were higher, in which the costs of voting were relatively lower, and in which the contest was closer, whether that closeness affected voter decision making directly or influenced it indirectly through the actions of strategic parties. What remains is the question of how Van Buren solved the prior and perhaps more important collective action problem. That problem was securing the participation of other elective office seekers, officeholders, and benefit seekers who commanded the extensive resources necessary to join his plan and create this new Democratic Party.

THE MOBILIZATION OF THE ELECTORATE BY JACKSONIAN DEMOCRACY

Turnout among adult white males jumped from 26.5 percent in the presidential elections of 1824 to 56.3 percent in those of 1828. Early scholarship provided three explanations of this increase that would be referred to in such terms as a "mighty democratic uprising" (Schlesinger 1947, 36) and a "roaring flood" of new democracy (Beard and Beard 1933, vol. 2, 550). These explanations were the assertion by the common voter of his newly won suffrage, the democratizing influences that arose from the western states and their frontier spirit, and the magnetic attractiveness of Old Hickory as a candidate to—and of—the common man.

McCormick (1960) demonstrated the failings of all three.[9] First, there was no newly won suffrage to be exercised for the first time in this period by any substantial proportion of the electorate.[10] Second, turnout was slightly lower on average in the western states than in the rest of the nation, so they could not be leading the nation in this exercise in democracy. Finally, he found little evidence that Jackson's personal popularity accounted for increased rates of voting. In 1828 Jackson carried three but also lost three of the six states with the greatest turnout. Also, when Van Buren ran at the top of the ticket in 1836, turnout actually increased slightly from 1832, even though the height of Jackson's popularity had been in 1832.

McCormick accounted for the increased turnout in presidential elections by three factors: heightened interest in presidential politics, greater competitiveness of the two parties in many of the states, and increased structuring of the parties in this period. Interest in presidential politics had waned during Monroe's elections, and if anything, the complicated, multicandidate contest of 1824 that would be resolved only in the House amid charges of corruption added alienation on top of apathy. As he notes, every state had already had much higher turnout in some election before 1824 than it had in 1824. Many times, this was even higher turnout than in 1828, 1832, or 1836 as well. It was only when turnout increased again in 1840 to the high 70 percent levels, on the full development of a two-party system, that many states recorded new highs in turnout.

McCormick analyzed closely the impact of increased competition on turnout in the various states. The vote in 1824 was quite one-sided in most states. Add greater interest and a few more competitive states, and it is not surprising that the turnout rate doubled in 1828 and stayed at that level in succeeding elections. It was only when the Whig party presented a strong candidate in 1840 that the vote between Whig and Democrat was close in most states, and it was this competitiveness that, in his account, led to the high rates of voting in the 1840s.[11] Later he would carefully study the development of party organizations in the states (McCormick 1966), and these data serve as the basis for the analysis in this chapter.

He anticipated these findings in his first study, however, and argued that "the key to the relatively low presidential vote [in 1828–36] would seem to be the extreme political imbalance that existed in most states as between the Jacksonians and their opponents. Associated with this imbalance was the immature development of the national parties in connection with the Jackson elections" (McCormick 1960, 107). He concludes that it was the existence of "balanced and organized parties" in each state that stimulated voters "by the prospect of a genuine contest" and led to marked increases in turnout. This was not generally true throughout the nation until 1840, "and then at last the 'mighty democratic uprising' took place" (108). My next task, then, is to assess the arguments Van Buren offered for the creation of the Democratic Party that resulted in the "extreme political unbalance" between Jacksonians and their opponents and see how this led to the first increase in turnout from 1824 to the period 1828–36.

THE ORGANIZATION OF THE JACKSONIAN DEMOCRATIC PARTY

The Historical Context

The social context had become conducive to mass-based parties by 1828. The national infrastructure, especially its transportation and communication systems, was rapidly improving. Growing population pushed the frontier ever westward, and six new states had been added since 1812. A national, mass-based party was therefore becoming technologically feasible, and the increasingly far-flung population required a similarly far-flung organization if it was to be mobilized.

McCormick correctly pointed out that the franchise was not extended significantly between 1824 and 1828, but *presidential* suffrage, the key to the new party, did expand greatly. From 1812 through 1820, nine states selected electors through the state legislature rather than by popular voting. With expansion in the number of states, the percentage of states using the state legislature fell from 50 percent in 1812 to 38 percent in 1820. In 1824 a quarter of the states (six of twenty-four) still used the state legislature. Only Delaware and South Carolina did so in 1828, and only South Carolina failed to use popular voting four years later. In other words, presidential selection was an exercise in popular voting nationwide by 1828, when for the first time over 90 percent of the states used popular voting to choose electors.[12] As a result, although the percentage of white males who voted in 1828 was about double that in 1824, the absolute number of voters tripled in 1828, breaking the one million mark, up from 365,000 in 1824. A presidential party could fairly be called democratic by 1828.

Van Buren's Rationale for a New Form of Party

Remini reports that "several of the most important leaders of the [forming] party earnestly sought a reaffirmation of the Jeffersonian principles of states' rights as the fundamental philosophy of the Democratic party" (1963, 53). The most important of these, Van Buren, decided not to "go over" to Jackson publicly until his reselection to the Senate in February 1827 and until he had received assurances from Jackson men. On December 22, 1826, he wrote home to the Regency, "My language here to our friends is that we will support no man who does not come forward on the principles & in the form in which Jefferson & Madison were brought forward & this they will in the end all assent" (in Remini 1963, 53–54).

On January 13, 1827, he wrote to Thomas Ritchie, editor of the Richmond *Enquirer*, leader of the Richmond Junto, and a spokesman of the southern Radicals. The letter sought Ritchie's support in securing Jackson's nomination and assisting in the formation of a national party. His first reason for a national means of nomination is that "it is the best and probably the only practicable mode of concentrating the entire vote of the opposition [to Adams] and of effecting what is of still greater importance, the substantial reorganization of the old Republican party" (Remini 1972, 4). Second, he wrote,

> I have long been satisfied that we can only get rid of the present, and restore a better state of things, by combining Genl. Jackson's personal popularity with the portion of old party feeling yet remaining. . . .
> 3rd the call of such a convention, its exclusive Republican character, and the refusal of Mr. Adams and his friends to become party to it, would draw anew the old Party lines and the subsequent contest would reestablish them; . . .
> 4th it would greatly improve the condition of the Republicans of the North and Middle states by substituting *party principle* for *personal preference* as one of the leading points in the contest. (5; emphasis in original)

For the South, he offered,

> Instead of the question being between a northern and Southern man, it would be whether or not the ties, which have heretofore bound together a great political party should be severed. The difference between the two questions would be found to be immense in the elective field. (5)

He goes on to point to a similar advantage in New England, forcing them to choose between "an indulgence in sectional and personal feelings [or] acquiesce in the fairly expressed will of the party" (5).

> 6th its effects would be highly salutary on your section of the union by the revival of old party distinctions. We must always have party distinctions and the old ones are the best of which the nature of the case admits. . . .
> If the old ones are suppressed, geographical divisions founded on local interests, or what is worse prejudices between free and slave holding states will inevitably take their place. . . .

[Jackson's] election, as the result of his military services without references to a party and so far as he alone is concerned scarcely to principle would be one thing. His election as the result of a combined and concerted effort of a political party, holding in the main, to certain tenets and opposed to certain prevailing principles, might be another and a far different thing. (5–6)

In short, Van Buren combined an appeal to win the 1828 election with a commitment to forging a truly national political party, reviving Jeffersonian Republicanism by linking "planters of the South with plain Republicans of the North" (6). A strong commitment to principles, at least the principle of party, was expressed here.[13] Equally clearly, there was a very practical side. Jackson was the one whose personal popularity could be added to old Republican support to defeat Adams. This call came without *any* commitment to policy. The ambiguity of Jackson himself ("Indeed Genl. Jackson has been so little in public life, that it will be not a little difficult to contrast his opinions on great questions with those of Mr. Adams," 5), and the absence of policy stances that this call for a renewal of the old party lines and principles invokes, were crucial in forging the party in 1828. The only policy consequences discussed in Van Buren's letter were how the renewal of party would set aside sectional interests and in particular the slavery issue (see chap. 5).

The basic collective good at stake here was the creation of a new party to win the presidency in 1828 with a popular, if ambiguous, Jackson, based on principles few could object to. The new party leadership was to be drawn from the majority of Jackson supporters already elected to Congress in 1826. The collective action problem at that level could be overcome relatively easily. This anticipated leadership consisted of those already known to be opposed to Adams. Should they cooperate in forming this new party, they stood to benefit from Jackson's election and the consequent spoils of office. Moreover, if Jackson's personal popularity made him a stronger candidate than anyone else, and if there was some party organization able to induce party voting in the public, those running for office under his party banner would benefit electorally either personally or via the greater vote for their allies in their state. Thus selective benefits were available in addition to the collective goods, and those selective benefits would be available only to those who contributed to providing this collective good. Finally, Jackson's ambiguous policy stance made it possible for those in the new party to run on whatever platform they wanted to, perhaps taking the opposite position from those running in the same party elsewhere in the nation. His personal popularity was a tide that would lift all Democratic boats without committing them to anything in particular, only to Jeffersonian principles in general. There were both collective and selective benefits to contributing, perhaps without any great costs.[14]

Jackson's lack of public definition of any real policy platform was crucial in part because many of these state organizations would enter the party already constrained on policy. As we will see later, many Democratic state party organizations, especially those created in time for the 1828 election, were formed out of extant state and local parties, factions, and cliques. Often these prior groups had public policy platforms of their own, and getting them to join the new national party entailed convincing them that they did not have to put at risk extant electoral support, predicated in part on policy. Jackson's ambiguous public image was therefore crucial in the formative years, precisely to reduce the cost of joining the collective action enterprise of creating a national political party. Remini described Jackson's platform for 1828 thus:

> There were indeed many differences of opinion dividing the Jackson men, both in and out of Congress. The problem of settling on terms and conditions was complicated by the necessity of creating a national voting majority out of a patchwork of conflicting interest groups, classes, and factions. . . . Undoubtedly, if these Congressmen had attempted a settlement on national issues, the alliances would have been stillborn. Because they represented a wide range of diverse interests among coalescing Jacksonians, no basic statement of purpose and direction seemed wise or feasible. Their first objective was to win the elections, nothing more. (72–73)

He points out that Jackson himself solved this potential problem by failing to announce a program. As he puts it,

> Yet for all his double talk and concern for his public image [not speaking out on issues to avoid the appearance of campaigning], Jackson did subscribe to a national program, one he vaguely alluded to during the campaign (very vaguely) but one he later outlined in detail. . . . As he subsequently defined it, his program was neo-Jeffersonian and conservative, leaning toward states' rights and the economics of laissez-faire, but so bland and inoffensive that those previously disposed to follow him could not seriously object to a single point. (73)

And this was his detailed announcement after the election! Even after election, for example, Jackson declared that he favored a "middle and just course" on the tariff question. Representative Samuel D. Ingham of "protection-mad" Pennsylvania proclaimed that Jackson would "raise the tariff every time he touched it." Conversely, Ritchie and other southern Radicals insisted that he favored the tariff only to raise revenue, strengthen national defense, and reduce the national debt. Thus not only was his ambiguity genuine, but it also allowed leaders to tailor the collective good of Jackson's candidacy to their local concerns, thereby reducing the costs of participating in collective action in 1828. The new party did not constrain Jackson either, since it did not even attempt to write a platform in advance of the election.

The National Alliance and Caucus

Van Buren translated this rationale into a two-pronged organizational effort. I examine the first prong, the national Alliance and its associated Caucus, in this section. The Alliance was the centerpiece of his immediate objective, carrying Jackson to victory in 1828. The Caucus was its organizational counterpart, and this national organization was to raise the resources for implementing the second prong of his plan, organizing individual states to mobilize the electorate.

The first task was to form an alliance among key state leaders opposed to the Coalition, as Adams's congressional supporters were known, seeking their support for winning an electoral majority for Jackson.[15] The Alliance was initiated in December 1826 when Van Buren met with Vice President John C. Calhoun. Van Buren offered the support of the Radicals to add to that of the Jackson-Calhoun faction. That faction could be expected to carry Tennessee, Pennsylvania, North and South Carolina, Alabama, and Mississippi. Alliance with the Radicals could add New York, Virginia, and Georgia. This was therefore an essentially North-South alliance, the revival of Jeffersonian Republicanism.[16] Van Buren quickly redeemed his pledge to Calhoun by touring the South, meeting with Crawford in Georgia (who promised his support for Jackson), Dr. Thomas Cooper (a "fiercely radical Southerner, who was not above preaching the destruction of the Union whenever Congress spoke of raising the tariff"; Remini 1959, 144) in South Carolina, Governor Hutchins G. Burton in North Carolina, and then Ritchie in Virginia to secure the Alliance.

This Alliance was a coalition designed to win the 1828 election. It involved very little in the way of a collective action problem: these were generally states in which Jackson and Crawford had run strongly in 1824 and in which a Jackson victory in 1828 was highly probable. There would be little personal risk for those entering the Alliance and some potential benefit—both from the collective good *and* from such selective benefits as leadership in the winning party, the spoils of Jackson's office, and the added boost of Jackson's personal popularity to the Alliance member's own candidacy or his faction's candidates.

The Alliance therefore differed little from prior practice as a possibly short-term coalition of political elites seeking to win a particular election. Van Buren sought and won a significantly longer-term commitment from the elites in the Alliance, however. The Caucus was to serve as the national arm of the new party-as-organization, raising resources, coordinating efforts, and overseeing investment in building state- and local-level organizations for mobilization in 1828 and thereafter.

The Caucus was centered in Washington, drawing from Jackson men in office (while Jackson's personal "organization" and advisers remained in Tennessee). In addition to the Alliance, the Caucus added Jacksonians from Delaware, Kentucky, and New Jersey. Meeting regularly, they oversaw fund-raising, established and subsidized a chain of newspapers throughout the nation, and determined how and where to focus their efforts. Although each was expected to contribute his own resources (and many even used their franking privileges to mail campaign literature), the sums needed to create a party organization in the various states were considerable.

Three points are noteworthy. First, state-level party building would take time; not until 1840 would their initial efforts extend to all states (see table 4.3 below). Second, the resources would have to come from somewhere, and this would require tapping (and presumably responding to the interests of) high-level benefit seekers who commanded such resources. Ferguson (1983) argues that these benefit seekers were critical in shaping policy under the Jackson administration and helped create policy changes that were so significant that some claim 1828–35 was a critical or realigning era. For example, bankers were a key source of funds, and many bankers benefited from ending the second National Bank under Jackson. Third, the Caucus rationally allocated its resources according to the strategic parties hypothesis, as will be shown. The result was that they organized first where state and local politics were already more organized, making them less costly to develop, and where the benefits would be highest, which meant organizing in states expected to be the most competitive. This, then, is the argument.

The Alliance as the electoral coalition to win the 1828 presidential election. Three expectations follow from viewing the Alliance (and Caucus) states as a coalition forged to win in 1828. First, the coalition should be large enough to win an electoral vote majority. Second, the coalition should be built on states that Jackson could expect to win, only then turning to states where victory was less certain. Third, coalition leaders should be drawn from those who already supported Jackson (or opposed Adams) and who stood to benefit—or could be made to benefit—in a selective way from the revival of the old Republican party and the election of Jackson.[17] The Alliance and Caucus men were those who fit the third point. What of points one and two?

Table 4.1 provides a detailed look at voting in the Alliance and the Caucus states, and table 4.2 compares all states. The Alliance states offered 142 electoral votes, 11 more than the necessary majority.[18] The other three states offered another 25. Thus they were sufficiently rich in votes to ensure victory on their own. Table 4.1 demonstrates that these states were Jackson territory in 1824. He carried six of the nine Alliance states and New Jersey, often beating Adams by large pluralities. They provided three-quarters of his electoral votes in 1824 (74 of 99, or 83 percent, with 8 more from New Jersey), and that was over half the votes needed for victory. Adding Crawford's vote to Jackson's, they carried eight of the nine Alliance states, plus New Jersey and Delaware, and they carried them by huge amounts. In none of these eight states was the Jackson-Crawford plurality less than *twice* that of Adams's and Clay's votes added together. The only state in the Alliance that was not one of theirs in 1824 was New York. It above all was what Van Buren was able to offer to the Alliance.[19]

As hypothesized, these states went for Jackson in 1828. In the nine Alliance states, Jackson won 126 electoral votes, just 5 short of victory, and victory was secure with the 14 votes won in Kentucky. He

Table 4.1 The Electoral Base of the Jacksonian Democratic Party, 1824–28

State	Electoral vote	Jackson-Crawford plurality, 1824[a] (%)	Jackson plurality, 1828 (%)	
National Alliance				
New York	36	−66.6	+1.9	(EV)[b]
Virginia	24	+50.2	+38.0	
Georgia	9	+100.0	+93.6	(EV)
Tennessee	11	+98.0	+90.4	
Pennsylvania	28	+69.9	+33.3	
North Carolina	15	+99.9	+46.2	
South Carolina	11	+100.0	+100.0	(EV)
Alabama	5	+63.5	+79.8	
Mississippi	3	+32.4	+62.1	
Caucus				
New Jersey	8	+16.2	−4.2	
Kentucky	14	−45.6	+10.0	
Delaware	3	+33.3	−100.0	(EV)

[a]Entry is the difference between the total of the votes received by Jackson and Crawford and the totals received by Adams and Clay.
[b]EV denotes electoral votes, since there was no popular voting for electors in these states in these years.

Table 4.2 Relation between Jackson and Crawford Vote in 1824, Compared with Adams and Clay Vote, and Involvement in the Democratic Alliance and Caucus, 1828

	National Alliance state	Caucus member only	Not in Alliance or Caucus	N
Top half of Jackson-Crawford states, 1824	8	2	2	12
Bottom half of Jackson-Crawford states, 1824	1	1	10	12
N	9	3	12	24

Note: See text for explanation for determining which twelve states were most supportive of Jackson and Crawford in 1824.

won 88.7 percent of the electoral votes available in the Alliance states, and the Alliance made up 71 percent of his electoral votes (74 percent including Kentucky). In other words his victory in these states was substantial, and his victory in the election was heavily concentrated in just these states.

Although the Alliance states and Kentucky gave Jackson an electoral vote majority, these states were if anything less supportive of him in 1828 than of him and Crawford four years earlier. Eight Caucus states had popular voting in both years. Jackson's margin of victory was smaller in 1828 than the Jackson-Crawford plurality in 1824 in five of them, increasing in only three. In those without popular voting in 1824, Jackson's support appeared to increase only in New York. Overall, his support increased in four, stayed the same in two, and decreased in six of the Alliance and Caucus states. Organizational efforts by the Caucus therefore did not pay off at the polls in their home states. That was not the intention of the organizational efforts, because except for New York, these states already were known to be safely his. They were his margin of victory, but mobilization efforts went elsewhere.

The claim that the Alliance and Caucus were expected to be the basis of victory because of their voting in 1824 is addressed in table 4.2. All twenty-four states were ranked by the proportion of votes cast for Jackson and Crawford in 1824 compared with those cast for Adams and Clay.[20] This rank order was then divided into the twelve strongest and twelve weakest Jackson-Crawford states.[21] Only Indiana and Maryland were above average for Jackson in 1824 and not in the Alliance or the

Caucus.[22] Only Clay's Kentucky and NewYork were weaker than average Jackson states in 1824 and included in the national part of Van Buren's emerging party. The hypothesis therefore is strongly supported. This was an Alliance and Caucus designed to win the 1828 election for Jackson and the party, a design based on the results of the 1824 election.

Organizing the State Democratic Parties

The national Democratic organization did not face an undifferentiated political world. Many states had parties, factions, juntos, or cliques already competing for office. In this there was great variation from state to state. McCormick (1966) described the politics in the various states very carefully, and though he found substantial differences in each state, he also found clear regional patterns.[23]

New England states had strong, well-organized Federalist and Republican Parties in the first party system. Often the Federalists simply retired or merged with Republicans, leaving these as strong one-party states during Monroe's presidency. The new parties therefore emerged from splits in the old Republican Party. The Middle States also had long experience with two parties, although they were typically not quite as well organized as New England.[24] In these states many Federalists returned to partisan politics, often playing key leadership roles in the new parties. There was more variation here than in New England. New York had a strong two-party system (Clintonians and Regency), the old Republican Party remained strong in New Jersey and Delaware, politics was factional in Pennsylvania, and the Republican Party had essentially disintegrated in Maryland. In the Old South there had never been any real Federalist Party at all. It competed only in Virginia and North Carolina, and rather ineffectively at that.[25] As a result, there was often little in the way of prior party organization. The familiar pattern of informal rather than institutionalized politics was already typical, quite similar to Key's description of southern politics a century later (1949). In Georgia, Kentucky, and Tennessee there were parties of a sort at the state level, albeit not aligned with national cleavages. In the rest, state politics was "organized" around cliques and factions. The final group of states comprised those newly voting in 1824.[26] None of these had prior party organizations; voting coalitions were organized along sectional, ethnic, and personal lines. Although there were some leadership cliques, there was no organized partisan activity of even the simplest sort. In these states the presidential contest provided the strongest impetus to initial electoral organization, so state and local politics were structured in alignment with, and upon emergence of, the national Democratic and National Republican, and later Whig, divisions.

This differentiated political world provided the Caucus with an opportunity. Instead of having to create state parties from whole cloth, national Democratic leaders could minimize the cost of collective action by combining existing state and local parties, factions, or cliques with remnants of the old Jeffersonian party. Van Buren appears to have recognized the advantage of reviving the old and borrowing from the extant over inventing the new. In his letter to Ritchie he wrote, "The country has once flourished under a party thus constituted and may again. It would take longer than our lives (even if it were practicable) to create new party feelings to keep those masses together" (Remini 1972, 6). There was a cost to this strategy, however, since the existing state and local organizations had leaders in place, principles as their basis, and policy concerns already publicly stated.

The state organizational effort was directed at mobilizing the electorate. The crucial point, of course, is that Democrats were the only ones attempting to generate a mass-based political party at the state level. Since the party had the field pretty much to itself, it chose where mobilization occurred. Where it did not so choose, organized mobilization efforts did not proceed very far.[27]

If the purpose of the state-level organizing was to thrust the Democratic Party into a state, organize it, and mobilize Jackson's supporters in the electorate, where would it act first? The strategic party creator would seek to organize first where costs were lowest and benefits potentially highest. Those states cheapest to organize were those in New England and the Middle States, which already had more structured politics, whereas the Old South and the new states would be more costly to organize. The expected benefits of mobilization would be highest where there was a chance that additional turnout could turn them in Jackson's direction, and hence the benefits of mobilization would be greatest in the most competitive states.

One consequence of this strategic party hypothesis is that the Alliance states were not likely to be the first organized, because they had been strong Jackson or Crawford states in 1824 and were expected to go for Jackson in 1828, as we have already seen they did. Similarly, Adams's candidacy in 1828 made New England an unlikely target, even if comparatively easy to organize, because there was little chance that Jackson could win any of these states.[28] The South, for its part, would be costly to organize given its informal pattern of politics, *and* there would be little to gain, since it would likely go to Jackson anyway. The new states would be costly to organize because they lacked any political structuring. The Middle States, combining competitiveness with prior partisan structures, therefore stood out as the most cost-effective place to begin party building. In 1832, with Clay at the top of the ticket, the states of New England would combine relatively low-cost organizing with newly competitive status, making them the most effective target for party building that year.

The national organization placed what we would see from today's perspective as minimal demands on a state organization for incorporation into the national Democratic Party. The Caucus required only that a state grouping be sufficiently organized to pick a slate of presidential electors, ensure that they would cast their votes for Jackson if called on to vote, and agree to call itself the Democratic Party. Chambers and Davis (1978, 176–77, table 5.1), provide a measure of state party organization, derived from their reading of McCormick's state-by-state analysis (McCormick 1966). The dates when they consider a state as having an organized Democratic Party are listed in table 4.3. They base their calculations on the alignment of the state with the national party label and the degree of centralization of the party in the state (looking especially to see if it held a state convention).[29] This building of a party institution was difficult. By their count, six states were organized by 1828, four more in time for the 1832 elections, and most others by the 1836 elections, with the rest completed by 1840.[30] Inclusion in the national organization was unrelated to the success of efforts in the states. Three states in the Caucus were organized in time for the 1828 elections; nine were not. Three of the states outside the Caucus were organized by 1828; the other nine were not.

Although Caucus members did not concentrate their efforts disproportionately in their home states, the strategic parties hypothesis fares

Table 4.3 States Organized by Democratic Party, 1828–40

Organized by			
1828	1829–32	1833–36	1837–40
New Hampshire	Massachusetts	Vermont	Pennsylvania
New Jersey	Connecticut	New York	Louisiana
Maryland	Rhode Island	Virginia	Indiana
Delaware	Maine	Georgia[a]	Georgia
Ohio		Missouri[a]	Missouri
Kentucky		Tennessee	(Michigan)[b]
		Mississippi	(Arkansas)[b]
		Alabama	
		North Carolina	
		Illinois	
(6)[c]	(4)	(10/8)	(3/5 + 2)

Source: Chambers and Davis (1978, 176–77, table 5.1).
Note: South Carolina is excluded, since it did not choose electors by popular vote in this period.
[a]Georgia listed as 1836/1840; Missouri listed as 1835/1839.
[b]Denotes state first voting for president in 1836 and excluded from analysis.
[c]Number of states.

well. Three of the six states successfully organized for 1828 were in the most strategically appropriate region, the Middle States. Even the other three illustrate strategic allocations by the party. Isaac Hill, a gifted leader and editor of the *New Hampshire Patriot*, served as an indigenous entrepreneur in New Hampshire, with the Caucus only providing support for his initiatives. Kentucky, with a quasi-two-party system ("Old Court" versus "New Court"), was a more convenient target in 1828 without Clay running for president, and Ohio was perhaps the most established of the new states.[31]

Much the same was true for 1832. Already well organized, New England became an attractive target with Clay replacing Adams at the top of the ticket. Thus lower cost was coupled with greater potential gain. Both turnout and Jackson's percentage of the vote increased substantially in every New England state save Vermont, the single state in the region not organized by the national party by the 1832 elections.

State Organizing and Electoral Mobilization

The central questions, then, are how these state parties attempted to mobilize the electorate and how successful they were in doing so. Historical accounts of the era of Jacksonian Democracy are replete with evidence about the radical transformation of campaigns in this era to contests of high interest, involvement, and even drama. Although especially clear in 1840 with two mass parties competing for the first time, this transformation applied to the Jacksonian elections as well. Rallies, bonfires, and parades were conducted, hickory trees were planted and hickory poles raised, and barbecues, Fourth of July parades, and state and local fairs (conveniently held in the fall) were politicized. "Shouting, drinking, speechmaking, and huzzahing" (Remini 1963, 115) were the order of the day in 1828 as well as 1840. And it was the organized Democratic state parties and local Jackson clubs that carried these efforts through.

Table 4.4 provides data about two points. First, as part A shows, turnout shot up by an average of 42 percent in the states the Caucus successfully organized by 1828, compared with a far more modest 18 percent increase among those not so organized. Second, mobilization was purely a consequence of state organization and was not related to a state's inclusion in the Alliance or Caucus. Parts B and C show that turnout actually increased less than average in the Alliance states and that turnout in states organized and participating in the Caucus increased to about the same extent as in organized states not in the Alliance or Caucus.

In table 4.5 the impact of state party organizing on electoral mobilization is extended to cover the three presidential contests, 1828, 1832, and 1836, in which the Democrats were effectively the only mass political party. Turnout increased substantially in those states newly

Table 4.4 Difference in Turnout Rate, 1824–28, by State-Level Democratic
Party Organization and by Membership in National Alliance or Caucus

	Turnout difference 1824–28, average		*N*
	A. Turnout differential by state party organization		
Organized	41.7		5
Not organized	18.3	(19.7 less RI, VA)	13
Average	24.8		18
	B. Turnout differential by national party involvement		
Alliance state	17.9	(18.3 less VA)	6
Caucus only	42.6		2
Non-Caucus state	25.4	(27.6 less RI)	10
Average	24.8		18
	C. Turnout difference by state organization and by national party		
Organized			
Caucus	42.6		2
Non-Caucus	41.1		3
Not organized			
Caucus	17.9	(18.3 less VA)	6
Non-Caucus	18.7	(20.9 less RI)	7
Total average	24.8		18

Source: State party organizing data from Chambers and Davis (1978); turnout figures from
McCormick (1960).
Note: Rhode Island and Virginia had restrictive suffrage requirements.

Table 4.5 Increase in Percentage Turnout in Presidential Elections,
Compared with Preceding Presidential Election, 1828–36

Election year	This election	Four years earlier	Eight years earlier	Not yet organized	All states
		State First Organized by			
1828	41.68[a]	—	—	18.32	24.81
1832	15.08	−4.72	—	−10.47	−4.52
1836	12.90	−3.72	−5.42	1.17	3.70
1836a	12.79	−3.72	−5.42	6.04	3.70

[a]Entry is average change in turnout from the preceding presidential election.
Note: The row 1836 includes Georgia and Missouri as organized by 1836; the row 1836a includes
Georgia and Missouri as not yet organized by 1836.

organized for each of these elections, and that heightened mobilization was concentrated almost exclusively in these states, except for
the much smaller increases in not-yet-organized states in 1828. The
evidence indicates that Jacksonians organized first where the net payoff
was largest, that is, in states with some degree of structure to provide a
basis for incorporation and in states where it would be most beneficial
to mobilize because the contest was likely to be close. Most important,

organizing paid off by getting out more of the electorate in those states than in the rest.

MOBILIZATION OF THE PRESIDENTIAL ELECTORATE, 1828–44

The evidence so far shows that a high level of competitiveness in the election in a state and the Democratic Party's having successfully organized that state were correlated with massive increases in turnout. A fuller accounting of mobilization of mass-based parties in this era is needed to ensure, insofar as data permit, that competitiveness and mobilizing efforts were indeed the reason for increased turnout.

The calculus of voting equation (4.1) specifies that turnout is a function of P, B, D, and C. Although measures of these concepts are limited, there are some measurable aspects of each (at least counting B as a part of D, as in equation 4.2). Region (using McCormick's fourfold measure [1966]) provides at least a partial measure of collective benefits of various candidates and their parties to the states (e.g., slavery, economic and ethnic bases, home state or regional favoritism). The Whig Party nominated three candidates in 1836 on precisely these grounds: each would have strength in his home region.[32] Closeness (measured as in McCormick 1960, hence yielding an expected negative sign) measures the likelihood that one's vote is effective and may also be an approximate indication of interest and excitement in the contest in that state. The three states with the most restrictive suffrage requirements (Louisiana, Rhode Island, and Virginia) provide a partial measure of differences in costs of voting. The Democratic Party organizational variable, included for the years 1828, 1832, and 1836, is measured by the number of election years the state party had been organized.[33] This model was estimated by OLS regression for each election from 1828 through 1844. Two versions of the model are estimated for 1836, reflecting Chambers and Davis's (1978) uncertainty about whether Georgia and Missouri were organized by that election.

The results of these estimates are reported in table 4.6. The adjusted R^2 is high for each election, ranging from a low of .64 (or .66) in 1836 to a high of .89 in 1840. Competitiveness as a measure of P was significantly related to turnout in each year but 1844. Its magnitude was especially large in 1836 and 1840, although perhaps surprisingly small in 1828. Thus McCormick's argument (1960) partially withstands a more fully specified test. Turnout in New England was always significantly less than in the new states (the excluded category), but few other regional variables were significant.[34] The hypothesis of real

Table 4.6 Regression Estimates of Electoral Mobilization, 1828–44

	Turnout in year					
	1828	1832	1836	1836a	1840	1844
Constant	66.04	64.25	57.22	57.55	88.90	82.76
	(5.44)[a]	(6.14)[a]	(4.70)[a]	(4.40)[a]	(2.45)[a]	(3.27)[a]
Closeness	−0.221	−0.321	−0.413	−0.406	−0.507	−0.168
in state	(0.098)[a]	(0.080)[a]	(0.214)[a]	(0.208)[a]	(0.152)[a]	(0.257)
Region						
New England	−14.15	−9.97	−10.78	−11.58	−5.25	−12.74
	(4.86)[a]	(5.71)[b]	(5.89)[a]	(5.81)[a]	(2.89)[b]	(3.47)[a]
Middle States	−1.93	−5.26	+1.67	+0.89	−5.85	−3.19
	(5.83)	(6.47)	(5.93)	(5.84)	(3.07)	(3.88)
Old South	−3.09	−0.63	+0.92	+1.07	+3.85	+3.83
	(5.63)	(5.44)	(5.52)	(5.34)	(2.99)	(3.64)
Restricted	−25.76	−27.07	−28.51	−28.87	−38.72	−31.84
suffrage	(5.92)[a]	(6.07)[a]	(6.11)[a]	(5.90)[a]	(3.19)[a]	(3.69)[a]
states						
Length of	+13.36	+4.77	+3.60	+3.81	—	—
party	(6.04)[a]	(2.87)[b]	(2.16)[b]	(1.96)[a]		
organization						
Adjusted R^2	.770	.740	.640	.658	.890	.826
N	(22)	(23)	(23)	(23)	(23)	(23)

Data sources and definitions
1. Turnout from McCormick (1960, 292, table 1).
2. Closeness from Congressional Quarterly, *Guide to U.S. Elections* (1985), difference between percentages of vote received by the two candidates.
3. Region follows McCormick (1966); "new states" is excluded category.
4. Louisiana, Rhode Island, and Virginia are the states with restricted suffrage throughout this period.
5. Democratic Party organization from Chambers and Davis (1978, 176–77, table 5.1). Length is measured as the number of presidential elections the state has been organized (0 = unorganized, 1 = organized this election, etc.).
6. The 1836 column includes Georgia and Missouri as organized for the 1836 election; the 1836a column includes them as not yet organized.
[a]Significant at the .05 level or better, one-tailed (region, two-tailed).
[b]Significant at the .10 level, one-tailed (region, two-tailed).

interest concerns whether the set of regional variables (as measures of B), taken together, are collectively significant, and whether the associated hypothesis test is statistically significant in each equation. The hypothesized reduction in turnout in the three states with unusually severe restrictions on suffrage (or higher C) is strongly supported. Finally, the Democratic Party organizational measure increased turnout by about thirteen points in those states organized in 1828, and its effect is statistically significant even given controls.[35] The estimated impact was five points in 1832 for states newly organized by that year and nine points in 1832 for those organized in 1828. In 1836 turnout was estimated to be ten, seven, and four points higher in those states organized by 1828, 1832, and 1836, respectively, than in states not yet organized. In sum, the estimates indicate that the variables reflecting the calculus of voting model explain aggregate turnout patterns quite well and that each individual measure is significantly related to turnout in virtually every election.

CONCLUSIONS

This chapter allows us to paint a rich account of the rise of the first mass-based political party, ending with the first two-party system in which mobilization of the electorate played a central role. The expansion of transportation and communication systems made the mass party technologically feasible at about this time. The expansion of "presidential suffrage," that is, the spread of popular voting for presidential electors, had become all but universal in 1828. Antipathy to Adams, in part due to the 1824 election itself, had broken down the universal coalition first associated with Monroe's presidency, so that there was the potential for new party formation. Jackson's availability, his personal popularity, and the ambiguity of just where he stood on the issues of the day provided the potential for moving to organize the opposition to Adams's coalition.

Van Buren generated such an organized effort, motivated in large part by a desire to revive the old Republican Party—that is to say, its principles, its central focus on the presidency, and if not the Virginia Dynasty, at least a popular war hero as successor. To do so he created the Alliance and Caucus, the organizational centerpiece of the national effort to reestablish the old party and elect Jackson in 1828 by merging the Jackson coalition of 1824 with the Radicals. He thus revived the elite coalition that formed the basis of the Jeffersonians. He based the Alliance on those states that supported Jackson and Crawford, added his home state, and drew Caucus leadership from those in office who already supported Jackson. The states in this Alliance offered enough electoral votes for victory, and Jackson's victory came primarily from them. The Caucus raised funds, established newspapers, orchestrated the campaign, and organized state party development.

The state organizations proceeded as we would expect from a strategic party leadership. The first states organized into the Democratic Party were those where there were organizations of sorts already there for building and those where, owing to the likely closeness of the contest, mobilization would be most effective in seeking to secure them for Jackson. This effort helped organize the Democratic Party but did not impose fealty to the national party platform. Indeed, in 1828 there was no platform, and ambiguity reigned at the national level and about Jackson's own positions, thus permitting the various states, even if organized, to go their own way on policy. This became harder in 1832, since Jackson as incumbent had revealed his intentions, and it became impossible in 1836. The one-sided partisan organization nonetheless had the desired effect, and mobilization went up substantially in the states organized.

Still, by 1836 Jackson was retiring from the scene, and Van Buren was the party's nominee. His positions were well known, and his role in creating this modern political party was controversial. He could convince southern Radicals in 1828 to support Jackson but could not get many of those same leaders to support himself, a controversial New York politician of the modern stripe, in 1836 (especially after the nullification crisis). The Whig Party was formed out of this potential. It ran three opponents so that each region would have its own favorite. This strategy was essentially like that of the Democrats in 1828; candidates could appear whatever way the leadership of the region wanted the Whig Party to appear. Without any platform, and with no clear statement of principles other than opposition to Van Buren, the party lacked other critical ingredients held by Jacksonians in 1828: a popular leader and the principles of Jefferson and Madison. Although there was a second national party, evidently it was primarily an attempt to win the election per se or, even more, to stop the election of Van Buren. This lacked both the "principles and form" that the Democratic Party held in 1828. It was therefore a relatively ineffective force of mobilization and did not generate sufficient mass popular following to achieve its primary purpose—winning the presidential election.

By 1840 the Whigs had organized more completely, and they copied the Democratic strategy of 1828 more directly. They too ran a war hero without platform (also harking back to George Washington), and they won. With that they also completed their development into a major mass-based party, and the second party system was finally and fully in place. As a result, mobilization increased once again, just as it had when Jackson and Van Buren first took to their Alliance.

The collective action problem in the electorate was solved by creating party organizations to mobilize it. But though the party was a successful solution to the collective action problem of mobilization, the party as mobilizer presents a prior collective action problem. Van Buren solved this by moving first and most aggressively into areas that already had electoral groupings. Van Buren forged an elite Caucus of those who opposed Adams, and the Caucus raised the resources to make it possible for state-level supporters to unite under the label of Jacksonian

Democracy. The national Democratic bargain to them was, in effect, "Take our popular leader and no controversial policies. We will provide resources to you, so long as you agree to call yourself Democrats. For your part, you can continue to hold to your current policy positions." Thus a precedent of state and local party autonomy was set and became an American party tradition that was to continue and is only now eroding. The reason this bargain was struck was simply the collective action problem—to solve it, whenever possible the Caucus turned to extant organizations rather than building wholly new ones. To knit together those already in place in local politics, the national party had to yield them autonomy. Each local unit needed the freedom to establish its own definition of benefits in the collective good. That was essentially a selective incentive for joining the larger organization, required by the nature of collective action.

Van Buren called for creating a party "on the principle and in the form in which Jefferson and Madison brought forward." This chapter has provided a careful analysis of the form the mass party took and its success in achieving its immediate goal of winning elections through use of that form. But what of principle? A major principle was the primacy of the party over individuals within it, most importantly subordinating strong personalities of leaders to the party. By creating a national party consisting of relatively autonomous state and local party organizations, the principle of the party over its men had the ironic effect that coherent national platforms could rarely be attained, something that would plague parties from then until today. But in fact the assurance that no one person or faction could become dominant also meant that no one region, even one holding a majority of the nation, could dominate. In the second party system, the need to strike compromises with all regions meant that neither North nor South could dominate. As we saw earlier, this was explicit in Van Buren's letter to Ritchie, undoubtedly the key to his insistence on a North-South over East-West basis for creating his intersectional alliance and, as we shall see in the next chapter, institutionalized in an intricate web of rules and practices in the Democratic Party. In sum, the intersectional alliance of the Democratic and, eventually, the Whig Parties provided the means to hold together the two most divergent sections and the deepest social, economic, and political cleavage in the nation. "States' rights" in the structure of the Democratic Party meant controls to ensure national unity in the party, and in particular, controls to keep that "peculiar institution" of slavery off the national political agenda for as long as institutionalized partisan politics could do so.

The Whig Party was also an intersectional alliance, but like the Federalists in comparison with the Jeffersonian Republicans before it (and not unlike today's Republicans in comparison with Democrats), it created a smaller web of rules institutionalizing its procedures. In that sense it should have been no surprise that the growing pressures for putting slavery on the national agenda affected the Whig Party most strongly, wrecking it in the 1850s. With the collapse of even one of the two intersectional alliances, slavery could no longer be kept off the agenda. The Republican Party arose, capitalizing on the fall of the Whigs and the rising concern over slavery. The Republican Party was primarily a regional party of the North, and its successes there weakened the northern wing of the Democratic Party, making it more a southern party than a truly intersectional alliance. As we will see in the next chapter, the success of the Republican Party was no sure thing, and it was only with its emergence as the second major party that the dominance of the slavery issue on the agenda was assured. Although that issue was a critical part of the story of the rise of the Republican Party, it was, as we shall see, only one part of the story. A second part was the interaction of career ambitions of politicians with the slavery issue that made the Republican Party's rise possible, ensured that slavery would become the dominant national issue of the era, and precipitated secession and the Civil War.

5

WHIGS AND REPUBLICANS

Institutions, Issue Agendas, and Ambition

Democrats and Whigs were locked in close competition both nationally and in many of the states throughout the era of the second party system. Both parties, that is, were intersectional alliances that could well imagine victory or defeat in each campaign. The two parties were divided primarily along economic lines, typically contesting over the tariff, national development, and similar issues. Sectional issues, especially those related to slavery, rarely surfaced in national politics, and when they did, both parties struggled to maintain balance by active compromise within and between themselves. The Compromise of 1850, for example, was carefully wrought, nearly line by line, on the Senate floor, led by the ambitious rising Democrat Stephen A. Douglas and the Whigs' Great Conciliator, Henry Clay.

Clay died on June 29, 1852. His party effectively died that fall with the defeat of its presidential nominee, General Winfield Scott (VA). The second party system and its apparent equilibrium of twin intersectional parties was gone by 1854. The *Boston Courier* described elections that year by writing, "The foundations of the political deep were broken up—men floated about loosely, and all party ties and ligatures which bound them together were burst and cast away" (in Mayer 1967, 30). In the Northwest the Whig party utterly collapsed, replaced by the new Republican Party. The Whigs competed in the Northeast in 1854 with only minor incursions by Republicans.[1] Nonetheless, as the *Courier* indicated, they were but a shadow of a political party, even in a state where the Whigs continued to contest. The American, or Know-Nothing, party also won major victories in the Northeast in 1854, if often secretly. Thus the old party balance was forever "burst and cast away" in North and

South.[2] With the collapse of this apparent equilibrium, Democrats also were torn, if not irrevocably, into regulars and anti-Nebraska Democrats or along other lines and names, such as the "Hards" and "Softs" in critical New York State. With the end of two-party equilibrium, that is, the Democrats were also riven by sectional issues, notably slavery.

Intersectional alliances all but disappeared, and the economic line of cleavage supporting them was transformed. With the country rent by slavery, nativism, and temperance issues, a realignment began that fundamentally restructured the parties and led to a new party system. The victory of the slavery issue in combination with a newly drawn line of economic concerns as the basis of the new cleavage meant that the system would be primarily sectional, North versus South. With Lincoln's victory in 1860, the Republican Party solidified its position as the second major party and demonstrated an ability to win national elections based on a voting coalition all but exclusively in the North. The consequent loss of the South's power in the national government and the threat to slavery were critical ingredients in the South's decision to secede and in the initiation of the Civil War.

The slavery issue in the 1850s tore both major parties apart, demolished the Whigs, and served as the basis for the rise of the Republican Party to majority status, ushering in the third party system. The slavery issue was not a new one, however. It was the basis of one of the major compromises at the Constitutional Convention, and most founders recognized that it would inevitably need to be solved and that doing so would entail great pain. Heretofore, however, ambitious politicians had managed to compromise whenever the issue surfaced. Compromise would last be possible in 1850: in the next decade, too many ambitious politicians would be unable or unwilling to negotiate on slavery.

In this chapter I examine the interplay between ambition and the slavery issue. I argue that though slavery was brought to the fore and was a necessary ingredient for understanding the partisan politics of the period, so too was ambition—the ordinary career ambition of elective officeholders and office seekers—a necessary part of the story. Although it was these ordinary career decisions that, along with slavery, induced dramatic change, this was ordinary ambition set in extraordinary circumstances.

Before turning to the events of the 1850s, we must ask a prior question: how was the slavery issue kept from dividing the nation under the second party system? The answer lies in the institutional arrangements of the government and of the parties, especially those of the Democratic Party. The previous chapter focused on the elective goals of Van Buren's new party. The second part of his design was the principles he, like others, raised to justify the development of the new form. Institutional arrangements meshed smoothly with these principles. The concrete manifestation of Van Buren's "principle and form," then, was not what happened, but what did not. That is, it was the set of principles, and the forms of institutional arrangements consistent with them, that solved the problem of how to keep the most divisive issue in American history off the active political agenda throughout the second party system.

THE "PRINCIPLE AND FORM" OF PARTIES AND GOVERNMENT IN THE SECOND PARTY SYSTEM

Van Buren wrote to his Regency in 1826 that he sought to build a new party in "principle and form." The party he created was, as we saw, a powerful force for electoral mobilization that combined careful calculation of where presidential majorities could be won with state and local organizations that impassioned and mobilized Democratic voters. Although winning elections was central to the new form of party, winning was not the (or not the only) principle Van Buren was invoking. As we saw in chapter 4, the Democratic Party could hardly be said to have been founded on principles of what was good or just policy: there was too much disagreement among Democrats. What principle, then, could Van Buren have been pursuing?

The principle was that the new political party was to be more important than the men in it. This basis for what we will soon see to be many specific institutional mechanisms solved two problems. First, only by putting the "party over its men" could Van Buren ensure that the new form could avoid becoming the instrument of dominant individuals, much as his foes in New York were dominated by George and DeWitt Clinton. At the same time, only by putting the party over its men could a truly intersectional alliance be forged. Only by maintaining an intersectional alliance, one that blended "plain Republicans of the North with planters of the South," as Van Buren put it, could the party avoid dominance by one section and seek policies in the common interest of the nation. That meant, in particular, that only an intersectional alliance of this form could keep the slavery issue from coming to dominance. If this attempt failed, it seemed certain that the nation would divide and that the great experiment in democracy would be put in jeopardy. The stakes were high, with no less than national unity hanging in the balance.

The problem was that the South was a minority when the second party system was established, and it would become an ever smaller proportion of the nation. In 1828 the states that eventually seceded supplied eighty-three electoral votes, or only 32 percent. Even adding in the rest of those south of the Mason-Dixon Line yielded only 44 percent of the electoral votes. Moreover, by 1848 the full set of eleven Confederate states held only 31 percent of the electoral votes, declining to 29 percent in 1860. The problem was that a nonslave majority existed and could exercise its majority status to limit or even end slavery. The trick, therefore, was how to give the South an effective and credible veto over substantial change on the slavery issue. The problem was resolved by a complex set of institutional arrangements: it was these forms that gave substance to the principle.

The first element was the "balance rule" for admission of free and slave states (Weingast 1991). The Missouri Compromise in 1820, for example, brought in Missouri as a slave state and Maine as a free state, leaving balance preserved at twelve states each. Throughout the second party system, there was either an exact balance or one more slave state than free state in the Union. Because states are equally represented in the Senate, the intended effect of the balance rule was to give a senatorial veto to the South. The Wilmot Proviso of 1846, for example, was passed in the House with the regional vote won by the more populous North. With fifteen slave and fourteen free states at that time, the Proviso failed in the Senate.[3]

Largely owing to the Compromise of 1850, the South's veto power in the Senate was lost. By 1860 Texas was the only new slave state, but California, Oregon, and Minnesota had entered as free states. In part the end of the balance rule reflected the lack of viability of a slave economy in much of the new territory. Quite simply, not only was slavery increasingly seen as immoral, but the South was also running out of potential areas that would desire to come into the Union as slave states.

Even when there was a balanced Senate, however, the intended veto for the South was often effective, but it was not certain or, in the terminology of the new institutionalism, was not a fully "credible commitment." First, with exact balance, exercise of the veto required that all southern senators be united if those from the North were. Although highly probable, that was not a certainty over the long run. Where slavery was less important, in Delaware perhaps or in other peripheral slave states, defection was imaginable, and only one senator need defect, perhaps just once, to forever alter the balance on the issue. The most evident example is that only eleven of the slave states seceded. Second, since there were often equal numbers of slave and free states, a strictly North-South division would yield a tie vote. The Constitution provides that ties are to be broken by the vote of the vice president. Equal numbers of Senate votes alone, therefore, would not give the South the veto it needed.

The vice president, of course, could vote with the South, yielding them an effective veto over House actions. If that failed, so that the House and Senate passed antislavery legislation (presumably with vice-presidential support), the president could veto it. Given the constitutional checks and balances, a southern minority held a credible veto if it was able to muster a majority in the House, or in the Senate, or in the White House.[4] With the House reflecting a majority of the population, the South would need a majority in the Senate, or an equal number there coupled with a tie-breaking vote from the vice president, or the one vote cast by the man in the White House. In other words, keeping the number of free and slave states equal would yield the South an effective veto if either the president or the vice president supported it. A balanced Senate, coupled with regionally balanced partisan tickets for president and vice president, would therefore provide that veto power to the slave states.

Thus we are led to political parties. Both Jacksonian Democrats and Whigs did, indeed, choose balanced tickets (see table 5.1). Except for regional nominees in 1836, the Whigs nominated a balanced ticket, North and South, in every year but 1852. In that year Winfield Scott of Virginia ran with William Graham of North Carolina, but even that ticket was effectively "balanced," since Scott was suspected to be anti-slavery.[5] Besides, the question is whether the southern minority was protected, not the northern majority. Democratic tickets were always regionally balanced from 1828 through 1860, except in 1840. In that year the Democrats renominated Van Buren but chose no running mate. Perhaps foreseeing defeat (if not ensuring it by this action), they left the decision to each individual state.[6] With that exception, the Democrats were as careful as the Whigs to ensure that nominees were balanced by region. It was only the Republican Party that failed to balance its tickets by selecting non-Southern running mates in 1856 and 1860.

Balanced party tickets were better understood as symbolic, public affirmations of the party's continuing commitment to maintain its intersectional alliance for electoral purposes than as actual assurances that a southerner would be able to cast the tie-breaking vote in the Senate or to veto legislation in the White House. The genuine commitment was to maintain the alliance to ensure that neither strongly antislavery nor diehard proslavery leaders would be chosen. More moderate views were the order of the day, and the genuine commitment in each party was to refrain from extremist views on this divisive issue. Certainly this moderation greatly hindered the Democratic administrations of northerners Franklin Pierce and James Buchanan from dealing effectively with the changing circumstances surrounding the slavery issue, owing in part to the breakup of the second party system in the 1850s.

Table 5.1 Regional Balance in Party Tickets, 1836–60

	Democratic Party		Whig, Republican Parties	
Year	President	Vice president	President	Vice president
1836	Van Buren (NY)	Johnson (KY)	Webster (NH)	Granger (NY)
			Harrison (OH)	Granger (NY)
			White (TN)	Tyler (VA)
1840	Van Buren (NY)	None[a]	Harrison (OH)	Tyler (VA)
1844	Polk (TN)	Dallas (PA)	Clay (KY)	Frelinghuysen (NJ)
1848	Cass (MI)	Butler (KY)	Taylor (VA)	Fillmore (NY)
1852	Pierce (NY)	King (AL)	Scott (VA)	Graham (NC)
			Whig-American	
1856	Buchanan (PA)	Breckinridge (KY)	Fillmore (NY)	Donelson (TN)
			Republican	
			Fremont (CA)	Dayton (NJ)
1860	Douglas (IL)	Fitzpatrick (AL)	Lincoln (IL)	Hamlin (ME)

[a]State parties chose their own vice-presidential nominees.

Selection of consistently balanced tickets therefore had the desired effect of guaranteeing an effective veto in government no matter which major party won election. The next question, then, was how the parties made sure that they would, for the foreseeable future, select balanced tickets. The Democratic Party solved this problem by yet another institutional design, this within their own party, to ensure the commitment to maintaining their intersectional alliance. The adoption of a national convention was justified in the first place in part on just such an assurance. The original call for convention in 1832 came from the New Hampshire legislature, and one of its members called the first convention to order by saying in part (Bain and Parris 1973, 17):

> [The] object of the people of New Hampshire who called this convention was, not to impose on the people, as candidates for either of the first two offices of the government, any local favorite; but to concentrate the opinions of all the states. . . . They believed that the example of this convention would operate favorably in future elections; that the people would be disposed, after seeing the good effects of this convention in

conciliating the different and distant sections of the country, to continue
this mode of nomination.

This call for a national partisan consensus was coupled with adoption of a rule that representation at the convention would be proportional to each state's electoral votes (a rule unchanged until 1940).
This had the effect of guaranteeing substantial representation for the
South (still at 40 percent for the whole South as late as 1860). It also
ensured a majority for the North, however. To render this majority
ineffective in selecting two of their own as nominees, the 1832 Democratic convention adopted a rule, maintained continuously until 1936,
that nomination required a two-thirds majority vote. Thus, as in veto
overrides in the Senate, the South held an effective veto over nominations in the Democratic Party for president and vice president in the
face of a free-state delegate majority.

This two-thirds rule effectively ensured that the South would have to
agree to any nominee; made certain that no extremist, whether pro- or
antislave, could be nominated; helped produce balanced tickets; and
effectively maintained the requisite intersectional alliance in the Jacksonian Democratic Party. This partisan institutional arrangement coupled
nicely with the governmental mechanisms already described, and with
the comparable moderation and balanced tickets within the Whig party,
to guarantee that sectional issues would not dominate the national polity and divide the nation throughout the life of the second party system.
Van Buren's party was thus able to deliver what he promised Thomas
Ritchie of Richmond, Virginia, in 1827 (Remini 1972, 5):

> [The proposed new party's] effects would be highly salutary on your
> section of the union by the revival of old party distinctions. We must
> always have party distinctions and the old ones are the best of which the
> nature of the case admits. . . . If the old ones are suppressed, geographical
> divisions founded on local interests, or what is worse prejudices between
> free and slave holding states will inevitably take their place.

The two-thirds rule was critical, but it was also controversial and
at times costly to the Democratic Party. Nominations under this rule
could take as many as 103 ballots, as happened in 1924 (in a fight
between North and South), and such rancorous and lengthy divisions
could only hurt the party at the polls. It exacted a price from the party
and its principal founder in the second party system as well. Van Buren
secured a majority vote on the first ballot for presidential nomination
in 1844 (with 146 of 266 votes). When he failed to win the required
two-thirds majority, his support waned, and the convention eventually turned on the ninth ballot to the original dark horse candidate,

James K. Polk (NC). Although Polk won election, it was surely true that bitter divisions and lengthy balloting are not elements of the public image of choice for any party.

This complex set of institutional arrangements suppressed the slavery issue, but all of these together still did not make a truly credible commitment to keeping a northern majority from working its will. Most important, the Democrats' two-thirds rule was subject to approval or rejection by national convention delegates at each convention, and when questioned, it was maintained by the vote of a simple majority. For example, in 1844 an amendment to the Democratic rules to reaffirm their commitment to the two-thirds rule was voted on the floor of the convention. It passed by a vote of 55.6 percent of the delegates (148 to 118), and so a simple majority voted to adopt a rule that defeated Van Buren, the choice of a simple majority of delegates.[7] In principle, then, an antislavery, northern majority in the party could have voted out the two-thirds rule and nominated an antislavery ticket, just as the 146 delegates who supported Van Buren could have voted down the two-thirds rule and won nomination for him.

Perhaps even more striking was that in 1836, the first time the two-thirds rule could have been reconsidered, it was. It also lost by a (less than two-thirds) majority of 231 to 210. It thus appears that a simple majority of delegates did not favor the principle of the two-thirds rule for selecting nominees when considered in isolation. This defeat of the rule appears to have surprised everyone involved, however, suggesting that the delegates also recognized its importance for holding the intersectional alliance together. Whatever their true beliefs may have been, the party leaders reacted to the defeat by calling for immediate reconsideration and declaring the two-thirds rule reinstated by voice vote.

The commitment, then, was not binding by rule or procedure. It was instead the repeated agreement of at least a simple majority of Democrats to maintain the requirement of extraordinary majority, thereby purposefully forgoing its potential decisiveness in favor of granting the slave states, or any other substantial minority, veto power. In other words, it took the support of at least some number of northerners to choose forbearance from acting as a united North against the interests of the southern minority. The northern House majority had not shown such restraint, as it did not on the Wilmot Proviso.[8] Convention leaders and delegates did maintain such forbearance, however, perhaps in part owing to their supposition that their Whig opponents would also maintain moderation and balance. With the breakup of the Whig party such calculations by ambitious politicians would change.

What, then, of the Whig party? They (and later the Republicans) required only a simple majority vote to select nominees. Thus a critical institutional guarantee used by Democrats was not used by Whigs. And yet the Whigs did nominate balanced tickets. As just noted, however critical the two-thirds rule was to the Democrats, it was not a decisive, credible commitment, because it could be reversed by a simple majority at any convention, as "accidentally" happened in 1836. Thus it was simply the personal commitment of a sufficiently large number of Democratic leaders that was the ultimate assurance of balanced and moderate tickets. And thus it was also in the Whig party.

In 1836, at their first appearance, the Whigs nominated three separate tickets for appeal to three separate regions. This tripartite balance of North, South, and West was characteristic of Whig party politics generally, with the western wing dominated by Clay. In addition to nominating Clay in 1844, the Whigs nominated four other candidates for president between 1840 and 1856. Three of these, William Henry Harrison, Zachary Taylor, and Winfield Scott, were generals without experience in national politics. They were therefore removed from partisan politics and presumed to be moderates. The fourth and last Whig nominee was Millard Fillmore. Ascending to the presidency after Taylor's death, he demonstrated his moderate position on slavery through his support of the Compromise of 1850 and other actions in office. Indeed, he was the southern favorite for nomination in 1852, even over Scott from Virginia. His selection in 1856, therefore, once again demonstrated the Whig Party's commitment to the choice of a moderate.

Although the Whigs lacked one element of the institutional commitment to intersectional alliance that the Democrats had adopted, the reality of the agreement was the same in both parties—forbearance of extremists and a principled rather than an institutional commitment to moderation, intersectional alliance, and national unity. The two-thirds rule served to assist Democrats when under strain, but on the Whig side it was more the personal commitment and leadership of moderates, most of all Clay, that held the Whig alliance together. It was no mere coincidence that the Whig party was torn apart and effectively collapsed the same year Henry Clay died.

THE COLLAPSE OF THE WHIGS AND THE RISE OF THE REPUBLICAN PARTY

The 1852–53 elections were very bad for the Whigs. Scott won 44 percent of the vote, unusually low for the second party system. The uniformity of the vote throughout the nation meant that he won only 42 electoral votes to Pierce's 254. The Whigs held only 71 House seats in the Thirty-third Congress, down from 88, setting a second party system low, and 22 seats in the Senate, one more than the lowest total. This very bad showing dashed early hopes of victory in 1852 and signaled to many that the Whigs were doomed.

They were. Two years later the Democrats increased their majority in the Senate (up 2 seats, to 40), but they lost nearly half of their congressional delegation (falling from 159 to 83). The Whigs did not gain from the Democrats' misfortune in the House, however. Instead, the newly emerging Republican party caucused in the House with an outright majority (108 seats) and became the largest minority party in the Senate (with 15 seats). Two years later the decline of the Whigs to third-party status would be seen not just in congressional elections but also at the presidential level. The Whig-American Party nominee, Fillmore, received 22 percent of the popular vote, carrying only Maryland's 8 electoral votes. Democrat Buchanan won the presidency with 45 percent of the popular vote and 174 electoral votes, and Republican John C. Fremont came in second with 33 percent of the popular vote and 114 electoral votes.

The emergence of the Republican Party was all but exclusively northern. Fremont, for example, was not even on the ballot in 12 of the 15 states south of the Mason-Dixon Line, and he received only 2.1 percent of the vote in Delaware and 0.3 percent in Maryland.[9] In 1860 Lincoln was on the ballot in a few more southern states, but he exceeded 10 percent of the vote only in Delaware (23.7) and Missouri (10.3). Focusing on the presidency is misleading, however, for the Republican party rose first at lower levels, as their congressional majority won in the 1854–55 elections shows.[10] The emergence of this new party was necessarily due to slavery and (increasingly) related issues, but it was also necessarily due to the calculations of these midlevel, ambitious office seekers, calculating in particular that it had now become in the career interests of large numbers of them to capitalize on antislavery sentiment by moving into a new party based on sectional issues.

AMBITION THEORY AND PARTY AFFILIATION

Joseph A. Schlesinger (1966) argued that ambition, the ordinary hope of a long, successful, and rewarding career, is the crucial ingredient for tying elected officials to the wishes of the public in a republican democracy. Ambition theory has been applied, with great empirical success, primarily to account for which offices political careerists seek.[11] This literature takes the party affiliation of the careerist as given, typically not even considering it a matter of choice for the politician. Here

I reverse that consideration, for the demise of the second party system made choice of party the critical decision.

The choice of party affiliation differs from the choice of office in two important ways. First, although a great deal can be learned about office choice by examining only short-term considerations, the choice of party necessarily involves both short- and long-term factors. Senator William Seward (NY), for example, reasoned as late as 1855 or 1856 that the Whig party retained substantial chances for long-term viability, even if on an altered basis. As a result this antislavery advocate remained a Whig longer than others, even given the successes of the Republican Party elsewhere. Those others, conversely, believed that the Whig Party was not viable in the long term and joined the Republicans or another third party sooner.

Second, the choice they faced was which party might attain or maintain major-party status. The success or failure of any of these parties therefore turned not only on what the individual candidate chose, but also on the decisions of many other ambitious politicians. Seward's belief, for example, depended on other Whigs continuing to believe in the viability of their party. When others acted against that belief, some dropping out of the Whig Party and new candidates running in a new, third party, he could no longer believe in the Whigs' viability, and he switched to the Republican side. A party can become a major party only if it attracts many strong and effective candidates. Rohde's analysis of House members' decisions about running for reelection of for higher office can meaningfully be studied independent of the actions of others.[12] The choice of party cannot be studied as an independent decision, but only as one depending on the choices of many others (see chap. 2).[13]

Suppose for the moment that potential candidates are assumed to be motivated by the desire for holding office per se, and for no other end or use of office (as in, e.g., Downs 1957). This allows us to trace out the implications of careerism by itself. In accounts such as Rohde's of the choice of which office to seek, the value of the office varies by its position in the "opportunity structure" (to use Schlesinger's term); that is, higher office is preferred to lower office. The decision to run for higher office therefore trades off this positive attraction against the higher costs, higher risks, and lower likelihood of success in running for it compared with running for reelection to the currently held office. By holding office constant and examining party choice, the value of holding that office as a member of one party or another is a matter of indifference to this pure office seeker. All that matter are differences in costs, risks, and probabilities of success in seeking office as a member of one party or another. The differential costs of running for office under one party banner or the other may be ignored here, since the office is the same and since any increase in costs for either party may be assumed to be due to lower probabilities of success or higher risks. In other words, the only consequential variable affecting the choice is the probability of winning as a member of one party or the other. The ambitious politician would choose to run for office in whichever party offers the most probable access to office.[14]

The conclusion above holds for ambitious politicians who place no value on policy or other nonpersonal uses of the office they seek. Suppose, then, that politicians value both holding office and policy. Policy enters the picture in two ways.[15] First, a candidate may value running for office on an attractive platform regardless of its effect on his or her chances of victory. The candidate may desire to "send a message" to the government or to the people, for example. In this case, policy advocacy yields a direct value to the candidate for choosing one party over others, regardless of outcome.

The more important effect of policy is for the politician who may prefer to hold office as a member of a party that is, or could reasonably hope to become, one of the two major parties, and thus play a critical role in shaping legislation. Thus an abolitionist politician would presumably have preferred the Free Soil to the Republican platform, but he might prefer election as a Republican rather than a Free Soiler if he believed the Republicans had a better chance of becoming a major party and therefore were more likely to enact an antislavery policy, even if weaker than ideally desired. Charles Sumner (Mass.), for instance, was an outspoken Free Soiler who switched to the Republican Party early on.

In this second case, the value of policy is affected both by the probability of winning office and by the probability of enacting that policy when in office. This case means that a candidate might choose to run in a party that is more costly or risky or that provides a less likely avenue to office, depending on the probabilities of electoral success for himself *and* for others in the party. The ambitious yet policy-motivated candidate, that is, weighs the probability of success only modestly less than the purely office-seeking candidate in choosing party affiliation.[16] Note, however, that the desire to affiliate with a major party in order to have a more significant chance to affect policy decisions also means that such a candidate's decision swings on other candidates' probabilities of winning as well as his own.

In either case, the choice of party depends more or less heavily on the probability of winning office. If the aspirant runs at all, it is as a member of the party offering the most likely access to office. This conclusion helps undergird the power of major-party status, for access to office is ordinarily much higher as a member of a major party than in any third party. This effect is what gives Duverger's Law such force for the existence of exactly two major and lasting parties in plurality or majority rule electoral systems (see Riker 1982b). In a competitive two-party system, such as that of the second party system, the strength of the Democratic and Whig Parties and the party system they formed was due to the reasonably probable access to office that either party offered the ambitious politician. The relatively broad range of policy stances within each major party made ambitious careerists with policy motivations comfortable within these two parties.

The exception was, of course, the slavery issue. Southerners likely were fairly content, since the status quo was about as proslavery as could be plausibly imagined. Antislavery advocates, however, could reasonably be quite frustrated with the at best glacial change in the status quo, especially since slave states constituted a minority of the population. The Liberty and Free Soil parties reflected that dissatisfaction.[17] With few exceptions, however, ambitious politicians could not expect to hold long and successful careers in anything but the Democratic or Whig Party. There was nothing that individual antislavery advocates could do to alter the power of the two-party system in the 1840s for maintaining the duopoly that the Democratic and Whig Parties formed over access to office and that they wielded in keeping the slavery issue from resolution.

The 1850s changed this situation in two ways, one amenable to a standard individual decision-making model, the other requiring analysis through strategic interaction. The first of these changes was the decline in electoral success of the Whig Party about 1852, coupled with the general expectation that the decline would continue (see, e.g., Gienapp 1986; Mayer 1967). Such a decline would make running as a Whig less and less attractive for an ambitious politician even if he was also concerned about policy. If the decline continued, it would inevitably reach a point where access to office as a Whig would become so improbable as to undermine the Whigs' standing as a major party. Perhaps in a way similar to the decline of the Federalist Party in national politics, ambitious politicians would perforce choose to go elsewhere.[18]

In a purely two-party system, a declining probability of election as a Whig (or in any major party) is accompanied by an increasing probability of election for the other major party. This decline, therefore, could represent just another of the ebbs and flows in relative attractiveness of the two parties. If a short-term ebb, it might represent little more than, say, 1840, in which an apparently unpopular incumbent, Van Buren, challenged by a popular war hero, William Henry Harrison, brought the Whigs to unified control of the national government for the first time, only to see it lost shortly thereafter. Realignments, however, are often associated with a new line of cleavage dividing the two parties, and with the ability of one party to capture the more popular side of this new cleavage. In and after 1852, neither happened. Neither party shifted along a new line of cleavage. The Whigs, with declining prospects, struggled to maintain compromise on the slavery issue, because losing a significant additional bloc of support, whether North or South, would likely destroy the party. The Democrats, in part because of the complex set of institutional arrangements woven to maintain the intersectional alliance, were unable to change.[19] Thus the traditional economic issue, even if of decreasing relevance, remained the line of partisan cleavage, and thus the declining success of the Whigs was matched by increasing probability of election as a Democrat only in the narrowest definitional sense. It was not the case that the Democrats rode a wave of increasing popularity, nor did they attract great support from erstwhile Whig supporters backing bold new majority-preferred alternatives.

Instead, the declining attractiveness of the Whigs was matched by agitation for a new party, based on new policies, breaking up the competition between two intersectional alliances. With an expanding majority in the North (and status quo policies reflecting the influence of southern minorities), such agitation was concentrated there. It was unclear, however, whether a new majority, even if based in the North, would be predicated on the slavery issue or on what the new political historians call the "ethnocultural issue." In the 1850s the most salient ethnocultural issue was nativism. A party based on antislavery would have to be primarily, if not exclusively, northern. A nativist party might be primarily northern (and likely based on the great cities of the Northeast), but it could reasonably imagine attracting considerable support south of the Mason-Dixon Line. Indeed, by 1855 the nativist American Party was competing broadly and fairly successfully throughout the South as well as in the Northeast.

Central to this account is the declining success of the Whig party. We have seen this in terms of the "bottom line"—electoral results. But why was it that the Whigs were unable to adjust to changing circumstances and survive as a major party? The answer lies not so much in elections as in substantive politics.

THE DECLINING SUCCESS OF THE WHIG PARTY

In 1848 the Whigs won the presidency for the second and last time. They ran their second war hero, Taylor, and as with their selection of William Henry Harrison in 1840, they chose not to adopt a platform.[20] A later meeting ratified a series of resolutions, but even these failed to address issues. Taylor won a relatively close race, 47 percent to 42 percent, from Democrat Lewis Cass, with Van Buren acquiring 10 percent of the vote as a Free Soiler. Taylor's death made Fillmore the president, and with his assistance the Compromise of 1850 was effected. Although southern Whigs were grateful, the northern wing was less so. As a result, there was the irony of southern support for this New York native in the 1852 convention whereas northerners generally supported his major opponent and the eventual nominee, Winfield Scott of Virginia.[21]

Scott represented a third Whig effort to elect a war hero. The two previous ones had been unaccompanied by a platform, but Scott was burdened with only the second one in the party's history. This platform supported the Compromise of 1850 and the principle of limited powers for the national government, as well as increased tariffs and avoidance of international alliances. Thus it differed little from that of the Democrats (differences were greatest on internal improvements) and, if anything, leaned southward in outlook, reflected by dissenting votes coming from the North. Scott was supported by northern Whigs in part because of his ambivalence about the Compromise and in part owing to his support from strong antislavers, especially Seward. He could have repudiated or, perhaps better, ignored the platform. What that might cost him in the South might be made up in the North, especially since John P. Hale, the Free Soil nominee, was likely to do much less well than Van Buren did in 1848.[22] Instead Scott endorsed the platform, thereby attempting to hold the increasingly divided Whig coalition together. As Gienapp argues (1986), Scott might also have decided to adopt nativism and related positions on the ethnocultural issues, but here too he sent mixed signals at best and wooed Catholic and immigrant votes that often went Democratic. Thus Scott did not develop a clear alternative to the Democrats on policy.

More generally, the Whig party all but lacked national issues. The Compromise of 1850 and its fugitive slave bill had the effect of driving a larger wedge between North and South in the Whigs than in the Democratic Party. The Kansas-Nebraska bill in 1854 rendered the Compromise and tenuous intra-Whig compromise ineffective, and with that bill Douglas and the Democrats had taken the initiative. Opposing the Kansas-Nebraska Act would lose southern support. Taking a more proslavery position than Nebraska Democrats would lose the Whigs the North. Adopting the Democrats' position per se was chosen but made the party appear to lack conviction. And no one had any other ideas for policies that would find favor in both North and South. Clay was now dead (so too were Webster and Taylor—that is, much of the party's talented and famous leadership). Thus the slavery issue presented the Whigs with no positive options at all.

As Gienapp makes clear, Scott was not the creative, dynamic politician who could solve this dilemma in 1852 (nor would Fillmore be in 1856). His loss called the Whigs' "politically ambiguous war hero for president" strategy into serious question and left the Whigs in disarray. They were in disarray not just because they lost the elections, but because they had no electoral issues and, with that, no strategy for winning support nationwide. Riker concludes that the 1852 "election revealed to Whigs that they could not win as an intersectional alliance on conventional economic issues" (1982a, 228).

Although Whigs continued to differ from Democrats on these traditional economic issues, these concerns receded in salience in the period 1850–54. Slavery issues, nativism, and temperance rose to the top of the political agenda. The new issues were fundamentally sectional, and with their rise in salience, maintaining strong appeal to both North and South was increasingly problematic. Both Whigs and Democrats were wedded to their intersectional alignments, but the Democrats had the twin advantages of unified control of government and, by 1855, of having passed the first major bill about slavery that was not a bipartisan compromise. The Democrats had taken the initiative, and their attempts to maintain their intersectional alliance were therefore more effective, especially as it was reinforced by intraparty institutional design.

Even the economic line of cleavage was shifting to a more sectional basis. Migration had of course been primarily from east to west, and so the newly settled states tended to have populations drawn from those to their east. Heretofore transportation had been primarily by water, and the Mississippi River moved goods in a north–south direction. The newly developing railroads, however, promised to redefine transportation and the economy generally. Transcontinental railroads were to go predominantly east–west, and there was likely to be only one such line for some time. Competition ensued to see if that first line would be to the north (e.g., through Chicago) or the south (e.g., through New Orleans, with a line going through Saint Louis a potential "compromise"). Douglas, for his part, was concerned to have the railroad go through his home state of Illinois, tying it and the states of the Northwest to the populous cities in the Northeast with their rich markets and ports. As a result, economic concerns promised to reinforce the family, social, and eventually political ties of the Northwest with the Northeast. Industrial growth and expansion of transportation provided a new set of benefit seekers with the resources to play significant roles in party politics, especially Democratic and Republican (for more details, see Ferguson 1983; Weingast 1991). It was no more economic than political or social coincidence that the Republican Party, seeking to forge a northern majority, adopted the slogan, "Free Land, Free Labor, Free Men."

The inability to reach a position on slavery and increasingly related issues was bad enough in 1852. By 1854 it was a disaster. The Compromise of 1850 was Clay's last great pacification, and it was a bipartisan effort forged with Douglas. The Kansas-Nebraska Act, however, was Democratic, and it was the first major intersectional compromise on slavery that was not a bipartisan effort. The main point of the act was the principle of popular sovereignty of residents of new territories in deciding whether their area would be free or slave.[23]

As a partisan issue, it drove a deeper wedge into the Whigs than the Democrats. The act was understood to be more pro- than antislavery, thereby being acceptable to many southerners in both parties. The act did cost the Democrats support in the North, even though led into law by northerner Douglas. At the elite level, some anti-Nebraska Democrats ran under that title while some defected from the party entirely. Douglas was able, however, to keep most within the party. Although the act tilted the Democrats somewhat more southerly, its essentially compromise nature permitted the party to remain viable nationwide.

Southern Whigs supported the act. Northern Whigs were faced with either supporting it, and effectively turning the issue and leadership over to Douglas and the Democrats, or opposing it. Unlike the Democrats, the appeal to anti-Nebraska Whigs to swallow hard and stick with Douglas in the name of party unity was not viable. Public opposition to Nebraska, such as by Seward and others who were genuinely antislavery, pushed northern from southern Whigs, whereas Douglas and others worked hard to reduce such distance in the Democratic Party. This wedge was reinforced by the general lack of other issues around which to rally Whigs, in office or in the electorate.

With traditional economic issues and compromise on slavery out, the Whigs' intersectional alliance was in jeopardy. Only two broad issues were available to organize opposition to the Democrats. One was slavery; the other was the complex of ethnocultural issues, especially nativism. Nativism was of course a broad issue, in the sense that it related a large number of specific policy proposals under the banner of reducing the political impact of new, especially Catholic, immigrants. The slavery issue was broad in two senses. First, slavery was deeply embedded in the entire social-economic-political structure of the South. Second, it too tied together differing policies. Of special relevance were economic issues and the nature of western settlement.

Third parties developed around each issue—Free Soilers on slavery in the 1840s and Know-Nothings on nativism in 1853. A national party based on nativism had a major problem, however. The policy manifestations of nativism, as on temperance, were state and local, not national.

Registry laws, for example, were essentially early forms of voter registration. Although they had a good-government component for reduction of voter fraud, they were primarily anti-immigrant. Generally, registry proposals included a waiting period—as long as twenty-one years—before naturalized citizens could vote and were therefore not particularly subtle appeals to nativist sentiment. But registry laws were matters for state or local action, not national legislation. Slavery was primarily a matter for national action, whether an interstate fugitive slave law, regulating slavery in Washington, D.C., or matters of territorial governance or statehood. Thus, without national policies to propose, it would be difficult to use nativism as a major principle for organizing a truly national political party.

Slavery would, of course, create a sectional party, so it ran against the principles of a party—and two-party system—entirely built on intersectional appeal. Nativism had some intersectional appeal, but its strongest "bite" could be expected to be where immigrants were most numerous, the Northeast. Silbey (1985) argues for the difficulty of extending the appeal of nativism to the South, at least in its most virulent forms, because it was seen to be, he argues, a puritanical extension of the government into private matters, especially if it were to be accomplished at the national level and thereby also undermine states' rights principles. To be sure, Silbey is arguing about the later 1850s, when nativism was a Republican concern and thereby intermixed with slavery. Even so, the argument demonstrates the difficulty of centering a national party on the issue. In effect, then, if national development and other traditional economic issues were no longer an effective unifying force, the only ones left were those with more (slavery) or less (nativism) sectional basis. At least those seeking to defeat Democrats for office would be forced to choose a side on one or more sectional issues, and that would require a base in the more numerous section.

All of this is to argue that after 1852 it is very likely that the probability of winning as a Whig had been declining—and could reasonably be seen as likely to continue to decline. It may have lessened enough in some areas that it was rational for a lone individual to run in some other party. More certainly, it would have declined enough to make the question of party affiliation one of active choice, and perhaps one on which collective action could be taken.

THE EMERGENCE OF THE REPUBLICAN PARTY

By 1854 the declining success and prospects for revival of the Whig Party made it rational for ambitious politicians, whether currently affiliated with the Whig or Democratic Party or newly entering (or returning to) politics, to make party affiliation a matter of considered choice. But which party should they choose? The trade-off was between policy and ambition. The ambition question was which party, besides the Democrats, offered the highest prospects for a long and successful career, while the policy question, especially for those who sought to change actual policies in government, was partially similar. Which, that is, had the best chance of becoming a major party?[24] The answer to this question turned on two more. The first was a "local" consideration: which party's platform was most attractive to the particular constituency targeted? At the extreme, even if a southerner were antislavery, joining such a party would court electoral disaster. More realistically, in the North, anti-Nebraska sentiment appeared stronger in the western states, while nativism appeared more promising in the eastern ones. Thus such appeals, variable across the North, could serve as a basis for a particular politician's winning a particular election.

The second question concerns strategic interaction: Which party— Whig, Republican, or American—offered the best prospects for major-party status? This depended not just on "local" considerations, such as what the politician personally valued and what the prospective constituency desired, but also on what other ambitious politicians chose to do. No matter how plausible a case there was for the ascendancy of a party, it could not achieve that promise unless it attracted a large number of other attractive, ambitious politicians.

Let us suppose, more simply than was the actual case, that the choice for non-Democrats in the Northwest was between the Whig and Republican Parties. For the pure office seeker, all that mattered was which party offered the higher probability of success. With declining Whig and rising Republican prospects, these probabilities would cross at some point, and the Republican Party would be the more attractive option. Add policy motivations, and all that changes is that the switch in relative attractiveness of the two parties would come sooner for an antislavery politician. But though Whig prospects were observably declining, Republican prospects were only latent until politicians translated that potential into reality. That is, a potential "tipping point," altering some (maybe many) politicians' preferred choice of party from Whig to Republican, had to be made actual, and that required the coordinated actions of many ambitious politicians.[25]

These "local" and strategic problems were closely related in the 1850s. In today's era of candidate-centered elections, it might seem that individual candidates could choose their party in isolation from the decisions of other politicians, such as in the case of Bernard Sanders

(VT), who was elected to the United States House and Senate as an independent based on purely "local" conditions. Three forces weighed against this independence in the 1850s. First, the principle that the party was more important than the men in it not only discouraged such individual initiatives except in the extreme, but also meant that the public tended to view votes more in terms of party than of candidate. Second, this principle was reinforced by partisan institutions at the elite level (including those described above and more), but it was also institutionally supported in the electorate. The two most obvious examples were the absence of secret voting and the use of party-strip ballots, making party monitoring of voter choice easier and split-ticket voting more difficult. The result of these devices and others was that party voting was commonplace in this period. Coordinated choice of party was all but mandatory for candidates. The third reason, still applicable today, is that ambition for a political career requires affiliation with one or the other major party. Long careers as third-party candidates not only are extremely rare but even, in a case such as Sanders's, greatly reduce the impact politicians can have in office. If anything, this pull is even stronger for an ambitious politician concerned about effecting policy outcomes, for that is possible only with the support of many others and thus only with the support of one or both of the major parties.

In the following sections, I make these arguments and provide supporting evidence. First I show that the Republican ascendancy differed significantly in the Northwest (and Maine) and the Northeast. In the Northwest, or what I call the "strong" Republican states, the party appeared first at the congressional level, competed broadly in that region in 1854–55, and won a great number of those offices that midlevel career politicians sought. These ambitious politicians coordinated their actions and succeeded, often before the more famous leaders from that section moved to the GOP. The higher salience of antislavery than nativist sentiment made this rapid transformation relatively straightforward, in many individuals' direct self-interest, and not requiring significant leadership from "above" to achieve. It was also encouraged because the American Party did not develop significantly in that region, and the decision problem for ambitious politicians was therefore simpler: choosing whether to be a Whig or a Republican. Finally, the Whig party had been weaker and was hurt worse in 1852 in that region than in the Northeast or the "weak" Republican states.

In the Northeast, the Whig Party was stronger in the early 1850s and therefore remained a plausibly viable major party longer. With new immigrants more concentrated in this region, nativism was also a stronger force, and free land was a less immediately consequential concern than in the Northwest. As a result the Whig Party declined less precipitously in 1854, the Republican Party ascended less rapidly, and the American Party was a strong (and in 1854–55, stronger) third party. With intersectional alliance possible through the Whig or the American Party, and with a Northeast–Northwest alliance possible through the Republican party, the choice of party affiliation was far more complicated for midlevel ambitious politicians in the Northeast than in the Northwest (a choice further complicated by the secrecy of association of the American Party with the Democrat, Whig, and Republican Parties). Not only did few midlevel politicians break with their old party in 1854–55 in this region, therefore, but it also took active leadership of higher level politicians to effect significant party conversions and to create what would in time prove to be a viable Republican Party in the Northeast.

Republican Successes in the Northwest in 1854–55

Midlevel ambitious politicians succeeded in coordinating their actions in Maine and seven northwestern states.[26] Whether the GOP was born in Ripon, Wisconsin, or in Jackson, Michigan, is debatable precisely because ambitious antislavery politicians in these states independently called conventions. Two points about these conventions are significant here. First, the Republican Party was born in 1854 because of the actions of candidates ambitious for "midlevel" positions, such as United States House and state offices. It was not led by most of the major figures who had achieved national prominence or soon would. The Republican Party therefore differed from its major-party predecessors, which were initiated for the purpose of contesting for the presidency. The GOP, by contrast, began and won its initial national impact in the House. Second, even these initial converts moved with caution. They were not typically abolitionists, and they ordinarily tried to limit the influence of abolitionism and abolitionists within this new party. Moreover, as late as 1860 even the call to national convention avoided calling it "the Republican Party," or giving it any name.[27]

The dramatic success of their venture in the eight "strong Republican" states in 1854 can be seen in tables 5.2 and 5.3. In these states Republicans contested for every available House seat and governorship. They routed their Democratic competitors, winning over 80 percent of the House races with an astoundingly high 57 percent of the vote, and winning five of the six gubernatorial contests held in these states in 1854 and 1855. Moreover, the Whig Party all but disappeared from the scene. Only one Whig ran for the House in the northwestern states, and two did so in Maine. All three were soundly defeated. Three Whigs ran for governor (two in Maine's annual elections), but they fared even

Table 5.2 Republican Strength in Eight Northern States: Congressional
Elections, 1854

	Ill.[a]	Ind.	Iowa	Maine[a]	Mich.	Ohio	Wis.	Total/Average
Districts (N)	9	11	2	6	4	21	3	56
Republican candidates (N)	9	11	2	6	4	21	3	56
Republican victories (N)	5	9	1	5	3	21	2	46
Average Republican vote (%)	52.2	54.1	51.4	56.7	53.3	61.4	55.5	56.7 (N = 56)
Whig candidates (N)	1	0	0	2	0	0	0	3
Whig vote (%)	19.8	—	—	26.3 & 18.9	—	—	—	21.7 (N = 3)

Source: Congressional Quarterly, *Guide to U.S. Elections* (1985).
[a]In the three races with Whigs, the Republican won two (Illinois, second district; Maine, third district).
In Maine, sixth district, the Republican came in second with 38.7 percent of the vote.

Table 5.3 Republican Strength in Eight Northern States: Gubernatorial
Elections, 1854–55

State	Percentage of vote for Republican	Victor	Percentage of vote for Whig
1854			
Iowa	52.4	Republican	—
Maine	49.5	Republican	15.5
Michigan	53.0	Republican	—
Average	51.6		15.5
1855			
Maine	46.6	Republican	9.6
Ohio	48.6	Republican	8.0
Wisconsin	49.9	Democrat	—
Average	48.4		8.8

Source: Congressional Quarterly, *Guide to U.S. Elections* (1985).

more poorly than did their House counterparts. With fifteen Republican senators in the new Congress, Republicans clearly had substantial
successes in state legislative races as well.

The Slower Emergence of the Republican Party in the Northeast

The transition from Whig to Republican as dominant party in the
Northwest and in Maine was rapid, effectively accomplished in 1854,
the very year of their founding in these states. This dramatic change
was not mirrored in the remaining nine states in the Northeast. There,
exactly zero Republicans appear in the report of congressional votes
(in *Congressional Quarterly*, 1985) in both 1854 and 1855. Only one

Republican contested for governor in these states in 1854, winning in New York with 33.4 percent of the vote. Two ran for governor in these states in 1855, with the victor an incumbent Whig running as a Whig-Republican. Conversely, the Whigs remained a viable electoral force in the Northeast in 1854. They fielded a nearly complete slate of congressional and gubernatorial candidates that year (seventy-six of seventy-nine, and six of seven, respectively) and won almost two-thirds of the congressional seats and three of the seven gubernatorial races.

Why was there such a stark difference between these two sets of states in 1854? The slavery issue was surely a major part of the story. Anti-Nebraska sentiment was stronger in the strong than in the weak Republican states, with its centrality declining, roughly speaking, with distance from Nebraska (except for Maine with its temperance issue), while the pull of nativism increased as the proportion of immigrants increased.[28]

Sentiment on slavery also interacted with ambition. If ambitious politicians weigh policy concerns and probabilities of success, we would expect the Whig Party to collapse first where its prospects were weakest and in greatest decline. The data reported in table 5.4 illustrate that that is precisely the case. By all measures—by congressional and gubernatorial voting and by the proportion of House, Senate, and gubernatorial elections won—the Whig Party was weaker in 1850–53 in the strong than in the weak Republican states. As the 1854 elections neared, for example, the Whigs held 29 percent of the congressional seats in strong Republican states, compared with 38 percent in the weak states, and they held barely 15 percent of senators and governors, compared with 29 and 37 percent, respectively. For an ambitious politician the Whig party was significantly less attractive in the states that went Republican in 1854.

In the Northeast, not only was antislavery sentiment less salient, but nativism was more so. Ambitious politicians in the Northeast could imagine an alternative basis for a new party, and the American Party served as that alternative. American Party candidates emerged in 1854 in two states, Massachusetts and New York, along with a single Native American Party candidate in Pennsylvania. In Massachusetts, Americanists ran in and won all eleven House races and the gubernatorial contest. In New York they won fifteen of the twenty-two congressional races they contested (out of a total of thirty-three seats), and the American Party candidate pulled a quarter of the gubernatorial vote.

The New York case, however, differed from other third-party efforts. The American party is also called "the Know-Nothing Party," because its candidates often refused to acknowledge the existence of the party

Table 5.4 Whig Party Strength in Strong and Weak Republican States, 1850–53

	Percentage Received by Whig Party		
	Strong Republican states	Weak Republican states	Strong/ weak state difference
House, 1850–51 elections			
Seats won	32.1	46.1	−14.0
Votes received[a]	42.9	48.6	−5.7
House, 1852–53 elections			
Seats won	28.6	37.9	−9.0
Votes received[b]	45.4	49.0	−3.6
Governor, 1850–53 elections			
Victories attained	15.4	37.0	−21.6
Votes received	44.5	49.3	−4.8
Senate seats, 1850–53			
Percentage held	15.4	29.4	−14.0

[a]Entry is percentage of two-party vote in the electorate.
[b]Entry is percentage of two-party vote in the electorate. After the 1852–53 elections cycle, the Whigs held 10 fewer House seats in the strong Republican states and 1 fewer House seat in the weak Republican states than they held after the 1850–51 elections cycle. Percentages reflect changes due to redistricting as well as to changing votes.

or their affiliation with it. This was particularly important in New York, where none of these candidates ran solely as Americanists. They ran as Whigs in thirteen districts and as Democrats in nine. Their nativist message, even with unrevealed partisan identity, appeared consequential, since Whig-American candidates fared better than did those Whigs who remained outside the American Party.

The 1855 elections. The 1854 elections were transitional in these northeastern states. Connecticut, New Hampshire, and Rhode Island held congressional elections in 1855. The Whig party had effectively disappeared from these states by then. A full slate of Americanists contested Democrats in these states, and they won all the available congressional seats. These three states held annual gubernatorial elections. In 1854, none were contested by American Party candidates, but the Whigs ran in all three states, winning in one and losing badly in the other two. In 1855 these contests were won by American party candidates, with purely Whig votes dropping to near zero. The closest the Whigs could come to claiming victory was in Rhode Island, where the incumbent Whig, William H. Hoppin, won reelection overwhelmingly, but as a Whig-American. In 1856 he ran and won as an American-Republican.

The 1856 elections. The Whig Party was effectively gone in these weak Republican states by 1856, leaving the field to Americanists or Republicans to challenge the Democratic Party. In the six states holding congressional elections in 1856, the American party fielded candidates for forty-eight of the seventy-nine available seats but won only one race, in Massachusetts, and averaged under one-quarter of the vote. Republicans contested fifty-five seats, winning thirty-eight of them, spread over four of these states. There were two attempts to solidify Democratic opposition, the Fusion Party in New Jersey and the Union Party in Pennsylvania. Unionists ran for twenty of the twenty-five seats in Pennsylvania and Fusionists for three of the five seats in New Jersey. They pulled a substantial amount of the vote (averaging 47 percent in Pennsylvania and 52 percent in New Jersey) but won only six seats in the former state and two in the latter. On the gubernatorial side, the situation was even more complicated in 1856. Republicans ran in Connecticut, New York, and Vermont, winning the last two contests. The American Party also fielded three candidates, in Connecticut (won by the Democrat), in New York, and in New Hampshire (won by Ralph Metcalf, the incumbent Americanist). Hoppin won reelection in Rhode Island, this time as an American-Republican; a Fremont-American candidate won in Massachusetts (and won reelection as a "pure" American Party candidate the next year); and the Fusion Party nominee won in New Jersey.

The 1857 elections. By 1857 this complex scene simplified. The Whig Party was gone, and the American Party was nearly so. It fielded only one congressional candidate, a Republican-American victor in Rhode Island, while "pure" Republicans contested for all eight of the other seats up for election, winning six of them. The Republicans contested in all seven of the gubernatorial contests in the Northeast in 1857, losing only two of them to Democrats. The American Party fielded only three candidates, averaging under 20 percent of the vote.

Coordinated choice and leadership. In the Northwest, the rapid transition to the GOP was due to three factors. First, the Whig party was already weaker there than in the Northeast. Second, anti-Nebraska sentiment was more salient, and nativism less relevant, for public and politician than in the weak Republican states. Finally, the partisan choice reflected the dominant policy choice, and the coordinated actions of midlevel, ambitious politicians made it possible for the Republican potential to be effectively realized, where coordination was encouraged by the relatively simple problem of sticking with an old, declining party or moving to the only new party that could reasonably be viewed as viable in the region.

The situation was more complicated in the Northeast. First, the Whig party was stronger, and in combination with its southern appeal, politicians could well reason that it had greater long-term potential as a major party. Second, policy concerns were more complicated, since nativism and slavery were both salient, and one could imagine seeking both short-term electoral gain and long-term national party viability based on either issue. Finally, the Republican and American parties were potential alternatives. Obviously the choice of one or the other would, if successful, lead to very different coalitional alliances.

Although the move toward the Republican Party in the Northwest required coordinated action of ambitious politicians, the coordination problem was even more severe in the Northeast. Even if an alternative to the Whig party was a necessity, as it clearly was in time, both issues, along with their associated parties, were potentially viable. Which alternative would emerge, therefore, would depend on active leadership. Coordination was simply more complex, and electoral successes for both new parties made the problem even more severe.

The emergence of high-level leaders differed significantly between the two sets of states, broadly consistent with the argument that the rise of the Republican Party in the strong Republican states was accomplished through the actions of midlevel ambitious politicians or, perhaps more accurately, through the coordinated efforts of the full set of concerned politicians at all levels, whereas in the weak Republican states the emergence of the Republican Party took more active leadership intervention from the outset. To examine this, table 5.5 reports evidence gathered on key Republican candidates. Assuming that gubernatorial and senatorial positions were sought by the most influential politicians in the state, "key" candidates were defined as the first Republican candidate and the first Republican victor for governor in each state, and the first selected as senators for either or both of a state's seats in the period 1854–58 who were either selected as, or soon converted to become, Republicans. Thus those who sought or obtained the most important offices as Republicans are considered the key figures in each state. This procedure yielded twenty-seven individuals meeting this definition (the full set of all who fulfill one or more of the criteria above), ten in the strong and seventeen in weak Republican states.[29]

The emergence of key Republican leaders in the strong Republican states. In the strong Republican states, the key Republicans were slower to emerge than were congressional candidates. After all, full congressional slates ran in all of these states in 1854. Only four out of ten of these key leaders were certain converts to Republicanism in 1854. Moreover, one of them (Lyman Trumbull of Illinois) was a Republican candidate

Table 5.5 Key Republican Candidates for Governor and Senator in Strong and Weak Republican States, 1854–58

Office	Year of candidacy						Previous party			In office[a]	
	1854	55	56	57	58	(60)	Democrat	Whig	Free Soil	Yes	No
Strong Republican states											
Governor	2	1	2	0	0	1	4	2	0	1	5
Senator	1	2	0	1	0	0	1	2	1	2	2
Total	3	3	2	1	0	1	5	4	1	3	7
Weak Republican states											
Governor	0	1	2	3	1	0	2	5	0	4	3
Senator	0	4	0	6	0	0	3	6	1	5	5
Total	0	5	2	9	1	0	5	11	1	9	8

Office	Position on slavery			Year of conversion					
	Anti	Pro	?	1854	1854/1855	1855	1856	1857	?
Strong Republican states									
Governor	4	0	2	3	0	1	2	0	0
Senator	3	1	0	1	1	0	0	1	1
Total	7	1	2	4	1	1	2	1	1
Weak Republican states									
Governor	2	0	5	0	0	1	4	0	2
Senator	6	1	3	0	2	3	2	0	3
Total	8	1	8	0	2	4	6	0	5

Note: See text for definition of "key candidate."
[a]In office at time of key candidacy.

for the House in 1854. Thus only three were candidates for higher office in that year. Two, Anson Morrill and William P. Fassenden, were from Maine, converting in August 1854. Morrill had earlier broken his allegiance with the Democratic Party, losing his bid for governor in 1853 as a "Wildcat." The remaining one was Kinsley S. Bingham, who was elected Michigan's governor. Counting Trumbull, the seven other key Republicans converted after the party and its congressional candidates had appeared—and proved electorally successful—in their states.[30] Several, such as Salmon Chase and Benjamin F. Wade of Ohio, became Republicans only after securing office.[31] The key Republicans appear typically to have followed their (usually successful) House candidates to the Republican side rather than leading them there, or even joining simultaneously with them.

The emergence of key Republican leaders in the weak Republican states. The key Republican candidates in weak Republican states differed in several important ways from their counterparts in the Northwest. Most important, at least among the twelve for whom their dates of conversion are known, their conversions and often their candidacies occurred during the initial emergence of the Republican Party in their states. For many the actual day of conversion is included even in brief biographical statements, indicating that it was considered a major event in their political careers. Thus it does appear that these important leaders were instrumental in forming the new party.

These key leaders were as likely to have been Democrats as Whigs in the strong Republican states. In the weak Republican states, twice as many had been Whigs as had been Democrats. In part owing to the stronger condition of the Whig Party, this also represents a measure of the relatively lesser importance of the slavery issue in the Northeast. Antislavery positions were critical ingredients in the switch for most of the key Republicans in the strong states. For half of these key leaders in the weak Republican states, their position on slavery was not sufficiently important to them for us to ascertain their public stance in the 1850s.

Most of the key leaders in the strong Republican states were out of office at the time their actions led them to be classified as "key." One of those who was in office was Trumbull, who was elected to the House as a Republican in 1854 (and had been out of office before then). The other two were the two Ohioans Chase and Wade. All the rest entered (or reentered) the electoral arena at this high level from outside politics. There was about an even split of officeholders to non-officeholders in the weak Republican states. As with Chase and Wade, most of these were relatively secure before their conversion. Hoppin (RI) and Stephen Royce (VT) were incumbent governors, and Henry Wilson (MA) and Seward (NY) had just been reselected to the Senate when they switched to the Republican Party. Sumner (MA) switched as an incumbent senator, not immediately after reselection. Solomon Foot (VT) also switched as an incumbent senator, but the timing of his conversion is uncertain. James Dixon (CT) was a state senator when he converted. Nathaniel P. Banks (MA) and Edwin D. Morgan (NY) were elected to the House as Republicans in 1856 before election as governor (in 1857 and 1858, respectively). One final illustration of the importance of these leaders to their states is that nine of them were elected to their first major political office in or before 1845, whereas only three of the key leaders in the strong Republican states were such senior figures. For at least six of these leaders, their conversion was from a secure office, but they were nonetheless converted as their state's Republican party was forming and often before it had any electoral impact rather than after it had already demonstrated electoral success, as was true of their peers in the Northwest.

These key leaders in the weak Republican states, therefore, appear to be key in the development of their state's party and in solving the problem of coordinating the actions of ambitious politicians in the nine northeastern states. If it is possible to characterize the dramatic shift from Whig to Republican Party in the Northwest by the interaction between the politics of the slavery issue with career motivations of ambitious politicians, the situation in the Northeast provides a major second chapter in the Republican Party's rise to major-party status. To become a major party, the Republican Party needed to become not just electorally competitive with, but stronger than, the Democratic party in the Northeast. Republicans could win nationally on an intrasectional basis only by carrying most of that section most of the time. Clearly this required defeating not just the Whigs but also the Know-Nothings in those states. The American Party appeal was based on nativism, and it was possible to win elections in the Northeast on that basis. Thus the Republican Party had to expand its appeal from its antislavery position to a broader basis. This took longest, perhaps, in critical New York State. As Silbey clearly showed (1985), to do so the Republicans had to admit some nativist impulse. Although Seward and boss Thurlow Weed fought against nativism, they finally agreed to compromise sufficiently to win support of a large enough portion of the nativism-motivated voters to undermine the appeal of the Know-Nothings. They broadened their appeal, that is, just enough to win, but no more. The Republican Party would run on a platform that combined nativism and antislavery, but it would be a platform that was antislavery first, led by antislavery men and not nativists or Americanists. The delicate strategy was to broaden just enough to win, and the struggle would not be won completely until the 1850s neared their end.

What happened in the local conditions of New York happened in the North more generally. The Republican Party and most of its leaders were antislavery in outlook, but not abolitionist. It was a northern party, and it was a policy focused in appeal, but it was not an ideological party. That is, it was not solely antislavery or extremist. It was led by ambitious politicians who desired to see it become a viable, major party and who acted to see that that was accomplished. From a core of antislavery sentiment, it expanded broadly enough to achieve major-party status. It drew primarily from former Democrats and Whigs as well as from a few Free Soilers and, eventually, from politicians who entered elective politics as Republicans. If it started in the Northwest as primarily antislavery, its second movement was to the Northeast as a more mixed and balanced party. Its third and final phase of expansion to major-party status was exemplified by Lincoln's cabinet. Prominent early converts to Republicanism from the Northwest in 1854 were rarely to be seen. In their place were representatives of leading political figures, many of whom entered the party only after it had achieved electoral success in their home states. It was a cabinet of the Sewards and Chases, rewarding key supporters of Lincoln, but also reflecting and accentuating its broad appeal among the regular leading politicians of the time. It was, that is, designed to reflect and extend the Republicans' appeal as a broad party, and to secure the broadest support possible in the North to fight the Civil War, but also to secure their position as the leading party of the North and as one of the two major political parties in the third party system. It thus rewarded men who had supported Lincoln, who were antislavery, and who were ambitious politicians.

PART THREE

THE NEW POLITICAL PARTY IN
CONTEMPORARY AMERICA

PROLOGUE

The subject of the next three chapters is the contemporary
party, a jump of about a century. Much that was interesting and important in partisan politics happened in the interim. Indeed, the "golden
age" of parties (also known from another perspective as the most corrupt of partisan eras) is generally located in the late nineteenth century. From these heights, political parties entered a long, slow period
of decline, according to the magisterial account of Burnham (1970).
This decline would have been continual except that, as he argues, it was
broken by a short but sharp revitalization of parties in the New Deal
era. Skipping from the Civil War to the Cold War misses two dramatic
changes that are generally agreed to be partisan realignments (see especially Sundquist 1983 and Brady 1988 for accounts), as well as the
transformation from a state of parties and the court to the administrative state (Skowronek 1982) and many other changes and events.

Why make such a dramatic jump? This book is not a complete narra-
tive of party history. The primary purpose of part 2 was to provide clear
instances to assess the plausibility of the theoretical issues developed
in chapter 2; and the 1790s, the Jacksonian Democratic Party, and the
transition from the Whigs to the Republicans as its major competitor in
the 1850s happened to do so nicely. But there are substantive reasons
permitting this jump as well. The dramatis personae of the Democratic
and Republican Parties were already on stage by the 1860s, and their
basic coalitional division of North versus South, though varying over
time, was not shattered until the contemporary era. Of even more importance, as part 3 will show, is that the basic structure of the modern
mass political party was reasonably well established by the 1860s, and

this form remained intact—until about 1960. I will argue in part 3 that the contemporary party is at base quite different from the form of Van Buren's mass party that it supplanted. It will take three chapters to develop these differences, explain why they developed in and out of the critical era of the 1960s, and show how one can understand this new form of political parties. Part 4, comprising the final chapter in the book, will develop the comparisons among party forms, trace the dynamics of partisan history, and root the contemporary party more firmly in the theory developed here. So let us fast-forward to the post–World War II period.

I begin in a seemingly odd place, the mass electorate—odd because of my claim that members of the public, as citizens, are not a part of the party. It is, in fact, their looking at the political party from outside that provides a convenient vantage point. Moreover, since they are the consumers, we will be able to consider what it is they might be offered for consumption. Finally, because they are the target of electoral activities, we will be able to build an account of one of the most important components of the party, the electoral campaign. Central here is the development of a new breed of benefit seekers, motivated more by policy concerns than by the selective incentives of jobs, contracts, and the like typical of the machine age. These observations will build an account of why interparty divergence and cleavages should be expected to be commonplace in the contemporary partisan era.

This account will focus on social choice theory, seeking to explain how parties serve to overcome the disequilibrium in majority voting in elections. It will show why parties provide some coherence amid this potential incoherence; indeed, they offer a coherence of partisan cleavages. The explanation will also depend on the collective action problem, especially the incentives for individual participation and for larger-scale mobilization of a new breed of party activists. These more policy-motivated activists serve as the electoral arm of the party organization, and we will see how they reinforce party cleavages.

Chapter 7 will carry the empirical observations, and especially the theory of campaigns and elections, into office. Here I will propose a theory of the party-in-government that in part depends on the theory of what I call the party-in-elections. What I hope will be striking about these two parts of the theory of contemporary parties is how very different this picture is from the political parties that a Hamilton or Jefferson, a Van Buren or Clay, or a Lincoln or Douglas would recognize. The theory of the contemporary party is a theory about a party facing a candidate-centered electoral arena, and that story is about the rise of a coherent party signal serving as a second basis, along with candidate and especially incumbent characteristics, shaping the voters' choices and its effects in changing from an individualized, incumbent-centered government to a partisan, polarized government.

This theory of the party-in-government is also based on the social choice problem and attendant instability of majority rule, in this case over policy choice in legislatures. The theory will also focus on the problem of collective action, specifically how to make it in someone's self-interest (in this case, that of legislative party leaders) to find what is in the collective interests of partisan affiliates—and to act on those shared interests. These two questions are compounded by the ambition problem, which is especially acute in today's electoral era when office seeking is candidate centered, that is, in which candidates are much more autonomous and individually responsible for their own fates today than before the 1960s. Careers are, today, candidate and office centered in contrast with their historically party-centered structure. Thus these first two chapters bring together all three of the theoretical problems, heretofore studied separately.

Chapter 8 will examine changes in the party-as-organization, demonstrating that these have been strengthened at all levels and that the national organizations have developed to the point where we can, for the first time since the Federalist-Jeffersonian era, call them truly *national* parties. I then analyze just how it was that the partisan world changed so dramatically, focusing especially on the critical period of the 1960s and its aftermath. I will argue that this was a critical period that in some ways resembled a partisan realignment but that was especially similar to the first partisan alignment in the 1790s and the first realignment in the 1830s, in which the structure, purpose, and principles of parties were originally created and then fundamentally altered. I will argue that this critical era led to a redefinition of the structure, purpose, and principles of parties nearly as fundamental as, and ending the reign of, Van Buren's modern mass party. This chapter, especially in conjunction with chapters 6 and 7, will emphasize how the problem of political ambition and the new possibilities for candidates to realize their own electoral goals have led, perhaps above all, to the new form of political party that emerged in the 1970s and 1980s.

Part 4 will draw the second and third parts together, united through the theory developed in chapter 2. A more general account of the dynamics of partisan history will be shown to extend across nearly the entirety of the history of the American Republic. The theory helps explain this dynamic, and the theory of conditional party government will be used to provide a theoretical explanation of the changing role of party in elections and in governance over the last sixty years. In this case the theoretical account is based on the new institutionalism that sees outcomes as the product of goal-seeking agents acting within an institutional context and under a specific set of historical conditions. But though institutions may help achieve desirable outcomes, the historical dynamic results from the actors' designing institutions to realize those outcomes. The partisan institutions they design are those that these actors, under competitive pressures challenging their ability to achieve their goals, create in light of theoretical problems made most acute by the particular historical context. That this dynamic is not only applicable to the last sixty years but is also nearly coterminous with United States history will also be shown to be less than coincidental, because political parties are, I argue, intricately intertwined with democratic politics in an extended republic. I conclude by comparing the fundamentally new form of the contemporary period with the forms that preceded it and by drawing the understanding of the new form, as for the older ones, from the theory of partisan politics in a republican democracy.

Even though the intention of this book is to develop and apply theoretical notions about political parties and democracy, it is true that the last section happens to draw cases from the first seventy years under the then-new Constitution, whereas the next section uses the theory to explain partisan politics over the most recent seventy or so years. This book is not, therefore, a history of partisan politics in the United States. Still, the next chapters will be more meaningful with a little historical context about the intervening seventy-plus years.

The first critical point is that 1860 saw the emergence of the two-party system featuring the Democrats and Republicans. The durability of the two-party system is not surprising. The durability of the two particular parties is more so. After all, the seventy preceding years were quite different in this regard. The durability of our current parties is, in part, testimony to the flexibility of form (which we will observe in some detail as it varies over the contemporary period) and thus to the endogenous nature of party organizations. It is no small feat to develop organizations able to structure politics that can withstand the buffeting of such events as a civil war and two world wars (inter alia), Reconstruction, industrialization, the emergence of the American empire, and two great economic crises (in the 1890s and the 1930s). Perhaps the Whig Party collapsed in part because it was seeking to hold together such great diversity of preferences within a common party. No matter how big the tent, keeping abolitionists such as Daniel Webster in coalition with proslavery "Fire-Eaters" such as John C. Calhoun was a herculean task that collapsed about the time that the public figure who was the closest thing to Hercules, Henry Clay, died. In any event, the internal North-South coalitions within each party ended, with sectionally based coalitions taking their place in 1860. While both parties draw from and can win contests in any state and region in the country these days, there remains a sectional basis, in continuity from the Civil War. While sectional bases remain, the flexibility of endogenous institutions can be seen in the nearly total reversal of state support from 1860 and 1900 to now, led by the South's change from a solid Democratic bastion to one with a Republican majority. But that reversal of public voting coalitions is part of the story yet to come.

Parties did not remain fixed in organizational form between 1860 and 1960. Still, a major theme of the next section is that, in 1960, the two parties were greatly weakened, but their organization remained consistent with the modern mass party form Van Buren brought to the nation. To be sure, that form held strongest in the late nineteenth and early twentieth century, when machine politics was at its peak. Starting even before the Progressive Era, reforms in government were designed to undermine the strength of party bosses. In part because immigration slowed and because, by the second generation, onetime immigrant families needed less of what party machines could deliver, those reforms eventually worked, such that Van Buren's party form, as revised over the decades, was ripe for replacement. That changing organizational form is also a story for the following chapters.

That leaves the party in government. Here, several different threads weave a somewhat more complex story. We might start with the coming of the secret, or Australian, ballot. Skowronek (1982) claimed that national politics at that time was dominated by the two parties (rather than, say, Congress or the presidency) and by the Supreme Court. For politicians, the path to a long, successful, and rewarding career was to become a "party man." That is, particularly at the national level, only a few elected politicians were career officeholders. Most of the rest looked to the opportunity structure of the party rather than the government to channel their ambition. The secret ballot was a first step in changing that. By the turn of the century, the House was a professionalized body (something that didn't happen in a majority of the states until well into the post–War II era). We were industrialized and becoming an empire. National politics became more important and thereby rewarding. At the same time, the South enacted its Jim Crow regime, reversing the gains of former slaves in Reconstruction. The South became all but a separate nation politically, economically, and socially. It would have scored low on most measures of democracy. Republicans could win majorities nationally at that time without the South, however, undermining any felt urgency to stop such changes. And when the Democrats did attain lasting majority status, it was in the depths of the Depression, when the dominant national issues of the day united southern and northern Democrat. Accommodating two such different polities helps explain the emergence of what came to be called the "textbook Congress" (Shepsle 1989) that lasted into the 1960s and even the 1970s and early 1980s.

It was only after the Depression and World War II that the contradictions in beliefs within North and South would emerge undeniably and shape partisan politics in the 1950s and 1960s. The Depression and War had a second effect, which was to accelerate the importance of national politics. Political parties as, in Key's words (1964), a "congeries" of state and local parties, increasingly fit oddly with national, professional politicians. Still, the centrality of parties as the gateway to elections remained throughout this period. While it is correct that a degree of autonomy for candidates was opened by the series of electoral reforms that began with the Australian ballot, a characteristic all but unimaginable before then, the degree of autonomy was nonetheless slight by today's standards. This period offered more a promise of things to come for many, even professional, politicians, although the number who could develop their own electoral following did increase. Still, it took technological and other changes, again especially those of the 1950s and 1960s, to realize that potential sufficiently to redefine party politics. It is thus the intersection of these various threads that define the changed territory of 1960 compared to 1860 and even to 1900, that make, as we will see, the era around 1960 unique, even odd, historically. And, it was in part a reaction to the forced attention to the nondemocratic nature of the South in the 1950s and 1960s that so dramatically changed the nature of parties and partisan democracy from then to today. With this context of parties-in-elections, parties-as-organizations, and parties-in-government from 1860 to 1960, let us then turn to pick up the story in detail.

6

PARTY ACTIVISTS AND
PARTISAN CLEAVAGES

Senator Barry M. Goldwater (AZ), in accepting the 1964 Republican presidential nomination, proclaimed that "moderation in the pursuit of liberty is no virtue, extremism in defense of justice is no vice." The author of *The Conscience of a Conservative* (1960), one of whose campaign slogans was, "In your heart, you know he's right," Goldwater championed a clear, if not avowedly extreme, policy stance in the election. The clarity of his message was heard by the electorate, with his landslide defeat suggesting that he was seen not just as right, but as too far right. But Goldwater not only ran on a far more conservative platform than his Democratic opponent, then president Lyndon B. Johnson; he also took a decidedly more conservative stance than his rivals for the Republican nomination, such as Governors Nelson A. Rockefeller (NY) and William W. Scranton (PA). For two decades Republican presidential nominations had been struggles between the conservative and moderate wings of the party. The consistent victories of moderates over conservatives were ridiculed from the right as "me-too-ism." To whatever the Democrats proposed, conservatives argued, the moderate Republicans responded with "me too." According to another of Goldwater's slogans, "A choice, not an echo," his was a triumph of choice over echo within the Republican Party.

The presidential contest of 1972 was strikingly similar to that of 1964, only with the parties reversed. Republican Richard M. Nixon was the popular incumbent preparing to seek nomination to another term, all but uncontested, much as LBJ had done in 1964. Democrats had gone down to defeat in 1968 under then vice president Hubert H. Humphrey, a moderate Democrat in the context of 1968, much as a Republican had gone to a narrow defeat in 1960 under then vice president Nixon, a relative moderate. Defeat of moderates strengthened the claims of more extreme elements in both parties. Senator George McGovern (SD) played the Democratic equivalent of Goldwater, defeating his moderate rivals for the 1972 nomination, proclaiming his fealty to more liberal causes and policies, and paying the price of a landslide defeat in the fall. Like Goldwater's convention eight years earlier, McGovern's convention humiliated the former center of power in the party. In 1964, conservative Republican delegates had boisterously booed Rockefeller off the stage. In 1972, liberal Democrats unseated the last vestige of the old Democratic machine politics, Mayor Richard J. Daley of Chicago, replacing his delegation with the more liberal William Singer delegation that included activists such as the Reverend Jesse Jackson Jr. And in both cases, the ideological heart of the parties came to define their image, for good or ill, in and to the public. Although the Democratic Party had long been more liberal than the Republican Party in its perceived image and in the actual stances of its leaders, both parties had been controlled more by their centers than by their ideologically committed wings, at least in presidential politics. After these conventions, the two parties would continue to be diverse and umbrella-like, but both would be more clearly seen and accurately described as ideologically distinctive, presenting the electorate in these and most subsequent presidential contests with a choice and not an echo.

In the period 1964–72, new forces captured their national conventions, with both parties becoming more extreme in their publicly and nationally expressed definition of their central goals and values. Although the identity of delegates to national party conventions may be quickly forgotten, and the platforms they enact may be just as quickly ignored by their nominees, they are significant indicators to the public about what the party stands for and values. The 1964 and 1972 nominations left little doubt that neither national party was centrist, but instead the two became seen as increasingly sharply distinguished on policy. In time, the public came to know this and acted and reacted accordingly.

The path to power in this republican democracy begins in the electorate. If political parties are primarily concerned with ensuring that their ambitious office seekers obtain power from the electorate, and if the ambitious officeholders depend on the electorate to continue to realize their ambitions, then the place to begin to understand contemporary partisan politics is in that electorate. V. O. Key Jr. convincingly argued that the political party must be understood in its three parts: the party-in-the-electorate, the party-in-government, and the party-as-organization

(1964). Of these three, he placed the party-in-the-electorate first. This chapter begins there, in the electorate, as well. After considering the various ways the most important indicator of the party-in-the-electorate—its partisan identifications—has been defined, I turn to the questions that begin this chapter: Why is it that the two parties are distinct on policy? Why is "me-too-ism" the exception rather than the rule? Unraveling the puzzle of why a party would turn, with some consistency, to leadership that presents a "choice" rather than an "echo," in spite of the risk of massive landslide defeats when that choice is too clear, presents a view of the contemporary party, its activists, its campaign strategies, and eventually its officeholders that is very different from the view of the nineteenth-century party analyzed in the previous three chapters. The full revelation and understanding of those differences will take the next two chapters to complete, but it begins here, with the voters.

THE PARTY-IN-ELECTIONS

The first of Key's triad of party forms is the party-in-the-electorate. I begin by considering the various ways in which political scientists have come to understand this aspect of Key's party.

> Few factors are of greater importance for our national elections than the lasting attachments of tens of millions of Americans to one of the parties. These loyalties establish a basic division of electoral strength within which the competition of particular campaigns takes place. And they are an important factor in assuring the stability of the party system itself. . . . Most Americans have this sense of attachment with one party or the other. And for the individual who does, the strength and direction of party identification are facts of central importance in accounting for attitude and behavior. (Campbell et al. 1960, 121)

While there is little controversy over the centrality of party identification, there are considerable differences in theories that seek to explain how to understand party identification. Campbell et al. (1960) offered the first and likely still the most influential theory of partisanship. Defining party identification simply as "the individual's affective orientation to an important group-object in his environment" (121), Campbell et al. thus define the importance of party identification to the individual citizen, to campaigns and elections, and to the two-party system. Their theory of partisan identification is not a theory of voting per se. They see the vote as determined by more proximal and direct attitudes, their "components of an electoral decision" (Stokes, Campbell, and Miller 1958; Stokes 1966). One's party identification is not a direct voting determinant, but it is at once less directly tied to choice and yet more central to electoral behavior than those more proximate attitudes. Party identification is a lasting core value that shapes the more direct evaluations of the actions of parties in office, of the candidates on the campaign trail, and of the policies proposed by candidates and enacted by incumbents. It is, in this theory, by far the most important and commonly held long-term core value for most of the electorate. Party identification is typically acquired early and endures, for most, over one's lifetime. If not impermeable to change, it is, they argue, nearly so except under such extreme conditions as major changes in one's life circumstances or fundamental realignments of the parties. Finally, for most people party identification forms the key "structuring principle" or "lens" for viewing and understanding politics, especially partisan campaigns and elections. This view has long shaped the study of party and elections. It is not, however, the only view.

V. O. Key Jr. referred to partisanship as a "standing decision" (1966). By that he meant it is a durable guide for evaluating most candidates in most elections. Voters can reasonably assume that nominees will be typical of their parties in platform, views, and values. It is therefore a good first approximation for choice: partisans will back their party's nominee unless given good reason not to. Thus, for example, it is safe to assume initially that the Democrat is the more liberal and the Republican is the more conservative candidate unless there is evidence otherwise. Campaigns, of course, present information from and about the candidates. If attended to, such information might provide that good reason to decide otherwise. Until then, however, Key's version of party identification is a preliminary—and perhaps final—basis for choosing. Note how closely it accords with the more recent accounts of party reputation (see chap. 2). When a party's reputation is clear, it provides a focal point for the standing decision. It is, that is, a valuable signal about what the party stands for. And if that reputation or signal remains reasonably constant, the decision will typically stand still, as well.

Fiorina (1981) proposed thinking about party identification as a "running tally of retrospective evaluations" (89). To him party identification is simply the net memory of past political experiences: what good or bad outcomes one experienced under Democrats compared with experiences under Republicans. Socialization and initial experiences yield an early basis of party identification, a first tally. The accumulation of political experiences over the life cycle builds an ever larger reservoir for that tally. Although his theory is by design one that yields a malleable formulation, as the tally grows larger, for most people the chances of changing identification recede. Thus durability is also consistent with this view, provided that what the parties have accomplished and what the voter desires from government have been relatively constant, which is to say absent partisan realignment or major change in the voter's life circumstances. Achen (1989, 2002) has specified this view more precisely as a Bayesian model of party identification and voter choice. He is able to deduce from it many of the empirical regularities that flow from, and underpin the success of, the Campbell et al. conception, thus rendering this rational choice model empirically identical (at least in these areas) to the original social-psychological account.

Political psychologists have transferred ideas developed in the theory of social cognition to the political context. Lodge and Hamill (1986), for example, have used the concept of schemas to study partisan identification (on schemas, see Conover and Feldman 1984; Lau and Sears 1985). Such social-cognitive approaches have a primary focus on information processing, largely in the context of how schemas and the like help make complex information comprehensible and usable for decision making. It is of course a cognitive rather than an affective structure, differentiating it from the other social-psychological based theory of partisanship, that of Campbell et al.

All of the views discussed so far view party identification as a core concept, but view the party itself as a thing apart from the individual partisan. Campbell et al., for example, see the party as "an important group object in the environment," Key sees it as a basis for evaluating current choices, Fiorina as the basis for generating his running tally of experiences under the different parties, and Lodge and Hamill as seeing "meaningful distinctions between the policies that Republican and Democratic leaders prototypically espouse" (1986, 507). Thus parties are removed from the self, and thus we might better think of parties-in-elections instead of parties-in-the-electorate. Parties are, in these views, not *in* the electorate. Voters evaluate and choose from what the various parties offer them.

These may perhaps seem like rather emotionally cool accounts of partisanship. In this era of emotionally charged politics at the elite level, whether illustrated by candidates, officeholders, bloggers, or talk radio and cable news hosts, parties hardly seem to be "objects apart" or a purely cognitive set of appraisals. Identity, especially in its recent form of social identity theory developed by Tajfel, Turner, and others (see Huddy 2001), seems to capture the "blue/red" distinctions, "tea party" politics, and the like. If so, partisanship may be, at least for some voters, an emotionally charged identity rather than "merely" the result of a cognitive set of accountings.

Two important recent studies illustrate the contrast. One is the more cognitive. Erikson, MacKuen, and Stimson (2001, 2002) argue that, at least at the aggregate level, voters respond to information just as one might rationally expect. Thus, economic performances filter into choice (again, at least in the aggregate) as if voters were fully informed about and responsive to economic conditions. When partisan majorities in government move too far from the center, the electorate serves as a counterweight, pulling the government back to where most people are (perhaps only to see the government overshoot in the other direction, setting the public-as-counterweight back into operation). What this means for partisanship is that, in the electorate as a whole, partisanship responds to events as well, moving in favor of the incumbent party in good times, withdrawing support in bad times.

Green, Palmquist, and Schickler see it differently, calling their book *Partisan Hearts and Minds: Political Parties and the Social Identities of Voters* (2002; see also 2001). The stakes here are that, if their position is largely the story of partisanship, party identification would not be a "thing apart," but party would be "in" the electorate, rather than just "in" the small percentage of the most politically involved. And their explanation has firm roots in Campbell et al. (1960), as well. Their empirical work focuses mostly on stability of partisanship even in the face of changing conditions, and they provide impressive evidence of that stability.

These two more recent accounts engage primarily over this question of stability in the face of changing conditions. Each has brought considerable evidence to bear, with strong support thereby adduced for both positions. But stability is probably not the key question if one were to ask about the utility of social identity theory (as in Huddy 2001). First, all theories of partisanship yield an expectation of at least a considerable degree of stability. But secondly, the important question is whether emotional attachment is the source of that stability, or whether stability flows from the consistency of elite partisan actions, Democrats always on the left, Republicans on the right. At bottom, how emotionally deep are the ties?

Let us consider one example. After the Supreme Court decision in *Roe v. Wade* (1973) thrust abortion toward the top of the national political agenda, the two parties began what some call an "issue evolution" (Adams 1997) in which the Democrats moved from a somewhat pro-life position to a clear pro-choice position, and the Republicans did just the reverse. Adams argues that the partisan elites led the change, with the public responding to them. The decision also began the political mobilization of what came to be called the Christian fundamentalist movement. As a result, some partisans not only confronted ambivalence over policy, that is, positively held values that conflicted over abortion itself (e.g., Alvarez and Brehm 1995), but also with partisan ambivalence, that is, a conflict between their partisanship and their issue beliefs. Perhaps the greatest of that sort of ambivalence was among southern Democrats, many of whom were also members of fundamentalist Christian churches.

Layman and Carsey (2002) use panel studies of the electorate (1958–60, 1972–76, and 1992–96) to demonstrate that some people changed their party identifications to conform to their issue preferences (over a range of issues), but that others did the reverse, changing their issue preferences to align with their party elite's positioning. I will return to their argument about parties and what they call "conflict extension" later. Carsey and Layman (1999) further show that much the same is true for party activists, too, and this time looking specifically at abortion. They find, for example, that about a quarter of state-level convention delegates altered their position on abortion between 1984 and 1988 to align with their party's position, while one in ten completely changed sides on the issue (i.e., moved from pro-life to pro-choice or vice versa).

One source of partisan polarization, therefore, is this resolving of the ambivalence that Alvarez and Brehm (1995) studied. Whether the public (and elite) change their partisanship to be consistent with their policy views or change their issue beliefs to align with their partisanship, the result is an electorate that moves toward a more coherent (or at least consistent) combination of party and policy. This more balanced alignment is at least one piece of what we mean by a more polarized nation—no longer are there large numbers of those who are pro-choice and pro-life in the same party. Even if no one became more extreme on policy, they would more be more neatly sorted into opposing partisan camps. Note that the period of the 1950s, 1960s, and 1970s could therefore have been less polarized because the nation was filled with moderates, and thus not deeply committed to "blue" or to "red"; or the lack of polarization could have been due to ambivalence, that is, both parties containing those holding views on both sides of critical issues. Thus, in this era, southern Democrats might have held "blue" partisanship but "red" beliefs on abortion (and other issues, notably racial policies), while others were more likely to be "blue" on partisanship and on policy. The result was a "big tent" with many and diverse opinions. What we observe as polarization could have consisted primarily of sorting of the elites and then the public so that party and policy align, without (necessarily) anyone becoming more extreme. A viable alternative view is that polarization consisted of elites both sorting into more consistent groups and also becoming more extreme, leading the public to be more aware of any inconsistency between party and policy views and thus sort themselves toward more consistency to resolve that heightened ambivalence (see especially Levendusky 2009).

What are the distinctive characteristics of the party that might lead the public to develop a sense of partisan identification? They are, first, the goals and values of the party, and the directions, usually understood as policy directions, in which the parties want to take the nation. They are, second and perhaps most important, the candidates the parties offer to the voting public and their records—both in terms of where they stand on the policies, values, and goals of the party that may, collectively, be referred to as the party's "reputation" and the records of success or failure the party offers, most prominently as seen through the performance of their incumbent officeholders. The rest of this chapter focuses on these two, in particular on the differences between the two parties, their leaders, and their activists, seeking to understand why parties might be seen as offering distinctive choices or indistinct echoes of each other.

PERCEPTIONS AND REALITIES OF PARTY DIFFERENCES

George Wallace was fond of saying in his third-party presidential campaign of 1968 that there wasn't "a dime's worth of difference" between the Republicans and the Democrats. This sentiment was not unique to those outside the two major parties, as Wallace temporarily was. In that era, pundits regularly raised the charge of "Tweedledum and Tweedledee" parties. Scholars more typically emphasized that the two major parties were collections of many, diverse people and therefore encompassed broad ranges of opinion. Others, however, in effect echoed Wallace, arguing that the parties needed to moderate and seek the policy center, for in Willie Sutton fashion, a party has to go where the votes are. This argument flows formally from the "spatial model" of elections, initiated by Anthony Downs (1957), reinforced by Scammon and Wattenberg's (1971) claim that the Democrats had lost control of the policy center in the late 1960s.

The empirical fact is that the public's perceptions of the policy stances of the two parties in this period were never all that similar. Even so, from about 1952 to 1964, coinciding roughly with Converse's (1976) "steady state" period in partisan identification, there was a fair amount of "confusion" (to use Pomper's term [1972]) about the stances of the parties. This confusion waned, and indeed the public has perceived the parties as quite distinct since the 1980s. As we will see shortly, there is a good reason for this perceived clarity and distinctiveness of the two parties. The good reason is that the parties actually are distinct, and the public in the aggregate perceives that with reasonable accuracy.

Pomper (1972, 1975) analyzed National Election Studies (NES) data on this point over the period 1956–68. He found that beginning in 1964 there were substantial increases in the proportion of voters who saw differences between the two parties on a variety of public policy items. We can pick up the story in 1972, using data from seven-point scales of various issues and of liberal–conservative ideology as gathered in the NES surveys. Respondents were asked to place themselves, presidential candidates, and the two parties on these scales. The results are summarized in table 6.1, which reports the median placements of parties and nominees, and the average self-placement of the electorate on these scales in the various years.[1] These data, like Pomper's, rely on the proportion who actually placed the item on a scale. The data clearly show that the electorate as a whole typically perceives clear differences between the two parties. On the ideology scale, for example, the overall placements are nearly 2.5 points apart (about 42 percent of the maximum possible difference). Moreover, these differences have, if anything, increased from the 1970s to the 1980s and later. Although perceptions of party stances have been consistently distinct, perceptions of the stances of the candidates has been more variable, with the two candidates in 1976, for example, seen as noticeably more moderate than their two parties.

We can tie the two time periods together as in figure 6.1, which reports the proportion of the samples who responded positively to whether the respondents saw major differences between the two parties. In the 1960s there was an even balance between those who did and did not claim the two parties were different (as there was in 1952 [not included in the figure]). Beginning in 1980, however, the proportion that claimed they saw major differences climbed to about six in ten and then jumped again to about three in four in 2004 and 2008. Thus the public has seen differences between the policy stances of the two parties, and this perception of party differences has grown, especially recently, to truly significant levels.

Respondents who claimed to see differences between the two parties were also asked, from time to time, which party was more conservative. The proportion saying the Republicans were is also reported in figure 6.1, and this proportion parallels the increase in seeing differences very closely. In 2008, clarity of these perceptions reached a new height as over three quarters saw differences between the two parties

Table 6.1 Perceived Issue Positions of Parties and Candidates: Seven-Point Issue Scales, 1972–2008

Issue	Democratic activist	Democratic Party	Democratic candidate	Republican activist	Republican Party	Republican candidate	Self-placement
1972							
Jobs and standard of living	3.04	2.78	2.04	5.21	4.56	4.43	4.28
Aid to minorities	2.81	3.78	2.36	4.45	4.72	4.09	4.18
Busing	5.54	3.79	3.22	6.89	5.05	5.47	6.83
Vietnam War	1.80	2.49	1.27	4.36	4.40	4.51	3.74
Rights of accused	2.89	3.48	2.96	4.64	4.19	4.28	4.29
Taxation	3.24	3.01	2.46	4.01	4.44	4.31	3.83
Average	3.22	3.22	2.39	4.93	4.56	4.52	4.53
SD	1.13	0.50	0.63	0.95	0.27	0.45	1.05
1976							
Jobs and standard of living	3.66	2.74	3.15	5.22	4.52	4.45	4.45
Aid to minorities	3.65	2.91	3.17	4.45	4.15	3.91	4.23
Busing	6.64	3.44	3.93	6.77	4.18	3.98	6.78
Health insurance	2.95	2.77	2.94	6.01	4.80	4.51	4.02
Rights of accused	3.52	3.29	3.57	4.85	4.01	3.73	4.44
Taxation	3.20	3.36	3.38	4.62	4.51	4.42	4.09
Average	3.94	3.09	3.36	5.32	4.36	4.17	4.67
SD	1.24	0.29	0.32	0.82	0.27	0.30	0.96
1980							
USSR	3.67	2.91	2.42	3.63	4.56	4.75	3.93
Jobs and standard of living	3.73	2.93	3.22	5.64	4.93	4.89	4.43
Aid to minorities	3.88	2.93	3.10	4.98	4.95	4.97	4.46
Government spending/services	2.22	2.76	3.01	5.14	4.54	4.58	3.68
Defense spending	4.32	3.93	3.71	5.66	5.38	5.51	5.37
Inflation/unemployment	3.33	3.31	3.65	4.43	4.35	4.36	3.93
Tax cut	1.92	3.41	2.31	4.66	5.76	4.79	3.80
Equal rights for women	1.42	2.71	2.78	2.29	4.15	4.21	2.40
Average	3.06	3.11	3.03	4.55	4.83	4.76	4.00
SD	0.99	0.39	0.48	1.06	0.51	0.37	0.79
1984							
Jobs and standard of living	3.54	3.25	3.24	4.99	4.91	5.14	4.23
Aid to minorities	3.47	3.03	3.07	4.64	4.63	4.63	4.09
Government spending/services	3.24	2.94	2.87	4.87	5.07	5.41	3.97
Defense spending	3.10	3.39	3.32	4.57	5.48	5.96	4.05
USSR	3.30	3.41	3.32	4.58	4.89	5.22	4.16
Central America	2.95	3.48	3.53	4.11	5.08	5.51	3.24
Socioeconomic status of women	3.26	3.18	3.02	4.29	4.48	4.58	2.57
Average	3.27	3.24	3.20	4.58	4.93	5.21	3.76
SD	0.19	0.19	0.21	0.28	0.30	0.45	0.57

1988							
Jobs and standard of living	3.57	3.38	3.29	5.84	5.16	5.17	4.52
Aid to minorities	3.38	3.28	3.31	4.00	4.74	4.86	4.48
Government spending/services	3.30	3.01	2.70	5.02	4.46	4.52	3.89
Defense spending	2.97	3.70	3.23	4.39	5.34	5.35	4.00
USSR	3.13	3.59	3.42	4.94	3.94	4.11	3.78
Health insurance	2.92	3.18	2.96	5.61	5.26	5.14	3.90
Equal rights for women	1.38	3.10	2.73	2.43	3.87	3.78	1.92
Average	2.95	3.32	3.09	4.60	4.68	4.70	3.78
SD	0.68	0.24	0.27	1.07	0.57	0.55	0.81
1992							
Government spending/services	3.37	2.87	2.88	4.96	4.79	4.84	3.89
Defense spending	3.10	3.44	3.30	3.92	4.88	4.91	3.60
Guaranteed job/standard of living	3.76	3.26	3.44	5.13	4.34	5.29	4.36
Aid to blacks	3.97	n/a	n/a	5.14	n/a	n/a	4.60
Women's role	0.31	n/a	n/a	2.17	n/a	n/a	0.43
Average	2.90	3.19	3.21	4.26	4.67	5.01	3.38
SD	1.49	0.29	0.29	1.28	0.29	0.24	1.69
1996							
Government spending/services	3.57	2.91	3.04	5.47	4.97	4.90	4.09
Defense spending	3.64	3.83	3.97	4.48	4.80	4.73	4.04
Government health insurance	3.20	n/a	2.71	5.75	n/a	5.12	4.01
Guaranteed job/standard of living	3.77	3.37	3.27	5.86	n/a	5.12	4.55
Environment vs. jobs	3.17	n/a	3.44	4.08	4.68	4.47	3.56
Aid to blacks	4.22	n/a	3.30	5.83	n/a	4.94	4.83
Women's role	0.38	n/a	1.92	2.34	n/a	3.46	1.51
Average	3.14	3.37	3.09	4.83	4.82	4.68	4.18
SD	1.27	0.46	0.64	1.3	0.15	0.58	1.09
2000							
Government spending/services	2.86	2.76	2.83	4.41	4.61	4.44	3.59
Defense spending	4.45	3.99	4.11	5.42	5.00	5.07	4.73
Government health insurance	3.38	n/a	n/a	5.01	n/a	n/a	3.77
Guaranteed job/standard of living	3.89	3.39	3.58	5.94	5.09	4.91	4.79
Environment vs. jobs	3.60	n/a	3.25	3.86	n/a	4.67	3.77
Aid to blacks	4.13	3.26	3.47	5.60	4.96	4.73	4.77
Women's role	0.26	n/a	2.29	1.95	n/a	3.37	0.37
Average	3.22	3.35	3.26	4.60	4.92	4.53	3.68
SD	1.41	0.51	0.63	1.37	0.21	0.61	1.55
2004							
Government spending/services	2.76	n/a	n/a	4.22	n/a	n/a	3.49
Defense spending	4.14	n/a	3.63	5.40	n/a	5.95	4.66
Government health insurance	2.67	n/a	n/a	4.81	n/a	n/a	3.67
Guaranteed job/standard of living	3.22	n/a	3.14	5.69	n/a	5.37	4.29
Environment vs. jobs	3.06	n/a	4.13	4.30	n/a	4.23	3.67

Table 6.1 *continued*

Issue	Democratic activist	Democratic Party	Democratic candidate	Republican activist	Republican Party	Republican candidate	Self-placement
Aid to blacks	3.74	n/a	3.37	5.58	n/a	4.95	4.58
Women's role	0.28	n/a	2.62	1.66	n/a	3.85	0.34
Average	2.84		3.38	4.52		4.87	3.53
SD	1.24		0.56	1.39		0.85	1.48
2008							
Government spending/services	2.76	n/a	2.48	4.97	n/a	4.41	3.55
Defense spending	3.63	n/a	3.50	5.08	n/a	5.70	4.26
Government health insurance	2.38	n/a	2.61	5.57	n/a	5.41	3.63
Guaranteed job/standard of living	3.20	n/a	2.95	5.64	n/a	5.29	4.47
Environment vs. jobs	3.57	n/a	3.72	4.38	n/a	4.56	3.99
Aid to blacks	3.91	n/a	2.78	6.02	n/a	4.89	4.92
Women's role	0.21	n/a	2.16	0.27	n/a	2.99	0.27
Average	2.81		2.89	4.56		4.75	3.58
SD	1.26		0.56	1.97		0.90	1.54
Ideology							
1972	2.93	2.96	2.16	4.93	4.99	5.02	4.15
1976	3.62	2.75	3.08	5.33	5.16	5.11	4.21
1980	3.00	3.12	3.71	5.57	5.46	5.66	4.31
1984	3.51	3.14	3.29	5.64	5.29	5.58	4.23
1988	1.23	3.10	2.99	4.95	5.53	5.52	4.35
1992	3.30	2.96	3.04	5.30	5.53	5.48	4.23
1996	3.60	3.08	2.99	5.68	5.30	5.43	4.28
2000	3.38	2.55	2.50	5.74	5.59	5.56	4.20
2004	3.16	2.77	2.76	5.62	5.62	5.71	4.24
2008	2.81	2.61	2.54	5.75	5.54	5.43	4.24
Average	3.05	2.90	2.91	5.45	5.40	5.45	4.24
SD	0.70	0.22	0.44	0.31	0.21	0.22	0.06
Grand averages							
1972	3.22	3.22	2.39	4.93	4.56	4.52	4.53
1976	3.94	3.09	3.36	5.32	4.36	4.17	4.67
1980	2.97	3.10	3.11	4.69	4.72	4.70	4.00
1984	3.27	3.24	3.20	4.58	4.93	5.21	3.76
1988	2.95	3.32	3.09	4.60	4.68	4.70	3.78
1996	3.14	3.37	3.09	4.83	4.82	4.68	4.18
2000	3.22	3.35	3.26	4.60	4.92	4.53	3.68
2004	2.81	n/a	2.89	4.56	n/a	4.75	3.58
2008	2.81	2.61	2.54	5.75	5.54	5.43	4.24
Average	3.15	3.16	2.99	4.87	4.82	4.74	4.05
SD	0.34	0.25	0.33	0.41	0.35	0.37	0.38

Source: ANES surveys, compiled by author.

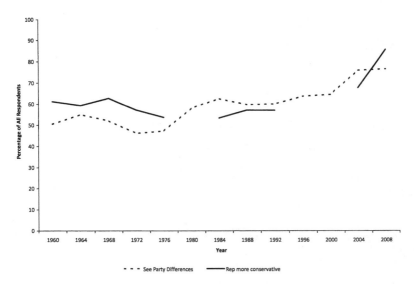

Figure 6.1. Perceptions of party differences by the electorate, 1960–2008.
Source: American National Election Studies (ANES) surveys, various years
(http://www.electionstudies.org/). Compiled by author.

with nearly nine in ten respondents seeing the Republicans as the more
conservative party. Not included in the figure are data showing that
the proportion not knowing which party was more conservative declined from one in five to about one in twelve since 1972. Thus, not
only is there a good case for clarity but also for accuracy of perception.
The parties have a much more widely perceived reputation currently
than they did a generation ago. How does this increase in ideological
reputations of the party affect partisanship? One way is in increasing
coherence of partisanship and ideology. The correlation between these
two variables (where ideology is measured by self-placement on the
seven-point liberal–conservative scale, used for the first time in 1972)
for each presidential election year is reported in figure 6.2. In the 1970s
and 1980s, that correlation was in the 0.3 to 0.4 range. In the realm of
correlations among political attitudes, that level is actually reasonably
robust. However, it is relatively low in comparison to the 1990s and
2000s. The correlation increased from 0.35 in 1992 to 0.50 in 1994
(not included in the figure), the year of the "Republican Revolution," in
which that party achieved majority status in the House for the first time
in forty years and selected Newt Gingrich (GA) as their Speaker. The
correlation stayed at that quite high level through 2008. The correspondence in people's minds between liberals and Democrats and between
conservatives and Republicans is now very strong by any standard.

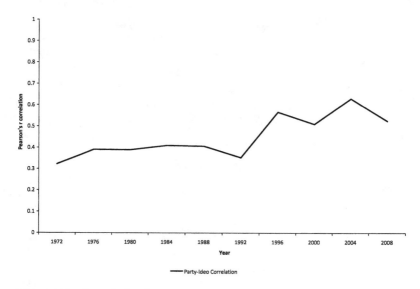

Figure 6.2. Correlation between party identification and ideology, 1972–2008.
Source: ANES surveys, various years (http://www.electionstudies.org/). Compiled by author.

Baumer and Gold (2010, especially 81, fig. 3.10) offer a similar conclusion. They look at the effect of party identification and ideology (as well as abortion and income) on presidential vote choice, simultaneously, from 1972 through 2008. Party identification has the largest marginal effect in every election, followed always by ideology. However, party identification had a much larger marginal effect, especially from 1980 through 2000. In 2004, the effect of ideology jumped dramatically, and by 2008, ideology and party identification had essentially the same (strong) effect on the vote, according to their analysis.

To this point, we have seen the emergence of a much clearer perception of the ideological reputations of the parties in minds of the public, and this greater clarity appears to explain the enhanced consistency in the public between their policy views and their partisanship. Partisanship also appears to be more closely tied to voting choices. The proportions of the public who vote in line with their partisanship for House and Senate are reported biannually in figure 6.3. The approximately eight in ten who did so in the 1950s declined over the 1960s and 1970s to about seven in ten in 1980, and then began a slow rebound to its original level in the 2000s. By 2008, the proportion voting along party lines reached new highs, if only slightly so. The similar quadrennial

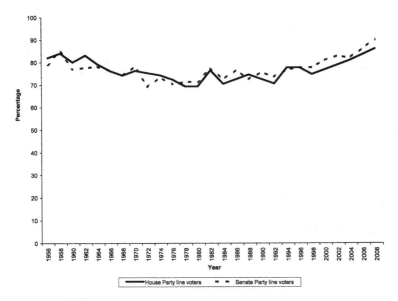

Figure 6.3. Party-line voting in House and Senate elections, 1956–2004. *Source:* ANES surveys, various years (http://www.electionstudies.org/). Compiled by author.

figure for presidential voting is reported in figure 6.4, with nearly identical results. In that figure, we also show the proportion who report voting a straight ticket for presidency and House, and this proportion also appears to follow a very similar pattern over time, with more than four in five voting for the same party for presidency and House in 2008.

Finally, this perception of party differences has a plausible basis for the public in terms of the actions taken by party elites. We have already seen that the public has seen differences in the policy stances of their standard-bearers, the presidential nominees, in most elections. Of course these may be perceptions of differential promises that go unfulfilled. Fishel (1985), however, has shown that presidents typically do try to fulfill their campaign promises, and that they succeed more often than not. Moreover, their success in Congress typically depends on their ability to maintain a substantial level of support from their partisans in both chambers. It is difficult to imagine health care reform legislation passing if John McCain were president instead of Barack Obama, and nearly impossible to imagine passing if Republicans had also won majorities in Congress.

The partisan basis of the presidential coalition in Congress will be examined more fully later. We will also see that party affiliation serves

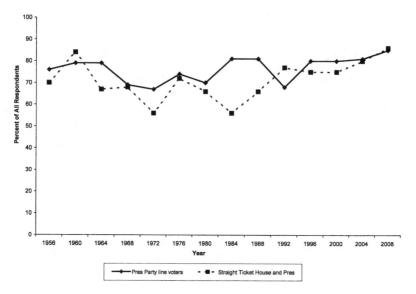

Figure 6.4. Straight-ticket and party-line voting in presidential elections, 1956–2008.
Source: ANES surveys, various years (http://www.electionstudies.org/). Compiled by author.

as the most common basis of voting coalitions in Congress and that throughout this era, party has always been a more common basis of voting alignments in Congress than its most common competitor, the "conservative coalition."[2] And beginning in the 1990s, there has been no competing basis for coalitions at all, as the incidence of the conservative coalition fell to near trace levels, whereas the frequency of party voting has increased substantially since then.

If, then, there are major differences between the parties, and the partisan gap has widened considerably over the past few decades, why are there such growing differences? The answer I propose is a theory of parties-in-elections that leads to the existence of party cleavages in equilibrium, and to incentives for candidates to diverge along those lines of cleavage in spite of the countervailing incentives to converge to the policy center for attracting mass popular support.

THE SPATIAL MODEL OF ELECTIONS AND THE POLICY MODERATION HYPOTHESIS

The theory of voting and its more general formulation, social choice theory, was discussed in chapter 2. One of many contributions by Anthony Downs (1957) was the development of the logic of the competition between two candidates for votes from the public.[3] In his theory candidates compete for votes by adopting positions on a single dimension, such as a left/right dimension (or in his case, a dimension indicating the degree of government involvement in the economy). Candidates are free to pick whatever position they like. Voters react by supporting that candidate who offers them the greater expected utility. Assuming that all have single-peaked preferences over that dimension, it follows that citizens prefer policy options, and therefore candidates, closer to themselves over those further away. In the literature on policy voting this is called "proximity" voting: one votes for the option more proximate to one's "ideal point." In two-candidate races, therefore, one votes, if at all, for the closer candidate.[4] Later work (e.g., Hinich and Ordeshook 1970; Ordeshook 1970; McKelvey 1975) examined the turnout decision. To the extent that the turnout decision rests on the positions advanced by the candidates (rather than on other factors such as the intrinsic costs and benefits of voting), one might abstain from spatial "indifference" (if the two candidates' platforms yield too small a difference in expected utility to outweigh the costs of voting) or from "alienation" (if the most preferred option offers too little to be worth supporting). For now what is important is that spatially related abstention typically has no effect on the location of optimal positions for the candidates.

With voters' choices now completely specified, the crucial question of electoral democracy becomes what positions rational candidates would adopt. As we saw in chapter 2, there are two answers. When there is an equilibrium position for a candidate, it is always to adopt the position of the median voter, provided candidates seek only to win the current election. In Downs's original unidimensional model, such a median voter always exists, and therefore so does a pair of equilibrium positions for the candidates.[5] And theorems that yield an equilibrium in multidimensional spaces hold only when there is a multivariate median.[6] The first answer is twofold: (1) Rational candidates will adopt the same policy position (convergence to each other);[7] and (2) the candidates will adopt a central or moderate policy position corresponding with the ideal preference of the median voter (that convergence is to the center of electoral opinion).

The second answer is that in multidimensional policy spaces there is generally no equilibrium at all. If there happens to be one, it will be as above, but the implication of Arrow's theorem in this spatial context (see chap. 2) is that there will rarely if ever be such an equilibrium. If anything can be said about the positions of candidates in the absence of equilibrium, however, it appears that they will tend to converge to the policy center (see, for example, Kramer 1977; McKelvey and Ordeshook 1976).

In spite of the Arrovian problem, many (e.g., Jackman 1986) conclude that spatial theory predicts policy moderation in two-candidate, and even multiparty, systems. This conclusion raises the "who governs" question (e.g., Garrett and Lange 1989): does it matter which party (or candidate) governs if all offer similar moderate policies?

It might be thought that the policy moderation implication follows because it is assumed that candidates care only about winning the election. Candidates claim—and sometimes act as though—they care about policy as well as about the election. Wittman (1983), for example, proved that if the two candidates care about policy, they will not converge. Calvert (1985) subsequently demonstrated, however, that though Wittman was correct, the candidates will diverge by only a very small amount. Thus it seems that the electorate imposes a very strong discipline on ambitious, office-seeking candidates, even those who also care about policy, pushing them toward the center. This pressure for moderation may even be a good thing for democracy, for as Schlesinger argues (1966), it is the desire to win election and reelection that harnesses ambitious politicians to the electorate, making them responsive to the public's concerns.

Moderation, moreover, is a good thing for the candidates. It yields them more votes in the general election. Wright (1994) reviews seven studies that document this moderation advantage. "For example," he writes (2), "in the U.S. Senate, running as a centrist rather than as a party ideologue (holding the position of the other candidates constant) appears to garner candidates between five and eight percent of the vote (Wright and Berkman 1986). For the general election, then, we have both strong theory and strong evidence for the rationality of candidate convergence."

As we saw earlier in this chapter, however, the public has consistently seen the presidential nominees of the two parties, and the two parties themselves, as far from offering convergent, centrist options. Instead they see party cleavages, with candidates and parties alike consistently seen as distinctly separated from each other and the policy center, and the evidence suggests that the actual behavior of elected officials is similarly distinct (as we will see in the next chapter). The challenge therefore is to develop a theory that accommodates the pressures toward moderation that electoral democracy induces and yet yields the consistent lines of partisan cleavages that the public perceives and the officeholders reveal.

PARTY ACTIVISTS AND THE SPATIAL MODEL

Schlesinger (1975, 1991) emphasized the importance of distinguishing the goals of a party's candidates from those of its activists. More precisely, he differentiated between office seekers and benefit seekers. The former are those whose motivation is holding office per se and who personally derive the benefits—power, prestige, and perquisites—that come from holding office. Benefit seekers derive their benefits indirectly from their party's control of political office, whether that is patronage, policy, or other rewards that a party's officeholders can bestow on their supporters.

Office seekers are motivated to win by the largest margin possible. Benefit seekers, though they want their candidate to win, of course, also prefer to be a critical component of the winner's coalition, therefore desiring very close victories. That way benefit seekers can most convincingly press their claims on the winner, arguing that their support was crucial to the victory so that the officeholder should reward them. The tension is in how constrained the victorious office seeker will be. With a substantial victory, officeholders are relatively free to use the perquisites of office as they see fit. With a narrow victory, they are more constrained to reward their faithful—and pivotal—supporters.

We can imagine two idealized types of benefit seekers. One type is motivated by patronage dispersed by successful office seekers—jobs, contracts, and the like, as in the old-style party machines. Patronage seekers care relatively little about the public policies the candidates campaign on in the election and that the incumbent seeks in office. Patronage seekers value only jobs or contracts. This benefit seeker sounds much like the cadre in the sort of party Van Buren created, in which loyalty toward party was rated above all else and platforms eschewed contemporary and controversial policies whenever possible (see chap. 4). The second type of benefit seeker is motivated by policy. Policy seekers hope to constrain the platforms candidates propose in elections and act on when in office.

James Q. Wilson (1962) described the rise in the 1950s of what he termed "amateur Democrats," distinguishing them from patronage-seeking, machine-type "professionals" whose jobs depended on the machine's continued hold on office. He called these policy-motivated activists "amateurs" because their political activities and policy concerns were not motivated by their jobs or, better said, their career goals were not dependent on officeholders. Later Wildavsky (1965) used the term "purists" to describe activists who demand that office seekers and holders stay as "pure" on policy as possible. Wildavsky used the term to describe the committed conservatives supporting Goldwater in 1964, but it also described the antiwar activists backing Eugene McCarthy or Robert Kennedy in 1968 and George McGovern in 1972. Indeed, as Goldwater's success brought the conservative purist to (near) dominance in the Republican Party, so too did McGovern's success bring the liberal purist to (near) dominance in the Democratic Party.

Not all campaign activists today are purists, but the proportion of those who might be called that has increased, most evidently in the two national party conventions.[8] Nor are purists insensitive to compromise, because even for them half a loaf may be better than none. But they may be more willing than professionals to lose now in the hopes of winning more of what they want in the future. Their jobs, unlike those of the ambitious office seeker and the party professional, are not on the line. Activists today may not always demand extreme purity, but they are more likely to have strong policy motivations rather than to be oriented toward winning elections just for the spoils of victory. The consequence is that office seekers and officeholders are more constrained on policy positions and actions to the extent that they depend on policy-motivated activists for access to office.

Machine activists might technically have been "volunteers" in a campaign, but their contribution of time, effort, and services was not truly voluntary, since their continued preferment depended on those efforts.[9] More to the point, they were expected to provide their services to the machine's candidates regardless of who they were or what they stood for.

Policy-motivated activists are typically under less pressure to support any particular candidate or party. Many are engaged in more nearly pure collective action, deriving benefits only from the policies espoused or enacted. As a result they are more nearly true volunteers—free to offer their time, effort, and services, or to withhold them, as they see fit. That typically means that the candidate must be acceptable to them before they take action. In this sense, then, policy-motivated activists are citizens turning to the political arena to achieve policy goals, with candidates serving more as instruments for achieving those goals than in the machine cadre.

ACTIVISTS AND PARTY DIFFERENCES IN SPATIAL ELECTIONS

To the extent that policy-motivated citizens turned activists have become more critical to party campaigns, we would expect to see them pressuring candidates and officeholders on policy. In this section I consider how, and under what conditions, this may be true, and what consequences this has for political parties and their candidates. Formal development of the theory described here can be found in Aldrich (1983a, 1983b) and Aldrich and McGinnis (1989). Robertson (1987) anticipated most of the theory and its understanding of partisan politics.

I argue here that what is missing from the classic spatial model (Downs 1957; Davis, Hinich, and Ordeshook 1970; McKelvey 1975) is the party and campaign activist. The addition of the political party can explain the emergence and the durability of partisan cleavages. For this purpose I am defining this part of the party as the set of benefit seekers in it, a significant part of what is meant by the party-as-organization.[10] The political role of this part of the party is to attempt to constrain the actual leaders of the party, its ambitious office seekers, as they try to become the party-in-government by appealing to the electorate.[11] That a party's benefit seekers were once more heavily the professional minions of ambitious officeholders made them less interesting to study, since they tended simply to carry out what the office seekers and holders desired. As they have been replaced by policy-type benefit seekers, activists have become a separate force, seeking to constrain the candidates. That is, their goals are more likely to conflict with the goals of office-seeking candidates rather than be so compatible.[12] Although they help explain the existence of contemporary party cleavages, elections have simultaneously become more candidate centered. The party is seen as less relevant, except indirectly, insofar as the benefit seekers are successful in constraining the actions of office seekers and holders. These benefit seekers are important as I seek to explain the origin and implications of cleavages and the simultaneous irrelevance to the public of political parties, qua parties, that seems to characterize the contemporary party.

Citizens, in spatial theory, are motivated by policy. That is, they have preferences about what the government should do, and those preferences motivate their actions. In the classic spatial model this means that their voting behavior is determined by their perceptions of which candidate seems more likely to do what these citizens believe best, and their turnout decisions are likewise policy related.

Citizens in this expanded theory can also choose to become involved in campaigns as activists, either in a political party or in a candidate's personal campaign organization. (This discussion will focus for the most part on party activists.) The central assumption is that such activity is policy motivated. Thus this is a theory of the "purist," or at least policy-motivated, activist rather than the "professional." I presume, in other words, that activists choose in the same way they do as voters. Citizens will become involved in the party they see as closer to them, and they will abstain from partisan activity if they are spatially indifferent or, perhaps, alienated. Of course the costs of activism are higher, so many more abstain from activism than from voting. Still, the decision rules, and the goals underlying them, are assumed to be identical.[13]

In the theory to be described here, citizens can become involved in campaigns either through a political party or through a particular candidate.[14] There may be relatively little to distinguish campaign workers motivated by choice of party and by choice of candidate, although a party worker may expend effort for more of the party's candidates. The more important distinction concerns long-term motivation. One motivated to work for, say, the Democratic Party may be expected to do so in more election campaigns,[15] because the choice does not depend on the presence of a particularly attractive candidate. Of course many of the party faithful become activists for the first time because of a specific candidate, then remain as potential activists for other candidates of that party even after that one has left the scene. What I presume is that a party activist is attracted to occasional or regular activity because of the relative stances of the two parties rather than those of the particular candidates. For example, Gary Hart claimed to have been attracted to politics by John F. Kennedy. He remained as an activist, eventually running George McGovern's 1972 presidential campaign and then becoming a U.S. senator and running for president himself. I assume in this instance that although JFK attracted Hart to politics in the first place, it was the continued attractiveness of other Democrats and what they stood for, compared to Republicans, which retained his loyalty and contributions. More precisely, then, citizens in this model compare their preferences with those policies supported by Democrats and by Republicans, choosing to become activists if neither alienated from nor indifferent to the two parties, and choosing to become active in the preferred, closer party.[16]

If this is the basis of choice, the "location" of the party is dynamic. As blacks became heavily Democratic in the mid-1960s, for example, the preferences of black activists shifted the party's center of gravity to a more liberal stance on civil rights and other issues. The Democratic Party therefore became more attractive to other liberals and less attractive to conservatives, encouraging more of the former to become activists and driving some of the latter out of the party. As the Democratic Party moved to the left on civil rights, not only did some conservatives drop out, but some switched to the Republican Party (as, later, the rise of "McGovern Democrats" led a number of Democrats who became neoconservatives to switch parties). Still other inactive conservatives, now less indifferent, might become active in the Republican Party. A different adjustment is that an activist who feels the party moving away from her on policy might change her policy beliefs to move along with the party. Carsey and Layman, as noted above, find evidence for this form of adjustment (as well as the reverse, in roughly equal proportions). While specific locations of the activist equilibriums may differ, it does not seem that this mixture of dynamic adjustments affects the formal results fundamentally, but that is conjecture rather than formal demonstration.

It might seem that there is no stop to this shifting of activists in the two parties. Perhaps the two parties are driven to extremes, or perhaps they continue to shift back and forth. In fact it turns out that pursuing this logic actually does yield a stopping point: there is an equilibrium to the distribution of activists in the two parties, with citizens choosing as outlined here. This result was shown formally for one dimension in Aldrich (1983a) and proved under very general conditions, in particular covering essentially all circumstances analyzed in spatial theory, by Aldrich and McGinnis (1989).[17] This means, most importantly, that it applies with any number of policy dimensions.

There are two important implications of these results. The first is the general existence of equilibrium. Although there may be no *voting* equilibrium, or equilibrium positions for candidates, amid this "chaos," the parties and their activists provide a sort of fixed point because there is an activist equilibrium. Given the existence of equilibrium, the second important implication concerns the nature and location of these equilibrium positions for the two parties. In particular the equilibrium distributions will be those in which there are party cleavages, that is, in which one party's activists are concentrated on one side of the policy center and the other party's activists on the other side. Thus the theoretical results are consistent with finding the Democratic Party activists to be "liberal" on issues while the Republican Party activists are "conservative." The exact location of the center of each party depends, among other things, on the distribution of spatial preferences in the electorate. Moreover, because the decisions of activists depend on the location of both parties, it is typical that the distribution of activists in one party will, on average, be about as extreme to the "left" as those in the other party are to the "right."[18]

The theoretical result is promising, because it is consistent with the kinds of cleavages observed. It has the potential for adding pressure toward divergence in a theory that otherwise mostly yields convergence. It may be, that is, that activists in a party provide a countervailing weight to the electoral pull toward the center for ambitious office seekers. Moreover, since there is an equilibrium distribution for the party activists, adding these parties to the spatial theory provides the potential for stability in a theory that, at least in multidimensional spaces, has so far typically yielded instability. The result reported above, however, provides only the potential for these two desirable properties. I will soon show how it can be the basis for yielding divergent candidates and some stability in elections.

EVIDENCE FOR THE SPATIAL THEORY OF PARTISAN CLEAVAGES AMONG ACTIVISTS

Before turning to these theoretical questions, let us examine the evidence in support of this theory of party activism. Generally surveys of elite activists, such as national or state convention delegates or, at a less elite level, caucus participants, show strong support for the theory. In particular there is a great deal of evidence that the two parties' activists are sharply divided from each other on policy preferences, as described above—there are party cleavages at these levels. When surveys include such questions, both policy and party loyalty, or party victory motivations, are elicited, as anticipated in the theory. Finally, research has shown that activists support candidates for party nomination in expected utility terms, weighing their attractiveness on policy along with their electoral prospects, as the theory predicts (see Stone and Abramowitz 1984; Abramowitz 1989).

It might, therefore, be more surprising to find the data lead us to reach the same conclusions about activists who are involved in campaigns but at lower levels of activism. The NES surveys have included a battery of questions tapping four activities respondents might have engaged in: attending political meetings, rallies, dinners, or the like; wearing a campaign button or displaying a bumper sticker; giving a party or candidate money or buying tickets; or having done "any other work for one of the parties or candidates." These questions are designed to tap the labor pool so essential for campaigning at the local level, ringing doorbells, and conducting get-out-the-vote drives. Elsewhere I report more detailed analysis of these data (Aldrich, n.d.).[19] The first (perhaps) surprise is how common such efforts are among the electorate. Typically, one respondent in five reports having engaged in at least one of these activities, which appear to be approximately evenly balanced between Republicans and Democrats.[20] Second, there is a clear demarcation between the two parties' activists, with virtually none choosing to be active in the further party. The more detailed estimates in Aldrich (n.d.), for each election year survey from 1972 to 1988 support the basic assumptions, yielding results consistent with choosing to be active in the closer party and "abstaining" from activism owing especially to relative indifference between the two parties and, to a lesser extent, being alienated from the closer party.

In table 6.1 I have included the estimated mean position of such activists in the two parties, along with the median (samplewide) perceptions of the positions of the two parties, their respective nominees, and the median self-placement for the full sample, on the various seven-point issue (and ideology) scales. These data reveal several things. First, ordinarily there are clear differences between the two parties' activists, overall more than 1.5 out of 7 possible points apart (and over 2.5 units apart, on average, on the ideology scale). Never are Republican activists to the "left" of Democrats.[21] Second, there is reasonable consistency in these positions over the various years.[22] Third, the positions of the activists are fairly comparable to the positions of the two parties as perceived by the full samples. And finally, the differences between the two parties' activists are often of the same order of magnitude as those of their presidential candidates. The exception was 1976, when the differences between the perceptions of Carter's and Ford's positions were typically much smaller than those between the perceptions of the parties' positions or those actually held by its activists. Combined with the evidence of others on more elite activists and the more complex estimation of equations testing the rational choice formulation reported more fully in Aldrich (n.d.), there is considerable support for the basic conclusions of the theory of policy-motivated party activists. Wright tested the claim that "the difference we commonly attribute to 'party' in roll call voting (on non-procedural votes [in the United States House and Senate]) are *primarily* due to candidates' needs to satisfy the policy preferences of the party activists in districts and states" (1994, 6; emphasis in original). His statistical analysis of the One Hundredth Congress strongly supported his claim (see especially his tables 2 and 3).

As a final empirical demonstration, consider the data in figure 6.5, which ties together data about a number of different kinds of activists (these data and their interpretation are taken from Aldrich and Freeze, forthcoming). In four years, 1972, 1988, 2000, and 2004, donors to presidential election campaigns were surveyed, and in three of them, delegates to both parties' national conventions were also. Figure 6.5 reports the difference between the average positions where Democrat and Republican activists placed themselves on the seven-point left–right scale. Also added were the partisan identifiers and campaign activists of table 6.1. We can see two important things. First, with the exception

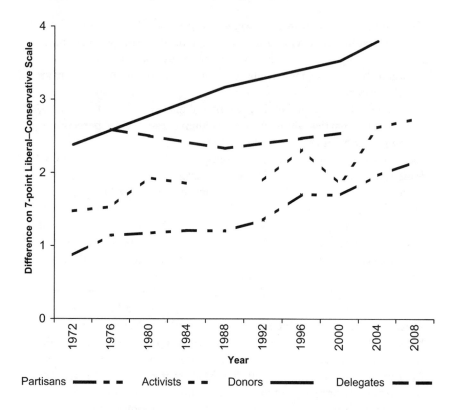

Figure 6.5. Ideological polarization among party activists, 1972–2008.
Source: ANES surveys and surveys of donors to presidential candidates, various years (details of donor surveys available on request). Compiled by author.
Note: Party activists in 1984 measured through noncomparable question formats.

of national convention delegates, the polarization of partisans in each of the four groups increased from election to election (and for the three available groups, jumped dramatically between 2000 and 2004). The exception of the convention delegates in 1972 could either reflect different wording of the ideology scale or the sharply left-leaning position of McGovern and perhaps of the delegates who supported him. More likely, it was both. The second major observation is that the higher the level of activity, the more polarized the partisan activists. Thus, identifiers are less polarized in each year than the activists—survey respondents and their often rather straightforward degree of activity (display a yard sign, etc.). Convention delegates and campaign contributors (those who gave enough to be required to have their names and addresses reported to the Federal Election Commission, that is, "large" contributors) are even more polarized. Indeed, in 2004, those who gave at least $500 to a presidential candidate's campaign were, on average, at points 2 and 6, which is to say nearly as extreme as possible on the 1–7 scale. Thus, the more demanding the contribution, the greater the polarization (see Kedar 2009, for careful theorizing about this phenomenon in a comparative perspective). And polarization is increasing at all levels of partisanship.

A critical question is why this polarization is happening especially within the electorate. The dominant view is that the public follows the cues of elites. The evidence that elites started out as more polarized than citizens and that their levels of polarization have increased dramatically over time, at least as much of that as partisans in the electorate, is at least consistent with this view. The second question is how polarization has proceeded. The two major options are that people have changed their partisanship to reflect their ideology or vice versa. Both have happened. Perhaps the most recent statement on this is that voters have "sorted" on ideology to reflect their partisanship more heavily than the reverse (see Levendusky 2009, 118; as he puts it, "sorting is party driven"; see also Baumer and Gold 2010).

THE IMPACT OF DIVERGING PARTISAN ACTIVISTS ON OFFICE SEEKERS

So far this theory tells us who are activists, and the presumption that they are policy motivated appears empirically plausible. The next theoretical question is what difference this makes. In particular, how might policy-cleaving parties shape elections, and especially the behavior of candidates? There are three major possibilities.

The first is candidate recruitment. As the example of Gary Hart illustrates, many candidates enter electoral politics as partisan activists and later seek office, whether on their own or through active recruitment by the party. Thus there is self-selection by policy motivation that reflects party cleavages. Candidates may be motivated in election campaigns by the desire to win. But outside the press of the campaign, even those with office-seeking goals are citizens too, and if citizens have policy motivations, so do those harboring office ambitions. They will choose the more desirable party, whether as activists first or directly as office seekers. Indeed, the comparative advantage of politics over many private careers is not financial. Many who hold high office could earn far more income in private careers (and often do, both before entering office and after leaving it). One of the major comparative advantages of a political career is the opportunity to shape public policy. Thus we would expect self-selection into political careers of those with relatively intense policy concerns.

In a competitive two-party system, both parties are viable routes to office. When this is so, as it is in an increasingly large part of the nation, the viability of a career in either party means that ambitious politicians will, by and large, self-select into the party closer to their policy concerns. This might not be true in a polity dominated by a single party, such as, historically, machine-dominated cities or the South. In the South, for example, a political career was unimaginable for a Republican before the 1960s. All ambitious politicians had to be Democrats, regardless of their policy views.[23] Much the same was true in longtime machine bastions such as Chicago. The effect of one-party dominance on careers could be seen when that dominance came to an end. The emergence of electoral viability for the Republican Party in the South, for example, was associated with an unusual amount of party switching among ambitious officeholders (see Canon and Sousa 1988; Castle and Fett, n.d.; Nokken and Poole 2004). The switching was invariably to the party more congenial to the switcher's policy views. Also, the breakup of the Daley machine in Chicago revealed that the Chicago Democratic Party contained a wide array of policy views, and the more conservative Democrats, such as Ed Vrdolyak, defected from the machine coalition.

This self-selection into partisan cleavages can also be shown more formally. House incumbents are among the most electorally secure: most win by large margins, few are defeated in the general election, and very few indeed lose in the primary election. Consider, then, an aspiring House candidate in such a district. He has the choice of running for nomination against a safe incumbent. He could run against the incumbent in the primary, but she is almost certain to win renomination. Or he could contest in the other party's primary with a far higher probability of success. Having that nomination, the chances of defeating the incumbent are at least significantly higher in the fall than in the spring. Aldrich and Bianco (1992) studied the implied game theoretic model, in which either candidate could in principle switch. We found that if the incumbent had a sufficiently high probability of nomination and election, similar to the one-party-dominant case, she would maintain her current affiliation. If it truly was a one-party-dominant district (in which the probability of defeating the incumbent with the other party's nomination was low), the challenger would remain in the dominant party and challenge the incumbent in the primary, even if motivated exclusively by winning. As the other party becomes more viable, however, the challenger might switch (indeed, under appropriate conditions, so might the incumbent), based only on ambition calculations. Policy motivations would not greatly affect the equilibrium outcome in a one-party-dominant case, but they would increase the likelihood of candidates' "sorting" themselves into the appropriate party in a competitive, two-party system. Thus even in an analysis of a highly truncated "career" decision, the formal logic supports the substantive argument.

As I noted earlier, Calvert (1985) argued that the "pull" of a candidate's personal policy motivations is weak, leading by itself to very little divergence from electorally induced policy moderation. But as the Aldrich-Bianco model reminds us, the candidate must first obtain a party nomination to have any realistic hope of winning the general election. The need to win nomination by party primary or convention, with policy-cleaved parties, provides the second possible source of divergence. Conventions that award nominations are filled with party activists, and a great deal of empirical research has shown that such delegates to state and national conventions are, if anything, more extreme and divergent than other partisans (as noted above). In nominations secured by primary elections (including the indirect primary selection of presidential nominees), the primary electorate consists preponderantly of party activists and loyalists. Although obviously much more like the distribution of policy preferences among partisan identifiers, such primary electorates also typically diverge along partisan lines of cleavage. To be sure, primary electorates differ from one electoral unit to another (e.g., from one state to another), and just as with state or local partisan activists, there may be more liberal and more conservative electorates within the same party. Still, within each relevant electoral territory there will be an equilibrium distribution of party activists, with lines of partisan cleavage appropriate to that unit. Although the data above emphasize the party as a national entity, it is a conglomeration of fifty state and many local units, organized along the geographic lines of electoral boundaries.[24]

The second impact of parties, then, works through the nomination process. Whether a candidate appeals for nomination support to party activists in a caucus-convention system or to a party's primary electorate, the policy preferences of those choosing the nominee will be very different from the preferences of those voting in the general elections. The best position for helping a candidate win in the fall is likely to be very different from the best position for winning nomination. Broadly speaking, the tension is between appealing for general election support by moving toward the policy center of the whole electorate and appealing for nomination support by moving toward the center of the party activists. If a candidate can adopt only one platform for both selections or is able to modify the spring platform only modestly for the fall, much of that tension must be resolved at the outset. The candidate will adopt the position that yields the highest probability of winning nomination *and* winning election.

This resolution might seem relatively simple, but it depends on the actions of others. For example, it obviously matters who is the opposition for nomination.[25] It also depends on the decisions activists make. It is plausible that primary election voters would be more likely to weight the proximity of a candidate's platform to their own preferences relatively heavily, much as spatial voters would do in the fall. Conversely, convention delegates might be more concerned with assessing how likely their prospective nominees are to win in the fall. They might be amenable to supporting more moderate candidates because of their higher chances of victory in the general election. There is indeed strong evidence that "electability" is an important consideration for convention delegates (see Stone and Abramowitz 1984). There is also ample evidence that primary voters consider electability in revealing their choices (see Abramowitz 1989; Abramson et al. 1992). Still, it is reasonable to imagine a heavier weighting of electability by delegates than by primary voters.

Even the most "sophisticated" activists in nomination campaigns are unlikely to weight closeness on policy at zero if they are motivated by policy rather than patronage. At the extreme, if both nominees adopted the median of the full electorate, there would be no advantage to having your nominee win other than the patronage value of holding office. And surely policy-motivated activists would rebel at nominating one further from their desires than the opposition! Formal treatment of the logic of the problem is limited. Aranson and Ordeshook (1972), in a unidimensional model, assumed that party activists are distributed with a line (or point) of cleavage—reflecting by assumption, that is, the results derived here. They concluded that the best position for a candidate is some compromise between the center of the party and the center of the electorate, with just where in that region depending on activists' weighing of electability (as well as the positions of nomination contenders and the other party's nominee). Their model has not been generalized to the multidimensional case. If generalization does follow along these lines, it is reasonable to conclude that nomination process "pulls apart" the candidates of opposing parties along the lines of cleavage.

The third impact of the party is its value to the candidate in the general election, and as in the two preceding cases, it "pulls" its nominees toward the party's position. A simple example illustrates the logic, which is shown formally in Aldrich and McGinnis (1989). Suppose that the party provides resources to a candidate so as to increase turnout. And suppose the closer the nominee is to the party's position, the more resources are made available. This is a most plausible assumption if the party activists must allocate finite resources to a number of nominees for various offices and if these activists are policy motivated. Imagine first that both parties' candidates are at or near the policy center, leaning only slightly toward their own parties. Both are slightly more appealing to about half the electorate. Suppose, then, that a candidate could increase turnout, through greater effort and resources from his or her party's activists, by taking a step toward that party's position. Doing so would mean that fewer in the electorate now favor that candidate. But if the gain in party resources means that sufficiently more of that (smaller) base of supporters actually vote on election day, the candidate might gain enough in increased turnout by this move to compensate for a somewhat smaller base of potential support. Thus if the party (meaning its resources—the time, effort, money, and such contributed by its activists) is sufficiently important, then the party will pull its nominee away from the overall center and toward the center of the party.[26]

There are, therefore, at least three ways a party filled with policy-motivated activists can generate candidates who reflect, at least in part, the policy cleavages separating the two parties' activists. They will recruit, in part by self-selection, candidates whose personal preferences reflect those cleavages. The need for the support of party activists to gain nomination and the value of those activists' working for the nominee in the general election will work against the incentive to moderate and pull toward the positions of the party. So, too, might concern that too much moderation would give room for a third party to begin to run candidates and cut into the party's base help keep the party's candidates from converging to the party center (as Lee [2008] demonstrates happens in congressional politics). And for ambitious politicians seeking a long career in elective office, given a long-term equilibrium in party activists, this pull away from the electoral center toward the party center will continue, generating incentives to act in office as they advocated on the campaign trail. Moreover, by the time an office seeker is in a position to run for high office, such as the presidency, the long-term effect of these partisan pulls toward divergence will have resulted in a career record of stated and actual divergence that would be very hard, if not impossible, to credibly disavow. Could, for example, Walter Mondale in 1984 and Ronald Reagan in 1980 have credibly claimed to have been other than a liberal and a conservative, respectively? In these ways, then, a party filled primarily with benefit seekers motivated by policy-induced partisan cleavages, induces a reflection of those partisan cleavages in its nominees, and may induce long-term cleavages among ambitious politicians not only on the campaign trail but in office.

CONCLUSION

The theory of party activists developed in this chapter is based on policy-motivated "amateurs" or "purists" who choose to become involved in campaigns because of the attractiveness of a party's views compared with those of the other party. This formulation had as its major consequence the existence of equilibrium distributions of activists in the two parties even under conditions that, in voting, yield no equilibrium at all. Moreover, the activist equilibrium yields lines of partisan cleavage that the data show to be durable and consistent, whether in the positions of activists themselves, in the perceptions of the stances of the two parties by the electorate as a whole, or in the positions of candidates as seen by voters and as revealed by their actions when in office. The party activists, I argued, can induce divergence along that line of cleavage among ambitious politicians by a combination of attraction of candidates with such personal policy views to run, the imperative for candidates to secure resources as well as the votes needed to win their parties' nomination, and the assistance that party activists can provide their nominees in the general election. Since officeholders must continually seek reelection, it also follows that they will reveal policy positions in office that reflect those partisan pulls along the lines of cleavage in their constituency and its party. The result is that the politician seeking election faces two competing pressures. The centripetal pressure is the pressure to seek votes in the middle, among those most torn in their decision between the two parties' candidates. The centrifugal pressure is that which emanates from the party activists; in generating policy goals for the many candidates who entered politics concerned about public policy; in being the core constituencies for nomination, whether in primary or caucus; and in being the source of the resources needed to compete effectively in the general election. Resolving these competing pressures is the difficult matter of balance that politicians must determine consistently as they consider the election. We will see a parallel pair of pressures in office, as well, in the next chapter.

The theory of parties offered here views the electorate, even the party loyalists, as external to the political party, consisting instead of the targets of partisan actions. If we can equate "strong partisan identifiers" with party loyalists, what makes the consumer of the party's product loyal is the consistency with which its "brand name" provides greater benefits than the opposition, and the higher the degree of consensus among party elites, the more precise and therefore useful the party's reputation, or brand name, is for citizens in rendering their political judgments. That is, it is the enduring relevance of partisan cleavages and candidates whose positions reflect them that makes a "brand name" meaningful and underlies Key's standing decision role of partisanship. As I noted earlier, policy-motivated partisan activists are freer than patronage-motivated activists to offer or withhold their support. And in this candidate-centered electoral era, candidates are freer to develop their personal careers but at the same time must continually win the support of policy-motivated activists. With candidates building their own bases of support, it is no surprise that they are more independent of the party in office. The modern mass party of Van Buren held allegiance to the party as its highest value, and this included candidates and officeholders as well as activists and voters. The preferment of office, as of patronage, depended on party loyalty. "Loyalty" in Congress today is induced electorally, by the combination of the voting public and the pull of party activists outlined in this chapter. That is, officeholders vote with their party when it is in their electoral-career interests to do so. There is a collective aspect to this. The more individualized the candidates' positions are, the less value and meaning there is to the party's reputation. Only if homogeneity is relatively high, i.e., only if candidates across the country take reasonably similar stances—and act on them when in office—is there a high value to the party's reputation. As we also saw, however, the measures of party voting and party loyalty are variable in the contemporary Congress: the party-in-government has differing degrees of revealed strength. This variation is also reflected not only in the meaning and thus decision-making value for the party, but it is also reflected in the construction of party institutions in the government, which in turn reflect and are reflected in the kinds of forces outlined here. It is time, therefore, to examine the party outside of the electorate.

7 POLITICAL PARTIES AND GOVERNANCE

James Carville put up a sign with three focus points in Bill
Clinton's campaign headquarters during his 1992 presidential campaign: "1. Change vs. more of the same; 2. The economy, stupid; 3. Don't
forget health care." While part of the focus was on critiquing George
H. W. Bush's economic performance, the first and third points of focus
(sounding remarkably like those of Barack Obama in 2008) typified a
candidate running at the center of the Democratic Party, that is, as a liberal Democrat. Four years later and after seeing his party lose the 1994
elections in the "Republican Revolution" that ended a forty-year reign of
the Democrats in the House, Clinton positioned himself as a moderate
candidate, albeit often by emphasizing those issues on which he retained
a more moderate stance rather than those on which he held more liberal
positions. He referred to this strategy as the "third way," by which he
meant neither liberal nor conservative but centrist (as Australia's Labour Party had run in the 1980s and as Britain's Labour Party soon
would). Conversely, George W. Bush sought the presidency in 2000
as a "compassionate conservative," offering proposals to reform social
security and education, among other "Democratically owned" issues
(Petrocik 1996; for application to 2000, see Aldrich and Griffin 2003).
In this manner, he sought to be seen as a moderate conservative. Four
years later, he ran from the right, with his chief strategist, Karl Rove,
noted for his emphasis on appealing to the party's ideological base.

Presidential-level politicians may be freer than those seeking and
holding other offices to define their (or their opponents') positions. And
they can apparently redefine these positions as suits their purposes, as
well. It is, perhaps, through their greater ability to shape their own repu-

tations rather than relying on (or being burdened by) their party's that we can see the different ways in which presidential candidates balance the appeal of the center for winning votes and the contrary appeal of the party's base, which is more toward the extreme, for winning nomination and seeking resources. In this chapter, we will see that the need to navigate between contending pressures is not unique to the electoral arena, but is found just as clearly in office, especially the Congress.

CENTRIFUGAL AND CENTRIPETAL FORCES IN LEGISLATURES

Candidates face a number of forces inclining them to the center and a number of forces inclining them away from the center, toward the extreme. Their master plan for their campaigning must therefore consider what balance to strike between these centripetal and centrifugal forces. Sometimes it is important to mobilize the base, to fend off nomination challenges, or to seek support from activists, all of which, on average, incline the candidate to move away from the center of the district's electorate. These centrifugal forces may be reinforced by the candidate's own policy preferences, especially if the candidate entered politics as a policy activist, or may be reinforced by the felt need to protect the flank from third-party or independent candidacies (see Lee 2008). But then, the candidate will feel the countervailing push back toward the center to win votes. This force is often doubled, in comparison to winning votes from the extreme. The more extreme voter is choosing between voting for this closer candidate or for no one, while the more centrist citizen's might well not only be a vote not won, but one actually lost to the other side, and thus a doubly harmful defection. The more extreme the candidate, the more vulnerable the center is to capture from an opponent less extreme on the other side. Thus, some candidates choose among these risks and rewards by going toward the extreme, others move to the center, but many balance these competing forces with moderate divergence.

In this chapter, in which a theory is developed for understanding the actions of the successful candidate when in office, we find that there are analogous competing centripetal and centrifugal forces at work in the Congress—and likely in state legislatures and perhaps other legislatures around the world. Of course, some legislators are from districts with centers far from those of the center of the nation as a whole (and presumably, therefore, the center of the Congress). For them, the balancing of competing forces is different in the district than in the nation. For others, with constituencies similar to Congress in this respect, which means especially having policy centers that are closely aligned to that of the nation as a whole, the forces in Congress are similar to those they face in the district. However, the reasons for the forces are different, and therefore even the legislator facing comparable forces in Washington and at home might wish to balance them differently. That is, these are different, but parallel, centripetal and centrifugal forces in Congress and in the electorate. In the next chapter I will consider the correspondence between the forces in the two settings and seek to explain how this helps us tie tighter the party-in-elections, with its candidates and voters, with the party-in-government, with its power, policy and re-election seeking officeholders, through the party-as-organization.

As Schlesinger has pointed out (1991, 1–2), the number of independent and third-party members of Congress dropped to a historical low in the postwar era. Both houses of Congress are organized by the parties, which is to say that they are organized by affiliating MCs (members of Congress) themselves. Both parties appoint their members to committees, and the majority party consistently ensures that it holds a majority on, and chairs, every committee and subcommittee.[1] In the House, a straight party vote selects the Speaker. Each party in Congress has its own organizational structures, such as the whip system, and both parties, through their Caucus (Democrats) and Conference (Republicans), base their organizational structures, leadership powers, and policy initiatives in the preferences and actions of their respective affiliates.

In this sense the two major parties dominate Congress as much as at any time over the last fifty years, or even more than ever. The partisan affiliations of officeholders and the partisan organizations in Congress are potentially important for giving strength to the parties-in-government. Both affiliation and organizational forms however, are merely formal properties. Neither must necessarily and logically shape policy outcomes in any particular fashion. Either or both *can* be vacuous or consequential.

Rohde (especially 1991 as well as in work with me, Aldrich and Rohde 1997–98, 2000, 2001, 2008, 2010) developed what we call the theory of "conditional party government" (CPG) to explain circumstances under which a partisan legislature will choose to strengthen the power of its organization and leadership, making them consequential, and when it will choose not to do so. These circumstances relate to the two of the components that define the condition (or the "C") in CPG. First, the party in Congress will want to act in a unified manner to fend off the opposition party when the two parties are distinct from each other (similar to what is currently referred to as "polarization" in

Congress). Having this differentiation from the opposition is particularly important for blocking their initiatives, what Cox and McCubbins (2005, 2007), with their "party cartel" theory, call "negative agenda control." Even with differentiation from the opposition, there may remain considerable diversity of opinion within the party. Even so, the party can agree that they do *not* want what the opposition seeks under differentiation (or "polarization"), even if they cannot agree on what they would like to do for themselves. Second, if the party is relatively more homogenous, there will be more that they collectively can agree that they want to achieve. It is of course possible that the party may be homogenous without there being much polarization. It is, thus, the combination of internal agreement and policy differentiation from the other party that makes possible "positive" agenda seeking and what we mean by the relatively higher satisfaction of the condition in CPG.

But there is a third aspect. Positive agenda control (rather than merely positive agenda seeking) requires the ability to influence outcomes, and thus positive agenda control is a question asked primarily about the majority party, for if the condition is well satisfied, the majority party has policy desires different from the minority's, due to differentiation; it has a more highly shared set of particulars it would like to achieve, due to homogeneity; and, finally, it has the potential to enact that set of consensual party goals due to its majority status. Of course, the smaller the majority, the greater is the need for the condition to be well satisfied. The Senate differs from the House in these regards primarily in not being a majority-rule-based institution, and so the majority must either be sufficiently large or the minority sufficiently diverse in their views to provide opportunities of winning the supermajority votes needed to pass legislation in the Senate. Conversely, both parties may have negative agenda control in the Senate, and this would be increasingly likely to be true the greater the extent to which the condition is satisfied. This is often called "gridlock," although there can be gridlock without there also being partisan polarization (for accounts of gridlock without parties, see Brady 2006; Krehbiel 1998).

Finally, whether even a unified majority in a partisan, polarized Congress will act on its positive agenda control depends upon what the status quo policy is. When newly elected to majority status (as for the Republicans in 1994 or the Democrats in 2006, for example), there may be a great deal to act upon, as the status quo is likely to be what the minority enacted when they were in the majority. Over time, however, the majority will have passed many of its desired policies and thus will have less reason to use its positive agenda control capabilities.

These various characteristics of the number and preferences of legislators in the two parties tell us much about intent and possibility. When the "C" in "CPG" is well satisfied, there is potential for parties, especially the majority party, to govern. In the next section, we look at whether the C being satisfied has led to voting on the floor that appears as if CPG were explaining the outcomes; that is, voting is what we would expect if parties were governing. With consideration of the C and the appearance of something like PG, we will then turn to study what happens in between these two types of voting, of citizens voting for representatives and of representatives voting for policy on the floor. That hard work to connect the two is precisely the task of the party organization in Congress. This will require, first, the building of theoretical expectations about institutions, and then their application for understanding the observed patterns of behavior from elections through floor voting over the last sixty years.

EVIDENCE OF PARTISAN CLEAVAGES IN GOVERNMENT

Legislation requires the formation of majorities on the floor in each chamber to pass bills to the president to sign (or, two-thirds majorities are needed in both chambers to override a veto). Social choice and voting theory provides the formal logic of instability in majority rule (see chap. 2), but one need not understand this formal logic to know that there are many ways to fashion majorities and that any majority coalition is always fragile. Political parties are one basis on which majorities can be formed, and they can provide long-term stability to such a majority. But these too can be defeated and majorities fashioned on other bases, as, for example, through formation of the conservative coalition, which was common in the 1950s, 1960s, and 1970s.[2]

In the political science literature, a vote is defined as a "party vote" (or, more precisely, a "party unity vote") when a majority of Democrats is opposed by a majority of Republicans, just as a vote is said to reflect formation of a conservative coalition when a majority of northern Democrats is opposed by a majority of southern Democrats and a majority of Republicans. Note two things about these standard definitions. First, these are minimal standards, the barest of majorities. We will, however, also examine the much more demanding standard of 90 percent of Democrats opposing 90 percent of Republicans. Second, these measures examine only roll call votes. They do not reveal why MCs voted as they did. A party vote might reflect strong partisan efforts, members' voting their preferences independently, or even mere coincidence. Roll call voting patterns do not tell us what did *not* make it to the floor or show whether the content of a bill that did make it was shaped by strong party control, recalcitrant committee leaders, presidential lobbying efforts, anticipation of what the other chamber or the president would support, or massive compromises and vote trades within that chamber. They tell us little about agenda control and coalition formation. These measures do tell us, however, who voted with whom.

In figure 7.1, I report the percentage of votes that were party votes from 1953 through 2009 (the Eighty-Third through One Hundred Tenth Congresses), comparing both measures within the House (the Senate looking quite similar). The shape of these data are influenced by a variety of factors, such as the number of unanimous votes and of votes that were not conducted via a call of the roll. Still, they provide a plausible first indication of patterns over time. And, there has been considerable variation over time in these data, with lowest ebb coming

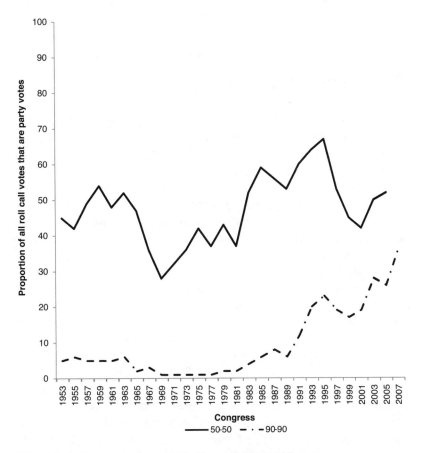

Figure 7.1. Party unity votes, U.S. House, 1953–2007.
Source: Malbin et al. (2008). Compiled by author.

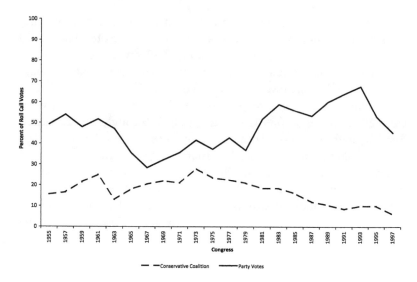

Figure 7.2. Party unity and conservative coalition votes, U.S. House, 1955–1997.
Source: Malbin et al. (2008). Compiled by author.

in the late 1950s and the 1960s, followed by a building in these measures through the 1980s, peaking in the One Hundred Fourth Congress (1995–96) when Republicans seized power. Party voting declined a bit over the rest of the 1990s but then gathered strength again through the current period. The second decline may be less important than the first, however, because the proportions of 90–90 votes in the House (and in the Senate) were very low throughout this period until the 1990s, and, with only modest wiggles, have been increasing sharply since then. There were, for example, a greater percentage of 90–90 party unity votes in the One Hundred Tenth Congress than there were 50–50 party unity votes in the Ninety-First Congress.

In figure 7.2, I report a different comparison, this being 50–50 party unity and conservative coalition votes in the House for Congresses from 1957 to 1999 (when conservative coalition votes became so rare they were no longer worth counting).[3] In every Congress, there were more party than conservative coalition votes. These differences were small in the Nixon administration, however, with party unity being barely more common than conservative coalition votes. Changes in these coalitions over time are inversely related: when party unity is relatively high the conservative coalition rarely forms, and vice versa. Thus party votes were rather common in the first and last decades displayed in figure 7.2, with half or more of all votes cast in the House being party votes, but they dropped sharply to about one in three in the first years of the Nixon administration and climbed slowly over the 1970s to about two votes in five. The conservative coalition formed on about one vote in six in the 1950s and early 1960s, increased to about one in four from the mid-1960s to the late 1970s, and declined to one in ten by the end of the 1980s before tailing off to near zero in the 1990s. In the 1970s the conservative coalition rivaled party. Before and after that time, party votes were far more common than conservative coalition votes.[4] The reason for these patterns lies with the choices of southern Democrats.

Figures 7.3 and 7.4 report the average party unity scores (that is, the proportion of times the partisan affiliate, on average, voted with his or her party on 50–50 party votes) for partisan groups in both houses, looking especially at the southern Democrats.[5] In both chambers southern Democrats were substantially less loyal to their party from the end of the Eisenhower administration (or even earlier in the House) until the Carter years. By 1986, however, southern Democrats had become as loyal to their party as Republicans were to theirs. Why southern Democrats "defected" from, and then came to resemble, their northern counterparts will be important throughout this chapter. Note, however, that southern Democrats remain at least somewhat distinct and more moderate than many other Democrats today. There is even an organized presence. As of this writing (2010) there are 51 members of the "Blue Dog

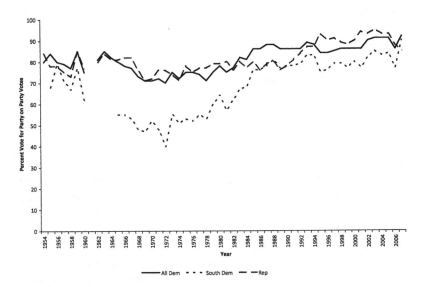

Figure 7.3. Party unity scores, U.S. House, 1954–2007.
Source: Malbin et al. (2008). Compiled by author.

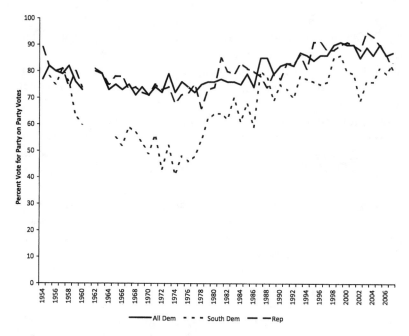

Figure 7.4. Party unity scores, U.S. Senate, 1954–2007.
Source: Malbin et al. (2008). Compiled by author.

Democrats," moderate Democrats, many (but far from all) of them southern. This organization formed to give them a voice with the Democratic Caucus in the House (which is, notably, a different thing than defecting on the floor, as in voting along with the conservative coalition).

Another way to assess partisan voting is to examine the success rate, and partisan support for, the president's position on policy. This focuses attention on some of the highest-profile legislation, since it is the set of matters the president went public to support, and it focuses attention on bills that actually became law. Figure 7.5 reports the percentage of the time the two chambers gave the president a victory on legislation on which he took a public position. The (unsurprising) story here is that Democratic presidents fared reasonably well with their party's unified control of the government, with success rates in the range of 75–85 percent, and the same held true when Republican majorities supported George W. Bush at comparable levels.

It may not be surprising that presidents are successful when their parties hold unified control of the Congress. The major change comes from the sharp decrease in success for presidents facing a Congress with at least one chamber controlled by the opposition. Eisenhower was quite successful, for example, until the 1958 congressional elections were held amid a sharp recession. Nixon and Reagan began their administrations with reasonably high success rates, but with considerable decline over their terms and those of the partisan successor of each. Clinton never did well with a Republican House, and the decline in George W. Bush's success rate upon losing control of Congress in 2006 is dramatic. These data indicate that there are clear differences in the voting behavior of partisan officeholders. Seriously contested votes are most likely to divide Democrat from Republican, whether or not the president has taken a position on the issue. Southern Democrats did, however, defect from their party significantly, especially from about 1965 to 1977. During the Nixon and Ford administrations, in fact, the conservative coalition was a genuine rival to the parties, perhaps providing the only systematic option for victory for a Republican president facing a Democratic majority in Congress. The 1980s and beyond saw a substantial revival of partisan voting patterns: southern Democrats have come to vote with their northern allies and not with the opposing party. As a result, the number of party votes has increased; party unity on these votes has strengthened, especially among southern Democrats; and presidential support is more sharply partisan than in earlier decades. The Democratic legislative majorities have also become more successful. Rohde, for example, reports that the percentage of party votes won by the Democrats in the House increased from 55 percent

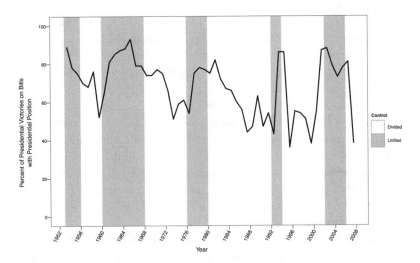

Figure 7.5. Presidential victories in House and Senate, 1953–2007.
Source: Malbin et al. (2008). Compiled by author.

in 1981, through 63 percent, 77 percent, 73 percent, and 73 percent, to a substantial 86 percent in 1986 (Rohde 1989, 161, table 7; see also Rohde 1991, 152–54). In the One Hundredth Congress (1987–89), House Speaker Jim Wright (D-TX) announced an unusually extensive agenda, and all of it passed the House and much into law (see Rohde 1991; Sinclair 1990). In short, it appears that there really is something to the partisan affiliation of legislators and that this "something" has had considerable teeth, even by the middle to late 1980s, let alone the last two decades. And in this there is genuine contrast with other times such as the Nixon-Ford era. Just what that "something" is that the parties have more of at some times than at others is the theoretical question of this chapter, through which I seek to explain these empirical patterns.

THEORIES OF LEGISLATURES AND POLITICAL PARTIES

Institutional Theories of Congress

Several institutional theories are helpful in developing a theoretical account of parties in the legislature. Almost invariably, these theories draw their inspiration from the House of Representatives. Scholars have turned more recently to study partisan institutions in the Senate (Monroe, Roberts, and Rohde 2008). Comparatively little has yet been examined on the effect of bicameralism (but see, for example, Sin 2007 and Lupia and Sin 2008).

Shepsle (1979) launched the "new institutionalism" as a self-conscious enterprise. His account began with the Arrovian problem and its extensions to the instability of majority rule (see chap. 2). The House, as a pure majority-rule body, should be expected to be unusually subject to that instability. Shepsle noted that the House has added great complexity on top of simple majority rule. His model developed one of the most significant of these rule emendations, the committee system. Most legislation is referred to one or more committees, where hearings are held and the actual bill is shaped, and the committee's product stands as the principal alternative to the status quo. Such actions provide numerous points at which committees (or subcommittees) can exert substantial influence on the shape of legislation and the structure of the agenda.

Deference to committees, long considered an important norm in Congress, suggests that what the committee does will have a great bearing on what Congress chooses.[6] However, deference needs to be explained, not assumed. Thus, for example, the Ways and Means but not the Appropriations Committee often reports bills that receive a closed rule (meaning that there can be no amendments), making these bills take-it-or-leave-it propositions. This gives Ways and Means stronger positive-agenda-shaping powers than Appropriations. The important next step, then, would be to explain why this is so. Perhaps even more important, committees possess substantial negative, or "gatekeeping," powers: they can, that is, keep legislation bottled up. They can simply refuse to report a bill out of committee, ending legislation in that jurisdiction, except in atypical circumstances, such as a successful discharge petition or referral to multiple committees, in which case another committee can put legislation on that subject on the floor.

Whether positive or negative, committees provide significant potential for agenda control. Shepsle demonstrated that committees with control over policy jurisdictions and appropriate amendment rules can combine to yield an equilibrium (called a structure-induced equilibrium, or SIE) where there would be none in the absence of these rules (and thus in the absence of an equilibrium based solely on preferences, or a preference-induced equilibrium [PIE]).

Theoretically, this is a clever way to take a potentially complex, multidimensional policy space and decompose it into subsets of committee jurisdictions. If done all the way to "simple jurisdictions" (that is, to jurisdictions of exactly one dimension each), one can then rely on Black's median voter theorem and Romer and Rosenthal's agenda control extension to unravel this complexity. It may well be that these various theoretical simplifications are representative of the actual situation. As noted earlier, however, the median voter and agenda control results are themselves very fragile. Moreover, committees typically have multidimensional jurisdictions, in which case a theory of committee decision making in the absence of an equilibrium needs to be developed.

Other kinds of institutional arrangements besides committees, jurisdictions, and amendment rules can induce SIEs in the absence of a PIE. For example, Hammond and Miller (1987) and Miller and Hammond (1990) have analyzed conditions under which bicameralism, presidential veto power, or both can do so. Later I will do the same for the political party.

This sort of analysis tells us about institutional equilibriums but not about equilibrium institutions (see chap. 2; Shepsle 1986). One answer to why such a committee system has been adopted (one consistent with, but different from, Shepsle's SIE account) is that this arrangement serves MCs' electoral interests. In this argument committees tend to be composed of members who have relatively extreme preferences for policies within the committee's jurisdiction (e.g., Shepsle and Weingast

1987; Weingast and Marshall 1988). MCs have substantial control over their committee assignments (Shepsle 1978). Different constituencies exert different needs and demands on their MCs. Assignment to a committee with jurisdiction relevant to the special needs and concerns of the district (or reelection constituency) is therefore desirable. The result is that members of the Agriculture Committee primarily represent agricultural districts, and so on. Committees in this argument are "preference outliers"; that is, they contain MCs with preferences different from those of the House as a whole. If committees do have positive agenda power, we would expect that legislation they propose would reflect their more extreme concerns, and if they have negative power, the status quo should not change in ways harmful to those more extreme concerns. This is in short an account of distributive politics, in which committees serve to institutionalize distributive gains along jurisdictional lines. Consequently "gains from trade" across jurisdictional lines are possible, by establishing a more permanent basis for institutionalizing logrolls over time through "trading" across committee proposals, owing to their agenda powers, norms of deference to them, and so forth. This, then, is a more institutionally complex view of a kind of universalism that we considered in chapter 2 (see Weingast 1979)

Krehbiel (1991) has a different view of the formation and role of committees, building on the elegant work he has done with Gilligan (e.g., Gilligan and Krehbiel 1987, 1989, 1990). In his view, committees can be seen as a division of labor and specialization of expertise designed for efficiency. Members know what outcome they would like to achieve. Someone, however, must spend the effort to become sufficiently informed to specify the problem precisely, consider alternative solutions, hear testimony, and draft the proposed legislative means to achieve the desired outcome. It is far more efficient from an informational perspective to empower a small number of individuals to craft the bill than to prepare it within the full House. Critical to Krehbiel's view is that there be some relatively clear definition of what Congress as a whole desires. Indeed, the formal work assumes that legislation is unidimensional so that there is also a PIE, via Black's median voter theorem (1958). The central idea of this approach is that, to put it most simply, floor rather than party "majorities work their will," getting pretty close to what they want—policies central to the distribution of policy views in Congress and presumably corresponding roughly to the policy center in the nation that elects them. His first question, then, is how to keep a Romer-Rosenthal-style outcome, one that is typically far from the median, from happening, rather than adopting the median as policy. This is done, in his account, through the appointment of committees that represent the whole House, rather than being preference outliers. The second question he examines is how to solve a collective action problem, giving incentives for someone to develop expertise so that the policy is crafted rather than everyone "defecting" from contributing to policy expertise, hoping to free ride on the efforts of others.

This view is especially apt for cases where there is clear consensus on objectives but little technical knowledge of how to achieve them. Consider national defense policy. All agree that a strong defense is necessary (although there are differing views of the trade-off between guns and butter). What the typical MC does *not* know is how best to spend defense dollars: which missile system is best, how best to balance a standing versus a reserve force, and so on. The typical MC might well say that such questions should be left to the experts on armed services, and defense committees who have studied these matters closely. Grant them leeway on the details, but let the floor set the basic parameters.

This is why, in this theory, committees are not likely to be "preference outliers." Creating such extreme committees raises the risk of these experts' exploiting too greatly their informational advantage (through what is known as a problem of "moral hazard"). They can then combine this with their committee-based structural advantage. If, instead, committees have memberships with preferences similar to those of the floor as a whole, then the risk of their seeking more (or less) than the House desires is reduced. To be sure, experts may want something different than the floor does, at least from time to time. Even so, such problems are not that severe as long as the House retains the ultimate power of final approval of any committee proposal. Thus, if the central problem in Shepsle's model is the instability of majority rule, the central problem in Krehbiel's is solving the delegation and collective action problems of inducing willingness to develop expertise among generalists, managing a vast workload, and achieving a modicum of efficiency. The theory underlying this view works best when there is a high degree of consensus about what social outcomes people want (e.g., a growing economy). When that is less true, when there is diversity of opinion or values over outcomes, it is unclear how policy options, no matter how expertly written to achieve nonconsensual ends, solve the serious problem. Moreover, formally, this account also rests on the existence of fragile equilibriums, such as that of the median voter theorem.

Krehbiel develops his model on two premises. One is majoritarianism on the floor, which, as he puts it, is "akin to the positive components of Fenno's 'good public policy,' Maass's 'common good,' and Madison's 'popular government [with] popular information'" (1991, 99). The other is the uncertainty about exactly how to achieve majoritarianism, which requires specialization to discern and, by concentrating the crafting of proposals in the hands of a few, provides a collective good to Congress as a whole.

The view that chamber "majorities win out" also affects Krehbiel's view of political parties in Congress. In his book he purposely eliminates them from his theory (1991, 101–2, 260–61). In later work he has attempted to show that partisan institutions in Congress are not empirically consequential (1993). In his theory, party affiliation may indicate what preferences MCs bring to Congress, but their intralegislative organizations and leadership do not get in the way of reducing uncertainty and allowing the majority of the whole House to work its will.

The *formal* results of these two theories about a committee-dominated Congress are not incompatible. What are incompatible are the interpretations; especially problematic is the interpretation of "equilibrium institutions"—that is, the reason MCs created and continue to support or change the working arrangements within Congress. It could be, of course, that both theories are correct in part. For example, distributive policies, considered by some committees, may reflect the kinds of gains from trade that Shepsle and others have modeled, whereas legislation more concerned with public goods, often under the jurisdiction of other committees, may reflect the majority and efficiency criteria of Krehbiel (as he argues). The same institutional arrangements may have more than one use apiece. Indeed, the final votes toward majority are frequently won by adding distributive outcomes tailored to the needs of those pivotal voters, such as happened to ensure the votes of the final moderate Democrats who provided the pivotal votes on the Obama health care bill in the Senate. More theoretically, both social choice and collective action problems may affect the ability of MCs to achieve their ends, and the theory of parties-in-government to be developed here addresses both problems.

I noted earlier that Krehbiel's tests of parties (1993) and of committees (1990) found little support for their impact. These tests (typical of the literature) are empirically problematic, in part because they look at roll call voting at the end of the process. Such measures cannot easily distinguish between situations in which the floor majority got what it wanted and those in which the party or committee was able to control the agenda and get just as much as it possibly could on the floor.[7] Nor can they distinguish Krehbiel's account from vote trades, whether across committees (as in the Shepsle, Weingast, and Marshall models) or as managed by a party. But even if there were no empirical problems, such tests would be consistent not only with Krehbiel's model, but also with other quite different models of intralegislative institutions. The strategy followed here is not only to look at variation over time in the "C" in conditional party government to see if floor voting patterns at the end of the process vary as the theory predicts they will with changes in "C." It is also to look at patterns of behavior between congressional elections and roll call voting to see if there are empirical patterns of sufficient richness as to provide heightened credibility to the explanation and to make it unlikely other explanations would fit such rich, diverse observations.

Kiewiet and McCubbins (1991) and Cox and McCubbins (1993, 2005, 2007) present accounts of political parties based on the problem of collective action. Kiewiet and McCubbins point out that congressional parties delegate a great deal, both within Congress (to committees and subcommittees) and beyond (to the bureaucracy). One might conclude from this that the congressional party is weak, allowing others to legislate. Kiewiet and McCubbins argue that "it is possible to delegate authority to others and yet to continue to achieve desired outcomes. Indeed it is often the case that desired outcomes can be achieved *only* by delegating authority to others" (1991, 3; emphasis in original). Parties, they argue, have genuine electoral value to MCs, even in today's candidate-centered elections, by providing voters with a brand name. It is therefore in MCs' interests to make that brand name meaningful, reducing the costs of information acquisition by voters. Partisan MCs in Congress delegate authority to party leaders to help solve the "collective action, coordination, and social choice instability" problems they face (55). Party leaders in turn delegate authority to committees or elsewhere. If this perspective is correct, the more active the committees, the more effective the delegation.

Cox and McCubbins build on Kiewiet and McCubbins's observation (e.g., 1991, 41) that it is wrong to think there is necessarily some "contest" between the pulls of party and constituency, with constituency usually "winning." Instead, although partisans in Congress might share policy preferences, it may be in no individual MC's interest to act on those shared preferences. The question is how to make it in *someone's* self-interest to act on common partisan concerns, akin to Krehbiel's problem of how to internalize incentives to develop policy expertise. Their answer is to "internalize" the party's collective action problem into the self-interest of leaders. If such offices are valued and if selection and reselection are contingent on leaders' acting in the collective interests of the party, it becomes in their self-interest to do so. They argue that there are three components to the preferences of leaders: reelection, benefits from being a party leader, and benefits from being leader of the majority rather than minority party. Kiewiet and McCubbins demonstrate that congressional leaders have tended to be moderates in their parties (1991, 52, 53; tables 3.3 and 3.4).

If anything, contemporary results are more extreme. Republicans named three new figures to their leadership team after the 2008 elections (the Democrats did not). All three were more conservative than those whom they replaced and more conservative than the average Republican (see Aldrich and Rohde 2010). This implies that their policy (personal reelection) interests are not likely to be seriously jeopardized by acting in the shared policy interests of their party. Moreover, they typically are extremely safe, so that their own reelection interests are not greatly at stake anyway. Thus their variable goals are primarily to hold their leadership position and for their party to attain or retain majority status, both of which are best achieved by acting in the collective interests of their party. This internalization argument provides one answer to how a collectivity like partisans in office can overcome collective action or coordination problems. It allows the individual MC to avoid worrying unduly about collective interests, leaving it to the party leadership. Finally, Cox, Kiewiet, and McCubbins argue that the partisan makeup of committees means that these are, at least potentially, an arm of the political party. Partisans may also choose to appoint committee members, especially to critical committees, who reflect the collective interests of their parties, yielding committees that, when so appointed by both parties, are not much different from the House as a whole. Committees, however, vote by majority rule, so that the majority party, by holding a majority of seats on every committee, has the basis for winning any contended vote in the committee.

Rohde and Shepsle (1987) and Shepsle and Humes (1984) point out that party leaders can act decisively when their party wants to enact a collective interest (in this way, there is a similarity to the above comments about Krehbiel's model when there is a high degree of consensus over outcomes). This will be true when two conditions are met. First, there must be a policy position that most in the party desire, and second, achieving that policy must require action. The first point means there must be a modicum of consensus within the party, especially compared with the opposition. When Democrats were deeply divided over race and other issues, strong party leadership was effectively impossible. The second condition is that what the party as a whole desires must be different from the status quo. Thus, for example, when a party first captures a majority, it often seeks to pass a great deal of legislation. Once that agenda has largely been achieved, the party, collectively, would be more concerned with holding on to gains already won than with taking new initiatives. Of course, it may take leadership to preserve the status quo, but the device of committee gate-keeping powers often achieves the end of perpetuating the status quo without active central leadership intervention, leaving it to individual committees to do so.

It is, thus, the importance of reasonable consensus within a party that forms the core of CPG (see especially Rohde 1991). Applying this concept to the thrust of enacted reforms by the Democratic Party in the 1970s and 1980s, he wrote, "there would be responsibility *only if* there were widespread policy agreement among House Democrats" (31; emphasis in original). In conclusion he wrote:

> The obligation to support party positions, moreover, was not intended to apply equally to all members. There was no intention to create a system of party responsibility like those that operate in parliamentary democracies, imposing on every member the requirement to support every party position. Instead obligation was to be imposed on members "who held positions of power"—party leaders, committee chairmen, members of prestige committees. In effect, seeking and accepting positions of influence within the committee or party leadership meant accepting an implied contract: such leaders were obliged to support—or at least not block—policy initiatives on which there was party consensus. If these expectations were violated, members risked the loss of their influential positions. Party support was also expected from representatives who aspired to these positions. Taken together, these elements define the system that we have termed conditional party government. (166)

Conditional party government meshes well with candidate-centered elections that rest primary responsibility on the individual candidates to ensure their own bases of support. The party-in-government is in this sense basically a method of solving collective action and coordination problems—realizing what it is in the interests of the party as a whole to achieve.

It might seem that the party and its leaders are not "powerful" because all the action is in understanding when there will be a partisan consensus. The party leadership "merely" has to translate that consensus into legislation—important tasks, to be sure, but hardly the stuff of politics and power. But that is not correct. Floor majorities could be fashioned on any number of bases. Indeed, even in this era of heightened polarization of parties, as figure 7.1 shows, four in ten roll call votes do not reflect opposing party coalitions. Thus, leaders must help sort out what is and is not partisan. Only in these (often electorally central) cases, then, must they seek to ensure that a partisan majority is fashioned and held together.

With both Democrats and Whigs forming intersectional alliances in the 1840s, for example, the leadership task was to ensure that the legislative agenda would be based on internal improvements and the tariff rather than on regional issues such as those related to slavery. The party-in-government sought to ensure, that is, that policy would be based on issues on which there could be partisan majorities, both in office and (they hoped) in elections. And as we saw in chapter 5, it was often a struggle, one that the parties eventually lost, to keep a northern majority from, in time, "working its will." As Skowronek shows (1988), James K. Polk struggled mightily—and eventually barely succeeded—in leading his party to achieve a great deal by (barely) finding what it was that Democrats held in common. Conversely, in the 1960s and 1970s, an intersectional Democratic majority divided over a newfound Republican electoral threat in the South and regionally divisive issues such as race, Vietnam, law and order, and other social problems. And yet as the 1980s wore on, a congressional Democratic majority could more effectively hold its own, finding common ground in the face of the Republican threat, as civil rights receded from attention, and as a compromise agenda could be found between the two wings of the party. To put the point more theoretically, solving this kind of collective action or coordination problem is *also* solving the potential instability of majority rule, and the party will be "strong" when it helps its members win what they collectively desire as partisans rather than winning what might be achievable from a voting majority formed on some other basis.

Size and Consensus

A party may be thought of as strong if it wins a preponderance of elections. In the postwar era, the Democrats have held as few as 43 percent of the seats in the House in 1947–48 and 49 percent in 1953–54, and as many as 68 percent of the seats in 1965–66 and 67 percent in 1975–76.[8] The two maxima are associated with the very active "Great Society" Congress and the active (if in a very different sense) "Watergate" Congress, whereas Truman campaigned against the Republican "do nothing" Congress in 1948, the lowest point for Democrats from the 1930s through the 1980s.

A party may also be considered strong if it holds a relatively clear consensus in views and acts to realize them. The simplest indication of intraparty homogeneity among Democrats until recently was the relative balance of northern and southern members. Until the second Nixon administration, the worse the congressional Democratic Party fared in the nation, the larger the percentage of southerners in its delegation. Since there was an almost constant number of southern Democrats, a good Democratic year meant electing more northerners, whereas a bad year meant a bad year for the northern wing of the party. In the "do nothing" Congress, over 60 percent of the (minority of) Democratic seats were held by southerners, and they also made up a majority of Democrats during the party's other stint as minority party in this period, in 1953–54. Thus, in practice, size and homogeneity worked together. The unusually active "Great Society" Congress had an unusually large and relatively homogeneous (which is to say northern) majority as well as a popular president recently elected by a landslide vote and possessing uncommon legislative ambitions. The combination of size, homogeneity, leadership, and an ambitious agenda was enough to swamp the opposition, swamp the relatively strong and insulated committee system chaired by southern Democrats protected by seniority, and with all that, swamp the status quo.

Overwhelming electoral success, pent-up demand for new initiatives, and presidential leadership come together rarely. When they do, internal structures cannot block this strong a partisan majority from working its will. More generally, only some of those forces come together. In such cases rules may combine with preferences to shape outcomes.

Suppose there were truly a single dimension so that the median voter theorem applied. Rules would matter a great deal in this case, if the majority party is to seek to use its majority status to achieve something different than the floor median. Although the majority party as a whole might desire something different from the floor median, without some formal mechanism we would expect that the floor median would at some point be proposed and enacted. This reflects the result in chapter 2, where we saw that there was no reason to form a party when the median voter result applies. All SIE results I know of conclude that the PIE, when it exists, is an SIE.

If the party "matters" in this context, it requires that some rules, in combination with members' preferences, determine the outcome. For example, members of the majority party could agree to vote in caucus (perhaps selecting the party median) *and* agree to bind themselves to vote for that winning outcome on the floor. This is precisely what the Democratic Party's experiment with party-caucus government during the Wilson administration tried, and this experiment soon failed over how to enforce the agreement to vote for the caucus choice on the floor. Or the party could agree in advance to provide its leaders with resources for sanctions and rewards sufficient to enforce a comparable rule. This is what Cooper and Brady (1981) report was characteristic of "czar rule" (which will be discussed later in the chapter), and this approach worked until intraparty diversity (roughly approximating the divided majority party case) became too great for the Speaker's resources to outweigh the personal policy preferences of enough MCs, leading to the revolt.

Instead of seeking means to make partisans vote against their policy preferences on the floor (as they would choose independently to have them publicly revealed), partisans could agree to control the agenda so that they are never asked to vote for a feasible policy, such as the floor median, that is not in the party's collective interest. This is accomplished most easily (and perhaps only) when the status quo is already within the set of outcomes desired by the party (e.g., is near the center of majority party members' policy preferences). Some form of negative agenda control must therefore be derived to ensure that the floor median is never proposed.

Consider the Clinton impeachment vote in the House (with a Republican majority) in 1998 (see Aldrich and Rohde 2000; Caldeira and Zorn 2004). It appears that the floor median was to pass a measure of censure and not to vote to impeach (nor to miss the opportunity to impose any sanctions at all). In the event, the Republicans used a Romer-Rosenthal, agenda-control-like result, in which the Republican majority voted to propose an article of impeachment but to prohibit an amendment to censure the president instead. The article of impeachment was thereby passed and went to the Senate (which everyone knew would vote against impeachment anyway). If permitted, censure apparently would have defeated the article of impeachment (that is, the amendment of censure would have passed), and censure would have defeated no sanctioning at all, that is, the status quo. Thus, sanction was almost assuredly the median (or PIE), and the majority party was able to keep it from being proposed and thereby winning.

Size and Party Interests in the Absence of a PIE

The discussion above considered a unidimensional policy space. Krehbiel's argument that the floor majority will win has, as we saw, great plausibility. It requires extraordinary rules for the majority party, no matter how large or how homogeneous it is, to achieve an outcome that differs significantly from what would happen on the floor simply by majority voting.

In reality, of course, policy choices are essentially never unidimensional. Even if they were, Riker (1982a) has demonstrated that incentives ordinarily exist for strategic politicians to manufacture a (potentially artificial) secondary dimension to upset the PIE. In this account there is, for all intents and purposes, *never* a floor PIE.

To begin to examine this ordinary case, consider the two instances cited above of "party government," that is, of a majority party that has adopted the rule (such as in the "czar era" or during the Wilson administration) that binds partisans to support on the floor whatever the caucus adopts. This leaves open the question either of the basis for voluntary compliance or of the rationale for the party's granting its leaders sufficient resources to induce partisans to vote against their immediate policy interests.

The rule need not be that every partisan is required to vote for whatever the caucus chooses, only that those who do support the policy in caucus agree to support it on the floor. The task therefore is to find a policy that is agreeable to enough MCs in the majority party's caucus to ensure passage on the floor. What is needed, then, is a policy that attracts an extraordinary majority of partisans in caucus and so guarantees at least a simple majority on the floor.

If policy is indeed multidimensional, then there is no guarantee of a PIE not only on the floor, but also in the majority party. This is true in general. In his model of the committee system, Shepsle avoided this problem by analyzing committees with unidimensional policy jurisdictions ("simple" jurisdictions, in his terminology). This cannot be assumed for the theory of political parties. Thus the problem is that, if there is no PIE in the legislature as a whole, there is also no PIE in the party caucuses. More generally, there is no game theoretic "core" in either party or on the floor, at least when simple majority rule is used to choose outcomes.

Within the party caucus, however, a core may exist because of the use of extraordinary majority rule (Schofield, Grofman, and Feld 1988).[9] In one dimension the median voter result applies, which is to say that a core exists for any majority voting rule, simple or extraordinary. As the number of policy dimensions increases, the existence of the core becomes increasingly problematic. It can never be ensured for simple majority rule if there are two or more policy dimensions. As the size of the majority needed increases from a bare majority, however, the core exists for more and more dimensions. Indeed, if unanimity is required—that is, if the largest possible majority is necessary—a core always exists no matter how many dimensions there are.

To put this in terms of the majority party caucus, if the majority party holds all the seats, *a core never exists except in a unidimensional policy space* (see Aldrich 1989b for proof of this and the following results). The reason, of course, is that a simple majority in the party caucus is a simple majority on the floor, so that a party core exists only when a core exists in the legislature as a whole. Conversely, if the party holds a minimal winning majority, it needs unanimity within the caucus to ensure passage of its proposal on the floor. Thus, at minimal winning, *a core always exists in the majority party's caucus,* no matter how many policy dimensions there are. As the size of the party's majority shrinks from unanimity toward minimal winning, the core exists for an increasing number of policy dimensions. For example, the core exists in the majority party in the Senate for any number of dimensions when the majority holds 51 seats—that is, is minimal winning. The core necessarily exists if the majority party holds 62 or fewer seats for four dimensions, 67 for three dimensions, 75 for two dimensions, and 100 for one dimension (the median voter result). Comparable figures for the House are 218 (minimal winning), 272, 289, 327, and 435.

This result seems curious. The smaller the majority, the more likely the majority party is to have a well-defined sense of what the party wants on policy and can achieve.[10] The seeming curiosity is due to two characteristics. First, the core is not necessarily a single policy outcome, and it consists of a particular policy choice only when there is a PIE within the party (its median voter). As the required majority increases, so does the set of policy options in the core. If we drew lines enclosing the ideal points of partisan MCs, the smallest lines that included all ideal points (the "convex hull") would include the so called "Pareto set" of the party. For any point outside that set, there is a point inside the set that is preferred to it unanimously, but there is no point inside that is preferred unanimously to any other point in the Pareto set. At minimal winning, the majority party always has a core, but that core is (exactly) the Pareto set—that is, it includes all possible outcomes within the range of preferences of the majority party. Thus, although a core is more likely to exist as the size of the majority party decreases, it will be a larger and larger range of outcomes, ending at the full Pareto set.

The second characteristic is that the core is an equilibrium: once it has been adopted, the party will not act to change it. In this context that means it will act to maintain the status quo, if it is in the party core. There is no guarantee, however, that the party will be able to adopt it in the first place.[11]

Thus once again we see the power of the party more likely to be revealed in what it seeks to preserve than in positive actions it may take. This result is important in several ways, however. One is that, if the rule is adopted that those who support a proposal in caucus must vote for it on the floor, the majority party will (under the conditions of the results described) induce an equilibrium in policy outcomes when there is none on the floor. Moreover, it will be a policy outcome that is within the range of preferences typical of the majority party. Although at minimal winning, that may not be very restrictive, at more than minimal winning, the core will be increasingly central to the preferences of the majority party. Thus, in what I call below the set of "instructions," the party can agree to anything in the multioption core in its caucus and permit committee leaders discretion to select which particular option within that set they will seek to achieve on the floor. To see how the party's institutional devices can lead to its actively adopting a change to the status quo—and in the (ordinary) absence of a PIE—let us consider results from the full model outlined above.

Elements of the Theory of Parties in the Legislature

In this section I develop the theoretical concepts that will be employed in CPG (conditional party government), the theory of parties in the legislature that Rohde and I have developed.[12] The particular result appeared in Aldrich (1994) and Aldrich, Grynaviski, and Rohde (1999). A simplified model is reported in Aldrich, Rohde, and Tofias (2004). I draw from, and draw together, the various elements already considered. Like the literature reviewed above, I focus here on a single legislative branch, one that looks like the United States House. The two key elements are the policy preferences of MCs and their relation to their party affiliations, and the rules governing parties and committees that structure this otherwise pure, majority-rule institution. This is done to demonstrate a simple point. Legislators, free to vote however they choose on the floor, may act to restrict their choices to policies away from the center of policy on the floor and closer to policies at the center of the majority party. They do so, further, the more fully satisfied is the condition in CPG. Later, I will show that actual members of Congress act in the way predicted by this account.

In this model each MC was elected to Congress as a Democrat (the majority) or a Republican. The theory has room for all three of Fenno's goals (1973): reelection, policy, and power in the House. The self-selection of MCs into politics in the first place implies that they are likely to have personal policy preferences, and their self-selection into a party implies that these preferences are likely to be typical of their partisan allies' and different from their opponents'. Because they are ambitious careerists, the goal of reelection induces their policy preferences. The electoral mechanisms of party will also induce some variable degree of similarity in policy goals of fellow partisans and of differentiation from the opposition MCs'. These are propositions informally derived from the theory of parties-in-elections developed in the previous chapter. There partisan elite cleavages were derived for each electoral unit, the district (if House) or state (if Senate). Whether these intradistrict cleavages will yield consistent partisan cleavages at the national level when aggregated to the Congress depends on the similarity of the preferences across each electoral unit. This "composition" of individual unit cleavages relative to national partisan cleavages is one of the major variables explaining intraparty heterogeneity among Democrats from the New Deal into the 1970s and greater intraparty homogeneity in the 1980s and afterward.

Ambitious MCs may also seek power within Congress. All positions of importance in Congress are partisan, thus requiring selection and reselection by the party (which may be an actual decision or the application of an "automatic" rule such as seniority). Depending on the selection mechanism, then, ambition for leadership positions may induce policy preferences through the "internalization" mechanism outlined above. Selection mechanisms have, in the contemporary era, differed in the House over time and by party. In some important recent cases, they have become less automatic and created stronger forces for internalization. These will be examined later in this chapter and in the next chapter.

Thus all aspects of MCs' goals, but especially reelection, induce policy preferences that MCs reveal in their actions.[13] Policy preferences are defined over the (multidimensional) space that characterizes the possible policy outcomes and in turn induce a large variety of possible policy agendas. MCs are assumed to have single-peaked preferences over this space, typified by their ideal point location. These preferences may or may not be related to partisan affiliation. Three cases can be considered. Partisan policy preferences may be *heterogeneous*, which at the extreme would be when policy preferences are unrelated to party affiliation, but we will examine less extreme versions primarily, as the data suggest that some times have seen relatively greater and others relatively lesser homogeneity rather than observing any extreme of either. Parties may therefore also be *homogeneous* in policy preferences, that is, be similar within each party. The third consideration is how distinct are the preferences of the two parties. For example, is there a clear line of *partisan cleavage*, so that each Democrat's ideal point is on one side of the cleavage and each Republican's ideal point is on the other side?[14] However, there is the special case of a *divided majority party*, such as in the 1950s through the 1970s, in which northern Democrats were fairly homogeneous, with preferences at least somewhat distinct from the also relatively homogeneous southern Democrats, who were in turn distinct from relatively homogeneous Republicans. The relative salience of the cleavage between northern and southern Democrats, compared with that between Republicans and southern Democrats, determined whether southerners were effectively "closer" to northern Democrats or to Republicans.

Next, consider outcomes and how this Congress-like body achieves them. Floor voting is governed by the usual (albeit simplified) rules for amendments and voting. Congress opens with some status quo (or reversion) policy, q. The final vote in any sequence pits the proposal (with any amendments) against it. In any one round, therefore, the final outcome is limited to a binary choice pitting two options, q and any (possibly amended) bill. We know that in a binary choice there is no room for strategic voting (or rather, strategic and "sincere" voting strategies yield the same choices), so by this point, all simply vote for whichever option they prefer. Thus, outcomes are limited to being q or being a policy outcome in the set of points, called $W(q)$, the "win set" of q, that are preferred to q by at least a simple majority of MCs (see Shepsle and Weingast 1982 for proof).[15] If there is no policy in $W(q)$—if nothing can defeat q—then q is a PIE. The result of the majority voting theory extension of Arrow's theorem is that there (almost) always is something preferred to q.

Consider, then, an adaption to Shepsle's original specification (1979) of the committee system and related features.[16] There are three partisan components to the committee system. First, each party assigns members to committees, whether by simply ratifying members' self-selection (subject to availability) or by more active decision making to achieve partisan collective interests. Second, each party determines who will be its leaders on each committee, whether by an effective nonchoice (e.g., maintaining seniority) or a more active decision. In either case the majority party ensures that it holds a majority on every committee and subcommittee and that its choices of ranking members become chairs. Committees, at least in principle, enjoy the same sorts of potential agenda-control powers as in Shepsle, but there may be a third role of parties. Each party (whether through its caucus or its leadership) may provide instructions to its partisans on the committee, where by "instructions" (to be defined more precisely below) I mean the range of policies the party as a whole would like to see considered.

Committees, in this view, are potentially powerful or more tightly controlled, and they may be controlled by parties or by the floor. That is, the formal structure of the committee system is constant, just as are the formal specifications of the party structures. The independence of committees, the effectiveness of a party collectively, and the autonomous discretion of members on the floor are the variables for analysis. The question, in other words, is how many resources actors can employ in their various positions in the formal structuring of the legislature.

The two basic structures of a party are its caucus and its leadership. The caucus, its set of partisan MCs, may meet formally or may do so figuratively, such as through its whip system, more informal interactions, or other forms of delegation and representation. One task of the caucus is to select its leaders. The literal or figurative caucus also is a means of sharing information about policy preferences, to guide leaders in shaping the policy agenda in the name of the party.

Consider the caucus of the majority party.[17] At the beginning of the session, the majority party could seek to change the status quo, if desired. Defining what the party "desires" provides the instructions that the party gives to its party and committee leaders. One possibility is to consider what a majority of Democrats prefer to the status quo. While this may be defined in many ways, one obvious way is to imagine that the party collectively limits attention only to bills that at least a majority of the caucus prefers to the status quo. This is akin to the win set for the majority party, but we can think of it as the "possibility set," that is, the largest array of alternatives that the party might consider seeking to pass. It would not seek to pass, in the name of the party, any bill that a majority of its members would vote against. This is, of course, a minimal definition of what is in the party's collective interests. The major results discussed below were derived with this definition of what the party desires, although this set can be defined in many different fashions, such as what is consensually approved, the sense of the caucus, or some extraordinary majority, without affecting the qualitative results. The instructions that the party provides its leadership, then, are simply, "Get us something that we desire and that is feasible (i.e., something that can win; some element in $W(q)$). If there is nothing that is both feasible and desirable, do nothing in the name of the party." Formally, the relevant committee is to consider any—but only—alternatives that are both feasible (i.e., can win on the floor), and desirable (i.e., are preferred to the status quo by at least a majority of the majority party). If the chair and majority members of that committee cannot achieve at least that with the bill they report (and their best guess about what will happen on the floor), then they should keep the gates closed, that is, report out no bill at all, preserving the status quo. The caucus selects its leaders and may choose to provide sufficient benefits to make selection and reselection to such posts valued and subject to caucus control. Following Cox and McCubbins, such a means of selection at least partially internalizes the collective interests of the party in its leadership posts, making it in their interests to do whatever is necessary for fulfilling the party's instructions—that is, getting what is feasible and desirable. For committee leaders, internalization need only concern policy within the committee's jurisdiction. As noted, selecting leaders from within the center of the party also reduces the extent to which the collective interests of the party diverge from the personal preferences of such leaders. Finally, compliance with the party's instructions often allows some flexibility. If there is more than one outcome that is both feasible and desirable, leaders can choose among them, either to satisfy their own policy preferences or to provide "currency" for trades with others.

In this theory, no MC is asked to vote or to take a public stance against his or her own preferences as the MC would like them to be publicly revealed. All are free to vote as they please. This, then, is a theory about the discovery and formation of the party's legislative agenda. Just as with Shepsle's committee system, this formulation requires some means of agenda control, and the most likely form is precisely the same as through his model, except that power is delegated to the party's members and leaders on the committee, who exercise it in a partisan manner. We will see below that over the last three decades, the majority party does appear to have increased its use of special rules and other devices to assist committees' bills by defending them from minority challenges.

Both party and committee structures are ongoing, formal institutions. As described, in themselves they carry no particular consequences. How or even whether they will be used depends on the actions of individuals to empower them with the ways and means to affect process and outcomes. Committees can have gatekeeping powers, or they can be forced to discharge, encouraged to report, or worked around entirely, such as through multiple referral or the use of task forces. Chairs can be selected automatically through seniority, or they can be "brought to heel" through effective reselection devices and have their power trimmed, such as by the enacting of the "subcommittee bill of rights" (Rohde 1991). Similarly, party organizations can be granted more or fewer powers, and leaders can be given more or fewer resources. These basic structures persist, that is, but are of variable importance depending on the decisions of MCs. Perhaps more important, the party structures can be empowered for certain policy areas and allowed to lie fallow for others. The above review of previous work on distributive, partisan, and majoritarian systems illustrated that quite different results can be obtained from a legislature with a committee system. The question now is what kinds of results can be obtained from considering a legislature with a party system, and under what conditions partisan MCs might choose to employ that party structure.

As I showed in Aldrich (1994), there is always a game theoretic equilibrium and (subgame perfect) "solution" to this problem. In Aldrich, Grynaviski, and Rohde (1999), my coauthors and I showed, among other things, that in anticipation of the actions of the minority party, the majority party would be able, at least at times, to secure outcomes away from the center of the floor and toward the center of the majority party, and those times were more common when the condition in CPG was better fulfilled. In Aldrich, Rohde, and Tofias (2004), my coauthors and I developed a simplified model so that we could demonstrate more clearly the effect of increased satisfaction of the condition in CPG on policies likely to be chosen.

This simplified model begins with the election of members, all of whom are affiliates with one or the other party, just as in the other cases. The chamber is to consider a bill for possible change to the status quo. Members are free to vote their policy preferences unconstrained by any aspect of partisanship. However, they first vote on selection of a rule (a rather similar process to the way a rule is typically adopted in the House, specifying terms of debate and amendment possibilities). The rule is that the person who gets to propose the bill is selected at random either from the full chamber or from the members of the majority party. Depending upon the outcome, a member of the majority or of the legislature as a whole is chosen at random and proposes their most preferred policy. Members know everyone's preferences, so they can form expectations about what policy is expected to be proposed if the proposer is drawn from the majority party, and what is expected to be chosen if the proposer is drawn from the full chamber. We simulate this by actually running this process repeatedly, varying the location of the status quo for each distribution of member preferences. We continue the process over a range of partisan preferences, from those that do not approximate the condition in CPG very well to those that do so very well. The simulation results are just as predicted by CPG—the more internal homogeneity in the majority party and the greater the differences in preferences of the majority compared to the minority party's preferences, the more likely a floor majority will vote to restrict itself to bills proposed by the majority party. All of this merely is to demonstrate that the majority party can affect policy outcomes without having any carrots or sticks to use to encourage recalcitrant members to come to the aid of the party. By vote of the whole chamber, they very well might vote to constrain themselves to consider only policy changes closer to the majority party and away from the policy center of the full chamber.

Reasons for Creating Parties

Motivations for MCs to form parties in the first place, both within a legislature and within an electorate, were reviewed in chapter 2. Recall that these results demonstrated that the assumption of long-term ambition among politicians and the value of reducing uncertainty induced collective interests even in cases (such as purely distributive politics and candidate-centered elections) where there were no seeming collective interests in the short run. Conversely, we saw that the existence of a PIE in the legislature yielded no incentives per se for forming a legislative party, but that there were such incentives in the absence of a PIE through reduction of the uncertainty that the instability of majority rule induces, especially in avoiding the worst outcomes for members of the majority party. Since PIEs essentially never exist, this long-term incentive should be taken to be present ordinarily. Although not a demonstration that MCs would in fact create parties (and thus a demonstration of "equilibrium partisan institutions"), the results do demonstrate the possibility of establishing them—and in a context as devoid of shared policy interests as could be devised.

Given that there are partisan institutions in Congress, their very existence creates incentives for individuals to be affiliated with a party, even in the absence of its electoral value. For example, given the partisan organization of Congress and the resulting distribution of rewards, even with "automatic" rules, such as seniority, those rare MCs elected independently or as members of a third party have even short-term incentives to affiliate with a major party, just as Bernard Sanders (House, later Senate, Independent, VT) and James Buckley (Senate, Conservative, NY) sought affiliation with a major party. Longer-term incentives, such as seeking power within the chamber, further enhance these short-term incentives. Whether due to collective action, social choice, or (career) ambition theoretic problems, these are all incentives that come from MCs' seeking to realize their goals, in these cases through the agency of a political party.

We have now reviewed a large number of results indicating that parties, through access to the benefits of office, through agreements to vote together, or through collective partisan control of the agenda, *can* exert considerable influence on policy outcomes and on MCs' ability to realize their goals. Some incentives for partisan affiliation and even the creation of parties in the first place exist independent of shared political interests. The formal structures of party and committee are virtually unchanged in Congress, but MCs have at times empowered their parties with rules to promote joint action and given their leaders more resources for those purposes. At other times partisans have denied their party the rules and resources to effectively structure action in Congress.

INSTITUTIONAL STRUCTURES IN THE HOUSE AND THE RISE OF PARTY VOTING IN THE 1980s

In this section I apply the theory presented in the previous section to examine structures in the House and their changes over the past century in broad terms. I also apply the theory to explain the decline and rise of party voting in the House over the past four decades in more detail. The broader historical considerations suggest that, like contemporary party government, hierarchical (or "boss" or "czar" rule), party-caucus government, and the committee-centered, bargaining system that congressional reforms of the 1970s replaced are *all* conditional forms of intralegislative institutional arrangements. Not only that, but all of these forms are conditional on the *same* critical variable, the partisan distribution of policy preferences. Thus, as this variable changes over time, we observe broad and dramatic changes in the internal structures of the U.S. House. As we focus more closely on the era after World War II, we can observe the more detailed patterning anticipated by CPG.

Alternative Structures in the House

Not long after Woodrow Wilson (1885) wrote of a Congress dominated by "lord high baron" committee chairs overseen by an even more powerful Speaker, "Boss" Thomas Reed was elected Speaker of the House.[18] Boss Reed and "Czar" Joseph Cannon personified the hierarchical structuring of House politics. Reed literally rewrote the rules governing the House, and through Cannon's speakership the czar had great powers. He appointed all chairs and all members of committees for both parties, virtually controlled the flow of legislation through committees and onto the floor, and had equally great control over the agenda on the floor itself, not only through what Cooper and Brady (1981, 412) call his "powers of repression," but also through his ability to exercise more positive powers (for a brief enumeration, see Cooper and Brady 1981). Equal to Reed's formal power as Speaker of the House, they argue, was his power as party chief.

> Initiative in the definition of party policies belonged to him. Moreover, if he could not win the support of all elements in the party, he had at his disposal a powerful mechanism for enforcing adherence to his wishes—the caucus. Through a binding vote in the caucus, he could oblige opposition to support his policy positions out of party loyalty.

Further:

> Unlike the contemporary House [when Cooper and Brady were writing, at the end of the committee-centric era] where party leaders and committee chairs are separate, committee and party leaders were one and the same. Tensions between the two were accordingly greatly reduced. . . . It was thus not a mere figure of speech to refer to committee chairs as a "cabinet." Both structurally and behaviorally, committee and party leaders were a cabinet. (Cooper and Brady, 413)

They then go on to explore the bases of czar rule, which they summarize by writing,

> In sum, then, it is critical to note the correspondence between a [partisan] polarized electoral system and a highly centralized leadership structure. Though the Speaker's formal powers reinforced party strength, the polarized electoral bases of the party system provided an indispensable platform for Czar rule. Thus, when the electoral polarization began to decline, the centralized internal structure also began to come apart. (415)

The "coming apart" was of course the revolt against the Speaker, in which the growing numbers of progressive Republicans combined with Democrats to overthrow at least some aspects of hierarchical control. These powers of party bosses therefore appear to have emanated from the rise of the Republican Party to control of the House and then to unified control of government after the realignment of the 1890s. As Cooper and Brady's analysis suggests, the GOP was rather homogeneous in policy preferences at the outset, heterogeneous by the time of the revolt.

The boss form of governing, therefore, is, according to Cooper and Brady's analysis (1981), effectively a form of CPG. It differs from the form observed in the contemporary era for a number of historically contingent reasons, but most especially because of the electoral connection. The boss era coincides with the introduction of the secret ballot and other changes (as discussed above) that initiated the very beginnings of candidate-centered campaigns, the first signs of the personal vote (McGerr 1986), and the reforms initiated within the chamber that marked the coming of the professional Congress. The truly candidate-centered campaigns of today were simply beyond reach for nearly all incumbents. Their ability to campaign, therefore, remained disproportionately party centered and thus their electoral autonomy was significantly less than today.

Following that revolt against Cannon, Democrats held a majority in the House from 1911 to 1919. They dismantled the hierarchical control wielded by czar-Speakers, but instead of dismantling the influence of party, they elevated it. Their experiment in party-caucus government succeeded for a while, but only as long as there was relative homogeneity in policy preferences. The normative appeal of party government and party loyalty, however, frayed "as the direct primary and ballot reform made it both possible and necessary for each member to paddle 'his own political canoe'" (Price 1977). More to the point, Price continues, "The Wilsonian Democrats' agreement on substantive policy was exhausted by 1916, and the issues of World War I split the party sharply. Small wonder that by 1920 *neither* party caucus in the House amounted to much" (59; emphasis in original).

The rejection of party-assented autocratic control and of party-caucus government did not lead to equal distribution of power among all MCs, allegedly true of the 1970s, or to a return to floor-dominated decision making, such as in the original use of the Committee of the Whole. Seniority became the Democratic majority's operative rule for selecting committee chairs by 1918, and though the Republicans criticized that practice, they effectively used it on their return to majority status in 1919 (Price 1977). Seniority was the de facto rule until the 1970s. Although it would be difficult to imagine a committee chair having no power whatever, the position could be granted more or fewer resources for exercising influence. In fact committee chairs came to have substantial, if still variable, resources, at least within their jurisdiction. The House became characterized by a diffusion of power and bargaining among committee chairs and the Speaker, such as under Sam Rayburn, which Cooper and Brady (1981) contrast to hierarchical control under Cannon. Jurisdictions themselves were a key ingredient. The committee system became rather like the one Shepsle modeled formally, in which committee jurisdictions effectively were a mutually exclusive and exhaustive division of the policy space, proposals would be referred automatically to the specific committee with appropriate jurisdiction, and no policy in that area could emerge on the floor without its—and generally that meant the chair's personal—assent. This included the period in which Shepsle (1978) demonstrated the importance of self-selection onto committees. These three features (and more) were rather like "rights": the majority member with longest service on the committee had the automatic right to be the chair, all extant members had the right to maintain their committee assignments, and each committee had "property rights" over all legislation in its jurisdiction.

These "automatically operative" rules of assignment, seniority, and jurisdiction need not signal an impotent party. Consider, for example, the New Deal coalition. The solid South meant that southern Democrats had safe seats, accumulated the greatest seniority, and therefore were disproportionately committee chairs. The South was, however, a large and critical component of the New Deal coalition in elections and in government, since it was affected by the Depression as deeply as any region, and more than most. As a result, southerners were as likely to support New Deal legislation as any other Democrats (see Sinclair 1982).[19] Throughout much of the prewar years, the Democratic Party was relatively homogeneous in overall preferences, but even had it been more deeply divided, giving power to southerners was giving power to New Deal Democrats.

At least, the South was a full part of the New Deal coalition as long as Roosevelt and northern Democrats did not seriously address and therefore make salient the issues that did divide northern from southern Democrat. In 1936, FDR added northern blacks to the New Deal coalition, as small a voting bloc as they were. That year, Richard Russell (D-GA) ran for his first full term in the Senate as a supporter of the New Deal, defeating Governor Eugene Talmadge on that basis. But by 1937, he became a part of the conservative coalition (and eventually its effective leader in the Senate) in opposition to FDR's "court packing" plan, thus undercutting temporarily the president's ability to enact the more liberal legislation of the second New Deal.

It was only after World War II that the divisions between the North and South in the Democratic Party, always latent (and in the earlier period occasionally active), could no longer be kept off the agenda. Civil rights was foremost among the divisive issues, but the variety of issues that came to define what "liberal" meant in the 1950s and 1960s tended to divide the majority party by region. When the Democrats were in the minority in these years, the South constituted a majority of that party in the House. But that was true only about half the time before 1955 and was never again true after the 1954 elections. By then the North constituted a majority of the Democratic Party, and northerners had different preferences than their southern peers. Not until 1958 was that majority especially large, and by 1959 the majority in the majority party had policy preferences different from those of its southern wing, yet that wing effectively held power—power to block liberal initiatives in committee and, if that failed, to combine with Republicans to defeat the majority of the majority party on the floor.

Changing the Rules

Rohde (1991) traces the origins of the reforms of the 1970s to 1959, with the founding of the liberal Democratic Study Group. The DSG, an important base of support for Kennedy and Johnson in the 1960s, proposed reforms, and many were adopted in the 1970s. Rohde categorizes these into three tracks. The first concerned the power of committees and, especially, their chairs. The Legislative Reorganization Act of 1970 initiated these reforms with some relatively minor procedures. In 1971 the Democratic Party caucus adopted the recommendations of its Hansen Committee, including limited conditions for the caucus to vote for committee chairs and provision of some resources to subcommittee chairs, beginning to free them from the control of the committee chair.

In 1973 caucus voting for committee chairs became automatic, with the option for a secret ballot. More famous was adoption of the "subcommittee bill of rights," which, as its name suggests, gave the subcommittees and their chairs substantial independence, by "right," from the full committee and its chair. For example, subcommittee chairs were bid for based on seniority rather than appointed (or perhaps never filled) by the committee chair. Each subcommittee had to have a defined jurisdiction, and legislation was to be reported to the subcommittee with appropriate jurisdiction. Each subcommittee was also given its own budget and control over choice of its staff. In 1975, with election of the large "Watergate babies" class, the caucus exercised its power to select committee chairs by voting against seniority (and incumbency), rejecting three southerners: William Poage (D-TX) as chair of Agriculture, F. Edward Herbert (D-LA) as chair of Armed Services, and Wright Patman (D-TX) as chair of Banking and Currency.

The second track concerned strengthening the party and its leadership. The Steering and Policy Committee was created in 1973 as a reasonably representative body of the caucus and leadership, and charged with shaping the party's positions on policy.[20] Although not especially important in this role until the 1980s, in 1975 it became the Committee on Committees, replacing the Democrats on Ways and Means. It was of course also in that year that the caucus first exercised its power to select committee chairs. The previous year the Speaker's powers had begun to be enhanced, in this case by the permitting of multiple referrals. In 1975 the Rules Committee was dramatically brought back within the purview of the majority party. The Speaker was given the power to appoint its chair (with caucus approval) and all of its Democratic members. No longer could a Howard W. Smith (VA) use that chairmanship (along with other conservatives and Republicans) to block initiatives favored by Democrats, as he had done during the Kennedy administration. In 1977 the Speaker was granted the right to set time limits on each committee's consideration of a bill. In this period he was given greater control over the floor by two increases in the numbers of days the House could act under suspension of rules. Finally, the ratio of Democrats to Republicans on committees was strengthened and extended by rule to all subcommittees.

The third track concerned enhancing "the collective control of power," that is, strengthening the party as a collectivity and enhancing the power of its leaders to move party-supported legislation. Some of these methods, such as secret voting by the caucus on each committee chair, were mentioned earlier. The subcommittee bill of rights was strengthened by establishing a Democratic caucus for each committee and giving it a variety of powers. The four major committees—Appropriations, Budget, Rules, and Ways and Means—were targeted for special attention. The full caucus voted to ratify all subcommittee chairs on Appropriations. The chair of Budget was elected by the caucus in the same way party leaders are selected. Democrats on the Rules Committee came to be appointed by the Speaker, as noted. Ways and Means not only was stripped of its committee assignment powers but was enlarged by 50 percent to make it more representative of the caucus, and it was forced to create subcommittees. Whereas the Rules Committee had routinely given a closed, special rule to Ways and Means (barring any amendments at all), especially on tax measures, procedures were created to enable amendments approved by the caucus to be in order on the floor.

The thrust of these reforms justifies the earlier quotation from Rohde about the implicit contract between actual or aspiring party leaders, committee chairs, and members of the most important committees, on the one hand, and the party and its caucus on the other. Note, however, that these reforms were enacted from 1970 to 1977. Procedures have been modified since, but the only large-scale reforms in the 1980s were the massive expansion of the whip system and the creation of parallel task forces to oversee particular pieces of legislation. These more recent changes are important, creating a party strategy of "inclusion" that Sinclair (1991, 97) summarizes by saying about task forces, "By increasing the number of people working in an organized way to pass the bill at issue, the task force increases the probability of a bill's success on the floor. Working on a task force satisfies junior members' expectations of participation and fosters cooperative patterns of behavior among party members." Yet with these important exceptions, the major reforms in the House and the Democratic Party (and sometimes, in similar form or purpose, in the Republican Party; see Rohde 1991) occurred at the same time that party voting and party unity were decreasing, and at just the same time that party was seriously rivaled by the conservative coalition as the voting coalition most common in the House. Small wonder that the usual understanding of the reforms of the 1970s at that time was of their powerful decentralizing role. Much autonomy was granted to individual MCs, and power was diffused from relatively few committee chairs to a far larger number of subcommittee chairs and even to subcommittee members. The inability of a weakened Nixon, an unelected Ford, and a seemingly ineffective Carter to achieve legislative action, even with unified partisan control of government, strongly suggested that decentralization owing to reform was the culprit.

Yet action did begin, initially and significantly during the Carter administration. It seemed after Reagan's election that the first signs of a Democratic majority's taking action in the House were effectively lost to a conservative coalition in the House, a Republican Senate, and an active and ambitious Republican administration. Surprisingly soon, however, that too reversed, and by the middle to late 1980s the House majority party was apparently able to use its relatively newfound means of action to act in harmony, to oppose the president, and, in the One Hundredth Congress, to win a substantial and ambitious agenda in the House and pass much of it into law.

Changes in Partisan Preferences, Conditional Party Government, and Positive Agenda Control

With reforms mostly completed by the mid-1970s, the elements were in place for conditional party government to operate. If they wanted to, the Democrats in the House could exert this form of party government. The "if"—the "condition" in conditional party government—was not yet sufficiently well satisfied, however. In terms of the theory presented here, we can assume that policy change was feasible: it almost always is. Reforms newly in place made it possible that the structure of party and committee developed in theory could work in practice. The end of automatic use of seniority in selecting committee chairs signaled clearly that at least some responsiveness to party concerns was required to ensure that seniority would be honored, and changes in the powers granted to committee chairs, subcommittees, and Democrats on them reinforced the necessity to attend, at least minimally, to the concerns of fellow partisans. Even party leaders were not immune to such control. Thus it became possible to enforce compliance with party instructions. The caucus itself, or more often bodies that reasonably represented it, began to search for instructions to give—to determine what was desirable to the party collectively. In short, rules provided for determining what was feasible and desirable and for internalizing the collective interests of the party in the self-interest of its committee and party leaders.

What was missing, then, was simply a set of *desirable* policies different from the status quo. A Democratic Party divided over race and a variety of social issues, over the Vietnam War and subsequent defense policies, and over spending for new domestic policies that would extend the Great Society would likely find that what was feasible on the floor and also desirable to at least a majority of Democrats would be close to the status quo. This finding would be especially likely in the face of needing the support, however grudging, of a Republican president. For example, it was not until 1975 that the caucus exercised its powers to select committee chairs in violation of strict seniority. A conservative committee chair might well have reasoned that the formal powers of selection would not be used effectively with a caucus that still had difficulty ensuring a quorum at its meetings. Significantly, as figure 7.5 shows (and as the annual proportions reinforce), the presidential success rate in Congress (passage through both chambers) jumped from the 50 percent range of the preceding four years to 75 percent and higher over Carter's four years in office, essentially the same rate as at the end of the Johnson administration.

We cannot know the distribution of preferences of MCs in general, except through measures based on roll call voting. It is likely, however, that the policy preferences of Democrats changed over the 1970s and into the 1980s for two reasons. First, the policy agenda changed. Civil rights, which so evidently divided North from South, was increasingly rare as a voting issue, even by the early 1970s. Economic policy became more important, as stagflation, WIN ("Whip Inflation Now") buttons, and the misery index typified. Although Nixon might proclaim that "we are all Keynesians" and seek to impose wage and price controls, the mounting economic woes under Carter were accompanied by the tax revolt (e.g., Propositions 13 in California and 2 1/2 in Massachusetts) and, in Congress and then Reagan's campaign, by the Kemp-Roth tax cut and supply-side economics agendas. In the 1980s the escalating deficits not only became a voting issue but also constrained the ability to seriously consider any new or enhanced expensive spending programs for domestic or defense concerns. The bipartisan foreign policy consensus of the postwar era was shattered by the Vietnam War. Demobilization and heightened international tensions in such places as Iran and Afghanistan led first Carter and then Reagan to push aggressively and successfully for dramatic increases in defense spending, further decreasing flexibility for new domestic initiatives. In short, what MCs were asked to vote on differed significantly over time. Although it is true that the voting agenda—what proposals make it to the floor—is at least partially endogenous to the actions and thus the preferences of MCs themselves, it is also true that the agenda is shaped partially by exogenous forces, whether the USSR, Iran, OPEC, and the international economy or changing citizen activity such as the decline of the civil rights movement, rise of environmentalists, Jarvis and Gann (leaders of the Proposition 13 tax revolt in California), a new president, and so on. A different mix of issues, some imposed by forces beyond the immediate control of Congress, can make differing aspects of policy preferences more central, aspects that may enhance party unity and cleavage or accentuate the divisions within one party or both.

It is also likely true that the preferences of Democratic MCs changed over time. Although preferences probably changed in both parties and in all regions, most prominent were changes among southern Democrats. Enfranchisement of blacks after 1965 dramatically expanded the proportion of liberals in the southern electorate. In some districts, for example, blacks held an outright majority and elected liberal black Democrats to Congress, whereas in others their proportions were sufficiently large to weigh heavily. Fleisher (1993) shows that white liberal Democrats seem to have made the most substantial contribution to the increasing "liberalness" of southern Democratic MCs. The increasing success of the GOP's "southern strategy" led to the election of conservative southern Republicans in place of conservative southern Democrats, while some conservative southern MCs switched to the GOP directly. Simply by contesting in losing efforts, Republican candidates with, say, 30 percent of the vote shaved that much of the most conservative electorate from the electoral constituency of Democrats. Some erstwhile conservative Democrats came to reflect their electoral constituency with representation inducing more moderate policy preferences. Incumbency remained a strong force, and some conservative Democrats continued to be conservative. Their replacements, however, were more likely to be either moderate or even liberal Democrats, or they were conservative Republicans. In any event, they were less likely to be conservative Democrats. Changing agendas and changing electoral conditions, therefore, gradually changed the composition of the southern Democratic delegation.

In at least some instances, moreover, the reforms seemed to have had a direct impact on influential southern Democrats. Rohde (1991) considered the case of Jamie Whitten (D-MS), whose nomination to be chair of Appropriations had been unsuccessfully but strongly challenged in 1979. In that Congress his party unity score exceeded 50 percent for the first time since before the 1958 watershed elections. It was also the first time since those elections that his loyalty ratings trailed other southern Democrats by less than 10 percent and trailed all Democrats by less than 25 points. In Reagan's first Congress, Whitten's unity score climbed to 68 (more loyal than the average southern Democrat and fewer than 10 points less loyal than all Democrats), then to 78, 79, and by the One Hundredth Congress (1987–88), to 88 percent—more loyal than even the average Democrat.

Nonsouthern Democrats also changed. The Watergate babies, elected in 1974, typified the new breed of "neoliberal," "Atari" Democrats, who were more strongly disposed to new defense initiatives and less strongly disposed toward new government programs on the domestic side, preferring to focus on already successful programs or to depend more on the private sector and encourage economic growth through industrial policies. Collectively, the distance between northern and southern Democrats shrank, while the salience of the issues that most divided them, especially civil rights, receded.

Combined with the reasonably high level of support given to Carter, the southern Democrat in the White House, Democratic loyalty scores increased. Although northern Democrats' loyalty scores were essentially constant, Carter's proposals were on balance more moderate than Johnson's or even Kennedy's. If that is true, the high loyalty rates of northern Democrats reflect a somewhat more moderate voting record, albeit over a quite different agenda than in the 1960s. At the same time, the dramatic increases in southern Democratic loyalty reflect a mixture of their own net more-moderate stance and the change from opposition to a liberal agenda to support for a moderately liberal one.

Reagan's election changed this calculus in several important ways. First, the choice shifted from comparing the status quo with the proposals of a Democratic administration to comparing a conservative Republican proposal with the status quo on such issues as tax cuts, or a conservative Republican budget with a Democratic alternative. Second, the loss of the Senate meant that the Speaker was now the only national Democratic leader in the government. Democratic alternatives or even simply opposition had to come from the House or nowhere. Third, in 1981–82 that majority was smaller than it had been for years—and that reduction came primarily from the party's northern wing. Remaining conservative Democrats and Republicans could carry the House. Senior southern Democrats, such as Whitten, could feel relatively safe in spite of the Republican threat. More newly elected conservative southern Democrats, largely making up what came to be known as the Boll Weevils (members of the newly created Conservative Democratic Forum and predecessor to today's Blue Dog Democrats), were far less secure. They could reasonably worry that opposition to the central tenets of the conservative president's agenda, a president who often carried their districts in 1980, could lead to significant Republican opposition in 1982—and defeat. In that Congress, if Republicans were united, only a little over half of the forty-seven Boll Weevils would need to defect from their party to pass a Reagan bill.

The Republican electoral threat, however, did not materialize for many of these MCs in 1982—or in 1984 or thereafter through the 1980s. Indeed, Republican congressional fortunes in the South waned. Perhaps owing to a failure to build an effective grassroots party in much of the South, the GOP congressional gains of the 1970s stalled. The proportion of southern seats the party no longer even contested increased over the 1980s, for instance. The result was that the electoral safety of remaining Boll Weevils increased. Republican losses in the recession year of 1982 were modestly replaced in 1984. Even so, after the 1984 elections, the combination of all 166 Republicans and the 35 remaining Boll Weevils added up to less than the 218 majority. As Rohde puts it, "As a consequence, more and more efforts to find a policy position that could win on the floor took place *within* the Democratic Party" (1991, 50; emphasis in original). Recapture of the Senate two years later only spurred such efforts, even though initiative remained primarily in the House and, especially in the One Hundredth Congress of 1987–88, with Speaker James Wright.

The result was that, after declining in the 1981–82 Congress, the proportion of party votes in the House jumped nearly 15 percent and remained over 50 percent throughout the 1980s—a rate of party voting higher than it had been for decades—while conservative coalition formation decreased over the decade to the lowest rates in this era. Significantly, although the decline of conservative coalition voting in the Senate closely tracked that rate in the House, the change in party voting in the Senate was far less than in the House. Although party voting in the Senate had consistently exceeded that in the House and had climbed slowly but consistently since the "Great Society" Congress, it leveled off in the Carter years and bounced erratically with no overall increase in the 1980s. The jump in party voting in the House after the 1982 elections was not found in the Senate, and House voting remained significantly more partisan throughout the 1980s (see figs. 7.1–7.4).

Similarly, Democratic Party unity in the House, which had dipped into the middle to lower 70s in the late 1960s (as did Republican unity) began to climb in the Carter years and, with only a slight setback in 1981–82, resumed its climb to over 85 percent, a point reached after the 1984 elections, and a rate higher than any since the revolt against Speaker Cannon. Moreover, it was precisely at that time that Democratic unity noticeably exceeded Republican unity for the first time. This average was made possible by the truly substantial increases in southern Democratic unity that began in earnest in the Carter years, was set back sharply in the first two years of the Reagan administration, resumed its climb, and matched that in the Republican Party after the 1984 elections. Democratic unity in the Senate had been much closer to constant, in spite of changes in southern unity of similar magnitude in the Senate as in the House. Conversely, the ascension to majority status (and beginning of Republican control of the presidency) increased unity to their party among Senate Republicans, something that did not happen at all in their House delegation. Perhaps more critical are Rohde's data, referred to above, that show substantial increases in Democrats' ability to win these party votes. Over the period 1981–86, recall, he showed that the Democrats increased from winning little more than half of party votes in 1981 to winning nearly 90 percent in 1986.

This evidence suggests that the strengthened party machinery, when finally combined with relatively homogeneous preferences over a new agenda, yielded a far more partisan governance of the House in the 1980s and, with that, Democratic success on a larger number of votes. It still does not demonstrate that what passed the House was different from what would have happened without the reforms of the party or, even more, based on MCs' preferences alone. Dealing with a counterfactual, there is never certain evidence of what would have happened if all decisions had been made on the floor. It is true, of course, that the only line of voting cleavage of any significance in this period was partisan, when it could have been some other basis as it often was in the 1970s. And it is true that the two parties played a great role in defining the policy alternatives based on that partisan cleavage. The House Republican agenda was largely (though not always) set by the White House. The alternatives were defined by the Democratic Party in the House. After the 1982 elections, for example, the relatively large class of freshman Democrats saw the deficit as the central issue for their election and for governance. Through the caucus or its representative bodies, an implicit agreement was struck, so that liberals did not push as hard for increased spending on the domestic side while moderate and conservative Democrats refrained from supporting, and sometimes actively opposed, increases in defense spending.

Control of the agenda was never more apparent, though, as the One Hundredth Congress opened after the 1986 elections. As Rohde put it (1991, 105), "The new Speaker startled many outside observers when, in his acceptance speech to the Caucus, he began outlining an agenda of legislative priorities for the House in 1987," which he further developed on national television in his reply to Reagan's State of the Union address on January 31 (Sinclair 1990, 234). These ten bills (listed in Rohde 1991, 110, table 4.2) were ambitious, covering the budget, action against the deficit, amendments to the Clean Water Act, highway construction, trade, aid for the homeless, welfare reform, aid to education, the (aptly named, ill-fated) catastrophic health insurance bill, farms, highways, and the savings and loan crisis.

As Sinclair said, Wright looked for what was feasible and desirable to the party: "In drawing up his priorities for the congress, the Speaker consulted with other members and also relied upon his judgment about what legislation [Democratic] members really wanted and needed to advance their goals, on the one hand, and what would pass on the other." It was also important to keep this agenda intact because, taken as a whole, it "contained items important to all segments of the party; a majority of those items had broad support throughout the party" (Sinclair 1990, 234). He used his leadership to keep attention on his agenda and employed a variety of devices to ensure that each piece of legislation emerged from the relevant committee or committees largely intact. Moreover, as Rohde shows (1991; see especially p. 111, table 4.3, and discussion thereof), he ensured that the Rules Committee provided special rules to limit amendment and other tactics that might erode support or delay action on the floor. The tactics worked, as every one of these priorities passed the House, with an average of only fourteen defections from Democrats. Again, this does not *prove* that these items would not have been enacted without the party rules and leadership, but that seems likely. Final passage into law had to negotiate a less structured Senate and an opposing president. Every one of these initiatives became law in one form or another. Two were passed over a presidential veto, but on three of them—the savings and loan rescue, welfare reform, and farm credits—the House and the presidency struck a compromise, each giving and each getting some of what it wanted (see Rohde 1991, 175–76, for more details).

Again this is only suggestive, but it strongly implies that the majority party in Congress shaped the agenda and achieved results that would not have happened without the combination of changed procedures and changed preferences among Democrats. As Rohde put it, "The majority party in the House *can* propose a program different from that offered by the president. The Democrats did so in the One Hundredth Congress. Moreover, under divided government the House majority *can* challenge (and defeat) the administration. On Wright's priority measures, the Democrats either secured a compromise result in which each side got part of what it wanted, or they prevailed outright" (1991, 176; emphasis in original). Sinclair (1990, 235) points out that, while promising cooperation with the newly elected president, the Speaker once again defined an alternative agenda for the succeeding congress. "Although not as extensive or specific as the 100th Congress' agenda, the leadership's engagement in counteragenda setting in the first year of a new president's term [1989] suggests that this has now become a normal rather than extraordinary leadership activity"—at least as long as the party can find new policies that are feasible and desirable.

I discussed this period closely because it marks the transition from the committee-centered era to the contemporary party-centered House. It seems fair to say that by the One Hundredth Congress, the "C" in

CPG was well satisfied and we could observe politics proceeding as expected by the theory. Because elections have only become more partisan since then, we can cover more recent events more quickly.

The "Republican Revolution," and Into the Obama Era

The Democratic majority seemed unassailable. Certainly, there were threats to their status. The aggressive, rising Republican leader Newt Gingrich (R-GA) was successful in bringing down Speaker Wright in an ethics scandal in 1989, which was followed by a series of other scandals that fell more heavily on the majority party. Still no one, not even Gingrich, anticipated that Republicans would win so many seats in 1994 that they would break the forty-year Democratic hold on the House majority. To be sure, Gingrich and other emerging Republican leaders in the House made possible their victories that year. They recruited candidates and resources to contest even where success seemed unlikely.

Gingrich developed the "Contract with America" for creating an electoral and legislative agenda for the Republican Party. Like Wright's agenda in 1987, a ten-point agenda was proposed. Unlike Wright's case, however, it was proposed before the elections and as a part of the party's national campaign strategy. Indeed, perhaps especially in midterm election years, the idea of a national plan complete with a platform for the public campaign was highly unusual, if not unprecedented. The only and much more modest recent precedent was the decision by the House Republican campaign committee in 1978 to require endorsement of the "Kemp-Roth" tax plan (cutting taxes by roughly 30 percent, a plan adopted by Ronald Reagan as part of his electoral strategy two years later) to receive their support. A high-profile signing on to the Contract by candidates, incumbents or not, was held on the steps of the Capital for public consumption. Candidates were free to run on all or only part of the Contract (or ignore it, of course, but few did). Still, regardless of its high level of organized activity, that the GOP actually won a majority of House seats took everyone by surprise.

Surprised or not, Gingrich took immediate control of the situation. While not yet even selected as Speaker-designate, he initiated numerous reforms (see Aldrich and Rohde 1997–98). Within a week of the election, for example, it was announced that three ranking minority members on major committees (Appropriations, Energy, and Judiciary) were being bypassed in violation of seniority, and this was even before the Republican Conference could meet to authorize new selection procedures or to endorse the new choices. Significant changes were also made to the powers of committees, including abolishing three of them. Republicans adopted term limits for their leaders (six years for chairs, eight for the party leader). The party leadership also brought committees to heel, through the use of task forces, to obtain major legislation without referral at all, and, in numerous instances on important legislation, with direct leadership intervention into committee proceedings. The leadership itself received greater powers than earlier, and in a variety of ways centralized control over the legislative process in the Conference and its leadership. For example, whereas Democrats tended to use special rules to shape agenda control when they were in the majority, Republicans initially resisted doing so, but having open debate and amendment processes ended quickly—while they sought to pass the Contract in the first one hundred days of the Republican majority.

Gingrich had emerged as a national leader, far more visible to the public than any recent Speaker, and he challenged the public influence even of the president. To be sure, he, and perhaps the party, overreached. Most of the Contract passed the House but little became law. Much of the public perception of the party being a force akin to the president was lost. They (and not the president) were seen as the problem in causing a temporary shutdown of the government in 1995 over inability to fashion a budget. While control of Congress obviously provided them with considerable leverage, such as their ability to force Clinton to accept a dramatic and pro-Republican change in welfare (ending "welfare as we know it" as Clinton put it), the 1998 articles of impeachment may have passed the House but impeachment itself failed in the Senate and led almost directly to the resignation of Gingrich and the scandal-tinged resignation of his likely successor, Bob Livingston (R-LA, who was the one who received the chair of Appropriations out of seniority in 1995).

A common question to ask concerning Gingrich's resignation was whether the evident importance that party took over committee under his speakership was due to the leadership capabilities of his and the other leaders or whether it was due to conditions that produced pressures encouraging centralization among Republicans. And with the ascension of Dennis Hastert as Speaker, the question became even more focused as Hastert promised a return to "regular" procedures. That did not happen, however (see Aldrich and Rohde 2008). Not only was there no reversion, Hastert oversaw the strengthening of central leadership even further. For example, Aldrich and Rohde write (2010, 248),

> In 2000, when the term limit was reached by many sitting chairs, the party (led by Speaker Dennis Hastert of Illinois) chose to vest the selection of their successors in the leadership-dominated Steering Com-

mittee, which conducted competitive elections among self-starting candidates from the committee in question. This process often chose someone other than the most senior candidate, and in many cases bypassed a more senior moderate to pick a more conservative but more junior member. Then in 2002, with the urging of Speaker Hastert, the GOP extended that selection mechanism to all subcommittee chairmanships on the powerful Appropriations Committee. In addition to influencing the initial selection of committee chairs, the Republican leadership demonstrated that they could penalize recalcitrant chairs. This happened in 2005, when Chris Smith of New Jersey was removed as chair of the Veterans Affairs Committee because his continuous efforts to increase spending on veterans programs conflicted with leadership priorities. Smith had been warned that he needed to be responsive to the leadership, and after he persisted in his efforts he was deprived of his position. Thus during the Republican era, the party leaders demonstrated that they could influence the selection (and even cause the removal) of committee leaders. Thus those committee leaders were forced to be responsive to the wishes of the leaders, who were themselves agents of the party membership.

As we will see in the next chapter, Republicans introduced competition for such important posts. Aspiring chairs were expected to create leadership PACs (political action committees) to fund Republican congressional campaigns. Rather than selecting chairs via an exogenous (or nearly exogenous) factor such as seniority, the party leadership was allocating posts based on contributions to party building. Incentives for leadership would therefore be dramatically different under the two regimes.

When Democrats regained majority status in 2006, they returned to the mechanisms they had in place before the "Republican Revolution" in 1994. But, while less leadership-centric than Republicans, they nonetheless did not revert all the way back to committee-centered governance. Nancy Pelosi (D-CA), the new Speaker, required John Dingell (D-MI)—a longtime, powerful Democrat, at this point chair of Energy and Commerce—to change positions on energy independence and global warming in legislation, which he did. Even that was insufficiently compliant to the Democratic Caucus after the 2008 elections, and he was replaced as chair by Pelosi ally Henry Waxman (D-CA).

Rules, Reform, and Conditional Party Government

There are many reasons for the dramatic increase in party unity in Congress. CPG highlights two of them. One is the changing nature of the kinds of legislators that voters choose to represent them. In the last chapter and this, I have placed greatest emphasis on the changing nature of southern Democrats, and I believe that incorporation of African

Americans into the southern electorate, after the civil rights and voting rights acts of 1964 and 1965, was indeed the most important impetus to change. This set in motion a long series of changes: liberalization of southern Democrats; creation of a viable and increasingly strong southern Republican Party; and in indirect reaction, the decline of the Republican Party's social liberal wing, the "Rockefeller Republicans." These changes resulted in the massive decline of Republicans elected to Congress in New England and lesser but still substantial declines in mid-Atlantic and Great Lake states. This not only sorted the two parties more fully by ideology, providing for more cohesive politics (exaggerated by changing agendas that deemphasized issues that cut either party internally), but also changed the kind of constituency that made up each party. Before Gingrich, the Republican leadership was almost exclusively northern. That changed dramatically and virtually overnight. As I put it (1999, 16):

> In the 103rd Congress, non-southerners were minority leaders in both chambers as well as the assistant leader in the Senate, and northerners were ranking members of five of the six key committees. In the 104th Congress, southerners held the top three leadership positions in the House (only Paxson of NY, who subsequently resigned under pressure, held a major post and was not southern). In addition, two of the top three leaders in the Senate (and all three if one counts Oklahoma) were southern, and the southern GOP delegation increased its holding from one to three of the six major committee leadership positions in the House.

The second reason for the increase in party unity in Congress is the internal structure of the party organization and leadership in the House. That is the subject of this section—how the increasing internal consensus and external differentiation led the party to adopt different and more party-centric rules. I have described some of these changes here. Because the historical pattern was switching from a committee-centered to a party-centered structure of the House, it might appear that this was a battle of opposing forces. To some extent, of course, there are tensions between party members and committee chairs. Yet, it needs to be remembered that a strong party, as Cox, Kiewiet, and McCubbins argue, acts whenever they can through the committee system, whenever their members can be counted on to be faithful agents of the party, as has been the case during the Pelosi speakership.

Figures 7.6 and 7.7 show this point through two complementary views. In figure 7.6, I report the first dimension of average Poole-Rosenthal scores based on roll call votes on the floor (the dimension most often referred to as "liberal-conservative" and most closely aligned with party

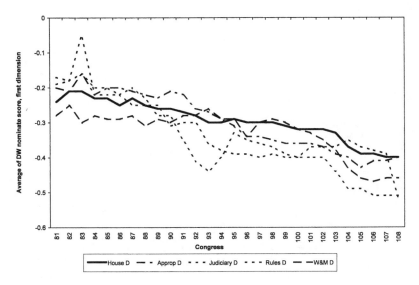

Figure 7.6. Comparison of roll call scores of Democrats on the floor to Democrats on selected committees, 1950–2004.
Source: Malbin et al. (2008). Compiled by author.

affiliation) for all House Democrats and for Democrats with assignments to major committees. Obviously, one story has been the increasingly liberal makeup of the Democratic Party overall. The heaviest line, for example, shows the increasingly liberal voting records of Democrats over time. A second story, however, is the move to create an even more liberal makeup to the most important committees. In the 1950s, Appropriations, Judiciary, and especially the Rules Committee members were more conservative than the party as a whole. Key committees were not only chaired but populated by the more right-wing part of the Democratic Party. Only Ways and Means was more liberal than the whole party. The change in makeup of Rules in 1961 (discussed above) is apparent. Over time, the basic flow has been to populate the most important committees in Congress with Democrats who are more liberal than the party as a whole. Figure 7.7 adds in the Republicans and reports the degree of differentiation between the two parties. Polarization is clearly visible (again, the heavy line indicates the increased polarization between the two parties in the Congress as a whole). The special role of Appropriations in often looking like the floor as a whole is also evident. But, after the expansion of Rules in 1961, and the bringing of Judiciary (where many important civil rights issues were considered) under party control during the Great Society period, the basic pattern

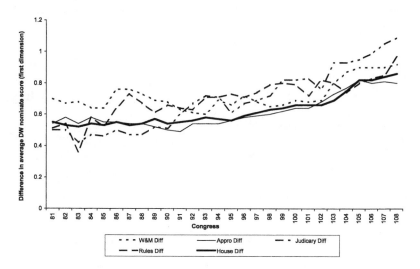

Figure 7.7. Party differences on selected House committees compared to floor, 1950–2004.
Source: Malbin et al. (2008). Compiled by author.

has been that polarization is greater on important committees than on the floor, and that is true even as the degree of floor polarization has grown substantially.

Committees, of course, continue to have gatekeeping power. The exceptions discussed above refer to ways in which the majority party has sought to ensure that its initiatives reach the floor, even if a committee or its chair (e.g., an Appropriations Committee as a whole early in the Republican majority, or a Dingell committee more recently) is recalcitrant. For the minority, committees simply need keep the gates closed. But parties also seek to pass legislation, and CPG anticipates (indeed, its special claim is) that rules and structures are needed to translate those preferences over goals that party affiliates would like to see achieved into forms that are actually able to pass the chamber.

A favorable committee can open the gates (and the basic lesson of figures 7.6 and 7.7 is that the important committees not only have a majority from the majority party but a majority even more disposed to support policies away from the center of the floor), but the party needs to be able to keep the legislation favorable to the wishes of the party on and through the floor. The most important and systematic method for doing so in the House is through adoption of special rules, proposed by the Rules Committee (and voted on the floor), that limit the ability of the minority to alter the proposal too severely. Rules are adopted under all systems. But the evidence suggests that the increasingly polarized House has turned to increasingly partisan special rules. First, the sheer incidence of special rules that require roll call votes has increased dramatically over the last sixty years (see fig. 7.8). Figure 7.9 (from Aldrich and Rohde 2010) suggests why. In that figure are reported the percentage of rules votes on the floor that were partisan unity votes, using both the 50–50 and 90–90 criteria. While many rules votes have also been partisan unity votes throughout the last fifty years and more, it is evident that there was a dramatic change in the 1980s and onward that continues to date. Most dramatic is the increase in 90–90 party votes. These went from occasional to, by the most recent Congress, nearly universal, and the dramatic increase began in the One Hundredth Congress (1987–88). It thus appears that members of both parties in Congress see the rules as favoring the interests of the majority party, and vote accordingly.

The story line, at least in the House, is now complete. Elections have changed in such a way that voters elect members who, when combined into a national legislature, reflect increasing satisfaction of the

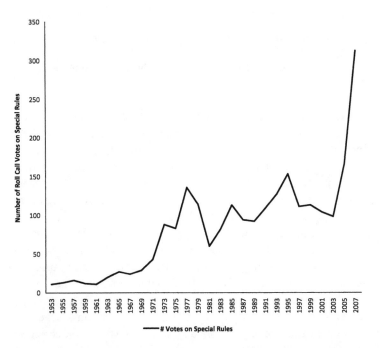

Figure 7.8. Number of votes on special rules, U.S. House, 1953–2009.
Source: David Rohde, Political Institutions and Public Choice House Roll-Call Database (Durham, NC: Duke University, 2010). Compiled by author.

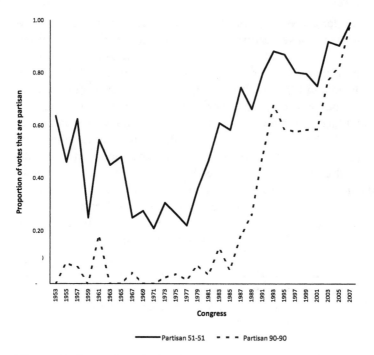

Figure 7.9. Proportion of roll call votes on special rules that are partisan unity votes, U.S. House, 1953–2009.
Source: David Rohde, Political Institutions and Public Choice House Roll-Call Database (Durham, NC: Duke University, 2010). Compiled by author.

condition in CPG. As this changed over the 1970s and especially into the 1980s, both parties, when they were in the majority, changed their procedures and rules in such a way as to strengthen the party caucus or conference and its leadership, and they appear to select leadership that reflects their party affiliates and not the Congress as a whole. They have appointed members to some of the most important committees that not only are typical of the polarized Congress as a whole but are even more polarized than the floor. They apparently have sought to exercise not just negative control through keeping the gates closed in committees, but also positive agenda control, by shaping the way committee or even task force proposals are able to be debated and amended on the floor. It is this combination that has led to the increases in party affiliates voting together and in opposition to the other party on a large and significant proportion of legislation. The House has, that is, changed from a chamber in which power was centered around committees and their chairs, to one in which committees are important, but they are important as arms of the majority party and its leadership. However, this cannot prove causation, of course. These changes could have been adopted for many different reasons, in principle. If, however, the changes in party voting and other indications of party strength in legislation are in fact no more than the reflection of changed preferences among members, the centripetal pressures would remain effectively the only force. Why then bother to spend as much effort in creating these rules and procedures if the parties were only to give in to the centripetal forces? Instead, it seems reasonable to conclude that the parties would go through the effort and cost of organizing and of applying these new rules only to create the centrifugal forces to counterbalance those of the pull to the center.

Party government is thus conditional, and it is primarily conditional on the policy preferences (and other goals) that members seek to achieve. But so too were boss-hierarchy, party-caucus, and seniority-related bargaining among committee chairs conditional, and primarily conditional on the policy preferences (and other goals) that members sought to achieve. Rule changes, as is perhaps especially illustrated by the need to revolt against the Speaker and to laboriously undermine seniority and related mechanisms of the committee-centered bargaining approach, come only with great effort. Conversely, the use of the party caucus or the kind of party government illustrated by the 1890s can quickly disappear. As soon as preferences within the majority party become diverse, there is little feasible policy change that the majority party would desire to use the potential of conditional party government to achieve. Still, the evidence suggests not only that those conditions can exist, but also that the rules assist in achieving those shared preferences to the exclusion of other possible preferences, and that they seemingly help achieve more than in a context that would be achieved with the same preferences but without these partisan-facilitating rules.

The conditions of party government, finally, should not be thought of simply as a set of preferences that members happen to have. They should be understood instead as the result of electoral forces, in the first instance, and of partisan forces operating in the electoral arena in the second. That is, the conditions of party government are more likely to be satisfied the stronger are the direct and, today more commonly, indirect effects of the party-in-elections. The greater electoral competitiveness of Republicans in the South created a more moderate Democratic representative, on average, in that region, and the GOP's efforts to woo more conservative voters in the South undermined their ability to elect moderate Republicans elsewhere. In this sense, nationally competitive elections help induce greater similarity among partisan victors and greater dissimilarity between the two parties. To that extent, broadly competitive parties-in-elections create the conditions needed for the party-in-government to operate effectively. The result may well parallel what David Mayhew claimed was true about the House in the era of strong committees and weaker parties, when he famously wrote (1974, 31),

> The organization of Congress meets remarkably well the electoral needs of its members. To put it another way, if a group of planners sat down and tried to design a pair of American national assemblies with the goal of serving members' electoral needs year in and year out, they would be hard pressed to improve upon what exists.

With changes in the nature of the electoral needs, we would expect a group of planners to revise that design, and as we will see in the next chapter, the members have actually done something very like a hypothetical group of planners might have done, and they might indeed now be hard pressed to improve upon what newly exists.

8   THE CRITICAL ERA OF THE 1960s

In 2006, Lincoln Chafee (R-RI) ran for reelection as one of the most moderate Republicans in the Senate and one of the few remaining Republican Senators in New England. He was challenged by Stephen Laffey, a "combative conservative" Republican (as the *Providence Journal* referred to Laffey), who took far more typical Republican policy positions. Chafee won the primary 54–46. Conservative activists in the Republican Party had come to have a deep dislike of Chafee (unlike their toleration of his father, who had held the seat for decades before him), and Laffey sought to capitalize on that dislike through "push polls" about late-term abortions and other issues. One might think that national Republicans would support the conservative challenger, but they did not. As the online version of the *Providence Journal* put it in their election night coverage (posted September 13, 2006),

> Washington's Republican establishment fought back. While Chafee may be a rebel in the Senate, party leaders saw him as the GOP's only chance to keep the seat in Republican hands. Sen. Elizabeth Dole, the North Carolina Republican who heads the campaign arm of Senate Republicans, has said the national party would not put any campaign money into Rhode Island had Chafee lost yesterday, in effect ceding the seat to Democrats. (http://www.projo.com/extra/election/content/projo_20060913_newgop.37563ed.html)

To no avail, however, as his Democratic opponent, Sheldon Whitehouse, argued, in effect, that though one may like what Chafee stands for and does, he will still be a part of the Republican delegation in the Senate, and so to support Chafee is also to support his party. And, that message that the Republican reputation was too conservative apparently carried the day, as Whitehouse won 54–46. Chafee subsequently mounted an independent candidacy for governor, and he won a three-candidate contest for that office in the 2010 election.

The reputation of a party as a guide to decision making in the public was introduced in chapter 2. Rooted in Key's notion of a standing decision, it was seen as valuable to the extent that it conveyed information to ease the voter's burden in making a decision by giving a single, continuous signal about where the party and (virtually) all of its candidates stand—and how they will act in office. Of course, party reputation is only an aid, and there are potential substitutes. The most important substitute is the reputation of the particular candidate. A reputation for a party might impinge upon a presidential nominee, but given the vast flood of information about the presidential contenders, voters will find less value, at least by election day, in relying upon what the party stands for, because they are likely to know what both candidates stand for—at least much more likely so for presidential nominees than for virtually any other pair of candidates. Similarly, such other candidates as famous figures, longtime incumbents, and the like are able to develop their own reputations. It is the little-known candidates, the newcomers, the aspirants for the relatively obscure offices, and the like who are the most likely to value the reputation of the party, because the voters are most likely to find that the party's reputation is a cheaper way to reach a tentative—and perhaps final—decision than learning about unknown candidates from scratch. It is precisely in this sense that the theory of party reputation from game theoretic models, such as signaling games, converges with V. O. Key Jr.'s notion of a standing decision (1964).

Consider the U.S. Congress. Throughout most of the nineteenth century, voting was public, not secret, and votes were often cast via a party-strip ballot (that is, a physical strip of paper that already had listed the names of the party's nominees on it). Developing a personal reputation was particularly difficult—and not particularly important, because votes were effectively cast for parties and not individual candidates. With the coming of the secret, or Australian, ballot in the late nineteenth century, and even more with a secret ballot organized by office (called, for evident reason, the office-block form of ballot) rather than party-strip format, it became at least imaginable that voters would, in time, have enough information about the candidates (especially the incumbents) to decide on the basis of his reputation rather than the party's. In the earlier period, candidates won if their party got enough votes, so they would do what they could to increase the vote for their party, and thereby for themselves. Around the beginning of the twentieth cen-

THE CRITICAL ERA OF THE 1960s 257

tury, a candidate-centered campaign at least became possible. And, it seems, not only did candidates (and presumably voters) adjust to these more candidate-centered campaigns, but so too did the structure of the Congress (see Katz and Sala 1996; Polsby 1968; Price 1977).

With the nearly automatic operation of the selection of chairs of committees and of the allocation of their powers, both via seniority within the House in the 1920s, incumbents gained access to increased powers simply by being reelected, not (necessarily) by working for the party. The committee- and seniority-centered era of the Congress (roughly from the 1920s through the 1960s) thus enhanced the forces strengthening the candidate as compared to the party as the center of electoral campaigns. And yet, the party remained a powerful electoral force, even for an office as high as the U.S. Congress. One crucial reason for this remaining importance of the party was that the party machines remained the principal source for the resources needed for actually conducting the campaign. While the House was not a particularly important office for the party machine (unlike the city hall or the state legislature), it was difficult for all but the most successful incumbents to develop the means on their own to run a strong campaign. If machines were to decline— as John F. Kennedy discovered they had in 1960—and if alternative means of running a campaign could be found, then at least the longer-term incumbents or otherwise already well known candidates (more commonly found in Senate or gubernatorial campaigns than among House contests) could develop their own personal "machines" for reelection. And by the 1950s and 1960s, as the personalizing media of radio and television came increasingly into their own, the growing strength of incumbency indeed made Congress into *The Electoral Connection*, as Mayhew titled his famous study (1974).

But a third fact, to go along with the rise of candidate-centered campaigns and the decline of party machines, was also true in the 1950s and 1960s. While never completely homogenous, the two parties in both the House and Senate were reaching a twentieth-century peak of internal heterogeneity in views. This was especially true of the Democrats who were divided largely between North and South, and yet were beginning what would prove to be a long run of majority status in the Senate and a very long run in the House. While, as we saw in chapters 4 and 5, the Democrats had always been divided regionally, the issues that long had so divided them were entering the national agenda in this Civil Rights era in a way they had not since the Civil War and Reconstruction. Thus, the Democrats' heterogeneity was especially politically relevant.

When there are such magnifications of internal divisions, the policy relevance of the party's reputation declines. Voters find party less informative for them, because being a party affiliate does not imply as much about where the candidate stands on issues or how the incumbent will vote in Congress, compared to the more internally homogenous party. Candidates, therefore, find it more useful to do something else, such as develop their own reputation and gather their own campaign resources than to run with and through the party as they would were they to remain "party men," to use Van Buren's locution. If the reputation of the party is less valuable to the incumbent in elections, it will be something incumbents respond to less while in office. And, therefore, there is less incentive to paper over differences within the party in Congress.

None of this is to say that the value of the party went to zero, only that it was of lesser value to the voters, and therefore of lesser relevance for candidates, for electoral activists, and thus for officeholders. It is this fraying that led to the observation of declining centrality of the party in the 1960s and into the 1970s. And, it is the increasing homogeneity of both parties and the increasing polarization growing since the 1980s that has increased the value of the party's reputation for public and politician alike. Note that the homogeneity increases the precision of knowing what a party affiliate stands for—that is, it gives a more meaningful reputation. And it is polarization, the increasing divergence between the two parties' reputations on policy, that makes those more meaningful reputations also more useful reputations for reaching judgments between the two parties and their candidates.

THE PUZZLE OF THE POSTWAR PARTY

This chapter begins with an analysis of what seems to be a puzzle in understanding the political party of the 1950s and 1960s. As we saw in chapter 6, party identification and related electoral aspects of the political party were entering a period of decline. But, just as Broder was declaring that *The Party's Over* (1972) and Price was seeking reforms for *Bringing Back the Parties* (1984), others began to analyze parties from other perspectives and concluded, as Kayden and Mayhe did, that *The Party Goes On* (1985) or even claimed, with Sabato, that *The Party's Just Begun* (1988). These scholars and others such as Herrnson (1988) were looking particularly at the party-as-organization, finding that it was strengthening at this time, especially in terms of organizing for electoral purposes.[1] The puzzle, then, is why Key's party-in-the-electorate was declining while the party-as-organization, especially those parts of the organization designed to affect the party-in-the-electorate, was strengthening at just about the same time.

The next few sections present some of the evidence that makes, I believe, the strongest case for the decline of parties-in-the-electorate (distinct from parties-in-elections) and for the strengthening of the parties-as-organizations in this period. The former completes the analysis of Key's party-in-the-electorate, begun in chapter 6, by focusing on the public's declining views of, and identification with, the two major parties. The revitalization of parties-as-organizations points to the exact opposite, the strengthening of the organizations as they become both more "nationalized institutions," to paraphrase Herrnson (1988), and more professionalized, better financed, and effectively stronger overall in performing their central tasks. These sections therefore have the additional virtue of completing the study of (significant aspects of) the Key-Sorauf triad of parties-in-the-electorate, parties-in-government, and parties-as-organizations.

The resolution of this puzzle is in one sense quite simple. The argument is that the old institutional form of the political party, the "modern mass party" invented by Van Buren and others a century and a half ago (see chapters 4 and 5), had collapsed in the 1960s. It was observing the more than century-long run of Van Buren's form of party that led Key to formulate the triad in the first place. With the end of the institution of parties as Van Buren created them, the integration of these three aspects no longer must hold. During the reign of the mass party, the three tended to move together. Thus, for example, the golden age of the mass party in the late nineteenth century saw high levels of party voting (and presumably strong levels of partisan identification) in the electorate, strong party organizations during this zenith of party machines, and unusually effective parties-in-government during the reign of the czar-Speakers undergirded by the norms and interests of party affiliates in the Congress, an instance of conditional party government. Conversely, it was the general weakness of the party in all three of its aspects a half century later that impelled the calls for stronger and more responsible parties by Schattschneider (1942) and the American Political Science Association committee he chaired (APSA 1950).

If the old institutional form of the modern mass political party was gone, so too was the relevance of Key's party in three parts for viewing it. A different institutional design for parties arose to take its place.[2] Thus, if the puzzle is how one aspect of parties as conventionally understood could decline significantly while another aspect strengthened, then that is a puzzle only because we are viewing parties as still the same form that Van Buren invented and Key and Sorauf analyzed. Although Key and Sorauf correctly understood the nature and form of a political party when they wrote, a new form requires a different understanding. Seen in the light of the new institutional form, the puzzle is no puzzle at all. In its place, then, is a new form of party, with a new equilibrium apparently emerging of polarized parties among candidates, activists, and officeholders, with therefore a relatively high degree of conditional party government and a resurgent relevance of party reputation in the party-in-elections, and highly resource-rich national party organizations tying these together.

THE DECLINE OF THE PARTY-IN-THE-ELECTORATE

The most persuasive evidence of the "decline of parties" thesis is the changes in the public's identification with the political party, and in its relevance. This is not evidence, I argue, for the decline of parties thesis. Rather, it is evidence for the changing form of the political party, from the mass party form invented by Van Buren and to which the Key-Sorauf party-in-the-electorate applies to a new party form that lacks what we understand to be a party-in-the-electorate but in its place offers service to candidates as they confront a candidate-centered electoral era.

In chapter 6, I reviewed the various theoretical understandings of partisanship and briefly assessed the changes in identification over the past four decades. Converse (1976) called the years 1952–64 the "steady-state" period because the aggregate distribution of partisanship changed very little over that decade, and because it reflected one of the most stable political attitudes at the individual level as well. Beginning in the middle of the 1960s, however, partisanship began to change more systematically, ending the steady-state period and beginning a period of overall decline in the strength of attachment to the two parties and a consequent rise in the more independent categories.[3]

The changes in partisanship were not unidirectional and in fact differed dramatically between blacks and whites. So profound are the racial differences that they point to a different understanding of partisan identification than originally offered. Black partisanship shifted rapidly in the mid-1960s, suggesting that partisanship needs to be understood as highly responsive to political events, at least when those events touch individuals in a way that is directly relevant for their stance toward electoral politics. The civil rights movement peaked in the early to middle 1960s. The national government, in response, took significant action, most importantly in the passage of the Civil Rights Act of 1964 and the Voting Rights Act of 1965. The two presidential nominees of 1964, in their roles as incumbent officeholders and as candidates, assumed very different positions. Democratic president Lyndon B. Johnson led both landmark bills into law, whereas Republican senator Barry Goldwater

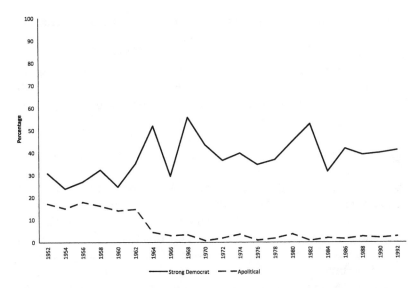

Figure 8.1. Strong Democratic and apolitical party identification among blacks, 1952–1992.
Source: ANES surveys, various years (http://www.electionstudies.org/). Compiled by author.

aroused considerable controversy during his presidential race by his vote against the Civil Rights Act in 1964. The result was rapid change in partisanship among blacks. The data presented in figure 8.1 illustrate two dimensions of these changes. With first the symbolic and then the actual inclusion of far more blacks in the political process, the percentage of blacks classified as "apolitical" fell sharply. Those so categorized, owing to their inability or unwillingness to respond to the party identification questions, dropped from about one in seven through 1962 to about one in fifty, two years later—essentially the same percentage as among whites. There was an equally sudden increase in their reporting of affiliation with the Democrats, a slight increase in expressed independence, and a virtual disappearance of Republican identification. For instance, the percentage of all blacks who claimed some identification with the Democratic Party increased from the 50 percent range to 60 percent in 1962 and then to the 70 percent range from 1964 onward. The immediateness of these changes, combined with their persistence thereafter, clearly shows that partisanship can reflect and be responsive to events in the larger political world. Thus Lincoln's party lost its majority support from those (few) blacks involved in politics during the New Deal, and it lost nearly all of its remaining substantial minority of support in the 1960s as Democrats pursued policies attractive to blacks whereas the GOP began its "southern strategy" in presidential politics that appealed to southern whites. The sudden change in black partisanship therefore was a plausible consequence and demonstrates that partisanship can alter quickly in response to partisan appeals. It also illustrates great permanence, as Republicans have not been able to do what is necessary to win back their support.

Partisanship among whites changed at about the same time, but less rapidly and in a very different way (see fig. 8.2). From the mid-1960s to about 1972, the proportion of the white electorate who considered themselves independents increased significantly. The balance of Democrats to Republicans, however, hardly changed at all at that time, and it did not do so until the mid-1980s. Instead, the weakening and outright loss of affiliation was proportionately equal in the two parties. The proportion of "pure" independents was a relatively constant 8 percent throughout the steady-state period, jumped to 12 percent in 1966, and increased slowly to about 15 percent in the 1970s before returning to about 11 percent from 1982 on. The proportion of

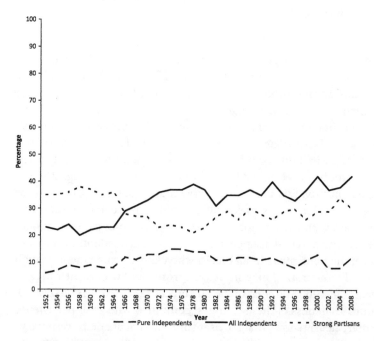

Figure 8.2. Independence and strong partisanship among whites, 1952–2008. *Source:* ANES surveys, various years (http://www.electionstudies.org/). Compiled by author.

"leaners" was also relatively constant over the steady-state period and, like pure independence, jumped in 1966 and continued to increase over the 1970s. By 1978 nearly 40 percent of whites were some form of independent.[4] Conversely, the proportion of strong partisans declined from a steady-state period 35 percent or so to a low of about 20 percent in 1978 before climbing back in the 1980s, only to decline again in the early 1990s to levels similar to the late 1960s.

Whereas changes in black partisan identification seemed closely tied to specific events and appeals, changes in white partisanship were not so easily understood, seeming more diffuse, remote in their causes, and therefore more alarming. They also were alarming to some because of the nature of the changes. If partisanship does indeed serve as the anchor for most of the public's understanding of electoral politics, that anchor was becoming less secure. This concern was compounded by two other factors. First, the decline was lengthy, lasting for over a quarter of a century. Second, the decline in partisanship was not the only sign of a growing detachment of the public from politics, and some of these additional indicators will be considered below.

Since whites make up a preponderant majority of the electorate, the move away from strong partisan loyalties among whites more than compensated for the opposing trends among blacks. That is to say, independence increased and strong partisan ties decreased among the electorate as a whole. Especially given the importance of partisanship and the remoteness of the decline from any specific political events, it became particularly important to understand its causes. After the major secular changes of the 1950s to the 1980s, patterns appear primarily to illustrate malleability. Just when pure independents return to the low levels of the 1950s, they bounce up again (notably in 2000 and 2008), while there has been a trend of increasing independence overall (thus, increasing proportions of those independents who "lean" toward a party), but an equally consistent upward trend in strong partisans as well!

Martin Wattenberg (1990; and pers. comm.) has argued that the driving force is the public's declining perception of the *relevance* of political parties rather than alternatives such as alienation from, or negative appraisals of, both parties. Since 1952 the National Election Studies (NES) surveys have asked respondents what they like and dislike about the two political parties. Coding in most surveys includes up to five "likes" and five "dislikes" for each party, so that a respondent could be recorded as offering up to twenty responses to this series of questions. Subtracting the number of dislikes from the number of likes mentioned reveals whether than individual's net response was positive, negative, or neutral toward that party (neutral only if the total score was exactly zero). Wattenberg examined three types of responses, looking from 1952–1992. One is what we would expect of a genuine "partisan," that is, one who is, on balance, positive toward one party and negative toward the other. A second type we might think of as the "alienated" respondent, who is negative toward both parties. The third category Wattenberg calls the "neutrals," those who are net zero in their responses to *both* parties. Although there are other categories, the totals for the three reported groups account for a hefty majority of all respondents.

In 1952 half of all respondents were "partisans," in the sense that their responses were, on balance, positive toward one party and negative toward the other. That proportion declined sharply in 1956, to about 40 percent, remained near that level through 1968, and declined again to the 30 percent range over the period 1972–84 before climbing to about 35 percent in 1988. Although there was an increase in those negative toward both parties in 1968, the proportion of respondents seemingly "alienated" from the party system is consistently low, 10 percent or less throughout the entire period.

The major increase therefore comes in the "neutral" category—those who were, overall, neither positive nor negative toward either party. Never reaching as much as 20 percent of respondents from 1952 through 1968, the proportion of neutrals jumped to about one in three and stayed at this new level through 1992. After 1972, that is, there are essentially as many whose attitude is one of neutrality toward both parties as those who are "partisan" in their responses. Even more striking, however, is that most neutrals are not those who carefully balance positive comments with negative ones. Overwhelmingly, these are citizens who have *nothing*, positive or negative, to say about either party. Wattenberg notes that in 1980, for example, 94.2 percent of those who were neutral offered zero positive and zero negative comments about the Democrats and zero "likes" and zero "dislikes" about the Republicans as well. That over a third of the entire sample had nothing whatever to say about the parties strongly suggests that, for a remarkable proportion of the public, the parties were provoking no response at all. No wonder Wattenberg and others have concluded that parties were simply irrelevant to much of the public.[5]

The data in figure 8.3 further document the argument that parties had become increasingly irrelevant but became at least as relevant to voters by 2008 as in the 1950s. First, neutrality toward each party is reported separately to demonstrate that growing neutrality affected the two parties in very similar ways. To be sure, respondents have typically been more neutral toward the Republicans than toward the Democrats, but the patterns over time are similar. In particular, the neutrality measures

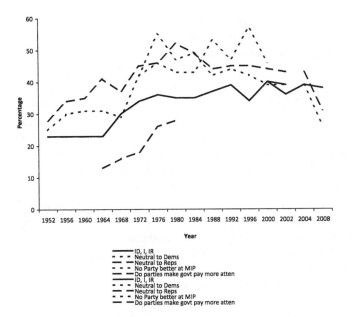

Figure 8.3. Indications of the irrelevance of political parties, 1952–2004. *Source:* ANES surveys, various years (http://www.electionstudies.org/). Compiled by author.

are at their lowest in 1952 and 2008. Thus, after peaking around the 1970s, fewer and fewer had nothing to offer about the parties. Instead, they increasingly returned to having something to like or dislike about each party. Second, the growth in independence is repeated here, to illustrate that it follows a pattern similar to that for neutrality, but the increase in neutrality preceded, and increased more than, the growth in independence. Third, from 1960 to 2000, respondents have been asked whether the Democratic Party, the Republican Party, or neither would better handle "the most important problem facing this country." About one in five thought neither party would be better during the steady-state years, a percentage that soared to about two in five in 1968 and increased to about one in two thereafter. As Abramson, Aldrich, and Rohde have documented (beginning in 1983, most recently in 2010), voters are very likely to support the presidential nominee of the party they believe is better able to solve the problem they consider most serious at the time of the election. Far fewer in the latter years of this time period, however, thought it matters which party holds power, at least in terms of addressing their most important concern. Finally, what made Key's parties-in-the-electorate relevant to the other aspects of parties was the critical linkage between the public and the elected officials the parties provided. From 1964 through 1980, the NES surveys asked whether the respondents thought political parties make elected officials pay more attention to concerns of the public. I have reported the percentages that replied that parties make officials pay "not much" attention to the public in figure 8.3 and discuss responses to it and the next most negative response here. In 1964 and 1968 about one in three reported that the parties pay only "some" or "not much" attention. That jumped to three in four respondents in 1972 and then to four in five in 1976 and 1980. Perhaps because of the increasingly one-sided responses to this question, the wording was changed in 1984 to "elections" rather than "parties."[6] Collectively, then, these data reinforce the claim that voters had withdrawn from partisan affiliation in large measure because they simply did not see the parties as relevant to their understanding of elections.

Combined with the analysis of parties-in-elections in chapter 6, two trends seemed strong but puzzling. People saw the parties and their nominees as holding very different policy positions than their opposition did, and if anything, this was increasingly so. And yet the public also believed, and increasingly so into the 1990s, that parties were irrelevant. The puzzle seems even more striking in light of the analysis in the previous chapter, which demonstrated that the legislative parties strengthened in the past couple of decades and that legislators are more likely now than earlier to vote with their partisan allies in Congress. The irony is that the public's affiliation with the parties was stronger and steadier precisely when the elite partisan electoral differences were smaller and partisan legislative coalitions were weaker.

THE EMERGENCE OF CANDIDATE-CENTERED ELECTIONS IN THE 1960s

The resolution of this puzzle is at one level rather simple. These data reflect the shift from a more party-centered to a far more candidate-centered electoral era in the 1960s. This often noted change has recently been illustrated in a compelling historical fashion at the presidential level by Shively (1992) and at the congressional level by Alford and Brady (1989a, 1989b; see also Gelman and King 1990). Shively analyzes changes in presidential voting patterns from 1846 to 1988, assessing whether changes in votes from one election to the next were due to differential mobilization of each party's partisans or to conversion of voters from supporting one party to supporting the other. Before 1960 changes in partisan success at the presidential level appear to be due more to differential turnout rates, but beginning with the 1960 election, changes have come to be due more to conversion (see especially p. 311, table 1, and p. 312, fig. 1). He attributes this shift primarily to the nominees' ability to appeal directly to the public as individual candidates, each able to provide substantial information to large proportions of the public and therefore to win or lose voters' support. Presidential elections, according to his analysis, became centered on the candidates and their appeals to voters rather than being a contest between the relative strength of the two parties in mobilizing their supporters on behalf of their nominees.

Martin Wattenberg (1990; and pers. comm.), in examining the likes/dislikes questions, noted whether respondents mentioned domestic policy concerns in responding only to the parties, only to the candidates, or to both (or neither). From 1952 to 1960, about two in three mentioned policy in responding (only) to the parties questions, while fewer than one in five did so for the candidates only. In the 1964–76 surveys about the same percentage, some two in five, cited some domestic policy in response only to the parties questions and only the candidates questions. Responses in the next four elections became more candidate centered. About half of those who cited any policy did so only for candidates, while only one in five did so for the parties questions only. Thus, as with his other measures, Wattenberg found a strong move toward candidate-centered responses over the first four post–World War II decades, which led him to examine the rise of candidate-centered elections in considerable detail (1991).

Alford and Brady have analyzed congressional contests from 1846 to 1986, essentially the same period as Shively, apportioning incumbency advantages in winning votes into those that come from partisanship and those that come from holding office per se (Jacobson 2008 extends their measure and the Gelman-King [1990] index up to date). Incumbents, that is, may be electorally secure because their districts have a large majority who identify with their party, or because they have developed a strong base of support for themselves as individual politicians, or both. They found that the advantage of partisanship has been substantial and essentially constant throughout the entire period (1989b). They also found that until 1960 there was *no* systematic personal advantage to incumbency. In House and Senate contests, however, they showed that a substantial and sustained advantage to incumbency emerged in 1960 and became equal in importance to the relatively constant partisan advantage.[7] Many scholars have documented the rise of candidate- and especially incumbent-centered elections at the micro level, grounding this general pattern in specific opinion and voting data (see Jacobson 1992 for details).

Together these studies show that there was an important shift in elections to all national offices in or about 1960, demonstrating that voters responded to candidates far more than previously.[8] It may have long been true that voters responded to the presidential nominees as individual candidates and personages, but this seems not to have been true even as these decades opened for congressional candidates. Stokes and Miller (1962) analyzed congressional voting in 1958 and concluded (545),

> Certainly the electorate whose votes they seek responds to individual legislative candidates overwhelmingly on the basis of their party labels. Despite our kaleidoscopic electoral laws, the candidate's party is the one piece of information every voter is guaranteed. For many, it is the only information they ever get.

Sometime, usually pegged at around 1970 or so, this changed. It was no longer a party-centered vote but an incumbent-centered vote (the pathbreaking articles were Erikson 1971 and Mayhew 1974). Holding the office was what mattered, not affiliating with the party with more identifiers in the district. To be sure, both often went hand-in-hand, but identifiers with the nonincumbent's party were far more likely to "defect" from their party to vote for the incumbent than were the other party's identifiers to "defect" to vote for the challenger.

A great deal of research went into the explanation of the incumbency advantage (Jacobson 2008 covers much of it). Explanations ran from advantages of office, such as the franking privilege, or the sending of congratulatory messages to constituents at key moments (births, weddings, and so on); through the use of office to channel pork barrel benefits to the district; to such electoral advantages as simply being a better campaigner than most, having access to more campaign resources, or having the ability to scare off potentially strong challengers, encouraging them to await an easier target. Indeed, all of these likely play a role. What was different about all of these explanations were that they were associated with the individual holding office, who was able to take advantage of these resources to build a clear, strong relationship with the constituents—in effect, a one-district electoral "machine" with the incumbent as "boss."

Voting thus became candidate centered,[9] and so parties as mechanisms for understanding candidates, campaigns, and elections became less relevant. The decline of Key's parties-in-the-electorate can apparently be attributed to voters' plausible perceptions that parties were indeed less relevant to them in elections than were their direct observations of the candidates. This clear and sustaining shift from party-centered to candidate-centered (or at least to party-and-candidate-centered) elections resolves the puzzle of how voters can perceive clear partisan differences in policy stances but care less about parties in themselves. They see parties as increasingly irrelevant to their decision making, or in effect they do not bother to "see" the parties much at all.

THE NATIONALIZATION AND STRENGTHENING OF PARTIES-AS-ORGANIZATIONS

As the views about perceived relevance of, and strength and frequency of, identification with parties declined among the electorate, the two parties initiated reforms of their organizations. Two sets of such changes are especially significant and are at the heart of the accounts of revitalized parties offered by Herrnson, Kayden and Mayhe, Price, Sabato, and others. One set of changes was the "nationalization" of the rules and procedures of both parties, so that the former description of the "national" party as little more than a congeries of many state and local parties no longer applied (see chap. 4). It became fair to speak instead of the existence of truly national political parties. The second set of changes was the strengthening of the resource bases and the levels of professionalization of the party organizations at all levels: local, state, and national. This strengthening has been of special significance for the parties in the electoral context.

The parties followed different paths to reform, although each party adopted at least some of the reforms initiated by the opposition. The Democrats led in adopting rules affecting the selection of delegates to their national conventions. These were rules created at the national level, imposing conditions on the state parties and at times on state governments. These reform efforts have been the more visible and controversial (see, for example, Kirkpatrick 1978; Polsby 1983; Ranney 1975). The Republicans' path to reform emphasized strengthening the party's resources and raising levels of professionalization, especially of its national party organizations. With each adopting, and adapting, aspects of the other's reforms, the two parties-as-organizations are reasonably similar today, and both are far different from the parties as they existed before the reforms. I examine this first set of reforms that led us into the 1990s. I then turn to examine their extensions, and in some cases critical revisions, that have reshaped party organizations even further since the 1990s. I focus particularly on changes in the organization and operation of the party in the U.S. House as the Congress has adjusted to its internal operations to reflect the new and more partisan campaign and electoral realities.

The Democratic Path of Reform

At a time that would in retrospect turn out to be almost immediately after the demise of the mass party form, Democrats began to reform their institutional structure by establishing the McGovern-Fraser Commission, the first in a long series of reform commissions. After the tumultuous 1968 Democratic National Convention, Humphrey appointed Senator Fred Harris (D-OK) chair of the Democratic National Committee (DNC), and he, with Humphrey's approval, appointed Senator George McGovern (D-SD) head of this commission. When he resigned to run for president in 1972, McGovern was replaced by Representative Donald Fraser (D-MN), a close associate of Humphrey's. McGovern had stood in for Robert Kennedy after his assassination, so there was little doubt where he stood in 1968. But Humphrey apparently saw that the process by which he had won nomination, largely the old-fashioned way of behind-the-scenes coalition building, could not be used again. For one simple example, about one-third of all 1968 delegates had been selected before that year, when Johnson appeared unassailable. Unsurprisingly, one reform proposal was to ensure more timely selection of delegates. More generally, however, these reforms emphasized opening up the party to provide greater opportunities for participation and included groups that had been underrepresented in its decision-making process. The overall goal was to make the presidential nomination more controlled by the public, with delegates chosen by them and for that purpose.

These reforms enacted national standards to govern state and local parties, a significant step in what Herrnson (1988) called the creation of "institutionalized national parties." Over time, national rules came to govern aspects of when and how delegates could be selected, and even who would become a delegate. Examples include mandating the time (or "window") during which delegates could legitimately be selected (adopted in both parties, sometimes with slightly different openings) and, in the Democratic Party, requiring closer and closer approximations to purely proportional transformation of popular support into delegate support, barring the selection of delegates through open primaries in which Republicans could vote, and creating "superdelegates," or seats reserved for party and elected leaders, totaling about one in five delegates in 1992 (for more on Democratic Party reforms, see, for example, Crotty 1983).

One of the most famous (although unintended) consequences of the initial reforms sponsored by the McGovern-Fraser Commission was the proliferation of primaries as means to select convention delegates. This proliferation combined with campaign finance laws to create the "new presidential nomination system" in 1972 that resulted in presidential candidates' winning nomination by campaigning for public support (see Aldrich 1980; Bartels 1988). In large measure these reforms and the resulting nomination system codified into party practice the candidate-centered campaign, organization, and election process that John F. Kennedy, Nelson Rockefeller, Goldwater, McCarthy, and Robert Kennedy had employed (see below). More directly, it effectively ensured that no new candidate could win nomination the way Humphrey did. The two principal consequences of this series of reforms were the nationalization of party standards and rules and the opening of the party and its nomination process to greater participation by the public, making voters, through the primary season, the effective choosers of the presidential nominees. Although Democrats have revised their procedures, such changes only modified specifics without seriously affecting these two consequences. And though Republicans have not reformed their procedures as extensively, greater nationalization of standards and opening of the party to participation characterize their rules as well.

The Republican Path of Reform

Longley (1992, 4) traces Republican reforms to the efforts of "two innovative RNC party chairmen, Ray C. Bliss (1965–69) and, to an even greater extent, William E. Brock (1977–81)," thus, under Bliss, predating the Democratic initiatives. Their path, however, also helped institutionalize the national party.[10] The apparent success of their reforms is a central part of the revitalized parties thesis.[11] The Republicans have furthered institutionalization by enhancing professionalization and by strengthening the resource base of the national party, so that they can provide ever greater services to candidates to assist their electoral fortunes. Herrnson defines the notion thus: "The recent institutionalization of the parties' Washington committees—which refers to their fiscal solvency, organizational permanence, and the growth and diversification of their professional staff—demonstrates that not only are parties no longer in decline, but they are in fact flourishing in today's cash-oriented, technologically sophisticated world of campaign politics" (1988, 30). Before reform, the parties' national committees had little autonomous power.[12] In many ways they still have little direct power, although even that has increased somewhat. They do, however, have significant power indirectly, through "their fiscal solvency, organizational permanence, and the growth and diversification of their professional staff." Herrnson writes of "Washington committees," by which he means not only the national party committees, but also the congressional campaign organizations for both parties in House and

Senate. These latter four committees have existed, at least sporadically, for some time, but only in recent decades have they come to be strong, organized, financially solvent, and professionalized; in short, only recently have they become institutionalized.[13]

Figure 8.4 documents the increasing institutionalization of these Washington committees from 1972 through 1990 by reporting the growth in the financial receipts of the three national committees for each party.[14]

It is clear that the two national parties had far more money in 1990 than they did in 1976. One could add the growth in the number of staff positions as well. The overall picture, then, is of two parties that had greatly increased the strength and resources of their national party organizations.

Hire enough professionals with technological expertise and provide them with millions of dollars, and they will find a dazzling array of ways to employ their expertise and money. Herrnson (1988) and Kayden and Mayhe (1985) provided many early examples. These new party professionals may perform many of the traditional tasks of party organizations, but they do so with technological sophistication.[15] These run the gamut from recruiting new candidates for the party, training them in the new methods of campaigning, to perhaps actually running their campaigns.

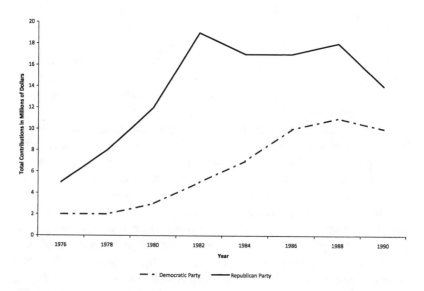

Figure 8.4. Receipts of national, House, and Senate committees, both parties, 1976–1990.
Source: Malbin et al. (2008). Compiled by author.

The new organizations differ from their predecessors in two ways. One is that the flow is "top down," from national headquarters to state and local levels, quite the opposite of the party Van Buren created. The second is that they offer services to the candidate. They are not the point of contact with the voter, the candidate is: it is the candidate's campaign. Only the closest follower of campaigns will even know about them except in the rare instances when the professional adviser's involvement becomes an issue in itself. And then the campaign issue is that these external forces are "manipulating" the candidate, controlling the campaign from behind the scenes. With those exceptions that illustrate the rule, voters will see and hear only the candidate. In former times they would see and hear the party and its spokesmen: it was their campaign as much as it was the candidate's—or more. Today, no matter how necessary the party professionals may be, they stay well in the background, and they will be successful to the extent that their efforts are unobserved (and unobservable) by the voters.

From the opposite perspective, Herrnson (1992) demonstrates that the more active the professional staff of the candidate's own campaign organization, the more money parties, political action committees (PACs), and individuals contribute. The interpretation is that the more sophisticated the campaign, the more "serious" it is and therefore the more worthy of support, even controlling for incumbency, party affiliation, and competitiveness of the race. He found, however, that it was the parties, not PACs or individuals, that gave somewhat more, on average, to nonincumbents than to otherwise similar incumbents.

It is important that the national parties have become increasingly consequential and able to constrain state and local party organizations, and it is also important that their resource base has grown and become increasingly independent of a particular president or candidate and of the state and local parties. The strengthened resource base of the organization is not unique to the national parties, however. The research team of Cotter et al. (see, e.g., Cotter et al. 1984) has demonstrated that state and local party organizations have also become more professionalized, with more substantial resources to employ. Huckshorne and Bibby (1982), for example, compared their data from 1979–80 with data from 1960–64, conveniently from just before or during the critical turning point and from sometime after it. They found that nine in ten state party organizations in 1979–80 had a permanent headquarters and a full-time chair or director and that three in four had voter mobilization programs in place. In the earlier period, barely more than half had the first two features, and only two in five had the third. They also concluded that the national parties have been important contributors to building these stronger state party organizations in both parties (Huckshorne and Bibby 1982). We will return to their research and update it later in this chapter.

This team also examined local party organizations (e.g., Gibson et al. 1983), arguing that the decline of parties thesis is not supported at the local level of organization. Their data show, for instance, that even though most county parties had done so in both 1964 and 1979, from one-fifth to one-third of the county parties performed one of their five programmatic activities in 1979 but not in 1964, whereas few did the reverse. They also surveyed party leaders in 1979, asking whether their party was stronger, had changed little, or was weaker in 1979 than "five to ten years ago." Under a quarter reported weakening, while nearly 60 percent reported strengthening. As Beck and Sorauf point out, what activity local parties engaged in "revolved around the election campaign" (1991, 84).

I use the term "parties-in-elections" to encompass the electorate's views of, and identification with, parties and the organizational arrangements parties design to affect the views, identifications, and most of all, voting behavior of the public in elections. These two aspects of parties-in-elections have changed, but in diametrically opposite directions. The electorate's identification with parties was higher in the 1950s and declined significantly in the mid-1960s. Their "views" of the parties declined dramatically in the same period, so that a great many no longer see the parties as particularly relevant or often do not "see" them at all. The organization of parties for electoral purposes at all levels moved in exactly the opposite direction, being weaker in 1964 (and presumably earlier) and strengthening over the 1970s and 1980s. They have become more truly national parties, better financed, more professionalized, and more institutionalized, with greater power to shape the actions of their state and local organizations. The question now is what happened to make these changes possible.

THE 1960s AS CRITICAL

The changes above took place in the 1960s,[16] a time of profound transformation in American politics. They were extensive, relatively rapid, and enduring. Although they were not confined to a single election, their extent and durability are sufficient to call the 1960s a critical era in American politics.

V. O. Key Jr. originated the theory of critical elections (1955). He defined a "critical election" as one that aroused unusual intensity and interest in the public; changed voting patterns substantially; and ended this period of change by ushering in a new era of stability, like the one that preceded the critical election but at a new and different level. Although no one argued that the 1960s were anything but a turbulent period in American politics, the lack of change in the balance of partisan identification between the two parties seemed to demonstrate that there was no partisan realignment of electoral loyalties. Indeed, that is so, but the absence of a net partisan swing does not mean the historical dynamics that Key called a critical era did not occur in the 1960s. A critical era is one of rapid change leading to a new period of relative stability. Such a description appears very similar to punctuated equilibrium (akin to Stephen Jay Gould's theory of evolution): long-term equilibrium punctuated by a short, intense period of rapid change, leading to a new long-term equilibrium. Note the similarity to Carmines and Stimson's use of punctuated equilibrium theory in their account of "issue evolution" in this period (1989). They quite correctly distinguish their account from a partisan realignment. I simply want to add that their analogy of evolutionary theory to American politics happens to coincide with Key's original definition once we relax the stringency of it being confined to changes in a single election.[17]

Richard Niemi and I argued at some length that the 1960s were just such a critical period as described here (Aldrich and Niemi 1990). That is, we argued that in the 1960s there were sweeping and fundamental changes in American politics and, perhaps especially, in public opinion and electoral behavior. These changes were relatively rapid and intense, and they covered a vast array of attitudes, values, beliefs, and behaviors. They occurred following an era of relative stability. Most significantly, the two decades that we studied, the 1970s and 1980s, are marked by substantial stability in these measures once again, but at a different level than before. The result adds up to a period of stability followed by a relatively short period of sweeping changes, followed in turn by twenty years (in that study) of general stability at a new level. This is precisely what we would expect from a punctuated equilibrium model. This pattern is also precisely what Key told us amounted to a critical era in American political history.

We analyzed a wide array of opinions and behaviors, including some already discussed here, such as the changes in both white and black partisanship. We also included such measures as changes in the New Deal voting coalition, declining trust and confidence in government, turnout, and split-ticket voting, among other public opinion and voting data, and roll call voting data of House and Senate parties from Carmines and Stimson's analysis of racial liberalism. Not all variables, of course, showed the exact pattern of change described. The central conclusion about the stability/rapid change/stability, akin to a "punctuated equilibrium" model, was based on an aggregate summary of twenty-seven of the measures available for most of the presidential election years. The three pre-1964 election years yielded an aggregate result that was nearly identical in each year, followed by a virtually linear change beginning in 1964 and ending in 1972. The value obtained in 1972 was almost the same as that obtained in the five succeeding elections, and the overall change between 1960 and 1972 was indeed substantial.

This description of changes is a rather sterile account of a most turbulent decade. This was a time of demonstrations, riots, and assassinations. Political changes were perhaps most vividly seen at the 1968 Democratic National Convention in Chicago, featuring acrimony on the convention floor and a police riot outside its halls, and in the tragedies of Watts, Detroit, and Kent State.

The principal claim I make is that these traumatic events were associated with a critical era that led to fundamental changes in the *institutional* bases of political parties, but there were also important elements of changes in partisan sentiments. As already noted, Carmines and Stimson (1989) have argued that racial issues present a case of their "issue evolution," that is, their application of punctuated equilibrium. They begin their account with the 1958 midterm elections, the same elections with which Rohde (1991) begins his development of conditional party government.[18] A large number of liberal northern Democrats were elected to Congress that year. Rohde notes that the increased proportion of liberal Democrats led to formation of the Democratic Study Group in the House and thus the beginnings of the reform era there. Whereas Republicans were, if anything, the more liberal party on racial issues in the 1950s, that partisan difference in roll call voting on the core issue of erstwhile division within the Democratic Party narrowed after the 1958 elections and reversed after the Democratic landslide of 1964 when the dramatic increase in liberal and northern Democrats led them to become the more liberal party on civil rights. In presidential politics, it was Goldwater who was the first Republican to win all of his electoral votes from the South, excepting his home state of Arizona. That was followed by Republican presidential campaigns adopting the "southern strategy" in 1968 and beyond, which made the South one of the strongest Republican regions in presidential elections. These events led to the dramatic change in black partisanship of such magnitude and rapidity that, if true of the whole electorate, it would have made 1964 a realigning election. As Stanley and Niemi (1989) have demonstrated, native white southern partisanship, once it is well modeled, shows a pattern that is also consistent with classical realignment theory, albeit in the opposite partisan direction from blacks. The resulting electoral forces in the South in turn led to the "nationalization" of southern Democratic congressional delegations, as Rohde showed (1991), thereby at least narrowing the internal divisions within the congressional delegation of the Democratic Party. On the GOP side, the 1964 contest effectively marginalized liberal Republicans, leading to their "decline and fall," as Rae puts it (1989). After this initial burst in Congress and then in the electorate, the full polarization of congressional politics took years to accomplish, but in turn the Republicans became the majority party in the South, but lost much ground in the Northeast and elsewhere.

The genius of Nixon's southern strategy in 1968 and later lay not in directly racial appeals, but in the complex of "social issues." Early on, these included calls for "law and order," such as stopping dissent against the Vietnam War, urban rioting, and the use of marijuana. These appeals tapped not just racial tensions, but patriotism and opposition to the lifestyles of "hippies and yippies." Scammon and Wattenberg (1971) provided an early warning to the Democratic Party that it was positioned out of the mainstream on this complex of concerns, risking loss of support among blue-collar workers, southern conservatives, and others. George McGovern in 1972 was sometimes disparaged as the candidate of "acid, amnesty, and abortion," that is, as supporting those who used or advocated the use of drugs, those who broke the law in resisting the military draft (to whom Jimmy Carter eventually did grant amnesty), and those who would come to be called pro-choice. The rise of feminism, environmentalism, and gay activism, and its impact on national Democratic politics, further supported this position. If the Democratic conventions seemed to be captured by extreme special interests on the left by 1972, the Moral Majority, fundamentalist Christians, prolife groups, and other extreme special interests on the right would come to play an increasingly important role in Republican politics over the 1980s, including, as some would argue, harming George H. W. Bush's reelection chances by their role at the 1992 Republican National Convention (see Abramson, Aldrich, and Rohde 1994).

Carmines and Stimson correctly note that even so salient a concern as the war in Vietnam passed and was, along with many of the 1960s and 1970s versions of "social" issues (save abortion), therefore not a potential "realigning issue" because it lacked sustaining importance. The Vietnam War did, however, have a long-term impact at the elite level. From the end of World War II until the Vietnam War, the mainstream position in both parties was an activist international policy seeking to contain communism. This bipartisan consensus on most foreign and defense issues broke over Vietnam, especially when it became seen as "Nixon's" (and the Republicans') war (see, for example, Destler, Gelb, and Lake 1984, and sources cited there). Opposition to the war became centered in the Democratic Party, with the result that since then the Democrats have labored under the general public perception that they were "soft" on defense and opposed to meeting the Soviet threat. Not only were Democratic presidential contenders Eugene McCarthy, Robert Kennedy, and George McGovern against the Vietnam War, but Jimmy Carter (with his international policy of cooperation and human rights), his vice president Walter Mondale, and Michael Dukakis (caricatured by George Bush as never meeting a weapons system he liked, and self-caricatured by a televised image of him riding a tank, looking like *Peanuts'* Snoopy) were vulnerable to Republican anti-Soviet rhetoric and appeals for strong defense. Although the end of the Cold War may have made it possible for Bill Clinton to weather charges of draft avoidance during the Vietnam War and still win election, the shattering of the bipartisan consensus on foreign policy was a major and lasting realignment of the parties that was a crucial part of this transitional period leading up to the mid-1990s.

Rabinowitz, Gurian, and Macdonald (1984) have presented some of the strongest evidence of a fundamental shift in the structure of presidential electoral voting patterns over the period 1944–80. In the nation as a whole, they found, the 1944–56 elections were almost directly aligned with the axis induced by party, the 1964–72 elections were aligned directly along an ideological axis, and those of 1960, 1976, and 1980 fell in between (625, fig. 4). The in-between status of 1960, 1976, and 1980, however, appeared primarily to be the product of southern voting patterns. They found (628, fig. 6) a cleaner break among nonsouthern states between 1956 and 1960. They interpreted these patterns as inducing a divergence between party and ideology, and they predicted, correctly, a new partisan equilibrium when party identification in the public would align with ideology, a prediction that we saw in chapter 6 has been borne out.

THE DEMISE OF THE "MODERN MASS PARTY"

The form of party that Van Buren and others created over a century and a half ago rested on the principle that the party was to be "above" the men in it. That principle led, when this "modern mass party" was working effectively, to the subordination of the wishes of all individuals—candidates, officeholders, activists, and voters—to the wishes of the party, and those wishes related primarily to winning elections to capture office and the spoils it provided. We saw in chapter 4 that this principle derived from the belief that the original form of parties could lead, all too easily, to their becoming dominated by individuals, such as the Clintons in Van Buren's New York. This principle of party above men was intended to ensure that there would be no such domination and that even an honorable individual like John Quincy Adams (whom Van Buren supported for president in 1824) would not be tempted, by the accumulation of too much power in his own hands, to corruption or tyranny. It thus followed that even the appearance of a "corrupt bargain" between Adams and Clay would be especially damaging to Adams's chances in 1828. This party principle, if adhered to rigorously, could exact great sacrifices, as it did from several of the Albany Regency's senators in New York who put their office at risk—and lost it (see Wallace 1968).

In theory, the wishes of the party were to be determined by applying the republican principle among members of the party, and the national convention was the institutional form designed to effect that principle by requiring that all national decisions be reached by delegates, representing all of the party throughout the nation, as determined by some fair means of apportionment. The convention was designed to be a more republican means of nomination than the congressional caucus (by then derided as "King Caucus") it replaced, as the modern mass party replaced the old party form. Insofar as this mass party could be said to have a genuine platform, it was to be selected via the same republican principle and procedure, reflecting whatever could be found that united all views and interests of the representatives of all of the party. And at least national candidates and officeholders were expected to honor such a platform, regardless of their personal views. Van Buren himself broke with the Democratic consensus on slavery, but only after being denied the party's presidential nomination in 1844 and only after he had left the party he created to become a member of the Free Soil Party. This seeking of intraparty consensus, and fealty to that consensus when found, was a norm and practice that undergirded czar rule in Congress and underlaid, even more directly, the Democrats' attempts at party government under Woodrow Wilson—and was thus like conditional party government of the 1980s.

For ambitious politicians, a political career was a party-centered one rather than an individual, office-centered career as in today's incumbency-oriented Congress. It was so because access to office required winning election, and the party had a virtual monopoly over the campaign needed to do so. For voters, the choice was far more than today a choice of party rather than a choice of candidates: straight-ticket voting was the rule. For decades, as we saw above, the nonsecret, party-strip ballot and other institutional devices made casting anything but a straight ticket so difficult as to be all but impossible. But even as these devices were eliminated at the end of the previous century and through the Progressive Era, straight-ticket voting remained common-place. As figure 8.5 illustrates, split-ticket voting was uncommon at the national level (10 to 15 percent) and relatively rare among state and local offices (30 percent or less) through 1960, but it increased substantially during the critical period. About twice the proportion reported casting split tickets in the 1970s and 1980s as in the 1950s. This percentage has been declining steadily over the 1990s and 2000s, back to levels associated with the 1950s. Indeed, as we have seen several times before, 2008 looks most like 1952 in these terms. If voters were casting a split ticket in the 1970s, they may have been doing so for any number of reasons, but it does necessarily mean that they were not voting strictly for the party.

Candidates in the nineteenth century played little overt role in their general election campaigns (and there were no primary elections to

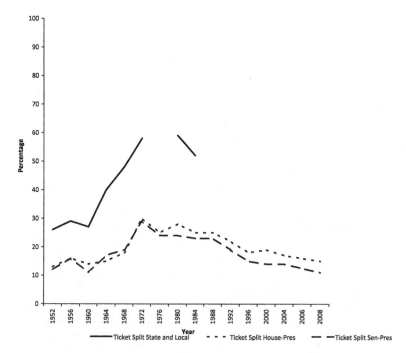

Figure 8.5. Split-ticket voting, 1952–2004.
Source: ANES surveys, various years (http://www.electionstudies.org/). Compiled by author.

contest). We saw in chapter 4 how constrained Andrew Jackson was owing to the traditional limits on what it was permissible for him to say in
public. Presidential candidates did not campaign in and to the public until populist (and Populist) Democratic nominee William Jennings Bryan
did so in 1896, to which Republican William McKinley responded with
his "front porch campaign" of periodically meeting with a few reporters
at his home. The campaign in the modern mass party was carried by
the party, not the candidate. Although this party-dominated campaign
became increasingly less common in the twentieth century, campaigns
remained party centered even at the presidential and congressional
level until 1960, as discussed earlier in this chapter. This party-centered
campaign likely helped keep the incidence of split-ticket voting low even
after most of the supporting institutional rules had been eliminated.

Reforms over the Populist and Progressive Eras undermined, bit by
bit, the control party organizations could wield over their office seekers
and over voters. New Deal legislation took over by policy and through
entitlement the kinds of services local machines had once made available to woo support on Election Day. As the waves of immigrants became established and as educational levels increased throughout the
nation, second- and third-generation immigrants needed less of what
machines could still provide. All of this contributed to what Burnham
(1970) has accurately characterized as the weakening of the major political party over the past century.

In spite of this weakening, the modern mass party had retained a virtual monopoly over one key component—access to office for ambitious
politicians—and with that political careers remained party centered.
It was this virtual monopoly that disappeared in the critical era of the
1960s, and with its disappearance, the modern mass party also disappeared as an institutional form. It was a casualty of social, political, and
technological changes and its own weakening institutions; but it was
above all the loss of its virtual monopoly control over campaigns as candidates were able to develop an alternative to the party-centered campaign—the candidate-centered campaign organization—that made the
modern mass party collapse at last. With that the century and a half of
party-centered elections ended and the contemporary era of candidate-
centered elections began.

THE RISE OF THE PARTY IN SERVICE TO
ITS CANDIDATES

Before the critical era of the 1960s candidates had no alternative to using the party organization to gain access to office. There was effectively

no technology by which an individual, except the very most well known, could create a personal campaign organization—other than capturing the local machine itself. There were no sources of capital extensive enough to substitute for the party, there was no effective technology at all akin to the television and computerized mailings of this period (to say nothing of e-mail and web-based campaigning more recently) to make it possible to "talk" directly to the voters, and there was no source of labor to do the campaigning—to ring doorbells, circulate literature, and such—save through the agency of the party. The party held an effective monopoly on the resources—the capital, the labor, and the flow of information—that were necessary to run an effective campaign for local, state, or national office. Ambitious politicians therefore could realize their long-term career ambitions and their ambition for election to office in the short term only through the agency of the party.

It is that effective monopoly that the party lost, finally, in the 1960s. It became possible, that is, for the ambitious candidate to create a *personal* campaign organization rather than relying on the party. I reviewed the change in the potential source of labor in chapter 6. Activists could be recruited based on the appeal of the individual candidate, either through great personal popularity or, more commonly, through policy appeals to the increasingly policy-motivated activist. Indeed, as I argued there, the typical policy-motivated activist should be expected to be attracted more to an individual candidate, who could be "purer" on policy, than to a majority-seeking party no matter how polarized the two parties (hence the fighting for the Republican nomination between the established and "tea party" Republicans, and other of 2010's "purists" on policy).

Large numbers of such activists, however, are there only potentially. The candidate must locate and mobilize them. Changes in technology first made such appeals—to activists, to resource providers, and to voters—possible in any significant and sustained way in the 1960s.[19] Television, above all, but also the nationalization of other media, the coming of high-speed travel, and eventually the application of computer technology to campaigns made it possible for the individual politician to contact the voter, the potential activist, and the potential resource provider directly in large enough numbers and short enough time to raise the capital and labor needed to make an effective campaign organization.

The growing importance of presidential primaries helped, of course. Their utilization by John F. Kennedy, Barry Goldwater, and then Eugene McCarthy and Robert Kennedy over the 1960s made primary elections an important staple of presidential nomination contests even before reforms induced their dramatic proliferation and their decisiveness. And the large national campaign organization created for nomination could be transferred to the general election campaign relatively easily.

In significant degree, one could mark the end of the mass party at the presidential level (and McCormick [1982] argues that the national party has always been primarily a *presidential* party) with the nomination and election of John F. Kennedy in 1960. Kennedy was the first candidate to win nomination who *needed* victories in presidential primaries. Although some form of presidential primary had been in use throughout this century, the candidate who relied on the primary to "go over the heads of the party to the people" was outside the party, and outside the party he stayed, unnominated. Kennedy, however, needed primary victories to go *to* the heads of the party. Such bosses as Chicago mayor Richard J. Daley and Pennsylvania governor David Lawrence were concerned that Kennedy's youth, glamour, inexperience, and most of all his Catholic faith would (like Al Smith's Catholicism and other liabilities in 1928) not sit well with the electorate. Although city and even state bosses might be Catholics, as Daley and Lawrence were, the only rule in choosing which candidate to support was to back no losers. Kennedy's task, then, was to show them he could win, and he did so with primary victories over Hubert Humphrey in Wisconsin (bordering Humphrey's home state of Minnesota) and then in the poor, heavily Protestant West Virginia. These victories helped Kennedy counter the argument that he would lose. He also discovered, however, that as powerful as Daley, Lawrence, and a few other bosses were, there were too few other bosses with sufficient remaining clout to deliver large blocks of convention delegates. Kennedy therefore built his own organization, developing lists of activists to approach (using the available technology of note cards instead of Excel), traveling the nation (with the newly available service of jet airplanes), and securing the services of a great number of experts, the "best and the brightest," to conjure up the strongest national organization to win delegate support. This organization, of course, served as the core of his general election organization and subsequent administration.

Four years later Barry Goldwater discovered that Republican Party organizations were, if anything, weaker than those on the other side. With the genius of F. Clifton White, who mobilized Young Republicans, Young Americans for Freedom, and other mostly conservative groups, he was able to woo regular Republican organizations to his side or, often failing to do so, simply outmobilize them. Only Governor Nelson A. Rockefeller (NY) was a serious obstacle, and he, like Kennedy, used his own wealth and power to attract a set of experts and develop a serious competing personal organization. Although the purist activists for Goldwater won the day, his nomination also required winning a very close race against Rockefeller in the California primary. In a sense the 1964 Republican nomination was the first one contested by multiple candidates of the new order, those able to build a contemporary, candidate-centered organization.

By 1968, although Humphrey would eventually prevail in the old-fashioned way, McCarthy's core of dedicated amateurs, dubbed the Kiddie Corps and motivated by his antiwar and anti-politics-as-usual stance, were able to convince the incumbent president not to seek renomination. Robert Kennedy entered the race having played a central role in creating his brother's campaign organization and having the power to mobilize blacks, youth, antiwar activists, and many others. Like the Republican contest in 1964, the Democratic nomination campaign was fought in and to the public by two candidates of the new order. One can never know whether Humphrey would have prevailed had Kennedy not been assassinated on the night that seemed to mark his certain defeat of McCarthy and, perhaps, his greatest personal triumph. When the campaign went on to Chicago without him, to paraphrase his last public words, the public campaigns he and McCarthy had helped set in motion so divided the party that, as noted above, Humphrey saw that the party would have to be reformed so that only campaigns of the new order could be effective. His method of seeking nomination could no longer be accepted. In this sense the reform path of the Democratic Party was designed to help the party organization catch up to the modern era, not to create it (which is essentially the conclusion drawn by Reiter, 1985).

In the party-centered elections of the mass party era, campaigns were labor intensive, relying little on capital or technology. What made the candidate-centered campaign possible was technology—from polling, to advertising, to fund-raising, to travel, to virtually all its aspects. National, and even many state and local, campaigns require experts in the use of this technology, so they have become dominated by professionals. Volunteers may still stuff envelopes, but the small importance of the tasks that can be done by amateurs compared with the advantages of computerized mailings and media campaigning means they now play a much less significant role. Political expertise was always valuable, but formerly it consisted of knowledge of local politics and how to knit together a coalition of support from the various state and local machines. Today's expertise rests far more on technology and is available for hire. Elsewhere (Aldrich 1992) I refer to this as the shift from a "feudal" structure of campaigns, rooted in the geography of electorally based party organizations, to a "bastard feudal" structure in which pollsters, media advisers, direct mail specialists, campaign finance and law experts, and all the rest are available to the candidate as an individual, based on the prospects for making the ambition of these "bastard feudatories" most likely to be realized. The ability of the candidate to acquire expertise, technology, and thus the information and resources needed to form a far-flung campaign organization, all but overnight and independent of the wishes, concerns, or even knowledge of local and state party regulars, is what makes for candidate-centered elections based on candidate-centered campaign organizations.

The key point, therefore, is not that the parties declined over the past century—although they did. It is that eventually it became possible for an ambitious politician to win nomination and election without relying on the party. The effective monopoly was broken: an alternative means was found. That, I argue, was the main effect (and likely an important cause) of the critical era in the 1960s. Not only did elections become centered on the person of the candidate, but so did organizations for achieving both short- and long-term career ambitions.

The critical era itself did not create a new institutional form of party; it simply meant the death of the old. Over time, however, the parties as organizations have adapted to the changing circumstances, and a new form of party has emerged, one that is "in service" to its ambitious politicians but not "in control" of them as the mass party sought to be. The party lost its effective monopoly, but it retained a significant set of resources. Most important, perhaps, it retained the affiliation of ambitious politicians. Seemingly, in fact, it serves their ambitions better now than earlier. Nomination by a major party, most fundamentally, remains an all but necessary condition for election to major office.

Shepsle (1989) has described the "textbook Congress" of the 1950s and 1960s as one defined by its committees and by the geographic imperatives of the electoral district, with political parties only in the background. He notes that the contemporary textbook Congress may see the parties more in the foreground. In similar fashion, we may define the "textbook campaign" of the modern mass party as one of voter and party, with the candidate only in the background. The contemporary campaign is now defined as having voter, media, and candidate front and center, with the party moving to the background of voter perceptions. This is so even though the party is reasserting itself in other ways, such as spending as much or more than the candidate's organization in a significant number of races in 2008.

If the party was in the background in campaigns, in elections, and in the voters' perceptions (or lack thereof), it remained important to the candidate by providing critical resources that initially only the Kennedys, Rockefellers, Perots, and movement leaders could otherwise possess. It could provide money, but, as we will see below, this was perhaps one of the least important and last elements to emerge in this era. More important, it could provide access to those who did have money. It could conduct polls for candidates who would not otherwise be able to use them, and supply access to advertising resources, whether expertise, facilities, or ads it created.[20] It ccould offer seminars or "campaign colleges" for candidates and their staffs and even find them managers if desired. The party could provide position papers, training on policy problems, and possible (partisan) solutions—and the means to advertise them. All of these services and far more could be offered by the parties to their candidates. The parties recognized this potential, first on the Republican side, but quickly on both, once Democrats discovered its value.

It is this set of attributes that defines the revitalization of the party organizations. One may assume, if not directly show (but see Herrnson 1992 for one demonstration), that candidates, especially the legions of candidates of lower profile than a Kennedy or Rockefeller, who make up the heart of the party in office at local, state, and eventually the national levels, rely increasingly on the services of a stronger party organization. One may further assume that ambitious politicians' continuing desire for office generates a continuing interest in those services. As Alford and Brady show (1989a, 1989b), even in the incumbent-centered era the value of the office to incumbent MCs has only come to match the value of the party in their reelection fortunes. Perhaps, then, the ambitious officeholders look to find what they have in common with their partisan peers and therefore seek to implement what is shared within the party before looking to create other forms of coalitions when in office.

But this party in service to its candidates lurks, often hidden, in the background. No wonder, then, that a revitalized, professional, well-financed, and seemingly much stronger party organization in campaigns appears largely irrelevant to the voters. The public sees the candidates, and sees them more often and more effectively the more they have availed themselves of the services needed to run a contemporary campaign. Perot's candidacy provides an exceptional instance of how this can be done without a major political party. For many candidates, however, those services come in larger measure from the party than from any other single source. Still, without an effective monopoly over the campaign, the party cannot expect to command the loyalty of its candidates and officeholders. A party in service can only help the candidate, who in principle has other sources for finding such help. The more effective and extensive the services the party offers, however, the more important they are to their ambitious candidates as they seek continual election and reelection. This party in service is, in short, an organization designed around the ambitions of office seekers—candidates now largely responsible for their own campaigns. They are responsible because it is practical for them to build their own organizations and then to take control over their own fates in a candidate- rather than party-centered electoral era.

One might well argue, however, that these sets of observations are time bound. They are, that is, the consequence of a politics built around candidate-centered elections—something still true today—but one in which the party is, as Shepsle observed, in the background. In the 2000s, it could be that the party has become so central that the "party-in-service" has itself collapsed and perhaps reverted to a more Van Buren–esque party, or perhaps to a new form. I conclude this chapter by looking at these changes. The "textbook Congress" has changed, and with it the role of the party—it has moved more to the foreground. But it appears that the party remains in service to its candidates, and thus the new form remains; it is just that the party has even more services to offer its candidates and appears to be a more important source of them. Indeed, especially in the contestation on the Republican side between the party regulars and the supporters of the candidates associated with the "tea parties," the parties are active in trying to recruit candidates, especially seeking those who can win and thereby increase the chances of attaining or maintaining majority status, rather than seek fidelity to policy views, regardless of their effects on the odds of victory.

TOWARD A NEW EQUILIBRIUM?

In the years since the "Republican Revolution" of the 1994 election, and the full flowering of the effects of CPG, party organizations have continued to develop. In many ways, they have continued to strengthen, and we will look briefly at a couple examples of this. In some ways, however, they have done more than simply continue to develop. There have been some changes in the way parties organize themselves, including in the Congress, that support the idea that the organization of the Congress is serving its members' electoral interests very well (as Mayhew [1974] famously wrote about the earlier era), but those interests have a stronger partisan-electoral component today.

Table 8.1 reports some comparisons between the degrees of development of state-level party organizations as discussed above for the

Table 8.1 Survey of State Party Organizations, Comparing the 1980 to the 1999 Survey

Party activity		1980	1999
Contributed to:	Governor	47	89
	Other constitutional offices	44	81
	Congress	48	85
	State senator	25	85
	State legislator	47	92
	Local candidate	70	
Held fund-raising event		19	98
Direct mail fund-raising			98
Conducted campaign seminars		89	95
Recruited full slate of candidates			91
Published a newsletter		80	91
Operated voter ID program		70	94
Conducted public opinion surveys		32	78
Typical election-year budget		340,000	2,800,000
Typical election-year staff		7.7	9.2

Source: Gibson et al. (1983); Aldrich (1999).

1960s through about 1980, in turn compared to a survey conducted in 1999. The 1999 survey (Aldrich 1999) replicated a good number of the questions Gibson et al. included in their earlier surveys (see Gibson,1983; this survey was actually conducted in the late 1970s, with responses covering the period 1960–80; these data are referred to here as the "1980 survey"). As I noted above, by the 1980s, the state party organizations had shown considerable increases in the actions and functions involved. By 1999, the state organizations reported nearly complete saturation of the states in terms of their professionalization and involvement in supporting their state's candidates. Particularly dramatic (due in no small measure to the various changes in campaign funding regulations) was the increase in state party organizations that held their own fund-raising events. In the earlier survey only one in five did so, while in the 1999 survey all but one did. As a result, the average of reported election-year budgets for the state party organizations increased eightfold, from $340,000 to $2,800,000. Thus, the standards for measuring the degree of professionalization of state parties needs to change, or we must simply conclude that all state party organizations are fully professionalized, because the established measures have reached their saturation point.

The formal apparatus of party organizations are thus fully extended at the state level across the nation. A second comparison is, if anything, even more dramatic. Figure 8.6 extends figure 8.4 through to 2008. The comparison is instructive. A look at figure 8.4, for example, suggests a general increase, but a possible tailing off of that increase if not anticipating actual decline in total fund-raising. It also suggests a noticeable Republican advantage. Figure 8.8, however, suggests something very different. Most obvious is that the increases seen in the first few years are now dwarfed by those of the last decade. The Republicans have essentially tripled their fund-raising success from the 1980s to the 2000s, while the Democrats increased sevenfold. Second, Democrats caught up to the Republicans. Whereas the Democrats raised about half what the Republicans did in the 1980s, the total income for the two parties was relatively even, in proportionate terms, in 2004, and the Democrats actually outraised (possibly for the first time in history) the Republicans in 2008.

Fund-raising at this level might be expected to have real effects on the candidates. Parker (2008, 23, fig. 2.1) reports that party expenditures grew substantially as a proportion of all expenditures raised by congressional candidates. In 1980, for instance, party expenditures made up less than ten percent of spending by congressional candidates. By 2000 (the last year of his data), they made up nearly 30 percent. Conversely, as party spending has increased, spending money contributed by PACs has decreased. In the early 1980s, it made up about 40 percent of all the money congressional candidates spent. By 2000

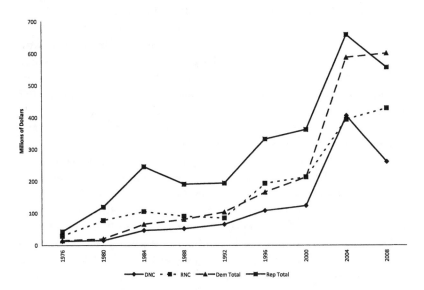

Figure 8.6. Receipts of national, House, and Senate committees, both parties, 1976–2008.
Source: Malbin et al. (2008). Compiled by author.

it was down to about one-quarter of all expenditures, and by 2006, under one-fifth (see Ornstein, Mann, and Malbin 2008, 98, figure 3-3). Looked at alternatively, the median amount spent by challengers to incumbents in the 2008 congressional general election campaigns was under $75,000, although of course, typical incumbents spent much more (as did the small number of well-financed challengers). The two parties spent nearly $100,000,000 on one hundred congressional races in 2008, or approximately $1,000,000 per race in which they invested (reported in Abramson, Aldrich, and Rohde 2010, 240, table 9-4).

Not only has the relative balance of the funding of campaigns shifted from an interest-group-based model to a partisan model, but that amount of fund-raising has also altered the nature of power in the Congress. There has been a rapid increase in expectations that those who want to become party leaders, whether within committees or in the caucus or conference, should contribute to the strength of the party. By that I mean that they should form what are known as leadership PACs that raise money for the purpose (or at least for one major purpose) of providing support to partisan peers running for seats in the House (or Senate). This activity (along with loyalty to the party's policy agenda) has grown effectively to replace seniority as the basis for allocation of powerful posts in the party-in-the-chamber. Figures 8.7 and 8.8 demonstrate the changes over the 1990s and into the 2000s for the U.S. Senate. Leadership PACs had existed for some time, but after the Republicans won majority control of the House and, as we saw above, weakened seniority as a path toward power, they began (in both chambers) to turn increasingly to expecting those seeking to attain, or even to continue to hold, committee chairs and other such posts to use their PACs to assist others (typically incumbents in their party) to win election. Figure 8.7 illustrates the numbers of PACs involved and the numbers that made contributions into the early 2000s. Figure 8.8 illustrates the dramatic changes in actual dollars circulating on this basis.

Heberlig (2003) showed that the data support his proposition that "congressional party leaders . . . use desirable committee assignments as a selective incentive to entice incumbent members of Congress to contribute [to] the collective good of the party's campaign efforts" (2003, 151). In particular he showed that the more incumbents contributed to party committees or candidates, the more successful their applications to transfer to prestige committees were. He, Hetherington, and Larson later wrote,

> We argue that the leadership selection system, which now gives significant weight to fundraising, helps explain the continuing polarization

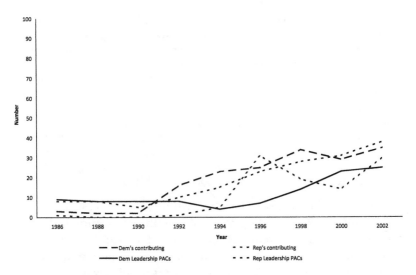

Figure 8.7. Number of senators with leadership PACs, and number contributing to other senators' election campaigns, 1986–2002.
Source: Malbin et al. (2008). Compiled by author.

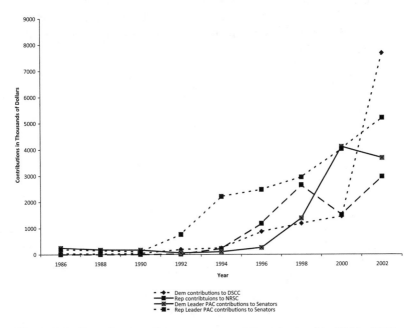

Figure 8.8. Contributions from senators and from leadership PACs, 1986–2002.
Source: Malbin et al. (2008). Compiled by author.

of the congressional parties. Focusing first on elected party leadership posts, we demonstrate that members will select ideologically extreme leaders over "ideological middlemen" when extremists redistribute more money than their more centrist opponents. We then show that redistributing campaign money also helps ideologues win posts in the extended party leadership, though appointment to such posts by the top leaders (rather than by the caucus) makes the role of money and ideology more complex. Specifically, we demonstrate that top leaders, who are now ideologues themselves, reward the contributions of ideologically like-minded members more heavily than those of ideologically dissimilar members. This produces a more polarized leadership in Congress. (Heberlig, Hetherington, and Larson, 2006, 992, abstract)

If Congress does in fact shape its institutions to meet its members' ambition for reelection, then how it shapes those institutions that are most directly under its control should reveal a great deal about how its members perceive the best way to achieve reelection. In this sense, then, the Congress that Mayhew described was built around Shepsle's "textbook Congress" of that era, one centered on individual opportunities to seek reelection, one in which committees loomed large, but parties hovered in the background. The current era suggests a different equilibrium, in which parties loom much larger and in the foreground, compared to the earlier era, and in which leadership includes direct and indirect contributions to the reelection chances of a Congress member's fellow partisans.

PART FOUR

CONCLUSIONS

9 POLITICAL PARTIES, HISTORICAL DYNAMICS, AND DEMOCRATIC POLITICS

I began this book by claiming that "political parties lie at the heart of American politics." By that I meant not only the individual parties but also the system of competition for control and use of elective office that the two major parties constitute. The former is for the most part what the theory of parties presented in chapter 2 and applications throughout the book have been about. The latter, however, is what animates the dynamics of American politics.

And, it is quite animated. While assessments of American party politics in the 1970s and 1980s were filled with the use of "de-" words, such as decline, decay, and decomposition (see chap. 1), assessments today are dramatically different. Ronald Brownstein wrote in the *National Journal*, under the title "The Parliamentary Challenge" (September 12, 2009, 66), early in the battle to pass health care legislation,

> So much for narrowing the divide.
>
> Whatever else happens, it's already clear that the struggle over health care reform has pulled the plug, at least for now, on President Obama's hope of defusing Washington's polarized partisanship. . . .
>
> America is steadily moving away from the ramshackle coalitions that historically defined our parties and toward a quasi-parliamentary system that demands lockstep partisan loyalty. It is revealing that Obama is facing nearly unanimous Republican opposition on health care just four years after President Bush couldn't persuade a single congressional Democrat to back his comparably ambitious Social Security restructuring. . . .
>
> Today, these centrifugal forces most affect the Republican Party. . . . But with Republicans operating as a parliamentary party of opposition, Democrats will have to pass health care reform virtually, if not entirely, alone [and, as it happened, in the Senate it was entirely alone]. That

leaves them with a binary choice: Democrats can either fragment into stalemate or function as a parliamentary majority party by unifying enough to advance their agenda.

Our final question is, therefore, how did we get from the "ramshackle coalitions" of our parties, regularly seen as in decline and decay, to "quasi-parliamentary" parties voting in Congress in "lockstep," as if in a nearly mythical version of Westminster-style democracy, akin to many of the aspects championed by those in favor of the responsible party thesis? To answer that question, we will have to pull together the strands of the theory of the major political party and America's two-party system, and then apply those insights to consider just how to understand the dramatic transformation of American democratic politics in the last half century. We begin with the question, what does the theory in chapter 2 tell us about the contemporary party?

Political parties are here understood as the result of choices made by rational political actors, most especially the ambitious office seekers and, only slightly less importantly, the associated benefit seekers. The rationality postulate assumes that actors have preferences and act to realize them. In this sense, rationality assumes self-interested behavior. It is easy enough to understand such self-interested behavior in a narrow sense. Moreover, the study of political elites, even by those scholars not strongly identifying their work as rational choice theory, often rests on the presumption of narrowly self-interested behavior. Mayhew (1974) and many who followed his impressive analysis, for example, have made a great deal of progress in understanding Congress by assuming that the primary, perhaps even overwhelming, goal of its members is reelection.

The rational choice postulate need not, however, be equated with such narrowly self-serving actions. Nor, for that matter, is reelection necessarily narrowly self-serving; it may serve as gateway to achieving other, non-self-centered goals. The rationality postulate is only that behavior is goal directed. Earlier I argued that, as Fenno (1973) instructed us, ambitious politicians have richer goals than merely reelection or, rather, that narrow self-interest is only part of the mix of goals, sometimes dominant, but sometimes not. I could not have made sense of the partisan actions analyzed in chapters 3 through 5, for example, without thinking that more lofty, or at least less self-serving, goals were critical to understanding rational, ambitious politicians' behavior. Perhaps this is not surprising. Political parties are large collective enterprises, and common goals may well be expected to include larger concerns than merely having a long, successful career. It is true, of course, that large collective enterprises are most likely to succeed when they are constructed to realize both shared and self-interested goals, and this may be especially true for political parties. Nonetheless, even a brief overview of partisan history highlights the consequential impact of more general goals in addition to the narrower ones.

Political parties, in this theory, are endogenous institutions. They are the creations of political elites, especially those who depend directly or indirectly on capturing office and using it to achieve their goals. These elites, and those striving to become elites, seek to win—that is, to attain their goals. Capturing and using office are, of course, contested. The impossibility results underlying the collective choice, collective action, and ambition theories reviewed in chapter 2 are, in this context, demonstrations that it is logically impossible to guarantee, in a liberal democracy in an extended republic, that any elites can maintain continued control over office, and demonstrations that any set of institutional arrangements consistent with the republican principle can be used to wrest office from them over the long run.

Political parties can be seen as coalitions of elites to capture and use political office. A coalition, however, may be only a temporary, convenient grouping of those with common interests. Thus, for example, the legislation enabling the North American Free Trade Agreement (NAFTA) passed in the House in 1993 with a largely centrist coalition of moderate Democrats and (most of the) Republicans. Opposition tended to come from liberal Democrats and from what was then the more extreme right in the Republican Party. These coalitions, however, were no more than a collection of House members expressing preferences for the same policy. It did not continue over very many issues or over any significant amount of time.

A political party is therefore more than a coalition. A major political party is an institutionalized coalition, one that has adopted rules, norms, and procedures. The Hamiltonians and Jeffersonians of the First and Second Congresses, for example, were coalitions that lacked all but the most elementary organization. Why did these political coalitions choose to create the rules and procedures of the first parties? The problem that brought them together was one that could be solved only over some reasonable length of time. And the problem—that is, the goal those in the coalition were seeking to realize through that coalition—was one that actions within the extant set of rules under the new Constitution were not solving. Thus this example suggests that shared interests may be necessary but are insufficient for the turn to parties.

Four conditions must be fulfilled if ambitious politicians are to turn to parties. First, there must be sufficient common interest for the politicians to seek to coalesce. As we saw in chapter 2, this is a very mild, easily fulfilled condition. Second, these common interests, composing the problem the potential party coalition seeks to solve, must be ones that its putative founders expect to require solution over a relatively long period. Thus for the great principle fought over in the 1790s, it would take continued actions over time to ensure the solution these potential coalition members sought. And thus Van Buren and others sought not just the election of Andrew Jackson in 1828, but a durable coalition to capture and use office in 1828, in 1832, and thereafter. So, too, might coalescing simply to win be a longer-term goal—if we win together today, let's stick together and win again tomorrow.

Third, the current institutional arrangements must be insufficient to solve their problem on terms suitable to their goals. Indeed, the current arrangements are usually keeping them from achieving their goals. It was in large measure the relatively pure majority rule structure of the First Congress that kept (or at least threatened to keep) the in-principle Hamiltonian majority from winning, owing to the ability of opponents to exploit Arrovian instability and upset the apparent majority coalition based on shared preferences alone, as Madison discovered how to do. The remnants of the old party system also were a major contributor to the problem that Van Buren sought to solve by invention of the modern mass party. And it was the complex set of partisan and other institutional arrangements that kept the regional issues, especially slavery, from being addressed at all, and certainly from being resolved on terms suitable to those who would soon become the Republicans.

Fourth, and implicit in all three conditions above, there must be opposition of sufficient (potential) strength to put winning—that is, realization of those collective goals—at risk. The liberal Democrats in 1965 had such an overwhelming majority that winning in the short term was not seriously in doubt. Great Society policies could be passed, therefore, without much need for institutional devices to achieve victory. Realignments yielded large enough majorities that institutional reforms for securing the new majority's aims were not needed until some years later, when that majority was no longer so substantial (see Fink and Humes 1989 for evidence). In short, a coalition institutionalizes to win what it is in its collective interests to win over time, in the face of current difficulties in achieving its goals, and in the face of usually formidable opposition.

As a highly endogenous institution, there is no one form of the major political party in America. Rather the major party is defined, at any point, in relation to the extant government and other political institutions of the time. It is also defined in a particular context—in terms of problems it is constructed to address. This is the meaning of the "fundamental equation" of the new institutionalism applied to political parties. The party is created to address a central, defining problem, and institutionalized to resolve it over the long term. But as we have seen, that problem changes over time, and with it the form of party that political elites create to seek to resolve matters in their favor.

To be sure, the constitutional form of our government has been nearly constant in many important respects. As a result, parties created partly in light of government institutions (as well as the problems presented by the historical context) will be similar over time. Most important, the necessity to win a majority of the electoral and legislative vote requires any party to expand its appeal broadly, and it constrains the system to be a two-party rather than multiparty system. But the historical context yields different concerns over time, and these well may have, and often have had, the consequence that particular sets of institutional arrangements within these very broad constraints are better choices for politicians seeking to resolve those differing problems on favorable terms. Thus the two major parties are organized in sometimes quite different ways at different times.

Although a study of political parties naturally focuses most heavily on cases when ambitious politicians turn to parties, there is no reason in this theory why politicians must do so. The apparently necessary conditions for them to want to do so may not be met. Indeed, the principle that parties are "merely" the creatures of politicians seeking to realize their goals means that what is fundamental is goal seeking. The particular institutional means to achieve those goals need not be political parties. As the theory in chapter 2 indicates, however, there are more or less continual incentives for ambitious politicians to consider party organizations as means to achieve their goals. In most general terms, these incentives flow from the very nature of liberal democracies in an extended republic, and in an immediate sense that means the ability to fashion and hold majorities. As a result, political parties often and regularly have been the chosen solution in America and in all other extended republics, even when politicians turn to a party new in form or content in opposition to the extant party and government arrangements.

THE CHANGING FORM OF POLITICAL PARTIES

The striking regularity of partisan realignments in the 1850s, 1890s, and 1930s (and perhaps in the 1820s) was what led many to expect that the New Deal era would end with a realignment in the 1960s. While there were elements of realignment then, the failure of a new partisan majority coalition to come to power meant that a partisan realignment as commonly understood did not happen. It turned out, however, that we were looking for the wrong changes. What we might want to think of as a "critical era" occurred right on time in the 1960s, but it led more to a change in partisan form than to a change in partisan alignment. Let us consider the dynamics of party forms over American history, then, alongside of the more typical review of the dynamics of partisan alignments over American history.

The first critical era was the 1790s, when national officeholders felt it necessary to move toward inventing the first form of parties. They did so with great hesitation, of course, because they believed partisan politics were baneful. Yet create them they did. Whether or not that was a partisan realignment (or more accurately, initial alignment), it was a critical era in partisan institutional form and initiated what would be called the first party system.[1]

That first partisan form had two components. The first was agreement within the party on principles. The partisan division, emerging from exploitation of the Arrovian problem, was difference over a central principle—what I call the great principle—of how strong a federal government was required to make the American experiment in republican government endure. The second component was the belief that partisan organizing and its inevitable impact on its members was at best a necessary evil. Parties were to be temporary alliances for securing the success of the American experiment, even if that required temporary use of "cabal and intrigue." Organizing to embed that partisan impulse in institutional form, however, was to be avoided. The result was that the early party, as an institution, was more informal than those that came later, and tended to be centered on the necessity of principle and the force of personality—of men such as Jefferson, Madison, Monroe, Hamilton, Washington, and Adams at the national level, and of local notables. The success of the experiment under Jeffersonian leadership over the next decades was not accompanied by the withering away of the institutions of party everywhere. Party retained its role in organizing governments and elections. That is why "King Caucus," for example, was despised by many by 1824. With the success of the American experiment seemingly assured, and thus the great principle effectively resolved, all that was left of party was the remnants of organization based on "cabal and intrigue" and centered on the strength of individual personality.

In 1824 the Caucus chose William Crawford, a choice contested, but by a method lacking organizational justification.[2] With the demise of the Federalist party, the Caucus was by then effectively a monopoly, selecting among themselves who the next president would be. Hence followed the felt need for contestation, but it first came without a requisite form to structure and justify it. By 1828 Van Buren saw the opportunity for a mass political party centered on principle, a revival of principles of the "true" Jeffersonian and Madisonian sort. It was to be a new party form designed to align with the success of the experiment in increasingly mass-based democracy, and based on the idea that no person would be more important than the party. It was not to be, that is, the personality-dominated party Van Buren had observed in New York or in the nation. In this case 1824 was the critical election, if any one election was critical, marking the death of "King Caucus" and the old partisan arrangements it represented. Unlike the critical eras of the 1790s or the 1960s, in which a new party form would emerge slowly, if not nearly unintentionally, at this time Van Buren had developed a blueprint for national parties, based on the successes of his Albany Regency, and Democrats followed his blueprint nearly step-by-step.

The Jacksonian critical era of the late 1820s could hardly be called a partisan realignment. At the simplest level, with only one national party left, there was little alignment to realign. Even after the rise of the Jacksonian Democratic Party there was no system of two parties competing for power. That would not occur until the Whigs became the second major party in the late 1830s, signified by the 1840 election's being what some consider the first "real" presidential election under the "full flowering" of the first two-party system (see McCormick 1960).

The critical era of the 1850s culminated in what is widely accepted to be a genuine partisan realignment. Equally important for understanding party politics, however, was the associated destruction of the old, both the old Whig Party itself and the set of inter- and intrapartisan institutional arrangements that had worked to secure intersectional alliances in both parties. As we saw in chapter 5, especially within the Democratic Party, maintaining an intersectional alliance required elaborate institutional arrangements. Not only was a new party created with the collapse of the Whigs, but the new set of arrangements ensured that the two parties would have to make sectional appeals, and their coalitions would be based on sectional loyalties. In this case the principle underlying the creation of intersectional alliances of the Jacksonian period, to keep regionalism and slavery off the national agenda and to permit unity within the young nation, gave way to precisely the issues it was designed to suppress.

The following two critical eras were close to purely partisan realignments with modest change in party form. The rise of the Republican Party from national parity to majority dominance in the 1890s and the succession of that majority dominance to the Democrats in the 1930s were clearly the central consequences of these two eras. Although the Democrats under William Jennings Bryan became a minority party in the nation, the populist impulse Bryan led and its progressive successor were not fully defeated. Many of the populist and progressive reforms eventually came to pass, setting in motion the elements that Burnham (1970) perceptively described as leading to the long-term decline of parties that, in effect, ended only in the last few decades. The revolt against Speaker Cannon in 1910–11 ended the Speaker's role as akin to a party machine boss in Congress. Local machines and their bosses came under serious attack, and the period of "party and Court dominance" was replaced by a more technical-bureaucratic or "administrative state" in the words of Skowronek (1982).

Burnham (1970) describes the New Deal as a short-lived reversal of the decline in parties that had been proceeding since the 1890s. Like all realignments, this one marked a dramatic change in the policy agenda and terms of debate over it—in this case, to the American version of the social welfare state. The long-term consequences of what was eventually to prove a bipartisan consensus on the responsibility of the government to provide a "social safety net" for its citizens—even if there was substantial disagreement over the extent and nature of that responsibility—had a significant impact on politicians' ability to provide those services directly to citizens in the name of the party. The result was to remove one more critical component of the mass political party and to set the stage for its eventual demise in the 1960s.[3]

The bonds of party that channeled the ambitions of politicians so as to put the party ahead of any individuals in it created a modicum of partisan integration and coherence, especially in and through the electorate. This coherence meant that the shifts in the popularity of one party and its nominees affected everyone in the party. Although these bonds were never utterly binding, they were relatively taut during partisan realignments, affecting the party's candidates across a wide range and number of offices. A reasonably close approximation of a "party in control," as I called it earlier, united the collective fates of its candidates and officeholders and made it possible to hold the party's politicians responsible for its actions.

The changes of the 1960s permanently loosened those bonds for the ambitious candidate and officeholder. The party still provided (and provides) useful services, but the politician's choice to accept those services became voluntary, or perhaps more regularly voluntary than before. Politicians since the 1960s have been responsible for their own fates in election and in office. The fragmentation of this party in control to a party in service may mean that a classic realignment is unlikely as long as the contemporary party form survives. Realignments have historically been rejections of a party's leading figures and the policies they have come to symbolize. All Republican politicians labored under the label "party of Hoover" after the New Deal realignment, for instance. More recently, the rejection of Lyndon Johnson and his policies and of Jimmy Carter and his administration brought Richard Nixon and Ronald Reagan, respectively, to power. Too many Democratic legislators, however, exercised responsibility for their own fates and secured their own reelection to have these and other landslide presidential defeats lead even temporarily to the election of a majority of Republicans to the House. Perhaps had Republicans carried Congress in 1968, the critical era of the 1960s would have been a realignment. The modern mass political party had died by then, however, and was slowly being replaced by what was either a temporary arrangement of a party in service to its candidates, or one more permanent.

Such a party form can be of great value to its candidates and officeholders. This form of party is (was?) far less visible to the public, however, than the mass party was, and it is or was of low visibility even when offering great services to the candidates the public votes for. Since it is no longer the point of contact between the governors and the governed, the contenders themselves do much of what the organizational muscle of the mass party formerly did. This is no longer a mass political party: it is the candidates and those activists seeking to benefit from their election who organize elections, and it is the candidates who appear in front of the public. Just how a new party centered on the ambition of autonomous political actors led to increased clarity of partisan cleavages, to greater intraparty homogeneity among party affiliates in office, and therefore to relative unity within the (conditional) party government will be reviewed later. Then we will ask whether changes in party form over the last fifteen years have been so great as to alter its form, or only to more clearly specify the party in service. The point for now is that the critical era of the 1960s ushered in momentous changes in the form that political parties have assumed.

Parties in the 1950s, 1960s, 1970s, and into the 1980s appeared to some to be decomposing before our eyes. To others they appeared to be strengthening to levels not seen in decades. Both views were correct, but comparing partisan realities in those decades to those before the 1960s assumes political parties in both time periods to be Van Buren's mass party form. The question is ultimately misplaced. We cannot compare the political party after the critical era with an earlier one using the terms of the modern mass party. It changed because the means by which politicians could realize their ambitions changed. They created a form that would better serve their ends, they sought a party in service to them, but it was they who chose to—who finally had the technological capabilities to—take responsibility for the conduct of their own campaigns and thus for achieving their goals.

THE FORM OF THE CONTEMPORARY AMERICAN PARTY

To assess the contemporary party form, we must begin with the form it replaced. Van Buren and others thus created the modern mass party, one version of that rational, legal entity that the American experiment in democracy in an extended republic seems to require.[4] This party became the "party in three parts," so well observed by Key and by Sorauf, closely integrating those parts into what would in time come to be a series of party machines. Based on the republican principle, it would have to have an institutionalized form with a base sufficient to reach throughout the nation, into as many of its states and localities as possible, and into the very fabric of life of the masses, that "great body of the people."

As we saw in chapter 4, the most difficult problem of collective action the mass party was designed to solve was creating the organization and resources to mobilize the electorate in the first place. The emerging Democratic Party was therefore led to adopt the most minimal standards for including already established state parties, factions, and juntos under the name of the national party. Substantial local autonomy was thus established. Resolution of the great issues structuring parties, first avoiding and then embracing regional issues, left primarily local autonomy and the extended spoils system as the basis of parties after Reconstruction. Selective incentives effectively drove out collective interests. As selective incentives came to define, disproportionately, the "interests" of the party—that is, the interests of those benefit seekers and office seekers in it—and as they used the government to achieve those incentives, there was little to distinguish one party or make it more attractive than the other. Either party, with control over the government, could provide selective incentives. That parties were driven primarily by these selective incentives had two consequences. First, local dominance by one party became commonplace. Second, New York City and Philadelphia, for example, could be controlled by a Democratic and Republican machine, respectively, and to the public it didn't much matter which. Either provided access to office for ambitious office seekers and, with it, access to the spoils of office for ambitious benefit seekers. Although the nation as a whole might be competitive, that was a two-party system of competition frequently composed of many pockets of one-party dominance.

This was a highly integrated and institutionalized system, relating its electoral, organizational, and office-seeking and spoils-controlling arms into a regularized system of party politics. Of this there is no doubt, although of course it was far closer to this "ideal" type at some times and further from it at others. It was on this understanding of party politics that political analysts' notion of the party in three parts was built. The importance of selective incentives and the difficulties of forging national intraparty consensus on collective interests led to the calls at various times and places for more responsible parties. But this now traditional form was in crisis itself, just when calls for more responsible parties, led by Schattschneider and the APSA committee he chaired, were at their strongest. This traditional view of parties was in crisis because the basis of its spoils system, the selective incentives that held this form of institutionalized party together, was being removed piece by piece over the end of the nineteenth century and the first half of the twentieth.

But weakened though it was, this party form retained an effective monopoly over a critical, even necessary, resource for its central actors—its ambitious office seekers and holders and the associated ambitious benefit seekers whose preferment depended on the capture of office by the party's candidates. There was no alternative for most such ambitious politicians, most of the time, other than to seek a major party's nomination and rely on that party to run the general election campaign. The parties may have been weaker in the 1950s than in the 1880s at solving that set of collective action problems in some absolute sense, but that was, broadly speaking, a weakness shared by both parties. The only consequential questions were, first, whether one's perhaps weak party could reasonably be expected to match the perhaps equally weak opposition in mobilizing the electorate, and, second, whether there was any alternative path to office. In fact, parties were reasonably balanced and remained more effective than any alternative for most ambitious politicians most of the time.

By the 1960s an alternative means to office became a viable alternative to the older form of parties-in-the-electorate. It became technologically feasible for a candidate—to be sure almost invariably a major party's affiliate—to substitute his or her own campaign organization for the party's. This became possible first at the presidential level, famously realized by John F. Kennedy in his 1960 campaign. That capability came to spread to lower levels of office, and the effective monopoly of the old-style party of Van Buren over access to office was broken. With that, Van Buren's creation finally collapsed.

In its place grew the "party in service" outlined earlier. Our questions will first be just what that form is and, secondly, whether the effect of elite polarization led to useful adaptations of that form to a polarized partisan era or whether the modifications have become so severe as to be yet another new form. With the last question not yet answered, I will write of the party in service in the present tense, until we conclude that it is no longer the correct form to describe today's political realities.

The party, as one in service to its candidates and officeholders, is structured to advance the needs and interests of ambitious politicians. That is, this is a party designed around the ambitions of effectively autonomous politicians, responsible for their own electoral fates and therefore responsive to the concerns of their individual electoral constituencies. Why then did party organizations and coalitions in office strengthen enough so that we can speak of a party in service to autonomous candidates and officeholders as a systematic and institutionalized form?

The most important forces are those in elections. Autonomous, ambitious candidates are nonetheless overwhelmingly partisans. With virtually every election actually or potentially contested by candidates of both parties, self-selection of political hopefuls into parties and recruitment of candidates by parties yield a sorting of the ambitious into the party whose "brand name" is the more congenial. That sorting of elites along the lines of partisan cleavages is powerfully reinforced by the informational and mobilizational collective action problems facing the candidates. With many voters seeing the general outlines of partisan cleavages through the stances taken by the parties' candidates, and with the candidates' electoral platforms reinforcing those cleavages, the brand name has increasingly clear meaning and value to the public. Party therefore has come to play an increasingly important role in structuring elections for voters.

With elections open to serious contest from either party, most voters today face a choice somewhere on the ballot in which partisan cleavages are meaningful and relevant. Although, for example, Republicans may rarely contest seriously within central-city House districts, voters there are likely to see keen competition for other offices such as governor or senator. All do so, of course, at the presidential level. Only in the last few decades has it become true that most southern voters can choose viable Republican candidates for most national, state, and local offices. The growth of two-party competition in the South—its nationalization—is perhaps the greatest force behind the rise of party as a voting coalition in Congress. Indeed it is at the very core of the partisan dynamics of the last half century.

Competition, therefore, makes partisan brand names valuable to candidates in solving, in significant if preliminary measure, the collective action problem of information in the electorate. Candidates still need substantial resources to reach a final solution to that problem. Jacobson (2008), for example, demonstrates convincingly that the incumbent advantage among congressional voters arises because many challengers lack the quality and resources to solve this information problem. He shows that voters often have few "likes or dislikes" about challengers; but he also shows that the value of incumbency, per se, disappears when they do, because voters base their choices on what they like and dislike about the particular candidates. And of course the candidates also need considerable resources to solve the second collective action problem: mobilization.

Here is where the party in service is especially valuable. As we have seen, such organizations today are more nationalized, have greater resources, and are staffed with more professionals. These professionals have the "capital stock" of technical information and expertise, as well as financial and in-kind resources, to help solve their candidates' collective action problems, similar to the value of the national convention for organizing Jacksonian Democracy. In both cases the actual mobilization requires activists—then of state and local factions, today those in service to the personal organization of the candidate, and increasingly with the national party, often contesting to define just what that national party will stand for. In the contemporary era, we have seen that these activists are primarily policy-motivated benefit seekers, and they are often located and mobilized through their connection to policy-motivated organizations and movements (or at least mailing [and e-mail] lists). These changes are perhaps most evident at national party conventions. As late as the New Deal, conventions were dominated by machine bosses, aided by the organized benefit seekers of those machines, such as unions in the Democratic Party and business interests in the Republican Party. Contemporary conventions are better described as combinations of issue and ideological movements: liberal groups representing African Americans, feminists, environmentalists, and the like in the Democratic Party; and conservative groups advocating pro-life, pro-family, and religious principles, and supporting other conservative causes in the Republican Party. The integration of such causes into the parties is an important component of what Denise Baer (1993) refers to as the "vitality" of partisan political life and "coherence and political identity" as Democrat or Republican at the national level. This vitality and coherence are often replicated within candidates' personal, often continuing, campaign organizations via the PACs (including their own leadership PACs) and other resource providers they put together from the outside and the coalition that constitutes their reelection organization inside their district or state.

Self-selection of ambitious candidates into parties, the partisan primaries or conventions as the nearly necessary nomination process for access to office, and the reliance on policy-motivated activists, groups, and resource providers create and maintain partisan cleavages. These mutually reinforcing forces make the partisan name valuable to the candidates and provide a basic informational cue for voters. Thus, though the campaign is no longer party centered in a direct, visible sense, and the electoral consequences of the two parties are less immediate, parties are no less powerful for structuring elections. And the revised and revived party organizations are designed to make the party-in-elections valuable to its candidates. Our question will be whether all of these trends have strengthened sufficiently to undermine the central defining basis of the party-in-service, which is the autonomy of the politician in the electorate, distinct from the party.

The nationalization of elections means primarily the spread of two-party competition, as at least always potential, broadly speaking, to all constituencies. It does not necessarily follow that the line of cleavage between Democratic and Republican politicians is identical everywhere. It does mean, however, that in ordinary circumstances the line of cleavage in districts facing two-party competition will be broadly similar, with Democratic politicians to the left of Republicans, where what we mean by "left" and "right" is what the party politicians and supporting activists decide they mean by "left" and "right." And this relative similarity is reinforced, especially in competition for national offices, by the nationalization of both parties' organizations. In this way the electoral forces have heightened the tendency for partisan affiliates to have policy stances in office that are broadly similar within one party and divided along a rough line of cleavage between the two parties.

Politicians are just as autonomous in office as they are in elections. The relative similarity of partisan cleavages in districts and states, however, means that their electorally induced policy motivations (and often their own policy preferences) tend to have much in common with those of their partisan peers. As such, the condition for the operation of conditional party government will often be satisfied. It will not always be so, of course. Some policy concerns, such as NAFTA, may not align with the cleavage. But the forces that create the tendency toward cleavages rest on policy motivations, so that it naturally follows that they form over salient and, often, recurring policies. Congressional reforms in the 1970s therefore can be understood as creating structures that make acting on common partisan concerns feasible, when the conditions of conditional party government come to be satisfied. Parties-in-government are not designed to force today's relatively autonomous partisans to act against their preferences. They are instead designed to select, out of all possible ways of forging majorities, those ways that align with partisan cleavages— that is, to create means for taking collective partisan actions when there is a collective partisan interest on which there is potential for acting.

In short, the party-in-service differs from the mass party-in-control by no longer resting on the "party principle" that the party is more important than the men and women in it. Rather, today's version is that the party is the men and women in it. The mass party-in-control was an integrated system of reinforcing forces in the electorate, government, and organization. The party-in-service is also an integrated set in which the party-in-elections, party-in-government, and party-as-organization are mutually reinforcing in support of the common interests of autonomous, ambitious partisan politicians. The contemporary party is therefore a systematic and institutionalized organization, and it remains so as long as the electoral forces align partisan cleavages in broadly similar ways throughout the nation.

There is some reason to suspect that the "party in service" was a transitory form, as the party (that is, its office and benefit seekers) adjusted to the changing realities following the 1960s. Thus, for example, as we saw in chapter 7, the congressional party has changed its form and role significantly. Gone is the autonomy of power allocated by seniority, and in its place is power allocated, at least in significant part, by the member's contributions to the collective welfare of the party, particularly the party-in-elections. Further, the national parties have now reached a point in resource allocation at which they are sometimes the major players in the electoral campaign in at least some congressional districts, and more commonly are a truly substantial source of resources. And, as the party reputation builds in the public, the Lincoln Chafees of the political world find, at least in such extreme cases, that they have lost the virtually complete autonomy to be able to run as they please, without regard to the standing of their own party in Washington. As I write this, numerous incumbents, some of quite long standing, have come under attack as members of their party "in name only," leading to serious electoral challenges. Perhaps these are sufficient indicators that the party is not just "in service" to its candidates and office holders, and that another form of party is emerging.

While that well may become true, we must remember that the question is a balance of forces. As Shepsle noted about his "textbook Congress" (1989), it was not that party was irrelevant in the textbook Congress of the Rayburn era, but it was that constituency and committee loomed relatively greater, while the party hovered more in the background. So too might the current conditions simply be a reminder that the party was never totally irrelevant. Rather it has strengthened to the point where the party-in-service may have reached the limits, with the balance of forces stopping and perhaps pushing back a little from the autonomy of the well-known, long-serving incumbent in his or her campaign. The forces might well be settling, in an under-damped way, toward the appropriate balance of personal autonomy and party reputation. We simply cannot judge, at this point, whether we are at this equilibrium of a balancing of forces or are still undergoing sufficient dynamic change as to lead to a new organizational form.

THEORETICAL CONCLUSIONS

This revision to the original version of *Why Parties?* makes several additions to the theory presented in the original. The first version emphasized the relationship between the institutions of republican democracy and the political party. Those connections were from democratic institutions to political parties, and they were connections made at the elite level, particularly among the various ambitious politicians—that is, first and foremost among those seeking elective office, with political activists holding an important but decidedly second position. In this case, the institutions of the political party appeared to complete the project of creating viable republican democracy. That is, they appear to be necessary conditions for viable democracy in a large and extended republic. By the relative rapidity with which ambitious politicians created the first parties and created new ones at a fairly high level of consistency, it appears that they found parties necessary for the achievement of their goals, and this appeared to happen sufficiently often that ambitious politicians were rarely without a political party to employ. It thus seems that goal-seeking career politicians (among others) find political parties very useful, if not necessary—and parties are not necessary primarily because there seems to be no logical necessity that there be a single structure by which ambitious politicians could achieve their goals. Indeed, that parties have assumed a diversity of organizational forms in the United States implies that no specific form is necessary, but that parties are necessary because there are persistent problems (of the ambition, collective action, and social choice theory sorts) and because political parties, as endogenous institutions, are sufficiently adaptable.

Party Systems and Effective Democracy

The reverse, however, might be true. Most scholarly views, whether analytical and empirical or synthetic and philosophical, have gravitated to the necessity of parties for making democracy effective. But here, it appears, the argument is that the necessary condition is that there be an integrated system of political parties. On the empirical side, while hardly unique, Key's *Southern Politics in State and Nation* (1949) provides one part of a very strong case for this claim of necessity. In particular, he looks at the one extended exception of the presence of a multiparty system in America (that is, one with at least two durable parties), the Jim Crow South (circa 1900–1965). There have been other times with fewer than two such parties in the United States. These were often also in the South. Political parties were banned from the government by the Confederacy, for example, and there was fairly chaotic party development during and immediately after Reconstruction through to the era of Jim Crow. Thus, the South lacked a party system for virtually the entire century from the Civil War to the Civil Rights era. Nationally, while today's Democratic party can trace its founding to Jefferson and Madison without major break, there was a gap between a viable Federalist Party (perhaps dated as ending in the second decade of the nineteenth century) and the emergence of an organized opposition to the Democrats, whether the National Republicans for 1828 and 1832 or the Whigs beginning in 1836. From thence, there was only a very short break between the collapse of the Whigs and the rise of the Republican Party to major party status. Except for the Jim Crow South, then, these were of short duration—indeed, their short duration is evidence for their perceived necessity on the part of political elites, although not conclusive demonstration of necessity.

Thus, Key's evidence is the most important. There, in the Jim Crow—or "Solid," or "Lily White"—Democratic South, there was a political party, but only one, and therefore there could not be, by definition, a competitive party system. Thus, his evidence that there was no democracy under those conditions is a powerful demonstration of the central syllogism of necessity. By necessity, I mean that a competitive party system is necessary for effective democracy, or in syllogistic form, p implies q. Observing p and q proves nothing, however, as conditions such as r might also lead to q holding, without violation of a relationship of necessity between p and q. However, the reverse, that $\sim p$ implies $\sim q$, is what Key observed. For if it is true that there was no democracy, it must mean that there was no competitive party system; otherwise a party system is not necessary for effective democracy. That is, we would have observed a party system and no democracy, and therefore a party system would not be a necessity. We can thus say that the empirical record offered by America, the world's longest running republican democracy, thus supports party system as necessary for effective democracy. We cannot, however, conclude anything about sufficiency.

Let me make a final note on this logical syllogism. I use the phrase, "competitive party system." By "competitive" I do not mean that a party regularly wins elections. While it could mean that, and scholars point to the Social Democrats in Sweden, the Christian Democrats in Italy, the Liberal Democratic Party in Japan, and Labor (Mapai and it successors) in Israel as examples of parties that had long, nearly or actually unbroken runs at winning national elections (following Duverger 1954), the evidence we have does not show that southern Democrats won elections so regularly because they were popular. Rather, they won elections because they were popular among that minority endogenously permitted to participate (and enforced elimination of a broad swath of the electorate by the brutal, illegal use of force). That is, one cannot distinguish in Key's cases between a failure of democracy because no second party was able to fashion a popular enough appeal, and a failure due to formal institutions that were simply undemocratic on their face. Given what we know about the opportunity for formulating a winning possibility against nearly any platform, we suspect that it is the undemocratic institutions that matters here, not unpopularity, but that is only an informed suspicion.

Notice that this set of claims about competitive party systems rests on the idea that it is a system that matters, not the existence of more than one distinct individual party (see Aldrich and Griffin 2010). Competitive parties interact. This interaction is, in fact, more evident in a two-party system than in one with a larger number of parties, where interaction is dispersed over that larger array of parties and thus is less obvious. Politicians, the core actors in political parties, are nothing if not strategic—about their careers and the achievement of their goals. And thus, party interaction, as the concatenation of the actions of many of these strategic actors, can therefore be thought of as a form of strategic interaction. The rise of the Republican Party in the South, blocked by nondemocratic means for a century, led directly, through the generation of a new party reputation, to the decline of its fortunes in the Northeast, especially New England, where that new reputation was not helpful. And thus, we can define a party system as a set of parties locked into strategic interaction. I suspect that this definition is general and can be used to understand not just two-party systems but competitive party systems through the democratic world (see Aldrich 2007).

Conditional Party Government and the Dynamics of American Democracy

The second theoretical advance is the strengthening of the microfoundations underlying the theory of "conditional party government" that

Rohde (1991) and I have developed, and in particular the development of an understanding of the effects of changes in the "condition" in conditional party government. The central argument is that the appropriate equilibrium concept is not (or not quite) game theoretic, and in particular, an equilibrium in the Nash family of equilibrium concepts. Those concepts are based on the idea that players are engaged in strategic interaction, and equilibrium is achieved when no one strategic actor wishes to change her strategy unilaterally. The equilibrium here is much more in the classical sense of physics, of a balancing of forces in the electoral arena but also balancing in the legislature, with the equilibrium determined by the relative strength of centripetal and centrifugal forces. In this sense, the changes over the last sixty years are primarily the study of the increase in centrifugal forces, thus moving the actions of politicians farther from the center.

I believe the electoral forces are foundational. Much of the empirical evidence that we have examined about these forces has been of the centrifugal sort. That is, the extremity of activists—defined for here as those with resources to offer a party's candidates—has been amply demonstrated. Activists provide one kind of tug, the ability to get resources (money, labor, even votes in primaries), and we have seen they have always been centrifugal, and that they have been increasingly so, that is, increasingly more ideologically extreme in their preferences. Of course, candidates need enough votes to fashion a majority of those voting, and that is the major source of the balancing centripetal forces. Further, while this construction leads us to think in policy dimensions that favor a left-right sort of interpretation, candidates (and perhaps especially incumbents) have many ways to soften the centrifugal forces in elections. Thus, if they claim to be unusually effective and competent at their job, that is an appeal that may reach across broad swaths of, if not completely across, party divides. Much the same is true if they campaign on their ability to bring home valued projects, pork, or other aspects of distributive politics. Those might, but often do not, have partisan or ideological bases. And, if incumbents can offer very specific assistance to important business, industry, or other sources of government on pet concerns (e.g., specific tax breaks, particular contracts, and the like), that support can cut across many spectrums, and thereby soften at least marginally the centrifugal pressures of resource acquisition. That is, "valence issues"—such as candidate competence and effectiveness, distributive policies (such as earmarks that were popular versions of targeted pork in the past few years), and genuinely public goods, such as a strong economy—rebound to the benefit or determinant of the incumbent, all but independent of the party identification of the voter.

Still, as we know from most studies of congressional voting, specific policy issues play only an occasional role in most voting decisions, but they play a more critical role in decisions of activists. Not only are those groups more extreme than the general (even than the partisan and voting) population, they have been becoming more so over the last decades. Further, there are more and more groups whose preferences tend to cluster together, providing an amplification of centrifugal forces. Finally, the party itself has changed from a modest source of resources, to a broker among contributors of resources, to, today, a major source of resources in their own right, at times even outweighing the combined magnitude of PACs. But "outweighing" is not the right word, because the more partisan focus of PACs and interest groups in recent decades indicates that parties and these other groups of activists reinforce more than they compete with one another.

Stokes and Miller (1962) famously argued that voters in congressional elections in the 1950s voted their partisanship. These voters did not know much about the candidates, but their partisanship was readily available. Party therefore served as the basic determinant of congressional elections. The congressional voting literature turned in the 1970s and 1980s to look at the various ways in which the incumbent could overcome those limitations, and use the advantages that incumbency brought to create an identity and personal reputation in the district. This was a relatively new feature of congressional elections, made possible by the various technological and other changes described above. When in a position to change the conditions Stokes and Miller had found, the incumbent could convince independents and opposing party identifiers to cross over and vote for the incumbent, at least more so than the less well known challenger. And thus grew what became known as a "personal vote" (as Cain, Ferejohn, and Fiorina titled their book, 1987), and thus ensued the lengthy study of the origin and nature of incumbency advantage in elections.

The next set of changes did not result from incumbents losing their ability to compete along those lines. Rather, a second force, that of the party, has strengthened from the 1980s onward. In particular, as we have seen, the party has developed a stronger policy and ideological reputation in the public. And it has done so because the party in the legislature is more coherent. The "stand" of the party is a more meaningful signal as to how votes are cast by its affiliates in both House and Senate. That is, the parties' reputations carry more consequences and so have more meaning and value to the voter. That means the well-supported incumbent offers two signals to voters, that of her or his own reputation and that of the party. Most of the time, of course, those two signals reinforce one another. Sometimes, however (as, for example, with Lincoln Chafee in Rhode Island), the signals are in conflict. This does not necessarily indicate a vulnerable incumbent (although in extremis, that may be true), but it does indicate vulnerability to serious challenge when the seat does open. Seats become vulnerable under several conditions. One is when the constituency changes (perhaps due to migration or to redistricting). A rare instance is when incumbents change their actions. The change over the last few decades, however, has come more from the parties changing, primarily by internal homogenization and external polarization, that is, with changes that have created a stronger, more fully satisfied "condition" in conditional party government.

Consider, then, the challenger. The typically less well supported challenger now starts with a more meaningful party reputation, even if there is little recognition of the challenger as a person in the district. This contrasts with the 1960s and 1970s, when challengers all too often started out with neither that party reputation nor a personal one. Party reputation, in either case then, provides today something that more closely approximates that "standing decision" that Key discussed (1966). And, indeed, as Chafee apparently discovered, that reputation affects voters, even if they know the incumbent and what he or she stands for very well. At least at the margin, then, reputation affects outcomes, which is how the rise of southern Republicans, especially as they assumed leadership in Congress following the 1994 elections, had the indirect effect of costing them positions outside the South. This was a system out of equilibrium, and those such as Chafee or Arlen Specter, the long-serving senator from Pennsylvania who served as a Republican, switched parties to avoid losing in the Republican primary, and then lost in Democratic primary instead, paid the price of being in the wrong place at the wrong time during a change in equilibrium.

The evidence suggests that the fundamental transformation of the party system was the change in the two-party system as found in the 1950s and 1960s to that found today. The theory of conditional party government provides a coherent explanation of the politics of this transformation. I conclude by considering the hypotheses this view suggests and the evidence in support of those hypotheses that has been presented here.

The explanation is that the terms of the condition in conditional party government are what changed. After World War II, the diversity in the two parties, long present, became electorally significant, as the agenda of issues changed from ones that tended to unite southern and northern wings of the Democratic Party (and of the Republican Party, for that matter). It is the increasingly salient internal divisions within both parties, but most especially the majority party, that make the

1950s and 1960s the truly unique period, at least from the perspective of political parties in the United States. Their adaption to this diversity was to create an anomalous and unique set of party organizations, in elections and in the Congress. They hovered in the background, as Shepsle said (1989), for a reason.

Let us begin with the Congress, to see what kinds of signals the parties were sending to the public. In chapter 7, we saw some of the ways in which we could see the changes in behavior of partisan politicians in both House and Senate from the 1950s to the first decade of the twenty-first century. We saw, for example, that the proportion of party unity votes (a majority of one party voting against a majority of the other party) decreased in the House over the 1950s into the early 1970s, from about half the recorded roll call votes to about a third, and then began to increase once again. In the most recent decade, over half of recorded roll call votes were party votes, but in the House, this figure was misleadingly similar to the 1950s. It turns out that in the 1950s, very few votes deeply divided the two parties (at least by using the more stringent rule of a 90 percent majority of one party opposing a 90 percent majority of the other). By the end of the most recent decade, however, about a third were such deeply partisan votes. There were slightly fewer 90–90 party votes in the Senate in that decade, but more 50–50 party unity votes. Otherwise, the two chambers look similar in these regards.

The late 1960s and early 1970s were not only a low point of party unity voting in the House, but also a high point for votes that formed a conservative coalition (a majority of northern Democrats, opposed by a majority of southern Democrats and a majority of Republicans). Indeed, the two trends nearly intersected in the House at that time. That is, one of the sources of low levels of party voting in the House was a regionally divided Democratic Party. This was less true in the Senate, but that is because the Senate divided in this fashion earlier, in the 1940s and 1950s, and was beginning a slow recovery toward partisan coalition formation. Their divisions came over the second New Deal and Roosevelt's "court packing plan" and over early civil rights contestations, such as Strom Thurmond's filibuster of the Civil Rights Act of 1957 (which eventually passed in weakened form). By the early 1970s, Thurmond had become a Republican, and other southern Republicans were being elected to the Senate (e.g., Jesse Helms, NC), differentiating it from the House in that regard.

And, as those examples illustrate, it was indeed the division of the Democratic Party that was the source of the variation in party unity voting. In both House and Senate, we saw (in figures 7.3 and 7.4) that there was modest change in the degree to which northern Democrats and Republicans supported their party on party unity votes, but there was a great drop in such loyalty among southern Democrats in both chambers. The recapturing of southern Democratic loyalty to vote with their party by the mid 1980s, at levels only slightly less than the other party groupings, is the major reason that party unity votes at the beginning of the twenty-first century approach the levels of the beginning of the twentieth century. That is to say that the major reason for the decline and then resurgence of party as the dominant voting coalition in Congress is the behavior of southern Democrats. Once issues arose to the top of the national agenda that led them to defect from the New Deal coalition forged in the Great Depression, the result was a substantial decrease not just in their own extent of party loyalty but also the extent to which party served as the major coalition structuring congressional voting. And, the resurgence was because either southern Democrats changed parties by becoming Republicans or they (or, more likely, their replacements) changed policy positions and thereby began to vote like their northern partisan peers.

All of this is to say that the two parties presented the voters in the middle of the twentieth century with a diffuse signal of what either party stood for, but that signal has sharpened and clarified substantially since then. The relatively greater internal homogenization of each party and external differentiation from each other has been sufficiently great for the clarity of the signals the two parties are sending now to be usable by voters as reputations. That is, both parties' signals more faithfully reflect what a voter should expect regarding how any Republican and any Democrat will vote on legislation when in office. And it is precisely these two features of internal homogenization and external differentiation that indicate how well the "condition" in conditional party government is satisfied. It is this connection that ties the party-in-government to the party-in-elections—and it is the party-as-organization (now greatly strengthened and more fully aligned with other electoral organizations such as PACs) that acts on that connection. It is, in contemporary discourse, the polarization of the parties in Congress that shapes the strength of the reputation of the party in the electoral arena, and this in turn shapes how partisans in Congress choose to organize themselves.

This change in behavior in Washington can be seen in the Congress-by-Congress change in the policy positions estimated by Poole and Rosenthal (or any similar scaling technique) over these years (see http://www.voteview.com/; Poole and Rosenthal 1997, 2007). These views are, as the website name suggests, a way of summarizing in a rigorous way just what policy stances the legislators are offering their constituents. We have used those results as our best estimate of the overall message the incumbent wants to send to the public (constituents, activists, potential supporters for other offices, and so on). Certainly, the roll-call record is a very hard piece of evidence that they—and their opponents—can point to about what they stand for. For incumbents seeking reelection, these positions can be taken as their effective platform. We have aggregated them according to the criteria of conditional party government to make an assessment about how well these positions satisfy the condition in conditional party government, using the two-dimensional scores as observable on the website Voteview.com. Figure 9.1 reports the results for House and Senate from 1877 to the most recently completed Congress (the One Hundred Tenth, 2007–8; see Aldrich, Rohde, and Tofias 2004, 2007). These scores for whole Congresses permit comparison among Congresses (but there is no absolute scale for these or for the Poole-Rosenthal scale scores on which they are based).

Consider first the House. Figure 9.1 shows that the gradual decline in the condition over much of the twentieth century escalated rapidly in the 1970s (over the end of the Johnson, then the Nixon, Ford, and Carter administrations, and into the early years of the Reagan administration). It then reversed equally as rapidly and climbed back to czar-era proportions. The dynamics of the Senate look quite like those of the House, except that the dramatic decline happened earlier, as described above.

If roll call voting patterns thus changed at the individual level and at the level of the party in Congress, then the final step is illustrated by the trend shown in figure 7.5. That figure demonstrates that presidents with a unified partisan control of the Congress virtually always win actual legislative victories. Their bills, however, in earlier times passed at reasonably high rates at least for the first few years of their administration under divided control of government, but that has not been the case in the last two decades. That is, parties structure how their members vote in Congress, and that structuring shapes what legislation passes and what fails.

The summation of all of this is that the incumbents in both House and Senate adopted very different patterns of behavior over the post–World War II period. Therefore, the signals they sent to the electorate were very different. They voted in quite different ways in the mid-twentieth century than at the start of the current century, and that means they voted as parties for different sorts of things. They collectively presented increasingly cohesive voting patterns, as partisans, to the public, and in doing so, they offered the citizens very different sorts of legislation enacted. By 2010, the signal they sent to the public was that Republicans voted alike, Democrats voted alike, they opposed each other often, and

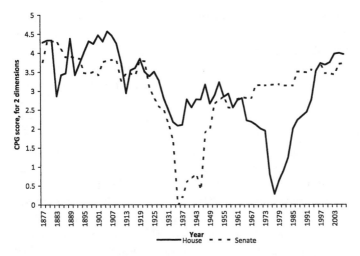

Figure 9.1 Conditional party government in House and Senate, 1877–2007. *Source:* http://www.voteview.com/. Compiled by author.

in doing so, the president gets about eight out of ten of the bills he supports enacted into law when his party controls Congress, and about five in ten when his party does not. The signal the parties send the nation is thus much cleaner, crisper, and more meaningful. The two parties offer, that is, different and meaningful reputations to the public.

As we saw in chapters 6 and 8, the public has seen and reacted to these dynamics. Figure 6.1 illustrated that, over the last fifty years, substantially more in the public see differences between the two parties, and they do so accurately, that is, identifying more completely that it is the Republicans who are the conservatives. Similarly, the relationship between partisan identifiers' own partisanship and ideological self-placement has increased dramatically, especially in the twenty-first century. If voters were receiving more diffuse signals of what the party stood for in the 1960s and 1970s than before or since, then we would expect that fewer voters would vote along party lines in that more diffuse period, since it stood for less, and that they would be more likely to vote for different parties for different offices, depending upon the particular mix of candidates in each race. Before or after that period, we should imagine observing higher degrees of voting along party lines and of voting straight party tickets. And that is just what we observed in figures 6.3, 6.4, and 8.5. Finally, although the number of questions that permit such over-time comparisons is limited, the kinds of indications that scholars, journalists, pundits, and politicians, alike, pointed to as worrying signs of the growing irrelevance of parties in the 1960s and 1970s, should show the same dynamic, that is, be increasing into that period and then declining again after, which is what figure 8.3 illustrates. No one worries any more about the irrelevance of parties.

If legislators take public stands by voting increasingly along party lines (as they do); if that leads to increased partisan regularity among voters, in response to that increasingly meaningful party reputation they are being presented (as it has); if party organizations have become stronger, more professional, more highly funded, and more fully coordinated with supporting activist organizations (as we have observed they have); then the increasing satisfaction of the condition in conditional party government should also mean that the internal workings of the legislature should change to reflect a more partisan government. We saw just such indications, especially in the House, in chapter 7. There we saw that the nature of power in committees, especially its chairs, was allocated in the "textbook era" purely by seniority. That changed to one in which party loyalty (often as measured by cash contributed to the party) became the primary mechanism of allocation of power. Certainly, it is true that polarized elections have led to more liberals among Democrats and more conservatives among Republicans, and the data presented there reflected that increasing polarization (satisfaction of the condition, in our terms). Even so, we saw that the parties (especially the majority party) appointed even more extreme members than the party as a whole to the most important committees over this period. The Rules Committee in particular went from an independent source of power for southern Democrats who then led it (thanks to the rule of seniority) to a committee that was but an extension of the majority party leadership. And that was important in the House, because the majority party, whether Democrat or Republican, has apparently used that committee to control the agenda on their terms. Thus, we saw that the number of bills reported to the floor with a special rule that required a roll call vote increased dramatically over this period, especially in the first decade of the twenty-first century (fig. 7.8). We also saw that these special rules were partisan, or at least that is apparently how members perceived them. In the last three available Congresses, almost every single roll call vote on a special rule was close to completely partisan—with almost every minority party member voting against, and almost every majority party member voting for the special rule (fig. 7.9). It does appear that the Congress is designed by its members to achieve its goals, as Mayhew argued (1974). It is just that today those goals—still quite often reelection goals—are achievable through a Congress organized by party, instead of in the fashion of the textbook era in which he wrote.

None of this goes directly to the content of legislation. So, let me close by considering the health care bill. On March 24, 2010, President Obama signed what had become known as the "Affordable Health Care for America: Reconciliation Bill" into law. On December 21, 2009, the Senate voted 60–40 to pass health care legislation. That was exactly the number needed to avoid a filibuster, and it was achieved by getting every Democrat to vote for it, because no Republican did. Of course, the pivotal voter was a Democrat and, by some theories, the bill would reflect precisely the desires of that sixtieth Democrat. The last to fall in line in support of the bill was Ben Nelson (D-NE), and he—or Blanche Lincoln, AR; or maybe Mary Landrieu, LA—was not the most liberal but the most moderate Democrat. And getting each of them to vote for the bill was not easy. Nelson, for example, not only got concessions on funding abortions written into the bill, but also got other concessions, most notably an agreement that his state, alone among the fifty, would receive full federal funding of Medicare beyond the three years all states were to receive. While the abortion funding changes are correctly understood as making the bill at least a bit more moderate than it was, and thus closer to his "ideal point," or most preferred bill, the special features available to Nebraska are most evidently understood as pure distributive politics. More generally, that the Democratic leadership had to entice, often with the use of pork barrel politics, their members in both chambers who would be pivotal (the median member in the House or filibuster pivot in the Senate) means that the bill was not at all close to their ideal policy. Rather, they were at the cut point, just where support turns to opposition. In the end, when several provisions were voted on in reconciliation (and thus filibuster free), Nelson, Lincoln, and Mark Pryor (AR) voted against the bill on March 25, 2010. Needing only a simple majority, the bill passed anyway, 56–43 (all Republicans voting no), indicating that Nelson did, indeed, barely favor the bill or perhaps did not favor it at all, and this appears to be true for the other moderate Senate Democrats.

In the House, requiring 218 votes to pass by simple majority, the final reconciliation bill passed 220–211 on March 21, 2010, with all 178 Republicans voting no. Thus, there was a very tiny margin left on the majority side. Some moderate Democrats in the House followed Bart Stupak (D-MI) and voted for the bill. Stupak had coauthored an amendment (along with Joseph Pitts [R-PA]) that would have made it impossible in the bill to provide federal funding for abortions. When that amendment originally passed, he voted for the original bill (Pitts did not). He announced opposition to the reconciliation measure when that amendment was stricken in the Senate, but ended up voting for the bill when Obama promised an executive order to achieve ends comparable to his amendment. Others, however, did not. Dan Lipinski (D-IL), for example, voted against it, only in part because of abortion. That is, in both House and Senate, legislators who were the "median voter," or were close to being so, faced agonizing rather than easy choices, indicating that the bill as enacted was not at all close to their position. It was instead a major policy outcome well away from the policy center in Congress and somewhere toward the center of preferences among Democrats. At least in this one instance, then, we can say with some confidence that health care reflected the wishes of the majority party and not the most moderate members of the Congress, just as conditional party government leads us to expect.

This example at least illustrates the final step in the cyclical process that is a two-party system in dynamic equilibrium. When the condition in conditional party government is well satisfied, and thus the Congress is run primarily as a partisan institution, policy is not likely to be at the center of legislative preferences and, one imagines, not at the center of electoral opinion. Rather, it will reflect the wishes of the majority party, and it will be the positive use of agenda control that makes passage possible. As we look at the historic patterns, such as in figure 9.1, we see evidence that implies that the contemporary pattern appears to be the historically common pattern, in which there is substantial partisan divide among officeholders and (presumably) the activists, that is, the benefit seekers who support them. The public factors that partisan reputation into their choices (no matter whether or not the public is polarized itself), and thus the circle of centripetal and centrifugal forces is complete, with outcomes likely to be a balance someplace between the pull of party toward the extreme, and the pull of moderation for majority-seeking toward the middle.

The 1950s and 1960s thus appear to be the historical anomaly. The era of the "textbook Congress" that so greatly shaped the writing of congressional scholars until relatively recently, that is, provided a unique, and even quite odd, base on which to build an understanding of American democracy. We are only now working out what was unique about that period.

I hasten to add that while today's elections, legislating, and partisan politics seem like the historically more common, and while the condition for conditional party government is more often fairly well satisfied rather than rarely so, that does not make democratic politics at the end of the twentieth century similar to that at the century's beginning. The technology (and hence institutional structuring) of elections, media coverage, and so on, are quite different, and that makes the working-out of conditional party government now distinctive from that of a century ago. Conditional party government, that is, provides one critical part of a theoretical explanation of democratic politics. It is not the only part.

What is general is the importance of political parties individually, and the party system they form collectively, to the effective workings of democracy. Whatever the institutional form of the major American party, the partisan impulse springs from the same forces today as in earlier eras—and these are likely to be the same forces into the future. These are the forces inherent in, and derived from, the very nature of democratic politics in an extended republic. That impulse is the combination of goal-seeking behavior of politicians, channeling and nurturing their ambitions for long and successful political careers, providing access to office and control over its use. The particular institutional manifestations of that partisan impulse are the further product of the political and government institutions of the time and of the historical conditions and setting that define the technological possibilities and shape the specific ambitions of those political elites. In America those ambitions require the formation of electoral and governing majorities. In America democracy is unthinkable save in terms of a two-party system, because no collection of ambitious politicians has long been able to think of a way to achieve their goals in this democracy save in terms of political parties.

NOTES

CHAPTER ONE

1. This is an intentional paraphrase of Joseph A. Schlesinger (1966, 1), for reasons that will become evident.

2. Granted, this literature includes important debates about the veracity of such claims.

3. I resist calling these theories, largely because some of them (especially the first view) are collections of sometimes quite different perspectives of particular scholars. For example, if the first view sees parties as "umbrella-like" organizations, including within them many and diverse views, so too are the scholars and their theoretical understandings many and diverse in this category I have constructed. This is less true of the responsible party scholars, and the competitive-party category is more uniform, consisting primarily of rational choice theories.

4. As they show, this was less true in the 1940s and presumably in the 1930s, when the New Deal coalition was at its strongest.

5. I use the term "platform" figuratively, as a set of policies proposed to be enacted in office.

6. Ranney is quoting Polsby and Wildavsky (1971, 225).

7. Jacobson (1992, 12n3) pointed out that thirty-two states chose at least one Republican and one Democratic senator between 1978 and 1990. Of the remaining eighteen, seventeen (all but Hawaii) have elected a governor of the other party. In other words, both parties have won at least one major statewide election, and often many more, in forty-nine of the fifty states in recent years. It is ironic that the only other period of geographically broad competition was in the second party system of Jacksonian Democrats and Whigs, an era with one of the strongest systems of parties, rather than the weak party period of the 1970s and 1980s.

8. That is, collective interests as partisans are necessary for there to be a strong party-in-government. Such interests are not a sufficient condition, however, owing to the collective action problem.

9. The justification for partisan use of political power, then, is that it is consistent with the republican principle. All power flows directly or indirectly from the great body of the people through elective office seekers and into the hands of the party. To be sure, partisan powers are often highly indirect and not very democratic. Indeed, major reforms of the political party are often sought to make the party a more republican-democratic institution in its own right. Thus was the invention of the convention system justified in the 1820s as more

representative than "King Caucus," and thus was the primary election method of nomination so justified (see Aldrich 1989b). Today, the nearly exclusive reliance on primary elections is rooted in the belief that all power should flow into the party more directly from the great body of the people. Nonetheless, primary voters do not choose party rules, platforms, organizations, or virtually any other form of outcome. They choose the leaders, but it is the leaders who will then choose the outcomes.

10. Office seekers, in Schlesinger's account, seek the private good of holding office, whereas benefit seekers, in addition to any value they, like office seekers, might obtain from good public policy, seek private preferments that come from the capture of office per se. Note that this distinction makes the most sense when speaking of benefit seekers in terms of the high-level resource providers or of the political machine, which had many private goods to allocate to its activists. The distinction becomes much less clear when discussing volunteer activists in general and especially the (purely) policy-motivated activist, as in chapter 6.

11. In chapter 4 I give a detailed account of Van Buren's idea of the importance of the political party, above and beyond that of any individual (himself included). Even here, though, the reason for desiring this form of political party (and for those who subsequently subscribed to this view of the political party throughout the "party period" [see McCormick 1979; Silbey 1985; and various places throughout this text]) was not for the party above all, even if for a party above men, but for the desirable effects such as party would have for democracy.

12. The reason these problems are recurring will be developed in the next chapter.

13. The allocation of n + k aspirants to n offices, at least for pure office-seeking candidates, defines an n-person, zero-sum game that, as such, lacks a core.

14. Riker's pathbreaking study of coalition formation (1962) that introduced many to rational choice theory began with a strong argument for the importance of winning in politics. Clearly, Schlesinger's ambition theory (1966) and its many related studies, such as those that follow Mayhew's emphasis on the importance of reelection in understanding Congress (1974) or those that follow Downs's accounts of elections (1957), place winning just as centrally as Riker does.

15. This result does not seem to depend heavily on the assumption that the alternative to universalism is the formation of minimal winning majority coalitions. What does seem to be crucial is the assumption that all coalitions are equally likely a priori.

16. At least they prefer this majority coalition to universalism if the costs of forming and maintaining it are less than the savings from not giving the minority any projects.

17. Once parties have organized, the current institutional arrangements will include those current partisan arrangements. Thus it may be that partisan institutions are part, even much, of the problem. By definition, these current partisan arrangements are at least insufficient to solve that problem. These three recurring problems share at their base something like an impossibility result. That is, no institutional arrangements, partisan or otherwise, that are

consistent with republican democracy can solve any of these problems in all circumstances. This logical consequence is the reason partisan institutions are always threatened by, or in a state of, crisis. The party is designed to solve what cannot be permanently solved. The solution is thus contingent. That is, it is the solution that works for the particular set of circumstances currently faced; the same arrangements may not work adequately under other conditions. And in a purely logical sense, any given set of partisan institutions will necessarily fail at some time, if these are indeed true impossibility results. It is in part for this reason that the historical context is so important for understanding political parties.

CHAPTER TWO

1. In fact, they are problems endemic to a far broader range of social settings than republican democracy.

2. Readers should be forewarned that though I will proceed mostly by example, some symbols remain.

3. Such recognition requires knowledge of the payoffs of the other player(s), unlike the personal incentive to defect based solely on consideration of the player's own preferences.

4. Commitment is generally achieved by imposing a punishment for failure to honor the commitment.

5. Defeating all three bills is not Pareto superior to the partisan outcome. The $(0, 0, 0)$ and the $(4, 3, -9)$ payoffs cannot be compared by the Pareto criterion (nor are $[4, 3, -9]$ and $[-2, -2, -2]$ Pareto comparable), since in neither pair does one alternative make all better (or no worse) off. In this sense there is no collective action problem with the party coalition.

6. To see this, there are three minimal winning coalitions, A-B, B-C, and A-C. Each legislator is in two of the winning coalitions, and all three coalitions are, by assumption, equally likely to occur. Thus there is a two-thirds chance of being a winner and a one-third chance of being a loser, a priori. Expected utility is determined by multiplying the chance of an outcome's occurring by its payoff and summing over all outcomes. In this case, each has a two-thirds chance of receiving a payoff of 2 and a one-third chance of receiving -2, yielding an expected payoff of $2/3$.

7. With geographic-based districting, we might also expect that legislators would favor bills that distribute benefits geographically, a feature consistent even with the intersectional alliances of the second party system, as well as with the regionally based parties of the later party systems and the contemporary era.

8. Arrow's theorem, of course, imposes conditions, so that it does not cover all possible methods of choosing. It does cover, however, all methods that choose between pairs, and thus all procedures used in legislatures. It also includes many other methods, such as the free market.

9. Preferences are single peaked if the alternatives can be arranged so that each voter's preferences increase monotonically, decrease monotonically, or monotonically increase to a peak and then monotonically decrease, moving across the dimension. Graphically, then, a single-peaked preference order looks like a single mountain peak. Generalization of single peakedness to multiple

dimensions is similar. In two dimensions, such preferences look like a topographical contour map of a single mountain peak, and so on.

10. Indeed, one definition of multidimensionality of the "choice space" is precisely when it requires more than one dimension to yield single-peaked preferences for all voters. Thus dimensionality is a function of the preferences held by members of the society, not the nature of the alternatives themselves. Such spatial models, especially in studying large electorates (e.g., Downs 1957), typically define dimensions by the nature of the alternatives. For example, alternatives may be arranged along one or more ideological dimensions, or by the amount of funds expended for a program, and so on. Preferences may not appear single peaked in such cases, even though they meet Black's definition. For example, alternatives for the Vietnam War issue might have been arrayed by the degree of United States involvement. Voters might have preferred a "win or get out" option, so that their preferences would not look single peaked on that dimension (they would, instead look like a V). But if all voters least preferred the middle option of continued involvement short of achieving a military victory, alternatives could be arranged (or rearranged) so that preferences were all single peaked.

11. Plott's and similar theorems are more general than this statement, but this gets at their essence.

12. See also Davis, DeGroot, and Hinich (1972), and Schwartz (1986). For the most general form of the spatial model of candidate competition and proof of the major theorems, see McKelvey (1975).

13. See Riker and Ordeshook (1973), who point out that Wilson's (1971) observation that Arrow's theorem is "essentially the observation that the core of a voting game is ordinarily empty" is also accompanied by the existence of a core precisely under the conditions of Black's median voter theorem.

14. "Anything happening" includes the possibility that the outcome might "wander" anywhere, including to Pareto inferior (unanimously opposed) outcomes. McKelvey's (1976) example of the "anythings" that can happen was of a single agenda setter who could exploit the chaos result to ensure that his or her ideal point was (always) selected. Thus another incentive for parties might be to capture control over agenda setting.

15. Other important results include Gibbard's (1973) and Satterthwaite's (1975) demonstration that whenever there was an Arrovian cycle, there were also incentives for at least one player to misreveal preferences, that is, to act "strategically" or "sophisticatedly" rather than to express preferences "sincerely." Riker (1982a) further argued that even when there was no cycle, there were incentives to create one, that is, to manipulate the agenda to concoct a cycle "falsely."

16. So far this review has pointed to the parallels between committees and large electorates. The information needed to vote in a sophisticated (or "strategic") manner is much more likely to be held by legislators in an ongoing, professionalized legislature than in mass electorates. This marks, therefore, one major divergence between these two settings.

17. In this sense Krehbiel's argument (1991; see the discussion of it in chap. 7) is strong: *if* there is a majority preference, the majority "works its will."

18. A similar argument holds for symmetric, multidimensional preferences.

19. This interpretation assumes that the candidate with the most votes wins the election and that all that matters is who wins. The winner might be able to accomplish more in office the larger the margin of victory, or the outcome might be valued in some way other than by who wins and loses. If so the interpretation becomes more complex, and the degree of the collective action problem is attenuated, but probably so little as to be irrelevant.

20. Especially for decision-making costs, C must be understood as the costs of turning out, net of the costs of abstaining. There may be psychic costs for failing to vote. More important, deciding to abstain is also costly, since it requires gathering information, processing it, and determining that R is indeed not positive. In a presidential election, in fact, these costs are usually very small (this may not be true for other contests, such as the less well known of the numerous proposals on the typical California ballot). As a result, deciding not to vote is nearly as costly as deciding to turn out and deciding whom to vote for together. This calculus also assumes that this is the only contest on the ballot. Time and effort costs of turning out are paid only once, even though the ballot typically includes a large number of contests. Thus, as Niemi has argued (1976), the costs of voting are typically very small for most eligible Americans.

21. The connection between the voting calculus and the prisoners' dilemma can be seen by comparing the row chooser's payoffs in the prisoners' dilemma (e.g., table 2.2) with the following decision table (developed more completely in Ferejohn and Fiorina 1974). Ignoring voting for the less preferred candidate, there are two choices: vote for the preferred candidate or abstain. There are four possible situations that hold before casting a vote: (a) the preferred candidate is ahead by one vote or more; (b) the candidates are tied; (c) the preferred candidate trails by exactly one vote; or (d) that candidate trails by more than one vote. The citizen's vote is ineffective if (a) or (d) holds, whereas it makes a tie if (c) holds and breaks a tie if (b) is true. Ignoring D, letting the voter's preference for the favored candidate be 1 and for the opponent be 0, and counting the value of a tie as $1/2$, the table below holds.

Choose to	Situation That Holds Prior to Choice			
	A	B	c	d
Vote	$1-c$	$1-c$	$1/2-c$	$-c$
Abstain	1	½	0	0

Abstention is preferred to voting if (a) or (d) holds. Voting is preferred under situations (b) and (c) (and if $c < 1/2$). If P is set to zero, one's vote does not make or break a tie, so that (b) and (c) cannot hold. Erasing them makes the payoffs to the voter identical in form to the payoffs to the row chooser in the prisoners' dilemma, as in table 2.2, thus showing that the individual decision-making model of the calculus, when $P = 0$, is identical to the individual's incentives in the prisoners' dilemma.

22. Although reinterpreted, the following example of the calculus of candidacy also provides more detail about the calculus of voting formulation. Similarly, the calculus of partisan affiliation in the next section adds further theoretical detail to these two calculi as well.

23. This calculus therefore represents a departure from Schlesinger's theory by making static and progressive ambition derivations from the theory rather than assumptions of it, as in Schlesinger's original account.

24. Duverger's Law does not depend on single-member districts, but it is clear that having single-member districts instead of at-large elections or multi-member districts accentuates the pressures plurality elections impose toward two-party systems. As we will see in chapter 4, it is probably not coincidental that legislation to require single-member districts in United States congressional elections was enacted after the very first appearance of a full two-party system in 1840.

25. Yet this may be true for only one of the two strongest candidates. In 1980, for example, Reagan was certainly not displeased to see Anderson attract votes that would otherwise have been cast for Carter.

26. The name derives from the attempt to blend the strengths of the traditional study of institutions in political science with the focus on the actions of individuals central to the "behavioral revolution" in political science in the post–World War II period.

27. It is thus no surprise that proposed rule changes that would materially affect the fortunes of presidential contenders are often determined by the preferences of the delegates for president rather than by their preferences for the rules per se. Voting on such rules, adopted before the presidential voting, typically tests the strength of the candidates, as in the Republican convention in 1976 or the Democratic convention in 1980 (see Aldrich 1993a).

28. These chapters therefore study only positive cases. They are not a full sample of cases, which would include instances of politicians' turning from parties or turning to solutions other than parties. In this sense there is a selection bias that means these chapters do not add up to a full test of the theory. See Hansen (1991) for an instance when politicians turned to devices other than parties. Although the decline of parties literature might suggest that the third section of this book studies a turn from parties in the contemporary era, the argument I make is more complex.

CHAPTER THREE

1. At least that is my count of roll call votes in the Inter-University Consortium for Political and Social Research data set.

2. The portion of his plan advanced in the first session concerned public credit, so debt assumption was evidently central. A second portion of the plan, including the creation of a central bank, was proposed later.

3. Jefferson cited Carroll and Gale as those who would be persuaded to switch votes in the vote agreement. Lee and White, it appears, were prevailed on subsequently by unknown parties, when their votes became critical because of changes among other representatives. The new capital was to be carved from the districts of these four, providing economic benefits to their districts, which implies some useful leverage in prevailing on them to switch.

4. Moreover, he argued that a compromise coalition on the capital issue in the House and Senate had already been forged before the dinner, without the intervention (and possibly knowledge) of the three principals.

5. It is, moreover, reasonable to assume that satisfaction with a position on the great principle would decline the further that position lay from one's ideal, and thus to assume that preferences were single peaked on this dimension. Note also that this description of preferences is more applicable to the ratification than to the convention period, that is, especially after the greatest concerns dividing large and small states and those concerning individual rights and liberties had been remedied.

6. If not direct application of the median voter theorem, then a different equilibrium based on the median voter theorem, such as Romer and Rosenthal's (1978), might apply. This and more general analysis from the perspective of ratification are developed in Aldrich (1989a).

7. Complex concerns, such as any fiscal policy, tap many different aspects of values and interests, implying that they are ordinarily multidimensional in themselves without even considering their implications for any greater principle.

8. Grant (1977) points to a number of key methodological issues that also affect, in part, the diversity of conclusions reached.

9. Martis (1989), for instance, reports pro-administration majorities of 36–28 in the House and 18–8 in the Senate.

10. Nomenclature can be confusing. The party founded by Jefferson was called "Republican" at the time, and I will therefore call it that myself (typically calling it "Jeffersonian Republican" if there is any chance of confusion with the current Republican Party or the National Republican Party of John Quincy Adams in the 1820s and 1830s). It was also sometimes called "anti-federalist," since it arose as an opponent to the Federalist party, but that risks confusion with "Anti-Federalist," meaning (and here used exclusively to refer to) opponents of ratifying the Constitution. Some refer to it as the "Democratic-Republican" party because Jackson and Van Buren claimed that their Democratic Party rested on and revived the principles of Jefferson and Madison (seen even today in such Democratic Party affairs as the annual Jefferson-Jackson Day dinners).

11. This is especially true if organizing was itself perceived to be illegitimate and risked effective criticism from the opposition.

12. Others also played leadership and entrepreneurial roles. Representative Robert Morris (PA), for example, was a key leader in debt assumption strategizing, thus nicely reversing roles with Hamilton from 1781 (see Cooke 1970, 1971), and so, certainly, were others.

13. Federalists never felt comfortable with even this tentative sort of campaigning. Republicans' principles, moreover, were more attuned to the exchange of information in an election. Here I am also arguing that committees were more expedient for Republicans at this time than for Federalists.

14. The constitutional role, if any, of the House in matters relating to treaties was, however, more directly a "great principle" question. Moreover, it makes sense that Hamiltonians would lean more toward Britain, with its government illustrating an extreme point on the great principle dimension, and Jeffersonians would lean more toward the French, whose government, such as it was, was at the other end of that dimension.

15. Missing data combined with the small universe of senators prohibit systematic analysis of that chamber.

16. As can be seen above, however, many important decisions were made in unrecorded votes, such as those reached in committee of the whole.

17. "Anti-Federalist" here means those opposed to ratification. Aldrich and Grant (1993) demonstrate that these Anti-Federalists provided a significant core to the Jeffersonian voting coalition in the First Congress. Anti-Federalist Theodoric Bland (VA) died in office, and neither he nor his replacement voted often enough to be included in the analysis.

18. These numbers, therefore, serve as the applicable n's for table 3.1.

19. I follow the usual definition of a "party vote" as one in which a majority of one party opposed a majority of the other party.

20. The mean position of the six Anti-Federalists on the first dimension (First Congress) is 0.048, that is, in the center. This seeming anomaly (since one would expect them to be more extreme than the Republicans) results because two of the six followed their states' instructions to vote as "Federalists" (reflecting the Anti-Federalists' preference for the Articles over the new Constitution, perhaps because representatives to the Continental Congress were bound to follow instructions from the state legislatures that selected them). Removing these two, the Anti-Federalist mean is, in fact, more positive (extreme) than that of Republicans. Further, the six-person mean has a large standard deviation (1.45) on this dimension, consistent with the effect of state instruction. Below, probit analyses of preferences alone on vote choices (those without party variables) include these Anti-Federalists to keep the number of cases as large as possible. Analyses that exclude them, however, show the same patterns reported here. These results are available from the author on request.

21. A negative sign was expected, and one-tailed hypotheses were tested. The t-statistics are $-1.77, -3.42$, and -5.43, respectively. Thus the test is barely significant at conventional levels for the First Congress.

22. The second dimension coefficient was significant, however, in the First Congress (0.476, 2.05 t-statistic), even though it divided partisans less sharply than did the first dimension (see table 3.1). The parameter estimates for the first dimension and t-statistics for the three Congresses are -0.323 (-1.37), -1.00 (-3.39), and -1.34 (-4.77), respectively. All other dimensions in the later two Congresses (and the third dimension in the First) had very small coefficient estimates and t-statistics. The percentages correctly predicted for the three Congresses are 72, 77, and 92, respectively. Part of the low effect of the first dimension in the three-dimensional model of the First Congress is the small and skewed distribution of partisanship and some collinearity between the first and third dimensions.

23. In such a case, the model cannot be estimated. Since discrimination is perfect, a single value for the coefficient estimate cannot be determined. Therefore this vote could not be analyzed further.

24. This is (appropriately) a conservative test of the hypothesis. Rejection of the null (based on chi-square test of log likelihood ratios) strongly supports the hypothesis. Failure to reject the null does not imply that the two other dimensions are irrelevant. For example, owing to collinearity, the first dimension might be "picking up" some of the effects of the excluded dimensions in the bivariate case. In one vote in the First Congress, the null is not rejected, but one of the other dimensions had a significant coefficient estimate, indicating

that it was an important component of the vote decision albeit undetected in the hypothesis test. See Aldrich (1989a) for details on the hypothesis tests.

25. Estimates are not reported here but are available on request.

CHAPTER FOUR

1. One "faithless elector" failed to vote for Monroe. Some argue that the reason was to keep Washington as the only unanimous choice, while others suggest that it was (or was also) dissatisfaction with Monroe that caused the defection (see Kolodny 1989).

2. In chapter 2, for example, the calculus of voting equation was shown to be essentially identical to Rohde's calculus of candidacy (1979).

3. Direct penetration of campaign organizations to the state and local levels yields a further direct benefit. Face-to-face contact with citizens, soliciting their support and encouraging them to vote, brings national politics literally to their doorstep. Quite often people are truly appreciative that someone—anyone— cares enough about them to ask for their support. This intrinsic benefit may explain why media advertising is apparently less effective in turnout drives than labor-intensive doorbell ringing.

4. It is not theoretically different from the original, because it is simply an interpretation of what constitutes the content of the original D term, where theoretically, D denotes any intrinsic value that comes from voting per se.

5. That Jackson did kill a man in a duel and that his wife was (unknow-ingly) not yet divorced when they married only gave the mudslinging greater credibility.

6. Thus this account is consistent not just with the calculus of voting but also with its major alternative in the rational choice literature, Ferejohn and Fiorina's "minimax regret" model (1974, 1975). As they show, their model of rational decision making concludes that turnout will be related to the B, D, and C terms only and not the P term. Although they exclude the D term from their analysis, their model may be extended simply to include it (see Aldrich 1976).

7. This explanation of "strategic parties" is theoretically similar to the well-known Jacobson-Kernell "strategic politicians" hypothesis (1983). They used their hypothesis to explain why individual voters do not seem to choose candidates in congressional races based on economic performance, but that at the aggregate level poor economic performance is strongly related to voting for nonincumbents. Their hypothesis is that in bad economic times strong challengers recognize that their chances of victory are higher than usual, and thus the opposition party fields an unusually strong set of candidates. Note that this follows from the calculus of candidacy described in chapter 2. Political action committees and other sources of campaign resources are also more willing to support these stronger challengers in bad economic times. Strong and well-financed challengers therefore attract more votes, so that the out party does better at the polls in bad economic times even though voters base their choice on which candidate is the better option and not on economic conditions. Their strategic politicians hypothesis requires an additional step because, as Born (1986) pointed out, there must be a reason that strong challengers and organized interests believe bad economic times are propitious for them. Jacobson

(1989) provided evidence that voters do base their choices in part on the state of the economy. The result, then, is that the impact of strategic politicians increases the already existing effect of economic circumstances on the vote. No such step is required in the strategic parties hypotheses presented here. Parties will rationally invest resources in close races because they are close, whether or not that expected closeness matters to citizens. Parties do so because they seek to win, and a close race is one that they can either win or lose.

8. Cox and Munger (1989) developed a very similar argument to explain turnout in congressional elections. They estimated a model of turnout that included measures of the closeness of the races and of the amount of campaign funds expended in each contest. Their estimates of turnout in the 1978 congressional elections showed that both variables were indeed significantly and strongly related to the participation rate. The closer the election and the greater the expenditures, the greater the turnout.

9. McCormick's paper is famous both for its substantive contributions and for its methods. In debunking prior accounts and offering a new understanding of mobilization in this period, he carried his argument by systematic data analysis. The substantive accomplishments he demonstrated to be possible through this method helped launch the "new" or quantitative political history movement.

10. Some states continued to have electors chosen by the state legislature rather than by popular vote. Of the remainder, in only three states—Louisiana, Rhode Island, and Virginia—were there significant restrictions on suffrage of adult white males, and these were not reduced until much later.

11. The difficulty with this account is that competitiveness in most states first appeared in the 1836 election. Yet turnout in 1836 was essentially the same as in the more one-sided contests of 1828 and 1832 and far less than in the similarly competitive contest of 1840. It is possible that party organizations did not strengthen much from 1828 to 1840, although the data presented later in this chapter (based on McCormick's later study, 1966) suggest otherwise. It is possible that organization strengthened between 1836 and 1840, and it certainly did on the Whig side at least. Also, the 1840 election of "Tippicanoe and Tyler, too," of "Log Cabin and Hard Cider," might have marked a substantial increase in the enthusiasm and drama of political campaigns. Although such comparative judgments are hard to make, I argue later that the basic nature of the new form of campaigning was first seen in 1828—and at rather high levels. Although the strengthening of party organizations and heightened drama of campaigns are plausible accounts, they are different from asserting that it was the increased competitiveness of the 1840 election that explains the increased turnout that year.

12. The number of states using a statewide, winner-take-all procedure for selecting electors also increased in this period. In 1824, twelve states used this at-large method while six used a district method. This increased to eighteen at-large and only four district states in 1828. The last state in this period to use a district method was Maryland in 1832. To the extent that Duverger's Law carries force, the growth of popular voting, winner-take-all methods would encourage not just a mass-based party form, but a two-party system as well.

13. One reader has pointed out that the principle may be little more than,

"it is good that our side wins." Federalists had never won a truly contested presidential election, so painting Adams as a Federalist like his father could be a winning strategy. Moreover, a revival of an alliance between New York and Virginia (as, for example, the first Republican presidential victory under the Virginia–New York ticket of Jefferson and Aaron Burr) would protect their interests against an alliance between Adams's New England and South Carolina (the home of Vice President Calhoun—Van Buren's early move to seek Calhoun's support for the new party could thus be seen as an attempt to break up that alliance before it become permanent). A new form was needed, then, to make an alliance, and therefore winning, as durable as possible. To do so required establishment of the principle of party over men (rejecting the Clintonian basis of organization) and the means to mobilize the electorate.

14. If the principles of the party included putting it ahead of the men in it, this principle could exact a cost for politicians agreeing to it. The exact nature of the cost was likely unclear at the time, but it implies potential constraints on the freedom of action of elective office seekers and holders in the Democratic Party. Wallace's fine study of the Albany Regency (1968) includes such an example that may have been known to potential Democrats in 1828. The Regency successfully persuaded seventeen of their New York senators to vote against popular voting for electors in 1824, defeating this popular bill. Most were defeated for reelection, which they knew their votes risked. The story also illustrates the value of this principle, as well as its costs, because the Regency acted to take care of those whose support of the party led to their defeat. Such action was of course crucial for a party built on ambitious careerists, but it served only to reduce, not eliminate, the costs of compliance with the principle that the party was more important than its men.

15. States included in the Alliance were Alabama, Georgia, Mississippi, New York, North Carolina, Pennsylvania, South Carolina, Tennessee, and Virginia.

16. Calhoun apparently preferred an East-West alliance, which effectively would be the second stage in Van Buren's plan. In return for the promise of Radical support, Van Buren might have received the assurances he desired from Calhoun that Jackson would support Jeffersonian principles. There is no evidence of this, however. Ritchie publicly claimed to have received assurances that Jackson was a "politician of the Richmond school" (Remini 1963, 54), but Remini reports that claim is unlikely to have been correct.

17. The break between pro- and anti-Administration supporters came in 1826. At the time it was not clear that the cleavage was so deep as to be irreconcilable. Perhaps for that reason, some (especially among the Radicals) became anti-Adams congressmen but simply did nothing at the time rather than moving directly to support Jackson (see Remini 1959, 124).

18. Four of these were not statewide, winner-take-all states. Two of them, Jackson's and Calhoun's home states, were nearly certain to go overwhelmingly to Jackson, and Delaware, with its three votes, was too small to worry about split electoral vote outcomes. This left the largest electoral prize in the nation, New York, with thirty-six votes. For 1828 New York was to use popular vote for selecting electors but would do so by the district method. In the event, Jackson won a narrow popular vote plurality and twenty electoral votes. It is reasonable

to conclude that Van Buren could offer a large bloc of electoral votes to the Alliance, precisely because it was a district-method election, even though he could not promise a large or even certain victory. Still, even a large minority of electoral votes won there would be a major improvement over the one vote Jackson and five votes Crawford won in New York in 1824.

19. At least he could offer the assistance of his Regency and its (and his own) popularity. He also knew that his opposition, DeWitt Clinton, favored Jackson. Kentucky was the other state not won by Jackson, Crawford, or their combination in 1824. Needless to say, it went for its favorite son, Clay. Without Clay running in 1828, it was the only one of the three additional Caucus states that went for Jackson.

20. Where possible, the ranking was based on popular votes cast. In the rest, the ranking was based on electoral votes.

21. Delaware and Illinois were the twelfth- and thirteenth-ranked states, and they had almost the same electoral vote percentages. Illinois is in the bottom grouping in table 4.2. If these two were reversed, Illinois would be in the upper right cell while Delaware would be in the bottom center category.

22. Van Buren had struck a North-South alliance—sensible if reviving the party of Jefferson—rather than an East-West alliance as Calhoun initially suggested. This might possibly explain why potential Jackson states such as Indiana (and Illinois, perhaps, which would be a third such state if included in the stronger group of states) were not part of the Alliance. Alabama and Mississippi were new states included in the Alliance, but their Deep South character might explain their inclusion.

23. He does not discuss South Carolina, because it did not have popular election of presidential electors until after the Civil War.

24. The Middle States are New York, New Jersey, Pennsylvania, Delaware, and Maryland.

25. The Old South included Virginia, Kentucky, Tennessee, Georgia, North Carolina, and South Carolina. Although McCormick does not discuss it, Federalists had some strength in South Carolina.

26. These states were Ohio, Indiana, Illinois, Alabama, Mississippi, Missouri, and Louisiana. Estimates (similar to those reported below) were also run with the region subdivided into the three new states of the Deep South and the remainder, but these are not reported here since the subdivision made little difference.

27. I worded this carefully, since especially in the state polity, efforts of the Democratic Party to organize might well be countered by another party or faction. The point is that where the Democratic Party did not organize, no other party did so either, at least systematically.

28. The long-term goal was to organize the entire nation. If a party could be organized easily and cheaply in a state, it might be done regardless of short-term electoral benefits. In New Hampshire, for example, a local political entrepreneur, Isaac Hill, undertook this effort in 1828, requiring little support from the national Caucus. See text at note 31 below.

29. Chambers and Davis do not provide enough information to reproduce their decisions about individual states with complete certainty. Van Buren made great efforts to have state conventions held as soon as possible in as many states

as possible. These conventions were to choose electors for Jackson and, where possible, to designate Jackson campaign leaders in the state. In several states, conventions were held for those purposes and little else. In other states, conventions also were used to nominate candidates for state offices or perform other state and local functions. The latter were therefore more closely integrated with the national party. Still, candidates—whether nominated at a state convention or not—might be free to run campaigns nearly or completely independent of the national party and its (minimal) "platform." It appears that this latter distinction plays a role in their coding.

30. Georgia and Missouri are listed in their table as "1836/1840" and "1835/1839," respectively. All analyses were run listing them both as organized in time for 1836 and as not organized until 1840. The text is written with them considered as organized by 1836.

31. According to McCormick (1966), the Democratic Party forged national identities in that state in 1828 but did not penetrate deeply until 1832.

32. More accurately, Senator Daniel Webster of New Hampshire ran in Massachusetts; Senator Hugh L. White of Tennessee ran in the South; General William Henry Harrison ran elsewhere in the nation. Francis Granger of New York was the vice presidential candidate running with Harrison and Webster, and John Tyler of Virginia was White's running mate.

33. Calculation from table 4.5 shows that, though turnout decreased in 1832 by five points for those states first organized in 1828, that decline still leaves their average turnout higher than even in states newly organized in 1832.

34. There is some evidence, however, that there was something to the argument that turnout was higher in the frontier states, at least in this more fully specified model than McCormick's.

35. Of particular importance is controlling for region, since organizing was associated with region as described above.

CHAPTER FIVE

1. The major exception was Maine, which went as strongly Republican as the Northwest. A Fusion Republican, Myron H. Clark, was elected governor of New York in 1854, but he won a three-candidate race with only 33.4 percent of the vote.

2. The 1854 congressional elections in the South were contested primarily by Democrats and Whigs, with a sprinkling of American party candidates. By 1855, however, very few Whigs ran for Congress in the South, with the contests (covering most of the southern states) being almost exclusively between Democrats and Know-Nothings.

3. The Wilmot Proviso would have prohibited territory acquired in the Mexican War from entering the Union as slave states.

4. The White House veto would have to be coupled with an ability to muster one-third plus one in either the House or the Senate to avoid override. With a balanced Senate, such an override would be extremely unlikely.

5. Moreover, what was truly critical was that at least one southerner be on the ticket, for the northern majority in the House was certain.

6. This incumbent vice president, Richard M. Johnson of Kentucky, was immersed in controversy over his personal life.

7. Four years later, Van Buren defected from the intersectional alliance he had created in part to suppress the slavery issue. In 1848 he was the presidential nominee of the antislavery Free Soil Party. It thus appears that he did indeed put party over his own interests and suppressed the ability of the government in the second party system to take action on his preferred option on the slavery issue.

8. The northern House majority that passed the Proviso may, of course, have reasoned that they could take an antislavery stance in the knowledge (or reasonable expectation) that the Senate would defeat the Proviso.

9. South Carolina still did not choose its electors by popular vote. All its electoral votes were cast for Buchanan.

10. This majority was exclusively northern, since no Republican ran for any congressional seat south of the Mason-Dixon Line in the period 1854–60.

11. Ambition theory was put formally by Black (1972) and Rohde (1979). See chapter 2. One possible (even likely) conclusion is that the political career-ist will often find it rational to run repeatedly for reelection to the same office. Thus those (e.g., Mayhew 1974) who have seen the "reelection imperative" as the major driving force for understanding legislatures (especially the United States House) and the behavior of legislators in it can be seen as investigating a special case of ambition theory.

12. Even here there may be concerns about strategic interaction. For example, a member might be more likely to run for the Senate if he or she believes it is unlikely that other members or prominent others (e.g., a current or former governor) are unlikely to run. Indeed, although a new party will be more attractive the larger the number of strong candidates it can attract, the decision to run for higher office will be more attractive the smaller the number of strong candidates seeking it.

13. Theoretically, the point is that choice of office can often be studied as a problem in individual decision making, thereby employing the technology of expected utility maximization. The choice of party, however, must be seen as a problem in strategic interaction, requiring the tools of game theory.

14. This conclusion is shown more formally in Aldrich (1990) and Aldrich and Bianco (1992). In the former, it is also shown that adding longer-term career calculations accentuates the effect of the probability of success on party choice.

15. That the public may predicate its actions on the policies advocated by a particular candidate or party is irrelevant here, for that simply becomes a part of the probability of winning term. Note that running as a candidate of a somewhat less attractive party may be compensated for by extra effort, providing another example of the probably rather strongly negative relation between costs of running and the probability of winning.

16. This is shown formally in Aldrich (1990). With either form of policy motivation, the aspirant is trading off between policy and ambition. For the politician motivated to effect actual policy outcomes, that policy concern must be weighted by the probabilities of election and of success in seeing policy changed after the election.

17. Put another way, the complex institutional arrangements described

above served to keep a potential and growing northern majority from "working its will." It is less obvious that this majority was uniformly and deeply committed to an antislavery policy, or even to cessation of slavery's extension.

18. This inevitability is shown formally in Aldrich (1990).

19. This is the most probable reason the demise of the Whig Party did not lead to a grand party in national unity, which the National Republicans under Monroe sought to achieve with the effective demise of the national Federalist Party. There was insufficient unity in the nation.

20. The first Whig platform was adopted in 1844 when Clay was presidential nominee. It was under one hundred words long.

21. Some New England delegates backed native son Daniel Webster, making the nomination long and contentious.

22. Hale received less than 5 percent of the vote.

23. A territory would be free or slave by vote of its residents—at least until statehood. This principle had been championed by Democratic presidential nominee Lewis Cass in 1848.

24. Of course the policy motivation also required answering the question whether the viable party was at least minimally satisfactory on policy or could become so.

25. Aldrich (1987, 1990) and Aldrich and Bianco (1992) show formally that this situation can be modeled as what Schelling (1978) called a game with a "tipping point" equilibrium change. For choice between two parties, it is shown that there are two such equilibriums to this coordination (or with policy motivations, an assurance) game, in which all such candidates run either in one party or in the other. This model is also extended to the multiparty case with similar results.

26. The issue in Maine was temperance rather than slavery, however.

27. This was in part to avoid association with the old National Republican Party.

28. Immigrants were, of course, concentrated in the coastal cities of the northeast, thus reinforcing the East-West geographic division. This relationship was imperfect, however, and where there were concentrations of immigrants (particularly Catholic immigrants), nativism was a potential issue, whether on the coast or in the heartland.

29. Dates of conversion could not be ascertained, however, for five of the seventeen.

30. The theory concerns the selection of party, which may be either the initial choice of party or the conversion from one party to another. I was able to ascertain a prior party affiliation for twenty-six of the twenty-seven key figures, so it is fair to speak of "conversion" of these key leaders to the Republican Party, which may not have been true for the House candidates.

31. Although Benjamin Wade became a Republican after being reselected as senator for the session opening in 1855, Chase's switch is a bit less certain. Mayer (1967), for example, reports that he ran for governor in 1855 as a Republican—and as a Whig, a Democrat, and even a Know-Nothing. That is, he appeared publicly in whatever guise seemed most useful at the moment. There is therefore at least reason to doubt that his public affiliation was with the Republicans before he won election in 1855. In table 5.5, three senators are

listed as becoming Republican in 1854–55, denoting their switch as coming after reselection to the Senate and thus after the 1854 elections.

CHAPTER SIX

1. The columns labeled "activists" will be explained below.

2. A vote is defined as an instance of the conservative coalition when a majority of northern Democrats are opposed by a majority of southern Democrats and a majority of Republicans.

3. Actually, Downs described the competition as between two parties. In his work parties were teams acting like single individuals. His parties were identical to competition between two candidates in any particular election, but as teams they could continue to compete for office over a very long period. Thus, although his theory should not be considered a theory of political parties, through this clever device he was able to analyze competition in a single election and competition over a virtually infinite series of elections at the same time. I will treat his theory of "party" competition in a single election as a spatial model of candidate competition.

4. Until recently, most spatial modeling examined two-candidate contests. In two-candidate races one votes (if at all) for the closer candidate, whether one is a "sincere" or a "sophisticated" (sometimes called "strategic") voter. With three or more candidates, the sincere voter continues to support the closest candidate. The sophisticated voter might, however, vote for some other candidate (here the second closest candidate) to avoid "wasting" the vote on a hopeless (but closest) candidate and to avoid election of an even less attractive alternative (the furthest removed candidate; see Farquaharson 1969; McKelvey and Ordeshook 1972 for formal development). As usual, Downs anticipated the work only recently being developed for multicandidate contests, such as Austen-Smith and Banks (1988) and Shepsle (1991).

5. Recall that this is an application of Black's median voter theorem (1958) to the electoral setting.

6. The theorems alluded to in the text presume that voters are certain about their perceptions of the platforms of candidates. With uncertainty added to this account, theorems typically yield equilibrium at the mean, rather than median, voter's ideal point (see, for example, Hinich 1977). Although obviously a different equilibrium position (and one that exists more commonly), it is still a convergence to moderation result. Erikson and Romero (1990) have developed a spatial model that includes forces other than policy considerations affecting voters' utilities and hence choices. They are able to derive the existence of equilibrium positions for the candidates—also involving convergence to policy moderation—under far more general conditions.

7. McKelvey (1972) proved that if candidates are in a zero-sum game (if what one wins the other loses, such as in plurality or probability of winning maximization) and there are any equilibrium positions for the candidates, at least one of the equilibrium pairs involves convergence. Moreover, the candidates always expect to tie in equilibrium, and they receive the same value for any pair of equilibrium positions, convergent or not, and hence are indifferent between converging and diverging, if there are any divergent equilibriums.

8. More accurately, perhaps, the number of machine-induced "profession-

als" has waned with the demise of most machines. The vacuum has been filled by nonprofessionals, with their most obvious goal being the public goods of government policy.

9. The past tense is used not because there are no "professionals" left today—there are professionals and remnants of machines as well—but to emphasize that the balance of professional versus policy-motivated activists has shifted heavily toward the latter.

10. Of course, the party-as-organization also includes its bureaucracies, such as the state and national party committees and the like. See chapter 8.

11. But recall that to my mind the electorate is not a part of the party-in-elections but is the target of the actions of the office seekers and, indirectly, benefit seekers that together constitute a political party.

12. Of course to the extent that candidates have policy goals, they may or may not be incompatible with the goals of benefit seekers. In the machine era, benefit seekers were concerned primarily with winning, making their goals more similar to those of win-oriented candidates, and indifferent to any policy goals of candidates, and public platforms taken by them, except insofar as these affected the probability of winning.

13. For systematic tests of this assumption and the model of party activism, see my manuscript "Parties, Candidates, and Citizens: A test of a spatial model." There is a collective action problem in this account just as there is in voting. As in voting, however, many do become involved in campaigns, even if minimally. Indeed, by the measures used below, as many as a quarter claim to have done some sort of campaign-related activity beyond voting. Thus there is, empirically, substantial resolution to the collective action problem. Although social and solidary incentives take us further in this case than in voting, it is unclear just why the collective action problem is not a greater barrier to participation, just as it is unclear why so many vote in elections, given the calculus of voting. See Aldrich (1993a, 1993b).

14. The formal logic of candidate-campaign activists is identical to that of partisan activists, except that the reference is to the candidate's position in the former case and to that of the party in the latter.

15. This may be true in different election periods or in different campaigns at the same time. Certainly, if the party is at all organized, the activist will make it onto lists that lead to repeated dunning for support.

16. Of course the set of current party activists yields a distribution of ideal points in the party. I assume that the potential activist assesses the positions of the two parties as the average position of activists already in each party. In effect, the single point where respondents place the party on issues scales, as in table 6.1, is their personal summary of this full distribution, which I assume is the mean ideal point position. Candidates and officeholders are likely to be "activists" for this measure. Further, all results described in the text hold for an average that may be weighted—for example, counting the position of a presidential nominee more heavily than one who occasionally rings doorbells.

17. Technically it is shown that there is a Nash equilibrium for citizens, in which no additional citizen desires to become, or to cease to become, active in either party, and none wants to switch parties. As a result, the full distribution of activists in each party stabilizes, at least until there is some change in prefer-

ences. It is easier to refer to the mean of this distribution of a party's activists as "the position" of the party. It should be understood, however, as no more than a summary measure.

18. The two distributions of activists will not in general be symmetric, however, unless the distribution of policy preferences in the electorate would happen to be symmetric.

19. Estimates are reported there for the 1972–80 surveys. Comparable analyses were conducted using the 1984 and 1988 surveys, and the results are available on request.

20. The NES began to ask a question about the income tax check-off provision once implemented, and I have eliminated such "contributions" from the determination of activism. The much more consequential problem is that there is no systematic attempt to measure whether activists were working for the party or for a particular candidate, or even which party they worked for! This forced me to use party identification as a determinant, which is why I have not reported statistical results in detail. The only check I have been able to devise for the plausibility of this procedure involves testing whether those who placed themselves closer to the Democratic (or Republican) Party (as measured by the samplewide median placement of the parties on the seven-point issue scales) were in fact estimated to be Democratic (or Republican) activists as determined by party identification. For the three years in which such estimates were conducted, the probability of "correct" classification was over .9 in 1976 and over .999 in 1972 and 1980. Nonetheless, the lack of definitive data on activists' choice of party or candidate limits the strength of the findings and explains the relatively brief description of what are otherwise strongly supportive results.

21. On busing, the two parties' activists, like the sample as a whole, are very conservative, whereas the sample and activists are skewed extremely to the "left" on the two scales of equal rights for women (1980 and 1988). In only two other cases are the averages (barely) less than one full point apart: taxation (1972) and aid to minorities in 1988 (but not other years), owing to the moderate positions of Republican activists.

22. There is little variation on the Republican side, although the activists in the 1980s were slightly to the right of those in the 1970s. There is more variation on the Democratic side. This is due mostly to 1976. In that year the Democrats nominated Carter, and (presumably for that reason) a larger number of more moderate southern Democrats reported engaging in campaign activity than in other years. Again, however, the differences are not that large.

23. Of course other party and electoral forces might have made it impossible for southerners with different policy views to reveal and act on them without harming their career prospects. It was also important to southern Democrats that, until recent decades, the presidency or other aspects of national leadership that required national support were all but closed off. There was, that is, little point in creating a broad national base of support. Ambition was effectively restricted to offices that rested on a southern electorate. This fact of life differentiates the old one-party South from many contemporary one-party locales. Ambitious politicians from one-party locales today might well want to position themselves to be able to appeal to a broad national electorate in case the opportunity arises.

24. It will be a theme in later chapters that the increasing party distinctiveness seen in the electorate in the 1980s and visible in the national legislatures in the 1980s is due both to the enhanced importance of the national party and its leadership and to the greater alignment of the fifty state parties, especially as the South has become more "nationalized."

25. Even the number of candidates will matter. A two-candidate primary might look much like the spatial model described so far (excepting considerations of electability). But in a three-candidate race, a moderate candidate, in a good position in a two-candidate race, might find votes siphoned off by one candidate slightly to the right and another slightly to the left (see Brams 1978 for demonstration).

26. Here is where the activists generated by the candidate per se might counter the party's activists. If a personally popular candidate can generate a great deal of support independent of the party and from those with policy preferences different from the party activists, then the "importance" of party decreases and, with it, the pull on the candidate in the general election. But if potential activists are policy motivated, they would be far more likely to be attracted to a divergent candidate than to one who calls for the same policies as his opponent.

CHAPTER SEVEN

1. The only exceptions are the House Ethics Committee, to emphasize the bipartisan or nonpartisan nature of ethical standards, and an occasional subcommittee.

2. Of course piecemeal formation of majorities one person at a time, regardless of party or ideology, is another possibility, albeit hard to measure systematically.

3. Unless otherwise noted, data reported in this chapter were drawn from Ornstein, Mann, and Malbin (1992).

4. Rohde (1991) shows the pattern of party votes in different policy and procedural categories. His work consistently supports the general conclusions reached here.

5. These scores represent the percentage of time a member of the party supports that party on party votes. Rohde (1991) reports figures for party cohesion (eliminating consensual votes) on both party unity and non-party unity votes for much of this period in the House. He shows that Democratic cohesion has been very similar on party and nonparty unity votes (51, fig. 3.2). Generally Republican cohesion has been significantly lower on nonparty unity than on party unity votes (126, fig. 5.2). He also shows that the Republican Party has its own regional tension. Northeastern Republicans began to break significantly with their party in the early 1960s and continued through 1988. Although their average unity score never dipped below 60 percent in this period (compared with 80+ percent, among other Republicans), it never reached 70 percent after the Eighty-Seventh Congress (1963–64), either.

6. Just why there is such deference is controversial, reflecting in part differences among the theories reviewed here.

7. Such measures include actual roll call votes, indexes derived from them, such as ADA or other interest group ratings, and the Poole-Rosenthal estimates

of spatial locations, as used in chapter 3. For one test of this, see Aldrich et al. (1994).

8. I thank David Rohde for providing these data, which I updated through 1992 from the *Congressional Quarterly Almanac.*

9. Under simple majority voting, a core is the PIE (at the median voter's ideal point). Thus the core is the general equilibrium concept that reduces to the PIE for simple majority rule.

10. This is of course conditional upon the rule that those who support the policy in caucus support it on the floor.

11. At minimal winning, the caucus would have to agree unanimously on a policy option. Only if some policy is preferred to the status quo by all would the majority party's caucus propose to change it. Moreover, the rule binding those who supported a measure in caucus to support it on the floor would have to be strong enough to ensure that the minority could not secure even one defection from the action adopted by the caucus.

12. I call this "parties in the legislature" because the account examines only intrachamber considerations. Development of a full theory of the party in the entire government is reserved for a later date.

13. Rohde (1991) calls the preferences that MCs would want to reveal on the floor their "operative" preferences, distinguishing them from the personal preferences that MCs individually believe desirable in themselves. In this context I use "personal" preferences to reflect both individual feelings and reelection-induced preferences, distinguishing these from policy preferences that may be induced by partisan leadership ambition and such.

14. I called this the "separation condition" earlier (Aldrich 1994). Note that moderate Republicans may be closer to moderate Democrats than to extreme Republicans under this condition, but clear partisan distinctiveness remains.

15. Technically, $W(q)$ is that set of policies *preferred* to q by a majority rather than the set that a majority actually vote for over q. In final, binary choices such as these, all voters, whether sincere or sophisticated (strategic), vote their preferences, so the difference in this case is moot. In fact, however, proposals may not be seen as "final" or as viewed in isolation from what else is expected to arise, in which case strategic voters may or may not vote their (immediate) preferences.

16. Perhaps more than any others, Shepsle's committee system differentiates formal study of the House from study of the Senate. Although the Senate has features comparable to the House committee system, the common use of unanimous consent rules and the absence of restrictions on amendments reduce the formal consequences of agenda control through committees in the Senate.

17. Similar reasoning holds for the minority party, although the exact details are more complicated and therefore more cumbersome to state (see Aldrich 1994).

18. To quote Wilson on the Speaker: "If I have succeeded, in what I have already said, in making clear the extraordinary powers of the Committees in directing legislation, it may now go without saying that he who appoints those Committees [the Speaker at that time] is an autocrat of the first magnitude" (1881, 84–85).

19. Of course their size and centrality to the New Deal majority helped shape Roosevelt's New Deal policies in the first place.

20. This was the first of a number of reasonably representative surrogates for the caucus (see Rohde 1991).

CHAPTER EIGHT

1. This strengthening of the party-as-organization in the 1970s and 1980s therefore precedes, but otherwise parallels, the strengthening of the party in Congress, as detailed in Rohde (1991) and in chapter 7 above.

2. The gradual emergence of the new form makes its evolution more like the emergence of the first two parties in the 1790s (see chap. 3) than the more literal and purposeful invention of the mass party from Van Buren's blueprint for the Jacksonian Democratic Party.

3. Converse (1976) dates the beginning of the changes to 1965, whereas Clarke and Suzuki (1994) point to mid-1967 as the beginning of these changes.

4. After dropping somewhat in the 1980s, the proportion of independents climbed in 1992, but the presence of Perot as an independent presidential candidate makes interpretation of this increase unclear.

5. Data for 1992 are reported in Gold (1994). Stanga and Sheffield (1987) call those who offer no comments about the parties "artificial" neutrals and develop models to assess what category (which they estimate to be primarily "partisan") these people would fall into if they did offer comments. Although it is plausible that very few who gave no responses to these questions would have offered exactly the same number of positive as negative comments for even one party, let alone both, it strikes me as inappropriate to consider these people as "artificially" not responding. First, there has been no comparable growth in the proportion of the public offering no comments about the candidates. Second, the dramatic change in the proportion of neutrals over time should be largely unaffected. Thus, though it may be that those who offer no comments are not actually neutral to the parties in the sense of having an even balance of things they like and things they dislike about the parties, if forced to say something, they have an effectively neutral stance toward the two parties in the sense that their evaluations are not important enough to them to bother stating.

6. Although not comparable to the parties question, it is noteworthy that the perceived role of elections as making officials pay attention to the public seriously deteriorated between 1984 and 1988. The proportion saying "not much" increased from 20 to 29 percent, while the percentages of those saying "some" or "not much" increased from 57 to 87! In 1992 the proportions returned to their 1984 levels (12 and 53 percent, respectively), perhaps in part owing to Perot's candidacy.

7. See especially Alford and Brady (1989b; see also 1989a, 161–62, figs. 6.3, 6.4). Shively's national analysis finds less impact of conversion in House contests, thus seemingly differing from the results that Alford and Brady obtained. The difference is likely due to the necessary aggregation over 435 separate contests in Shively's case.

8. It is perhaps no coincidence that 1960 marked the first presidential election in which a majority of households owned a television set.

9. There is of course far more evidence about the rise of candidate-centered elections than mentioned here. On presidential elections, see Nie, Verba, and Petrocik (1979) and Wattenberg (1991), and see Jacobson (1992, 2008) for a review of such arguments about congressional elections.

10. Longley (1992), following Herrnson, uses this term to characterize Democratic efforts in the 1980s and 1990s to catch up to Republicans along this reform path.

11. Kayden and Mayhe's book (1985) makes a strong case that is very consistent with (and that helped mold) the overall argument in this chapter. Herrnson's work (and Longley's updating) provides the most systematic data analysis and makes the strongest argument(s) about what I am calling the "party in service," while Price's (1984) and Sabato's (1988) books provide careful documentation of the need for stronger parties and develop extensive reform proposals (some of which have been implemented by the parties) that would if anything extend the service component of parties.

12. Cotter and Hennessy (1964), for example, titled their study *Politics without Power: The National Party Committees.*

13. See Caro (1982, chap. 31, "Campaign Committee") for a wonderful discussion of Lyndon Johnson's use of this committee to build power in the House in the 1940 campaign.

14. These data are adapted from Longely (1992), who updates Herrnson's data. See Longely's pp. 4, 8, tables 1–4.

15. Note the different sense of "professional" used here. Whereas "professional" in the mass party period was contrasted with "amateur" or "purist" and was meant in the sense of their profession's (as hack) being contingent on the spoils of office from party victory, in the party in service, professional is meant in the sense of possessing technical knowledge not available without special training or experience.

16. By "1960s" I mean not the numerical decade, but the set of events concentrated in that decade. As we will see, some mark the 1960s in this sense as beginning in 1958, and this critical era may have ended in 1972.

17. Sundquist, in the first edition of his important study of realignments, pointed out that the term has been used with varying meanings, but that "one element is common to all the stated or implied definitions. A realignment is a durable change in patterns of political behavior" (1973, 5). In the revised version he no longer used that definition but wrote that "a realignment is a shift in the distribution of basic party attachments, as distinct from a temporary alteration of voter behavior" (1983, 6). He is quite correct in his revised statement of the "one basic proposition" about realignments, but he is also correct in the earlier definition of a Key-like critical era that includes realignments as one special case and institutional change of parties as a second case of Key's original position that Niemi and I modified only slightly.

18. One might want to point to the origin of their "issue evolution" as beginning with the civil rights movement in the mid-1950s (or perhaps even to *Brown v. Board of Education* in 1954 and 1955), but its electoral impact did not begin until 1958.

19. I do not argue that the techniques employed were at all new, although the technology was. I only argue that the extent to which these techniques were

feasible and became available to the individual candidate was so much greater that the change in degree induced a change in kind.

20. The term refers to generic ads to encourage voting for the party's candidates (or negatively, against the opposition party's candidates).

CHAPTER NINE

1. William Riker (pers. comm.) has suggested that there was a realigning aspect to this critical era. He argued that "nationalists" had assumed dominance of government at least by the end of the Revolution and held it, eventually in Federalist form, until 1800. Madison's movement from allegiance to Washington, and therefore from alliance with Hamilton and Adams to association with Jefferson, indicates the shift to the Jeffersonian Republican point of view. That view raised the importance of states' rights, southern interests, and the yeoman farmer as alternatives to the nationalist impulse of Hamiltonians, and the Jeffersonian view secured electoral dominance in the elections of 1800.

2. In particular, state legislatures proposed candidates, but that form was "adopted" ad hoc and lacked justification (although justification was, in principle, possible). More important, such procedures lacked the ability to create the majorities needed to achieve consensus and coherence within parties and to forge the national majorities needed to elect a president.

3. The argument that the New Deal established it as the role of government to provide what the parties had heretofore provided has been made in detail by Milkis (1993).

4. In fact even "his" form of the modern mass party was quite variable over its century and a quarter long reign.

REFERENCES

Abramowitz, Alan I. 1989. Viability, electability, and candidate choice in a presidential primary election: A test of competing models. *Journal of Politics* 51 (November): 977–92.

Abramowitz, Alan I., Ronald B. Rapoport, and Walter J. Stone. 1991. Up close and personal: The 1988 Iowa caucuses and presidential politics. In *Nominating the president*, ed. Emmett H. Buell Jr. and Lee Sigelman, 42–71. Knoxville: University of Tennessee Press.

Abramson, Paul R. 1983. *Political attitudes in America: Formation and change.* San Francisco: Freeman.

Abramson, Paul R., John H. Aldrich, Phil Paolino, and David W. Rohde. 1992. "Sophisticated" voting in the 1988 presidential primaries. *American Political Science Review* 86 (March): 55–69.

Abramson, Paul R., John H. Aldrich, and David W. Rohde. 1983. *Change and continuity in the 1980 elections.* Rev. ed. Washington, DC: CQ Press.

———. 1987. *Change and continuity in the 1984 elections.* Rev. ed. Washington, DC: CQ Press.

———. 1991. *Change and continuity in the 1988 elections.* Rev. ed. Washington, DC: CQ Press.

———. 1994. *Change and continuity in the 1992 elections.* Washington, DC: CQ Press.

———. 2010. *Change and continuity in the 2008 elections.* Washington, DC: CQ Press.

Achen, Christopher H. 1989. Prospective voting and the theory of party identification. Manuscript, Department of Political Science, University of Chicago.

———. 2002. Parental socialization and rational party identification. *Political Behavior* 24 (June): 141–70.

Adams, Greg S. 1997. Abortion: Evidence of an issue evolution. *American Journal of Political Science* 41 (July): 718–37.

Aldrich, John H. n.d. Parties, candidates, and citizens: A test of a spatial model. Manuscript, Department of Political Science, University of Minnesota.

———. 1976. Some problems in testing two rational models of participation. *American Journal of Political Science* 20 (November): 713–34.

———. 1980. *Before the convention: Strategies and choices in presidential nomination campaigns.* Chicago: University of Chicago Press.

———. 1983a. A Downsian spatial model with party activism. *American Political Science Review* 77 (December): 974–90.

———. 1983b. A spatial model with party activists: Implications for electoral dynamics. *Public Choice* 41 (1): 63–100.

———. 1987. The rise of the Republican party, 1854–1860. Paper delivered at the annual meeting of the Midwest Political Science Association, Chicago, April 8–11.

———. 1989a. On the origins of the American political party: The endogeneity of the party in the legislature. Working paper 60, February 20. Duke University Program in Political Economy.

———. 1989b. Power and order in Congress. In *Home style and Washington work: Studies in congressional politics,* ed. Morris P. Fiorina and David W. Rohde, 219–52. Ann Arbor: University of Michigan Press.

———. 1990. A game-theoretic model of party selection: Ambition theory, two-party systems, and the rise of the Republican party. Working paper 101, March 21. Duke University Program in Political Economy.

———. 1992. Presidential campaigns in party- and candidate-centered eras. In *Under the watchful eye: Managing presidential campaigns in the television era,* ed. Mathew D. McCubbins, 59–82. Washington, DC: CQ Press.

———. 1993a. On William Riker's "inheritability problem": Preferences, institutions, and context. Paper delivered at the annual meeting of the Southern Political Science Association, Savannah, GA.

———. 1993b. Rational choice and turnout. *American Journal of Political Science* 37 (February): 246–78.

———. 1994. A model of a legislature with two parties and a committee system. *Legislative Studies Quarterly* 19 (August): 313–39.

———. 1997. The study of party politics in the twenty-first century. *Election Law Journal* 6 (2): 209–19.

———. 1999. Political parties in a critical era. *American Politics Research* 27 (1): 9–32.

———. 2007. The study of party politics in the twenty-first century. *Election Law Journal* 6 (2): 209–19.

Aldrich, John H., Steven J. Balla, John Brehm, and Michael Layton. 1994. Before the floor: Political parties and committees in the legislative process. Paper delivered at the annual meeting of the Midwest Political Science Association, Chicago, April 14–16.

Aldrich, John H., and William T. Bianco. 1992. A game-theoretic model of party affiliation of candidates and office holders. *Mathematical and Computer Modelling* 16 (8–9): 103–16.

Aldrich, John H., and Melanie Freeze. Forthcoming. Political participation, polarization, and public opinion: Activism and the merging of partisan and ideological polarization. In *The democratic experiment: Explorations in the analysis of public opinion and political participation,* ed. Benjamin Highton and Paul Sniderman. Princeton, NJ: Princeton University Press.

Aldrich, John H., and Ruth W. Grant. 1993. The Antifederalists, the first Congress, and the first parties. *Journal of Politics* 55 (May): 295–326.

Aldrich, John H., and John D. Griffin. 2003. The presidency and the campaign: Creating voter priorities in the 2000 election. In *The presidency and the political system,* 7th ed., ed. Michael Nelson, 239–56. Washington, DC: CQ Press.

———. 2010. Parties, elections, and democratic politics. In *Oxford handbook of American elections and political behavior,* ed. Jan Leighley, 595–610. New York: Oxford University Press.

Aldrich, John H., Jeffrey D. Grynaviski, and David W. Rohde. 1999. Three models of a legislature with two parties. Paper prepared for delivery at Conference on Parties and Congress, MIT, October 1999.

Aldrich, John H., Calvin C. Jillson, and Rick H. Wilson. 2002. Why Congress? What the failure of the Confederation Congress and the survival of the Federal Congress tell us about the new institutionalism. In *Party, process, and political change in Congress: New perspectives on the history of Congress,* ed. David W. Brady and Mathew D. McCubbins, 315–42. Stanford, CA: Stanford University Press.

Aldrich, John H., and Daniel Lee. n.d. A Duvergerian model in two-space. Manuscript, Duke University.

Aldrich, John H., and Michael McGinnis. 1989. A model of party constraints on optimal candidate positions. *Mathematical and Computer Modelling* 12 (4–5): 437–50.

Aldrich, John H., and Richard G. Niemi. 1990. The sixth American party system: The 1960s realignment and the candidate-centered parties. Working paper 107, May 9. Duke University Program in Political Economy.

Aldrich, John H., and David W. Rohde. 1997–98. The transition to Republican rule in the House: Implications for theories of congressional politics. *Political Science Quarterly* 112 (4): 541–67.

———. 2000. The consequences of party organization in the House: The role of the majority and minority parties in conditional party government. In *Polarized politics: Congress and the president in a partisan era,* ed. Jon R. Bond and Richard Fleisher, 31–72. Washington, DC: CQ Press.

———. 2001. The logic of conditional party government: Revisiting the electoral connection. In *Congress reconsidered,* 7th ed., ed. Lawrence C. Dodd and Bruce I. Oppenheimer, 262–92. Washington, DC: CQ Press.

———. 2008. Congressional committees in a continuing partisan era. In *Congress Reconsidered,* 9th ed., ed. Lawrence C. Dodd and Bruce I. Oppenheimer, 217–40. Washington, DC: CQ Press.

Aldrich, John H., David W. Rohde, and Michael W. Tofias. 2004. Examining Congress with a two-dimensional policy space. Paper delivered at the American Political Science Association Annual Meeting, Chicago, September 2–5.

———. 2007. One D is not enough: Measuring conditional party government, 1887–2002. In *Party, process, and political change in Congress: Further new perspectives on the history of Congress,* ed. David Brady and Mathew D. McCubbins, 102–12. Stanford, CA: Stanford University Press.

Alford, John R., and David W. Brady. 1989a. Personal and partisan advantage in U.S. congressional elections, 1846–1986. In *Congress reconsidered,* 4th ed., ed. Lawrence C. Dodd and Bruce I. Oppenheimer. Washington, DC: CQ Press.

———. 1989b. Personal and partisan advantage in U.S. House elections, 1846–1986. Manuscript, Department of Political Science, Stanford University.

Alvarez, R. Michael. 1989. The new republic and the new institutionalism: Hamilton's plan and extra-legislative organization. Working paper 85, August 23. Duke University Program in Political Economy.

Alvarez, R. Michael, and John Brehm. 1995. American ambivalence towards abortion policy: Development of a heteroskedastic probit model of competing values. *American Journal of Political Science* 39 (4): 1055–82.

American Political Science Association. 1950. *Toward a more responsible two-party system*. New York: Rinehart.

APSA Committee on Political Parties. 1950. A report of the Committee on Political Parties. *American Political Science Review* 44 (September): i–xii, 1–99.

Aranson, Peter H., and Peter C. Ordeshook. 1972. Spatial strategies for sequential elections. In *Probability models of collective decision making*, ed. Richard G. Niemi and Herbert F. Weisberg, 298–331. Columbus, Ohio: Charles E. Merrill.

Arrow, Kenneth J. 1951. *Social choice and individual values*. New York: Wiley.

Austen-Smith, David, and Jeffery Banks. 1988. Elections, coalitions, and legislative outcomes. *American Political Science Review* 82 (June): 405–22.

Axelrod, Robert M. 1970. *Conflict of interest: A theory of divergent goals with application to politics*. Chicago: Markham.

———. 1984. *The evolution of cooperation*. New York: Basic Books.

Baer, Denise L. 1993. Who has the body? Party institutionalization and theories of party organization. *American Review of Politics* 14 (Spring): 1–38.

Bain, Richard C., and Judith H. Parris. 1973. *Convention decisions and voting records*. Washington, DC: Brookings Institution.

Barry, Brian M. 1970. *Sociologists, economists, and democracy*. London: Collier-Macmillan.

Barry, Brian M., and Russell Hardin, eds. 1982. *Rational man and irrational society?* Beverly Hills, CA: Sage.

Bartels, Larry M. 1988. *Presidential primaries and the dynamics of public choice*. Princeton, NJ: Princeton University Press.

Barzel, Y., and E. Silberberg. 1973. Is the act of voting rational? *Public Choice* 16 (Fall): 51–58.

Baumer, Donald C., and Howard J. Gold. 2010. *Parties, polarization, and democracy in the United States*. Boulder, CO: Paradigm Publishers.

Beard, Charles A. 1941. *An economic interpretation of the Constitution of the United States*. Rev. ed. New York: Macmillan.

Beard, Charles A., and Mary R. Beard. 1933. 2 vols. *The rise of American civilization*. New York: Macmillan.

Beck, Paul Allen, and Frank J. Sorauf. 1991. *Party politics in America*. 7th ed. New York: HarperCollins.

Bell, Rudolph. 1973. *Party and faction in American politics: The House of Representatives, 1779–1801*. Westport, CT: Greenwood.

Benedict, Michael Les. 1985. Factionalism and representation: Some insight from the nineteenth-century United States. *Social Science History* 9 (4): 361–98.

Bianco, William T., and Robert H. Bates. 1990. Cooperation by design: Leadership, structure, and collective dilemmas. *American Political Science Review* 84 (March): 133–47.

Binkley, Wilfred E. 1962. *American political parties: Their natural history*. 4th ed. New York: Knopf.

Biographical directory of the United States Congress, 1774–1989. 1989. Bicentennial ed. Washington, DC: U.S. Government Printing Office.

Black, Duncan. 1958. *The theory of committees and elections.* Cambridge: Cambridge University Press.

Black, Gordon S. 1972. A theory of political ambition: Career choices and the role of structural incentives. *American Political Science Review* 66 (March): 144–59.

Black, Jerome H. 1978. The multicandidate calculus of voting: Application to Canadian federal elections. *American Journal of Political Science* 22 (August): 609–38.

Born, Richard. 1986. Strategic politicians and unresponsive voters. *American Political Science Review* 80 (June): 599–612.

Bowling, Kenneth R. 1968. Politics in the first Congress, 1789–1791. PhD diss., University of Wisconsin.

———. 1971. Dinner at Jefferson's: A note on Jacob E. Cooke's "The compromise of 1790." *William and Mary Quarterly* 28 (October): 629–40.

Brady, David W. 1988. *Critical elections and public policy making.* Stanford, CA: Stanford University Press.

———. 2006. *Revolving gridlock: Politics and policy from Jimmy Carter to George W. Bush.* Boulder, CO: Westview Press.

Brams, Steven J. 1978. *The presidential election game.* New Haven, CT: Yale University Press.

Broder, David S. 1972. *The party's over: The failure of politics in America.* New York: Harper and Row.

Burnham, Walter Dean. 1970. *Critical elections and the mainsprings of American politics.* New York: Norton.

Cain, Bruce E. 1978. Strategic voting in Britain. *American Journal of Political Science* 22 (August): 639–55.

Cain, Bruce E., John A. Ferejohn, and Morris P. Fiorina. 1987. *The personal vote: Constituency service and electoral independence.* Cambridge, MA: Harvard University Press.

Caldeira, Gregory A., and Christopher Zorn. 2004. Strategic timing, position-taking, and impeachment in the House of Representatives. *Political Research Quarterly* 57:517–27.

Calvert, Randall L. 1985. Robustness of the multidimensional voting model: Candidate motivations, uncertainty, and convergence. *American Journal of Political Science* 29 (February): 69–95.

Campbell, Angus, Philip E. Converse, Warren E. Miller, and Donald E. Stokes. 1960. *The American voter.* New York: Wiley.

Canon, David T., and David J. Sousa. 1988. Party system change and political career structures in the U.S. Congress. Working paper 41, June 27. Duke University Program in Political Economy.

Carmines, Edward G., and James A. Stimson. 1989. *Issue evolution: Race and the transformation of American politics.* Princeton, NJ: Princeton University Press.

Caro, Robert A. 1982. *The years of Lyndon Johnson: The path to power.* New York: Knopf.

Carsey, Thomas M., and Geoffrey C. Layman. 1999. A dynamic model of political change among party activists. *Political Behavior* 21 (1): 17–41.

Castanheira, Micael, and Benoit S. Y. Crutzen. 2009. Comparative politics with endogenous intra-party discipline. Paper delivered at the Research Group on Political Institutions and Economic Policy, Harvard University, December 5.

Castle, David S., and Patrick J. Fett. n. d. Party switchers in the House of Representatives: Conscience or calculation? Manuscript.

Chambers, William Nisbet. 1963. *Political parties in a new nation: The American experience, 1776–1809.* New York: Oxford University Press.

Chambers, William Nisbet, and Philip C. Davis. 1978. Party, competition, and mass participation: The case of the democratizing party system, 1824–1852. In *The history of American electoral behavior,* ed. Joel H. Silbey, Allan G. Bogue, and William H. Flanigan. Princeton, NJ: Princeton University Press.

Chhibber, Pradeep K., and Ken Kollman. 2004. *The formation of national party systems: Federalism and party competition in Canada, Great Britain, India, and the United States.* Princeton, NJ: Princeton University Press.

Clarke, Harold D., and Motoshi Suzuki. 1994. Partisan dealignment and the dynamics of independence in the American electorate, 1953–1988. *British Journal of Political Science* 24 (January): 57–77.

Clinton, Joshua D., and Adam Meirowitz. 2004. Testing explanations of strategic voting in legislatures: A reexamination of the compromise of 1790. *American Journal of Political Science* 48 (4):675–89.

Congressional Quarterly. 1985. *Guide to U.S. elections.* 2nd ed. Washington, DC: CQ Press.

Conover, Pamela Johnston, and Stanley Feldman. 1984. How people organize the political world: A schematic model. *American Journal of Political Science* 28 (1): 95–126.

Converse, Philip E. 1976. *The dynamics of party support: Cohort-analyzing party identification.* Beverly Hills, CA: Sage.

Cooke, Jacob E. 1970. The compromise of 1790. *William and Mary Quarterly* 27 (October): 523–45.

———. 1971. Rebuttal to Bowling. *William and Mary Quarterly* 28 (October): 640–48.

Cooper, Joseph, and David W. Brady. 1981. Institutional context and leadership style: The House from Cannon to Rayburn. *American Political Science Review* 75 (June): 411–25.

Cotter, Cornelius P., James L. Gibson, John F. Bibby, and Robert J. Huckshorne. 1984. *Party organizations in American politics.* New York: Praeger.

Cotter, Cornelius P., and Bernard C. Hennessy. 1964. *Politics without power: The national party committees.* New York: Atherton.

Cox, Gary W. 1997. *Making votes count: Strategic coordination in the world's electoral systems.* Cambridge: Cambridge University Press.

Cox, Gary W., and Matthew D. McCubbins. 1993. *Legislative leviathan: Party government in the House.* Berkeley and Los Angeles: University of California Press.

———. 2005. *Setting the agenda: Responsible party government in the US House of Representatives.* Cambridge: Cambridge University Press.

———2007. *Legislative leviathan: Party government in the House.* 2nd ed. Cambridge: Cambridge University Press.

Cox, Gary W., and Michael C. Munger. 1989. Closeness, expenditures, and turnout in the 1988 U.S. House elections. *American Political Science Review* 83 (March): 217–31.

Crotty, William. 1983. *Party reform*. New York: Longman.

———. 1984. *American political parties in decline*. 2nd ed. Boston: Little, Brown.

Cunningham, Noble E. 1971. Election of 1800. In *History of American presidential elections: 1789–1968*, ed. Arthur M. Schlesinger, 101–34. New York: Chelsea House, in association with McGraw-Hill.

Davis, Otto A., Morris H. DeGroot, and Melvin J. Hinich. 1972. Social preference orderings and majority rule. *Econometrica* 40:147–57.

Davis, Otto A., and Melvin Hinich. 1966. A mathematical model of policy formation in a democratic society. In *Mathematical applications in political science II*, ed. Joseph Bernd, 175–208. Dallas: Southern Methodist University Press.

Davis, Otto, Melvin J. Hinich, and Peter C. Ordeshook. 1970. An expository development of a mathematical model of the electoral process. *American Political Science Review* 64 (June): 426–48.

Demsetz, Harold. 1990. Amenity potential, indivisibilities, and political competition. In *Perspectives on political economy*, ed. James E. Alt and Kenneth A. Shepsle, 144–60. New York: Cambridge University Press.

Destler, I. M., Leslie H. Gelb, and Arthur Lake. 1984. *Our own worst enemy*. New York: Simon and Schuster.

Downs, Anthony. 1957. *An economic theory of democracy*. New York: Harper and Row.

Duverger, Maurice. 1954. *Political parties: Their organization and activities in the modern state*. New York: Wiley.

Eldersveld, Samuel J. 1964. *Political parties: A behavioral analysis*. Chicago: Rand McNally.

———. 1982. *Political parties in American society*. New York: Basic Books.

Epstein, Leon D. 1986. *Political parties in the American mold*. Madison: University of Wisconsin Press.

Erikson, Robert S. 1971. The advantage of incumbency in congressional elections. *Polity* 8 (4): 395–405.

Erikson, Robert S., Michael B. MacKuen, and James A. Stimson. 2001. What moves macropartisanship (revised). In *Controversies in voting behavior*, 4th ed., ed. Richard G. Niemi and Herbert F. Weisberg, 364–70. Washington, DC: CQ Press.

———. 2002. *The macro polity*. New York: Cambridge University Press.

Erikson, Robert S., and David W. Romero. 1990. Candidate equilibrium and the behavioral model of the vote. *American Political Science Review* 84 (December): 1103–26.

Farquaharson, Robin. 1969. *Theory of voting*. New Haven, CT: Yale University Press.

Feddersen, Timothy J. 1992. A voting model implying Duverger's law and positive turnout. *American Journal of Political Science* 36 (November): 938–62.

Fenno, Richard F. 1973. *Congressmen in committees*. Boston: Little, Brown.

Ferejohn, John A., and Morris P. Fiorina. 1974. The paradox of not voting: A decision theoretic analysis. *American Political Science Review* 68 (June): 525–36.

———. 1975. Closeness counts only in horseshoes and dancing. *American Political Science Review* 69 (September): 920–25.

Ferguson, Thomas. 1983. Party realignment and American industrial structures: The investment theory of political parties in historical perspective. In *Research in political economy*, vol. 6, ed. Paul Zarembka, 1–82. Greenwich, CT: JAI Press.

———. 1986. Elites and elections, or: What have they done to you lately? In *Do elections matter?*, ed. Benjamin Ginsberg and Alan Stone, 164–88. Armonk, N.Y.: Sharpe.

———. 1989. Industrial conflict and the coming of the New Deal: The triumph of multinational liberalism in America. In *The rise and fall of the New Deal order, 1930–80*, ed. Steve Fraser and Gary Gerstle, 3–31. Princeton, NJ: Princeton University Press.

———. 1991. An unbearable lightness of being: Party and industry in the 1988 Democratic primary. In *Do elections matter?*, 2nd ed., ed. Benjamin Ginsberg and Alan Stone, 237–54. Armonk, N.J.: Sharpe.

Ferling, John E. 2004. *Adams vs. Jefferson: The tumultuous election of 1800*. New York: Oxford University Press.

Fink, Evelyn C., and Brian D. Humes. 1989. Risky business: Electoral realignments and institutional change in Congress. Paper delivered at the annual meeting of the American Political Science Association, Atlanta, August 31–September 1.

Fiorina, Morris P. 1976. The voting decision: Instrumental and expressive aspects. *Journal of Politics* 38 (May): 390–415.

———. 1980. The decline of collective responsibility in American politics. *Daedalus* 109 (Summer): 25–45.

———. 1981. *Retrospective voting in American national elections*. New Haven, CT: Yale University Press.

Fishel, Jeff. 1985. *Presidents and promises: From campaign pledge to presidential performance*. Washington, DC: CQ Press.

Fleischer, Richard. 1993. Explaining change in the roll-call voting behavior of southern Democrats. *Journal of Politics* 55 (May): 327–41.

Fribourg, Marjorie C. 1972. *The U.S. Congress: Men who steered its course, 1787–1867*. Philadelphia: Macrae Smith.

Frohlich, Norman, and Joe A. Oppenheimer. 1970. I get by with a little help from my friends. *World Politics* 23 (October): 104–20.

Fudenberg, Drew, and Eric Maskin. 1986. The folk theorem in repeated games with discounting or with incomplete information. *Econometrica* 54 (May): 533–54.

Garrett, Geoffrey, and Peter Lange. 1989. Government participation and economic performance: When does "who governs" matter? *Journal of Politics* 51 (August): 676–93.

Gelman, Andrew, and Gary King. 1990. Estimating incumbency advantage without bias. *American Journal of Political Science* 34 (4): 1142–64.

Gibbard, Allan. 1973. Manipulation of voting schemes: A general result. *Econometrica* 41 (July): 587–601.

Gibson, James L., Cornelius P. Cotter, John F. Bibby, and Robert J. Huckshorne. 1983. Assessing party organization strength. *American Journal of Political Science* 27 (May): 193–222.

Gienapp, William E. 1986. *The origins of the Republican party, 1852–1856.* New York: Oxford University Press.

Gilligan, Thomas W., and Keith Krehbiel. 1987. Collective decision-making and standing committees: An informational rationale for restrictive amendment procedures. *Journal of Law, Economics, and Organizations* 3:287–335.

———. 1989. Asymmetric information and legislative rules with a heterogenous committee. *American Journal of Political Science* 33 (May): 459–90.

———. 1990. Organization of informative committees by a rational legislature. *American Journal of Political Science* 34 (May): 531–64.

Gold, Howard J. 1994. Third party voting in presidential elections: A study of Perot, Anderson, and Wallace. Paper presented at the annual meeting of the American Political Science Association, New York, September 1–4.

Goldwater, Barry M. 1960. *The conscience of a conservative.* Shepherdsville, KY: Victor. Reprint, New York: MacFadden-Bartell, 1964.

Grant, Ruth. 1977. The origins of American political parties: Antifederalists and Jeffersonian Republicans. Manuscript, Department of Political Science, University of Chicago.

Green, Donald P., Bradley L. Palmquist, and Eric Schickler. 2001. Partisan stability: Evidence from aggregate data. In *Controversies in Voting Behavior,* 4th ed., ed. Richard G. Niemi and Herbert F. Weisberg, 356–63. Washington, DC: CQ Press.

———. 2002. *Partisan hearts and minds: Political parties and the social identities of voters.* New Haven, CT: Yale University Press.

Grynaviski, Jeffrey. 2010. *Partisan bonds: Political reputations and legislative accountability.* Cambridge: Cambridge University Press.

Hammond, Thomas H., and Gary Miller. 1987. The core of the Constitution. *American Political Science Review* 81 (December): 1155–74.

Hansen, John Mark. 1991. *Gaining access: Congress and the farm lobby.* Chicago: University of Chicago Press.

Hardin, Russell. 1982. *Collective action.* Baltimore: Johns Hopkins University Press.

Heberlig, Eric S. 2003. Congressional parties, fundraising, and committee ambition. *Political Research Quarterly* 56 (2): 151–61.

Heberlig, Eric S., Marc Hetherington, and Bruce A. Larson. 2006. The price of leadership: Campaign money and the polarization of congressional leadership. *Journal of Politics* 68 (4): 992–1005.

Henderson, H. James. 1974. *Party politics in the Continental Congress.* New York: McGraw-Hill.

Herrnson, Paul S. 1988. *Party campaigning in the 1980s.* Cambridge, MA: Harvard University Press.

———. 1992. Campaign professionalism and fundraising in congressional elections. *Journal of Politics* 54 (August): 859–70.

Hershey, Marjorie Randon. 2009. *Party politics in America.* New York: Pearson Longman.

Hinich, Melvin J. 1977. Equilibrium in spatial voting: The median voter result is an artifact. *Journal of Economic Theory* 16 (March): 208–19.

Hinich, Melvin J., and Peter C. Ordeshook. 1970. Plurality maximization vs. vote maximization: A spatial analysis with variable participation. *American Political Science Review* 64 (September): 772–91.

Hoadley, John F. 1980. The emergence of political parties in Congress, 1789–1803. *American Political Science Review* 74 (September): 757–79.

———. 1986. *Origins of American political parties, 1789–1803.* Lexington: University of Kentucky Press.

Hofstadter, Richard. 1969. *The idea of a party system: The rise of legitimate opposition in the United States, 1780–1840.* Berkeley and Los Angeles: University of California Press.

Huckshorne, Robert J., and John F. Bibby. 1982. State parties in an era of electoral change. In *The future of American political parties*, ed. Joel L. Fleischman, 70–100. Englewood Cliffs, N.J.: Prentice-Hall.

Huddy, Leonie. 2001. From social to political identity: A critical examination of social identity theory. *Political Psychology* 22 (1): 127–56.

Jackman, Robert W. 1986. Elections and the democratic class struggle. *World Politics* 39 (October): 123–46.

Jackson, John E., and John W. Kingdon. 1992. Ideology, interest group ratings, and legislative votes. *American Journal of Political Science* 36 (November): 851–80.

Jacobson, Gary C. 1989. Strategic politicians and the dynamics of U.S. House elections, 1946–86. *American Political Science Review* 83 (September): 773–93.

———. 1992. *The politics of congressional elections.* 3d ed. New York: Harper-Collins.

———. 2008. *The politics of congressional elections*, 7th ed. New York: Pearson Longman.

Jacobson, Gary C., and Samuel Kernell. 1983. *Strategy and choice in congressional elections.* 2nd ed. New Haven, CT: Yale University Press.

Jillson, Calvin C., and Rick K. Wilson. 1994. *Congressional dynamics: Structure, coordination and choice in the first American Congress, 1774–1789.* Stanford, CA: Stanford University Press.

Katz, Jonathan N., and Brian R. Sala. 1996. Careerism, committee assignments, and the electoral connection. *American Political Science Review* 90 (1): 21–33.

Kayden, Xandra, and Eddie Mayhe Jr. 1985. *The party goes on: The persistence of the two-party system in the United States.* New York: Basic Books.

Kedar, Orit. 2009. *Voting for policy, not parties: How voters compensate for power sharing.* Cambridge: Cambridge University Press.

Key, V. O., Jr. 1949. *Southern politics in states and nation.* New York: Knopf.

———. 1955. A theory of critical elections. *Journal of Politics* 17 (February): 3–18.

———. 1964. *Politics, parties, and pressure groups.* 5th ed. New York: Crowell.

———. 1966. *The responsible electorate: Rationality in presidential voting, 1936–1960.* Cambridge, MA: Harvard University Press.

Kiewiet, D. Roderick, and Mathew D. McCubbins. 1991. *The logic of delega-*

tion: Congressional parties and the appropriations process. Chicago: University of Chicago Press.

Kirkpatrick, Jeane J. 1978. *Dismantling the parties: Reflections on party reform and party decomposition.* Washington, DC: American Enterprise Institute of Public Policy Research.

Kolodny, Robin. 1989. The several elections of 1824: The selection of President John Quincy Adams. M. A. essay, Johns Hopkins University.

Kramer, Gerald H. 1973. On a class of equilibrium conditions for majority rule. *Econometrica* 41:285–97.

———. 1977. A dynamical model of political equilibrium. *Journal of Economic Theory* 16 (December): 245–68.

Krehbiel, Keith. 1990. Are congressional committees composed of preference outliers? *American Political Science Review* 84 (March): 149–63.

———. 1991. *Information and legislative organization.* Ann Arbor: University of Michigan Press.

———. 1993. Where's the party? *British Journal of Political Science* 23:235–66.

———. 1998. *Pivotal politics: A theory of U.S. lawmaking.* Chicago: University of Chicago Press.

Layman, Geoffrey C., and Thomas M. Carsey. 2002. Party polarization and party structuring of policy attitudes: A comparison of three NES panel studies. Special issue: Parties and Partisanship, Part Two, *Political Behavior* 24 (3): 199–236.

Larson, Edward J. 2007. *A magnificent catastrophe: The tumultuous election of 1800, America's first presidential campaign.* New York: Free Press.

Lau, Richard R., and David O. Sears, eds. 1985. *Political cognition.* New York: Harcourt and Brace.

Lee, Daniel J. 2008. Life of the party or just a third wheel? Effects of third parties in U.S. House elections. Thesis submitted in fulfillment of PhD degree, Duke University.

Levendusky, Matthew. 2009. *The partisan sort: How liberals became Democrats and conservatives became Republicans.* Chicago: University of Chicago Press.

Libby, Orin Grant. 1912. A sketch of the early political parties in the United States. *Quarterly Journal of the University of North Dakota* 2 (April): 205–42.

Lijphart, Arend. 1984. *Democracies: Patterns of majoritarian and consensus government in twenty-one countries.* New Haven, CT: Yale University Press.

———. 1999. *Patterns of democracy: Government forms and performance in thirty-six countries.* New Haven, CT: Yale University Press.

Lipset, Seymour Martin, and William Schneider. 1987. *The confidence gap: Business, labor, and government in the public mind.* Rev. ed. Baltimore: Johns Hopkins University Press.

Lodge, Milton, and Ruth Hamill. 1986. A partisan schema for political information processing. *American Political Science Review* 80 (June): 399–419.

Longley, Lawrence D. 1992. The gradual institutionalization of the national Democratic party in the 1980s and 1990s. *Vox Pop: Newsletter of Political Organizations and Parties* (Ray C. Bliss Institute of Applied Politics, University of Akron.) 11 (1): 4–5, 8–9.

Luce, R. Duncan, and Howard Raiffa. 1957. *Games and decisions: Introduction and critical survey.* New York: Wiley.

Lupia, Arthur, and Gisela Sin. 2008. How the Senate and the president affect the balance of power in the House: A constitutional theory of inter-chamber bargaining. Unpublished paper, University of Michigan.

MacKay, Alfred F. 1980. *Arrow's theorem: The paradox of social choice*. New Haven, CT: Yale University Press.

Malbin, Michael J., Norman J. Ornstein, and Thomas E. Mann. 2008. *Vital statistics on Congress 2008*. Washington, DC: Brookings Institution Press.

Martis, Kenneth C. 1989. *The historical atlas of the political parties in the United States Congress: 1789–1989*. New York: Macmillan.

Mayer, George H. 1967. *The Republican party: 1854–1866*. 2nd ed. New York: Oxford University Press.

Mayhew, David R. 1974. *Congress: The electoral connection*. New Haven, CT: Yale University Press.

———. 1974. Congressional elections: The case of the vanishing marginals. *Polity* 6 (3): 295–317.

———. 1986. *Placing parties in American politics: Organization, electoral settings, and government activity in the twentieth century*. Princeton, NJ: Princeton University Press.

McClosky, Herbert. 1969. Consensus and ideology in American politics. In *Empirical democratic theory*, ed. Charles F. Cnudde and Deane E. Neubauer, 268–302. Chicago: Markham. Originally published in *American Political Science Review* 58 (June 1964): 361–82.

McCormick, Richard L. 1979. The party period and public policy: An exploratory hypothesis. *Journal of American History* 66 (September): 279–98.

McCormick, Richard P. 1960. New perspectives on Jacksonian politics. *American Historical Review* 65 (January): 288–301.

———. 1966. *The second American party system: Party formation in the Jacksonian era*. Chapel Hill: University of North Carolina Press.

———. 1982. *The presidential game: Origins of American politics*. New York: Oxford University Press.

McGerr, Michael. 1986. *The decline of popular politics: The American North, 1865–1928*. Oxford: Oxford University Press.

McKelvey, Richard D. 1972. Some extensions and modifications of spatial models of party competition. PhD diss., University of Rochester.

———. 1975. Policy related voting and electoral equilibrium. *Econometrica* 43 (September): 815–43.

———. 1976. Intransitivities in multi-dimensional voting models and some implications for agenda control. *Journal of Economic Theory* 18 (June): 472–82.

———. 1986. Covering, dominance, and institution-free properties of social choice. *American Journal of Political Science* 30 (May): 283–314.

McKelvey, Richard D., and Peter C. Ordeshook. 1972. A general theory of the calculus of voting. In *Mathematical applications in political science*, ed. J. Herndon and J. Bernd, vol. 6, 32–78. Charlottesville: University of Virginia Press.

———. 1976. Symmetric spatial games without majority rule equilibria. *American Political Science Review* 70 (4): 1172–84.

McKelvey, Richard D., and Norman Schofield. 1986. Structural instability of the core. *Journal of Mathematical Economics* 15:179–98.

Milkis, Sidney M. 1993. *The president and the parties: The transformation of the*

American party system since the New Deal. New York: Oxford University Press.

Miller, Gary J., and Thomas H. Hammond. 1990. Committees and the core of the Constitution. *Public Choice* 66:201–20.

Monroe, Nathan, Jason Roberts, and David W. Rohde. 2008. *Why not parties? Party effects in the United States Senate.* Chicago: University of Chicago Press.

Nie, Norman H., Sidney Verba, and John R. Petrocik. 1979. *The changing American voter.* Enl. ed. Cambridge, MA: Harvard University Press.

Niemi, Richard G. 1976. Costs of voting and nonvoting. *Public Choice* 27 (Fall): 115–19.

Nokken, Timothy P., and Keith Poole. 2004. Congressional party defection in American history. *Legislative Studies Quarterly* 29:545–68.

Olson, Mancur, Jr. 1965. *The logic of collective action.* Cambridge, MA: Harvard University Press.

Ordeshook, Peter C. 1970. Extensions to a mathematical model of the electoral process and implications for the theory of responsible parties. *Midwest Journal of Political Science* 14 (February): 43–70.

Ornstein, Norman J., Thomas E. Mann, and Michael J. Malbin. 1992. *Vital statistics on Congress, 1991–1992.* Washington, DC: CQ Press.

Page, Benjamin I. 1976. The theory of political ambiguity. *American Political Science Review* 70 (September): 742–52.

———. 1978. *Choices and echoes in presidential elections: Rational man and electoral democracy.* Chicago: University of Chicago Press.

Palfrey, Thomas R. 1989. A mathematical proof of Duverger's law. In *Models of strategic choice in politics*, ed. Peter C. Ordeshook, 69–91. Ann Arbor: University of Michigan Press.

Parker, David C. W. 2008. *The power of money in congressional campaigns, 1880–2006.* Norman: University of Oklahoma Press.

Patterson, Samuel C., and Gregory A. Caldeira. 1983. Getting out the vote: Participation in gubernatorial elections. *American Political Science Review* 77 (September): 675–89.

Petrocik, John R. 1996. Issue ownership in presidential elections, with a 1980 case study. *American Journal of Political Science* 40 (3): 825–50.

Plott, Charles. 1967. A notion of equilibrium and its possibility under majority rule. *American Economic Review* 57 (September): 146–60.

Polsby, Nelson W. 1968. The institutionalization of the U.S. House of Representatives. *American Political Science Review* 62 (1): 144–68.

———. 1983. *Consequences of party reform.* Oxford: Oxford University Press.

Polsby, Nelson W., and Aaron B. Wildavsky. 1971. *Presidential elections: Strategies of American electoral politics.* 3rd ed. New York: Scribner.

Pomper, Gerald M. 1972. From confusion to clarity: Issues and American voters, 1956–1968. *American Political Science Review* 66 (June): 415–28.

———. 1975. *Voters' choice: Varieties of American electoral behavior.* New York: Dodd, Mead.

Poole, Keith T. 1988. Recent developments in analytical models of voting in the U.S. Congress. *Legislative Studies Quarterly* 13 (February): 117–33.

Poole, Keith T., and Howard Rosenthal. 1985. A spatial model for legislative roll call analysis. *American Journal of Political Science* 29 (May): 357–84.

————. 1997. *Congress: A political-economic history of roll call voting*. New York: Oxford University Press.

————. 2007. *Ideology and congress*. Piscataway, NJ: Transaction Press.

Popkin, Samuel, John W. Gorman, Charles Phillips, and Jeffrey A. Smith. 1976. Comment: What have you done for me lately? Toward an investment theory of voting. *American Political Science Review* 70 (September): 779–805.

Price, David E. 1984. *Bringing back the parties*. Washington, DC: CQ Press.

Price, H. Douglas. 1977. Careers and committees in the American Congress: The problem of structural change. In *The history of parliamentary behavior*, ed. William O. Aydelotte, 28–62. Princeton, NJ: Princeton University Press.

Rabinowitz, George, Paul-Henri Gurian, and Stuart Macdonald. 1984. The structure of presidential elections and the process of realignment, 1944 to 1980. *American Journal of Political Science* 28 (November): 611–35.

Rae, Nicol C. 1989. *The decline and fall of the liberal Republicans from 1952 to the present*. New York: Oxford University Press.

Ranney, Austin. 1975. *Curing the mischiefs of faction: Party reform in America*. Berkeley and Los Angeles: University of California Press.

Reed, Stephen R. 2009. Party strategy or candidate strategy: How does the LDP run the right number of candidates in Japan's multi-member districts? *Party Politics* 15 (May): 295–314.

Reiter, Howard L. 1985. *Selecting the president: The nominating process in transition*. Philadelphia: University of Pennsylvania Press.

Remini, Robert V. 1959. *Martin Van Buren and the making of the Democratic Party*. New York: Columbia University Press.

————. 1963. *The election of Andrew Jackson*. Philadelphia: Lippincott.

————, ed. 1972. *The age of Jackson*. Columbia: University of South Carolina Press.

Riker, William H. 1962. *The theory of political coalitions*. New Haven, CT: Yale University Press.

————. 1980. Implications from the disequilibrium of majority rule for the study of institutions. *American Political Science Review* 74 (June): 432–46.

————. 1982a. *Liberalism against populism: A confrontation between the theory of democracy and the theory of social choice*. San Francisco: Freeman.

————. 1982b. The two-party system and Duverger's law: An essay on the history of political science. *American Political Science Review* 76 (December): 753–66.

Riker, William H., and Peter C. Ordeshook. 1968. A theory of the calculus of voting. *American Political Science Review* 62 (March): 25–42.

————. 1973. *An introduction to positive political theory*. Englewood Cliffs, NJ: Prentice-Hall.

Robertson, David. 1987. *Ideology, strategy, and party change: Spatial analyses of post-war election programmes in nineteen democracies*. Cambridge: Cambridge University Press.

Rohde, David W. 1979. Risk-bearing and progressive ambition: The case of the United States House of Representatives. *American Journal of Political Science* 23 (February): 1–26.

————. 1989. "Something's happening here: What it is ain't exactly clear"; Southern Democrats in the House of Representatives. In *Home style and*

Washington work: Studies of congressional politics, ed. Morris P. Fiorina and David W. Rohde, 137–63. Ann Arbor: University of Michigan Press.

———. 1991. *Parties and leaders in the postreform House.* Chicago: University of Chicago Press.

Rohde, David W., and John H. Aldrich. 2010. Consequences of electoral and institutional change: The evolution of conditional party government in the U.S. House of Representatives. In *New directions in American political parties*, ed. Jeffery Stonecash, 234–50. New York: Routledge.

Rohde, David W., and Kenneth A. Shepsle. 1978. Thinking about legislative reform. In *Legislative reform: The policy impact*, ed. Leroy N. Rieselbach. Lexington, MA: Lexington Books.

———. 1987. Leaders and followers in the House of Representatives: Reflections on Woodrow Wilson's congressional government. *Congress and the Presidency* 14 (Autumn): 111–34.

Romer, Thomas, and Howard Rosenthal. 1978. Political resource allocation, controlled agendas, and the status quo. *Public Choice* 33:27–43.

Rosenstone, Steven J., and John Mark Hansen. 1993. *Mobilization, participation, and democracy in America.* New York: Macmillan.

Ryan, Mary P. 1971. Party formation in the United States Congress, 1789 to 1796: A quantitative analysis. *William and Mary Quarterly* 28 (October): 523–42.

Sabato, Larry J. 1988. *The party's just begun: Shaping political parties for America's future.* Glenview, IL: Scott Foresman.

Samuelson, Paul A. 1954. The pure theory of public expenditure. *Review of Economics and Statistics* 36 (4): 387–89.

Satterthwaite, Mark. 1975. Strategy proofness and Arrow's conditions. *Journal of Economic Theory* 10 (October): 187–217.

Scammon, Richard M., and Ben J. Wattenberg. 1971. *The real majority.* New York: Coward, McCann & Georghegan.

Schattschneider, E. E. 1942. *Party government.* New York: Rinehart.

Schelling, Thomas C. 1978. *Micromotives and macrobehavior.* New York: Norton.

Schlesinger, Arthur M., Jr. 1947. *The age of Jackson.* Boston: Little, Brown.

Schlesinger, Joseph A. 1966. *Ambition and politics: Political careers in the United States.* Chicago: Rand McNally.

———. 1975. The primary goals of political parties: A clarification of positive theory. *American Political Science Review* 69 (September): 840–49.

———. 1984. On the theory of party organization. *Journal of Politics* 46 (May): 369–400.

———. 1985. The new American political party. *American Political Science Review* 79 (December): 1152–69.

———. 1991. *Political parties and the winning of office.* Chicago: University of Chicago Press.

Schofield, Norman. 1978. Instability of simple dynamic games. *Review of Economic Studies* 45 (October): 575–94.

Schofield, Norman, Bernard Grofman, and Scott L. Feld. 1988. The core and the stability of group choice in spatial voting games. *American Political Science Review* 82 (March): 195–211.

Schwartz, Thomas. 1986. *The logic of collective choice.* New York: Columbia University Press.

———. 1989. Why parties? Research memorandum, Department of Political Science, University of California at Los Angeles.

Sen, Amartya K. 1970. *Collective choice and social welfare.* San Francisco: Holden-Day.

Shepsle, Kenneth A. 1978. *The giant jigsaw puzzle: Democratic committee assignments in the modern House.* Chicago: University of Chicago Press.

———. 1979. Institutional arrangements and equilibrium in multidimensional voting models. *American Journal of Political Science* 23 (February): 27–59.

———. 1986. Institutional equilibrium and equilibrium institutions. In *Political science: The science of politics,* ed. Herbert F. Weisberg, 51–82. New York: Agathon Press.

———. 1989. The changing textbook Congress. In *Can the government govern?,* ed. John Chubb and Paul Peterson, 238–67. Washington, DC: Brookings Institution.

———. 1991. *Models of multiparty electoral competition.* New York: Harwood Academic Publishers.

Shepsle, Kenneth A., and Brian Humes. 1984. Legislative leadership: Organizational entrepreneurs as agents. Paper delivered at the Conference on Adaptive Institutions, Stanford University, 8–9 November.

Shepsle, Kenneth A., and Barry R. Weingast. 1982. Institutionalizing majority rule: A social choice theory with policy implications. *American Economic Review* 72 (May): 367–71.

———. 1984. Uncovered sets and sophisticated voting outcomes with implications for agenda institutions. *American Journal of Political Science* 29 (February): 49–74.

———. 1987. The institutional foundations of committee power. *American Political Science Review* 81 (1): 85–104.

Shively, W. Phillips. 1992. From differential abstention to conversion: A change in electoral change, 1864–1988. *American Journal of Political Science* 36 (May): 309–30.

Silberman, Jonathan, and Gary Durden. 1975. The rational behavior theory of voter participation: The evidence from congressional elections. *Public Choice* 23 (Fall): 101–8.

Silbey, Joel H. 1985. *The partisan imperative: The dynamics of American politics before the Civil War.* New York: Oxford University Press.

Sin, Gisella. 2007. Separation of power and legislative institutions: A constitutional theory of legislative organization. Unpublished PhD thesis, University of Michigan.

Sinclair, Barbara. 1982. *Congressional realignment, 1925–1978.* Austin: University of Texas Press.

———. 1990. The congressional party: Evolving organizational, agenda-setting, and policy roles. In *The parties respond: Changes in the American party system,* ed. L. Sandy Maisel, 227–48. Boulder, CO: Westview.

———. 1991. House majority party leadership in an era of legislative constraint. In *The postreform Congress,* ed. Roger H. Davidson, 91–111. New York: St. Martin's Press.

Skowronek, Stephen. 1982. *Building a new American state: The expansion of national administrative capacities, 1877–1920.* New York: Cambridge University Press.

———. 1988. Presidential leadership in political time. In *The presidency and the political system,* 2nd ed., ed. Michael Nelson, 115–59. Washington, DC: CQ Press.

Snyder, James M., and Michael M. Ting. 2002. An informational rationale for political parties. *American Journal of Political Science* 46 (1): 90–110.

Sorauf, Frank J. 1964. *Party politics in America.* Boston: Little, Brown.

———. 1988. *Money in American elections.* Glenview, IL: Scott Foresman / Little, Brown.

Stanga, John E., and James F. Sheffield. 1987. The myth of zero partisanship: Attitudes toward American political parties, 1964–84. *American Journal of Political Science* 31 (November): 829–55.

Stanley, Harold W., and Richard G. Niemi. 1989. The demise of the New Deal coalition: Partisanship and group support, 1952–1992. In *Democracy's feast: The U.S. election of 1992,* ed. Herbert F. Weisberg, 220–40. Chatham, NJ: Chatham House.

Stokes, Donald E. 1966. Some dynamic elements of contests for the presidency. *American Political Science Review* 60 (March): 19–28.

Stokes, Donald E., Angus Campbell, and Warren E. Miller. 1958. Components of electoral decisions. *American Political Science Review* 52 (June): 367–87.

Stokes, Donald E, and Warren E. Miller. 1962. Party government and the saliency of Congress. *Public Opinion Quarterly* 26 (4): 531–46.

Stone, Walter J., and Alan I. Abramowitz. 1984. *Nomination politics: Party activists and presidential choice.* New York: Praeger.

Storing, Herbert J. 1981. *What the Anti-Federalists were for.* Chicago: University of Chicago Press.

Sundquist, James L. 1973. *Dynamics of the party system.* Washington, DC: Brookings Institution.

———. 1983. *Dynamics of the party system.* Rev. ed. Washington, DC: Brookings Institution.

Taylor, Michael. 1976. *Anarchy and cooperation.* London: Wiley.

Wallace, Michael. 1968. Changing concepts of party in the United States: New York, 1815–1828. *American Historical Review* 74 (December): 453–91.

Wattenberg, Martin P. 1990. *The decline of American political parties: 1952–1988.* Cambridge, MA: Harvard University Press.

———. 1991. *The rise of candidate-centered politics: Presidential elections of the 1980s.* Cambridge, MA: Harvard University Press.

Weingast, Barry R. 1979. A rational choice perspective on congressional norms. *American Journal of Political Science* 23 (May): 245–62.

———. 1991. Institutions and political commitment: A new political economy of the American Civil War. Manuscript, Hoover Institution, Stanford University.

Weingast, Barry R., and William Marshall. 1988. The industrial organization of Congress. *Journal of Political Economy* 96 (February): 132–63.

Weisberger, Bernard A. 2000. *America afire: Jefferson, Adams, and the revolutionary election of 1800.* New York: William Morrow.

Wildavsky, Aaron. 1965. The Goldwater phenomenon: Parties, politicians, and the two-party system. *Review of Politics* 27 (July): 386–413.

Wilson, James Q. 1962. *The amateur Democrat: Club politics in three cities.* Chicago: University of Chicago Press.

Wilson, Robert. 1971. An axiomatization of voting games. Working paper 181. Stanford Business School.

Wilson, Woodrow. 1881. *Congressional government: A study in American society.* Baltimore: Johns Hopkins University Press.

Wittman, Donald. 1983. Candidate motivation: A synthesis of alternate theories. *American Political Science Review* 77 (March): 142–57.

Wright, Gerald C. 1994. The meaning of "party" in congressional roll call voting. Paper delivered at the annual meeting of the Midwest Political Science Association, Chicago, April 14–16.

Wright, Gerald C., and Michael B. Berkman. 1986. Candidates and policy in U.S. Senate elections. *American Political Science Review* 80 (June): 567–88.

INDEX

abortion, 174–75, 277, 321
Abramson, Paul R., 9, 58, 265
accountability, 3, 11–14, 26, 302
Achen, Christopher H., 172–73
activists and activism: amateurs versus
    purists and, 200; benefit seekers
    and, 307; centrifugal forces and,
    314; distribution of, 191–93, 200,
    341–42nn17–18, 342n10; electoral
    mobilization and, 307; extremity of,
    313–14; office seeking and, 195; par-
    tisan cleavages and, 192–200; party
    versus candidate and, 190, 341n14;
    polarization and, 194; policy positions
    and, 188, 193, 341n16; policy- versus
    patronage-motivated, 201, 282; spa-
    tial model of elections and, 188–92
Adams, Greg S., 174–75
Adams, John: elections and, 95, 97, 104,
    109; James Madison and, 347n1; vote
    trading and, 71, 74
Adams, John Quincy: accusations
    against, 107; corrupt bargain and,
    279; election of 1800 and, 97; elec-
    tion of 1824 and, 102; election of
    1828 and, 102, 107, 113, 115–18,
    120, 334–35n13; election of 1832
    and, 122; National Republican Party
    and, 331n10; opposition to, 116,
    126–27, 335n17
Adams, Thomas Boylston, 97
administrative state, 163, 302
agenda setting: after civil rights era,
    239; congressional committees and,
    212–14, 252, 344n16; counteragenda
    and, 244; positive versus negative,
    205; "Republican Revolution" and,
    246; revelation of preferences and,
    222, 229; Rules Committee and, 320
Albany Regency, 102, 119, 279, 301,
    335n14, 336n19

Aldrich, John H.: on activists' choice of
    party, 192–93; on allocation of party re-
    sources, 199; on anti-Federalist propos-
    als, 76; on campaign structure, 284–85;
    on conditional party government,
    229–30; on congressional leadership,
    248; on costs of candidacy, 53; on criti-
    cal era of 1960s, 275–76, 346n17; on
    equilibrium change, 339n25; on party
    affiliation, 54–55, 338n14; on party
    switching, 196–97; on plurality voting
    system, 60; on policy versus ambition,
    338n16; on "Republican Revolu-
    tion," 246–47; on socioeconomics
    and voting patterns, 9; spatial model
    of elections and, 189, 191, 341n13;
    theory of parties and, 225; on voters'
    presidential preferences, 265
Alford, John R., 266, 267, 286, 345n7
Alien and Sedition Acts, 83
Alvarez, R. Michael, 80, 175
ambition: ambition theory and, 21–22,
    28, 50–51, 139–43, 326n14, 330n23,
    338n11; calculus of candidacy and,
    53; candidate-centered elections and,
    165; coalitions and, 286; intraparty
    competition and, 19–20; party affili-
    ation and, 50–60, 139–43, 147–48,
    231, 338n11, 339n18; party-centered
    career and, 279; party forms and,
    303–4; party switching and, 197;
    public policy versus, 148, 338n16,
    339n24; pure, 52–54; slavery issue
    and, 129, 131, 152, 158–59
American Independent Party, 4
American Party: demise of, 154; early
    victories of, 130; election of 1856
    and, 154; formation of, 27; intersec-
    tional alliances and, 150; regional
    appeal of, 152–53, 155, 158; South
    and, 337n2; as third party, 146